The Lives of Ordinary People in Ancient Israel

The Lives of Ordinary People in Ancient Israel

Where Archaeology and the Bible Intersect

William G. Dever

WILLIAM B. EERDMANS PUBLISHING COMPANY
GRAND RAPIDS, MICHIGAN / CAMBRIDGE, U.K.

Published 2012 by

Wm. B. Eerdmans Publishing Co.

2140 Oak Industrial Drive N.E., Grand Rapids, Michigan 49505 /
P.O. Box 163, Cambridge CB3 9PU U.K.

Printed in the United States of America

17 16 15 14 13 12   7 6 5 4 3 2 1

Library of Congress Cataloging-in-Publication Data

Dever, William G.

The lives of ordinary people in ancient Israel: where archaeology and the Bible intersect /
William G. Dever.

p.   cm.

Includes bibliographical references (p.   ).

ISBN 978-0-8028-6701-8 (pbk.: alk. paper)

1. Jews — Social life and customs — To 70 A.D. 2. Palestine — Social life and customs —
To 70 A.D. 3. Bible. O.T. — Antiquities. 4. Community life — Palestine — History —
To 70 A.D. 5. Religion and culture — Palestine — History — To 70 A.D.
6. Cities and towns — Palestine. I. Title.

DS112.D48   2012

220.9′5 — dc23

2012002494

www.eerdmans.com

Contents

Preface

This book attempts to provide a new, original, lavishly illustrated handbook for students of the Hebrew Bible. It is written primarily for the non-specialist, but technical details for colleagues will be found in the notes and in the bibliography at the end.

This book is not a "history of Israel" in the usual sense. For one thing, it confines itself to roughly the 8th century B.C.E.: from the end of the Aramean incursions in the north toward the end of the 9th century, circa 810, to the Neo-Assyrian campaigns in Judah in 701. One reason for this limited scope is that this century or so is well defined as a discrete era chronologically. Another reason is that this period is exceptionally well documented archaeologically. The current disputes over the 10th-9th centuries need not distract us; the 7th century is ruled out simply because there is no longer an "Israel." It might be desirable to expand our coverage earlier and later. But that would make for an unwieldy work, since we now have a superabundance of recent data.[1]

What I intend to do here is to construct a parallel history of one era in ancient Israel and Judah — a sort of "secular history" of Palestine in the Iron Age — to supplement (and perhaps to correct) the portrait we have in the texts of the Hebrew Bible. But the *archaeological* data, not the textual data, will be the primary source initially. To be sure, the textual data will be considered later, in Part II of each chapter, wherever they can be shown to be historically accurate beyond reasonable doubt. But the biblical texts will be subsidiary and will often prove to be of minimal importance. In this

---

1. For convenient, brief, but up-to-date general surveys of the 8th century B.C.E., see now Campbell 1998; Cogan 1998.

sense, the present work will almost be "a history without the Bible," at least for the most part, even though some have declared this impossible. In Part III of each chapter, I shall move beyond facts to admitted speculation, in an attempt to ask what a good historian must ask: What was it really *like* in those days? That will help us to illustrate the lives of ordinary people, who are almost entirely invisible in typical histories of ancient Israel.

Thus this work is not another history of ancient Israel and Judah but rather what we might call a "phenomenology" — a broad description that does not claim to be a fully objective account. By phenomenology I mean a philosophical tradition that "focuses its attention on 'being' itself, on the lived world of human experience, on its unceasing ambiguity, its sponta- neity and autonomy, its uncontainable dimensions, its ever-developing complexity."[2]

My credentials for writing an archaeologically based history of an- cient Israel are that I am a professional archaeologist, although I originally had extensive training in Old Testament studies, or what I shall call here studies of the Hebrew Bible.[3] I have spent nearly fifty years in archaeologi- cal fieldwork in Israel, and I have published extensively on the relation of archaeology to biblical studies.[4] In many ways this lengthy experience seems to have constituted a prolegomenon to the present work. I want to stress, however, that I am a secular humanist, with no theological or other axe to grind. That is why this is a secular history. Although as a historian I must deal ultimately with the issue of truth in our historical sources (see the Conclusion), I gladly leave theological propositions to others.

There have been several previous books on what is usually called "daily life in biblical times." The best is that of Philip King and Lawrence Stager, *Life in Biblical Israel* (2001). One might also cite Oded Borowski's work *Daily Life in Biblical Times* (2003). But these are not really historical works, since they are topical, that is, synchronic rather than diachronic, and furthermore they do not attempt to be explanatory as history writing requires. And both still depend to a large extent on the biblical texts, not archaeology, as a primary source.[5]

2. Tarnas 1991, 357.

3. "Hebrew Bible," not "Old Testament," since the latter is a prejudicial term.

4. For a résumé of my career and a list of my publications, see Gitin, Wright, and Dessel 2006.

5. See now the popular book of my student Jennie Ebeling, *Women's Lives in Biblical Times* (2010), which although fictional is based on sound archaeological research. Karel van der Toorn's 2003 account of an Iron I village is similarly fictional, often imaginative but per-

One other work seemed promising, but it was of little use: Ferdinand Deist's *Material Culture of the Bible* (2000). Despite the title, it deals only with the biblical terminology for aspects of the material culture, and it is almost oblivious to archaeological data.

We are also fortunate to have had in recent years a number of extended works on specific topics that are relevant. Thus I have been able to make use of works by my fellow archaeologist Oded Borowski on animals and agriculture.[6] Nathan MacDonald's *What Did the Ancient Israelites Eat?* (2008) is a feast itself. In particular, we now have a number of specialized studies on aspects of women's roles in ancient Israelite society.[7] In addition to shorter works on baking, weaving, and cultic activity, we have a series of essays in a volume edited by one of my students, Beth Alpert Nakhai, *The World of Women in the Ancient and Classical Near East.*[8]

This work could not have been written without constant recourse to the monumental five-volume work *New Encyclopedia of Archaeological Excavations in the Holy Land,* edited by the senior Israeli archaeologist Ephraim Stern.[9] To avoid unwieldy documentation, I will often refer simply to the site entry in this work. There one will find an authoritative summary, often by the excavator, with extensive bibliography.

I have made extensive use of *The Sacred Bridge: Carta's Atlas of the Biblical World,* edited by Anson F. Rainey and R. Steven Notley.[10] This is much more than simply an atlas with maps; it is an authoritative historical geography, richly documented by both written and archaeological sources.

I am going to focus mostly in a nontechnical way on the results of archaeology, so I will not deal much with theory, which can be bewildering. As for my own position, I identify with the so-called post-processualist

---

suasive in the light of the archaeological data we now have. Neither work, however, is a real history. The fundamental sociology of ancient Israel — using *archaeology* as a primary source — is now Faust, *The Archaeology of Israelite Society in Iron Age II* (2011), a draft of which I had when writing this work, courtesy of my colleague. Faust's work supersedes all other sociologies of ancient Israel, valuable as they are, based as they are on the elitist biblical texts (i.e., Perdue, Blenkinsopp, and Collins 1997; McNutt 1999).

6. Borowski 1998, 2002, 2003.

7. Cf. for instance, works cited in Chapter VI by Ackerman, Meyers, and others.

8. (Cambridge: Cambridge Scholars Publishing, 2008). The introduction covers something of the growing interest in archaeology and gender studies, as well as some bibliography.

9. (Jerusalem: Israel Exploration Society, 1993, 2008). Site entries in this volume will be cited by individual authors; in the notes, but not in the general bibliography.

10. (Jerusalem: Carta, 2006).

school. Elsewhere I have treated this in some detail, but it will suffice to highlight some of the implications of post-processual archaeology for our purposes here.[11] Post-processual archaeology supplanted the "explicitly scientific" New Archaeology beginning in the 1980s. Especially significant in my earlier thinking was Ian Hodder's *Reading the Past: Current Approaches to Interpretation in Archaeology* (1986).[12]

Hodder's stress on "cognitive" archaeology — on finding meaning in things — is fully compatible with our phenomenological approach here. The metaphor of "reading" artifacts like texts, with similar interpretive principles, is one that in fact I had adopted earlier.[13] Hodder's description of the "language, grammar, and syntax" of artifacts is particularly apt.

Finally, post-processualism's understanding of history is strongly in the idealist traditions of R. G. Collingwood and others. In place of New Archaeology's vulgar materialism and impotent "laws of the cultural process," we return to the role of individual initiative, of art, symbol, aesthetics, and religion in culture and cultural change. Contrast this with postmodernism's nihilism.

A unique feature of this work is a series of specially commissioned drawings by Giselle Hasel. These will illustrate many aspects of the lives of ordinary people far better than words. Other illustrations are drawn from my own extensive collection of slides, evidence of my firsthand acquaintance with nearly every site I discuss, as well as with appropriate ethnographic analogies.

There is some unavoidable overlap between the chapters, both in text and in illustrations. Thus the famous Jerusalem water tunnel is mentioned in Chapter IV in the course of characterizing Jerusalem as an impressive capital. It is discussed further in chapter VII because its royal inscription is evidence of a literate, elite ruling class. And it is discussed yet again in Chapter X as an aspect of preparation for war. The alternative would have been to treat each site completely the first time it is mentioned. That, however, would have made this work an encyclopedia rather than a history.

A word about terminology is in order. I have already noted my preference, with most scholars, for "Hebrew Bible" rather than "Old Testament." I use "b.c.e." in keeping with current parlance. By "Palestine" I refer

11. See Dever 2003b. For a rare application in our discipline, see Bunimovitz and Lederman 2009.
12. (Cambridge: Cambridge University Press). For a later revision, less innovative in my view, see Hodder and Hutson 2003.
13. See Dever 1997b.

only to ancient Palestine of the Iron Age, without any reference to the modern political situation.

I dedicate this book to my parents, Lonnie Earl Dever (1908-70) and Claudine Watts Dever (1911-75). My father was a fundamentalist preacher in small-town churches in the South and Midwest. My mother was a homemaker, whose life revolved around the church and her family. They would not recognize nor approve of the worlds far beyond their own that I have come to inhabit after a long odyssey of my own. But they instilled in me a sense of values and a call to duty that have made me what I am and have enabled me to undertake this book, the culmination of a life's work.

I also want to thank my first wife, Norma Dever, who is unique in being able to transcribe my handwritten manuscript, complete with mistakes, into camera-ready copy. She has labored tirelessly over several drafts of this book.

I owe special thanks to my wife Pamela Gaber, without whom I would never have undertaken such a formidable work, one that many would have declared impossible. She urged me on repeatedly and survived many trial readings of troublesome passages.

CHAPTER I

On History and History Writing

What is history? Who writes it, how, and why? We must begin our inquiry about ancient Israel and Judah with these difficult but fundamental questions.

Defining History

First, what do we mean by the term "history"? There are as many definitions as there are historians. Clearly history is about the past but not, however, about reconstructing, much less reliving, the past, since that attempt would only create illusions. And it is equally clear to all except a naive few that history is also about the present. That is because we are the ones telling the story and doing so in part to define ourselves over against that past, real or imagined.

One way of defining history is to compare it with antiquarianism. For our purpose here that means asking whether the ancient writers of the Hebrew Bible were at least purporting to recount actual events or were simply antiquarians uncritically collecting and preserving old traditions.

One of the great historiographers of our times, Arnaldo Momigliano, has made the distinction clear. Antiquarians are engaged in "erudite research," while historians from the time of Thucydides on have attempted to put great political events in chronological order, to make sense of them, and to explain these facts in order to instruct the reader.[1]

For our task here, the primary source is the Deuteronomistic History

---

1. See the discussion and references in Kofoed 2005, 213.

(abbreviated "Dtr." below), the book of Deuteronomy plus Joshua through Kings. But are the writers, editors, or schools who produced this source storytelling, or attempting to "tell it as it was"? To put it another way, are the biblical texts facts or fiction?

There is a mind-numbing literature on the question of biblical and other historiography.[2] But here I will assume that in the Deuteronomistic History, as also in the relevant prophetic literature, our major sources have a mixture of fact and fiction, but a "core" of historical information that can be sifted out. Critical scholarship can never be completely unbiased in this effort, but we shall try our best.

This effort is compatible with a much-quoted definition of history by Johan Huizinga: history is "the intellectual form in which a civilization renders account to itself of its past."[3] Yet such an account can never be complete or completely accurate. That is due largely to our own biases and the limitation of our sources, even at best. But our inquiry can also be hampered by inadequate methods. So let us address in more detail what we have implied thus far about issues of sources, goals, and methods in history writing.

Sources for History Writing

A history is no better than the historian's sources. For most histories, the sources are texts, written records of past events that are supposedly factual (sometimes supplemented by oral histories). For our work here we possess written sources as well as archaeological artifacts, both assumed to be trustworthy witnesses to the past that we wish to portray. Each source, however, must be evaluated in terms of its validity, then compared with the other sources similarly evaluated.

Textual Sources

It is obvious that the texts at our disposal include both pertinent biblical texts and other texts, some of them contemporary, especially the Neo-

2. See Van Seters 1983; Halpern 1985; Millard, in Millard, Hoffmeier, and Baker 1994, 37-64; Brettler 1995; Long, in Baker and Arnold 1999, 145-75; and cf. Kofoed 2005 for discussion. See further below and n. 7.
3. On Huizinga's well-known definition, see Kofoed 2005, 16.

Assyrian annals. We shall subject all these texts, however, to the same critical evaluation. That is to say, we shall read the Hebrew Bible not as Scripture, preferentially treated, but simply as another written record.[4] In the
use of all texts, the following principles will be observed.

1. Texts are artifacts, too, so they must be treated just as archaeological artifacts so as to sort out reliable facts that can become useful data. It is
now clear that texts and artifacts can be "read" in much the same fashion,
interpreted on the basis of similar principles, once we learn the grammar,
vocabulary, and syntax of material culture. That is an enormous breakthrough in the attempt to create a dialogue between our two disciplines.
But few biblical scholars are aware of the potential, and thus they continue
to repeat the mindless description of archaeology as "mute."[5]

2. In using all ancient texts we must take into consideration obvious
shortcomings: miraculous stories that defy reason; biases either political
or, in the case of the Hebrew Bible, theological; and contradictions either
internal or in comparison with external data (such as archaeological data).

3. The dating of all our texts is crucial. Ideally texts should give us contemporary or eyewitness accounts. But even so, their reliability cannot be
assured, for reasons noted above. And with the biblical texts, we have a
unique problem: most texts, including the Deuteronomistic History we
shall utilize here, are later than the events they purport to describe, in some
cases centuries later (below). Thus it is sometimes argued that the biblical
texts are not reliable sources for writing *any* history of ancient Israel.

The specific biblical texts upon which we are dependent here constitute what is called the Deuteronomistic History (above). This is a compos-
ite work that includes the book of Deuteronomy plus Joshua through
Kings. Most scholars date its original composition to the 7th century
B.C.E., but it is clear that it was finally edited in the exilic period (6th century B.C.E.) or perhaps even later.[6]

Scholars may differ about the authorship and date of this epochal
work, but its intention is clear: to portray in a grand sweep the history of a

4. See the "comparative" model developed in Hallo 1990, 187-99; cf. Malul 1990. On
the flawed argument that the biblical text is held "guilty until proven innocent," see Dever
2001a, 128; cf. Niehr, in Grabbe 1997, 163.

5. See especially Hodder 1986. For an explicit application to Syro-Palestinian and biblical archaeology, showing similar interpretive principles in that field and in biblical studies,
see Dever 1997b. Hodder's later version, Hodder and Hutson 2003, is more radical.

6. See McKenzie 1991; Knoppers 1993/1994; Knoppers and McConville 2000; Na'aman
2006; Kofoed 2005, 113-63; Amit 2006; Na'aman 2006.

people united in a monotheistic faith and living a covenant life in a land promised to them by Yahweh. The question, however, is whether this scheme of things is history or myth. And in our case, we must ask further whether a work dated so late can have any relevance for our inquiry about the 8th century B.C.E. These are fundamental issues.

Again, the literature is too vast to survey here, but I shall follow in general the views of the distinguished Israeli historian Nadav Na'aman.[7] He reads the biblical stories as "historiography" rather than historical fiction, primarily because the writers were concerned with what had really happened in their view. But this is a didactic literature, which does describe the past, but which has a greater intent to use that past to impart certain moral lessons. Thus, despite postdating the biblical era, and having an agenda, the stories in the Deuteronomistic History may be cautiously used for historical reconstructions.[8]

This is where we disagree with the revisionists (Chapter II), who hold that there is no real history in the texts of the Hebrew Bible. We also reject the opposite extreme of fundamentalists, for whom the Bible must be literally true. Thus we regard both the biblical and the nonbiblical texts as genuine and equal sources for history writing, when used critically.

Archaeological Sources

There are as many definitions of archaeology as there are archaeologists. But an archaeologist can be regarded simply as someone who "writes history from things." I shall argue throughout that things — archaeological artifacts — now constitute *primary* data for writing new histories of Israel and Judah.

I have already argued above that archaeological evidence is similar to textual evidence and must be critically evaluated using similar methods of interpretation. But why might archaeological data be considered superior?[9]

First, artifacts often have a more tangible character than texts, which seem to present an ideal world. We can approach artifacts more directly: there is no need to translate them, at least at first glance. Of course, arti-

---

7. Amit 2006, 55, 56. See further Na'aman 2006. Cf. nn. 2, 4 above.

8. See nn. 2, 4, 5 above.

9. See Dever 1997a; and specifically on the nature and use of archaeological data as a source, see Dever 2001a, 53-95.

facts don't come labeled, so ultimately they, too, must be interpreted to give them meaning. But whereas an ancient text may seem inscrutable, the idea that it may contain a mystery, an ancient cooking pot can speak for itself. An artifact may thus seem closer to reality than a text.

Second, even though proper interpretation is required before an artifact reveals its full meaning, it is easier to control the interpretation. Both texts and artifacts contain encoded behavior. But ancient texts have been edited and reedited endlessly for centuries, so that what we now have is an interpretation of an interpretation of an interpretation. Finding any eyewitness information seems almost impossible.

By contrast, when an ancient artifact is first brought to light, it is pristine. Of course, interpretation begins the minute we touch it. Nevertheless, we do not have to cut through the accretions of centuries. So if "primary" means contemporary, artifacts trump our texts.

Another advantage of artifacts is that a group of them, when properly excavated, will have an original physical context. They then constitute what we call an assemblage. And when properly compared with other assemblages, they can be placed in an overall cultural context. With biblical texts, however, it is difficult if not impossible to know their original context.

The date of any written text also poses a problem. We have already noted the difficulties of dating the biblical sources. There are, of course, difficulties in dating some archaeological evidence as well (as biblicists are fond of pointing out).[10] But while biblicists may differ by as much as several hundred years in dating some texts (like the Deuteronomistic History), archaeologists today scarcely differ more than fifty years about even the most controversial finds, and the margin of error is usually much narrower. In any case, our dates are almost always sufficient for the broadbased history here.

Finally, the number of biblical texts we have, and always will have, is limited. The canon is closed. Even fantastic discoveries like the Dead Sea Scrolls do not change that picture much. But the number of archaeological discoveries is expanding exponentially. Twenty years ago, an archaeologi-

---

10. Even mainstream scholars, who should be better informed and more sympathetic, repeat the mindless charge that archaeology cannot date artifacts closely enough to make them useful; cf. Knoppers, in Baker and Arnold 1999, 211-12. See also, for instance, many of the authors in Grabbe 1997, such as Barstad (50), Grabbe (30), Carroll (90), and Niehr (159; archaeology is "mute"). The revisionists, of course, without exception, appeal to archaeology theoretically (the only source they have), but in practice distort or more typically dismiss it altogether.

cal history like this one would have been impossible. But I predict that twenty years from now, such histories will eclipse text-based histories. The sheer weight of the archaeological evidence will prevail.

The Goals of History Writing

No one writes history out of idle curiosity. The way people write history depends to some degree not only on sources but also on what they expect to accomplish. And that expectation in turn depends largely on personal motives, that is, ideology.[11] Many claim that it is improper to question another scholar's motives. On the contrary, I contend, it is often necessary to do so if we are to evaluate the history in question adequately. The only requirement is that our characterization is accurate and fair, that our argument is not simply ad hominem.

I shall define ideology here as "an overarching set of ideas in defense of a cause, claiming exclusive hegemony." Obviously everyone has a set of ideas, and most have an agenda in investigating the past. What then is wrong with ideology? I would suggest that ideology is a problem only when it becomes an obsession: going to extremes, ignoring all contradictory evidence, and escalating the polemics to demagoguery.

Much of the recent discussion of "maximalists" versus "minimalists" has to do with competing ideologies. The biblical revisionists, scholars on the far left, insist that mainstream scholars, and evangelicals in particular, are ideologues and thus put forward bogus arguments. Ironically, they seem blind to *their own* ideologies.[12]

In the next chapter, I shall survey the work of the biblical revisionists, where ideology is rampant and often seems like the only goal. Here, in

11. The literature on "objectivity" (i.e., ideology) in history writing is enormous. See, for instance, E. H. Carr 1987; Garbini 1998; Carroll 1997; Kofoed 2005; Provan 1995; Pippin 1986; Long 1994; Grabbe 1997; Pasto 1998; especially Barr 2000, passim, and Dever 2001a, passim. On revisionists and ideology, see n. 12 below and the conclusion of this book.

12. Barr takes ideology as the key to understanding recent Old Testament scholarship — in this case postmodern ideology. Its main target in its adopted form is traditional "positivist" or "historicist" biblical criticism and its claim to have discovered truth and meaning. Barr concludes that "the entry of the concept of ideology into biblical scholarship cannot be said to have been a happy event"; Barr 2000, 139. And as Brettler notes, "the understanding of ideology has become highly ideological"; Brettler 1995, 13. My own conclusion is that if everything is ideology, why is theirs any better than mine? On postmodernism and its impact on biblical and historical studies, see further Chapter II.

speaking of the goals of history writing in general, let us define ideology as above, a set of *fixed* ideas. But one might substitute "agenda" for "ideology." And since everyone clearly has an agenda, what is wrong with that?

The problem lies in the adjective "fixed." The ideologue is one whose agenda has become so obsessive that his or her mind is closed to all data that might be contradictory. In that case, ideology trumps scholarship, the defining characteristic of which is genuine open-mindedness. The historian, in particular, must be open-minded, since history writing is not a science, and the outcomes of the human enterprise are not predictable.

The most adequate histories, I would argue, are humanistic and positivist histories. Here there are, to be sure, subjective (i.e., ideological) factors at work; but not only are they up front, they are generally benign. For instance, mainstream history is usually written from a broad, liberal, humanistic perspective. It is neither reductionist nor determinist, but open-minded. More old-fashioned positivist histories are typically somewhat more theory-driven, but they nonetheless attempt to address facts, even though interpreting them in a maximalist fashion. But in contrast to these histories, ideological histories do not hesitate to ignore or even distort facts when they appear to be inconvenient for their cherished theory. Marxist histories (and some anti-Marxist histories) would be examples of the latter.

All this is not to say that any of our imagined historians are charlatans, only that all history writing is to some degree subjective, that ideology really *does* matter. So does motive; and some motives are better than others — better in terms of both practicality and the moral high ground. The lesson to be learned, however, is that we must constantly examine our own motives as well and be candid about our intentions. And above all, we must seek a balanced judgment.[13]

In three recent popular books I have described my personal background and set out my own presuppositions at the very beginning. In the present work, I duly note that I am a secular humanist, with no intention whatsoever of defending the Bible (or discrediting it). I am simply trying to be a competent archaeologist and an honest historian. Using all the

13. On the importance of balance, see the judicious observation of the distinguished Assyriologist and Near Eastern scholar William Hallo. He argues for a balance between credulity and extreme skepticism. We need to "stake out a place on the middle ground of sweet reasonableness," treating the "ancient texts critically but without condescension." See Hallo 1990, 187, 189. See also the biblical historian Marc Brettler, who speaks of "possible options"; Brettler 1995, 325.

tools at my disposal, I hope to grasp something of the reality of the lives of ordinary people in ancient Israel and Judah. I have tried to put aside my own worldview, in order to understand theirs. Where I do have an ideology, I can only hope that it is transparent and that it will not prevent me from seeing the full implications of the data I present.

Method in History Writing

If the outcome of our history writing depends on the sources we have at our disposal, on the feasibility of the goals that we have set for ourselves, and finally on a defensible ideology, all will depend ultimately on the methods we adopt.

Whether we are dealing with texts or artifacts, sound scholarly method is the same. It requires first of all appealing to facts rather than rhetoric, that is, a preference for statements that do not go beyond the empirical evidence, however caught up we may be in our subject. That means avoiding the extreme, which is the clue that inevitably unmasks the ideologue — the half-truth elevated to certainty.[14]

Related to that modesty is a genuinely open mind, a willingness to go wherever the facts may lead. That seems obvious and simple, but it is an enormous challenge. The lack of this openness is another mark of the ideologue, whose conclusions are usually presuppositions. Thus many text-oriented biblicists are oblivious to new archaeological data that might threaten their cherished notions about ancient Israel.[15]

Finally, the historian must exercise critical judgment, recognizing what we can and cannot know. That often means living with uncertainty, with partial truths, and with what several scholars have called "the balance of probability."

Given the sources we have, the goals we seek, and the most appropri-

14. Examples in revisionist discourse abound. Lemche declares that "the Canaanites did not know themselves that they were Canaanites"; this is patently absurd. What he *could* have said is that the modern concept of "Canaanite" is a construct that may not reflect the reality. Davies says that "everyone knows that history is not about the past but the present." What he *could* have said is that writing history is not entirely objective. When challenged, revisionists reply that they didn't really *mean* so and so. But it is fair to engage them on the basis of what they actually write.

15. See n. 10 above. Time after time the revisionists respond to my citing the archaeological data that they ignore by demonizing me. See further Chapter II.

ate methods we can employ, we shall try here first to examine each of our sources separately, reserving the biblical evidence until the last. Then we shall compare all our data to see where we can find what I call "convergences" between texts and artifacts.[16] It is here, where independent witnesses agree, that we are most likely to find, if not the truth, at least a reasonable and satisfying portrait of ancient Israel. That may be a modest goal, but it is attainable.

Ernst Axel Knauf, an extremely skeptical scholar, concludes of extracting information from texts: "I think, with the majority of historians past and present, that it can be done. Data from literary sources, though, have to be sifted as rigorously as data from archaeology; some are useful and others are not."[17] Knauf also makes an astute observation on the relationship of archaeological and textual data. To separate the two and to privilege philology will have a "devastating impact on archaeology and furthermore will guarantee that we will *not* understand what happened in the past." Knauf concludes that we need to demonstrate that "history can be written on the basis of archaeology, and, if need be, on the basis of archaeology alone; and also [to demonstrate] what kind of history would emerge from such an endeavor."[18]

Equally revealing are the observations of a distinguished biblical scholar, Lester L. Grabbe — founder of the "European Seminar," which has showcased so many of the revisionist biblical studies. He has produced a prolegomenon for any future history of Israel, in which he argues that the *archaeological* data, not the textual data, must be our primary source.[19] His *Ancient Israel: What Do We Know and How Do We Know It?* (2007) is in uncanny agreement with my *What Did the Biblical Writers Know and When Did They Know It? What Archaeology Can Tell Us about the Reality of Ancient Israel* (2001).

Now that a consensus may be emerging on the importance of archaeology, there will be more works like the present one. Better still, there will be much more teamwork, in which the archaeological data will be fully respected and integrated. In anticipation of that development, archaeology will take pride of place in the present work. I hope that it will be a harbinger of things to come.

16. Dever 2001a, passim. Grabbe 2007 similarly seeks "convergences." See my review, Dever 2010.

17. See Knauf 2008, 82.

18. See Knauf 2008, 85.

19. Grabbe 2007, 10, 35, 220, 224. Cf. nn. 16, 17 above.

In what follows I will assume throughout that the relatively late, elitist, and tendentious texts of the Hebrew Bible are not representative of the lives and concerns of the ordinary people of ancient Israel and Judah. These folk are mostly ignored in the Bible, or mentioned by priests, prophets, and reformers only to be condemned by them. In using the independent witness of archaeology to give back to these masses their voice, their history, I caution that I am not making any value judgments. As a "historian of things," I am simply trying to describe what it was really like for most people, in one particular time and place.[20]

20. I am well aware that in the Hebrew Bible there are laws protecting the rights of ordinary people, as well as prophetic protests against social injustice. But these are nevertheless the voices of elitists, and it is obvious that they represent the ideal, not the reality. Finally, the reality of women's lives is scarcely represented at all in the biblical texts.

CHAPTER II

The Challenges of Writing a History of Ancient Israel

Twenty years ago there was no challenge like the one presumed in our title. Biblical scholars wrote histories of ancient Israel as a matter of course. But in the interval, Hebrew Bible and Old Testament studies have made what is called the "literary turn" — the turn away from historical (and even theological) studies, toward reading the Bible simply as *literature*. That development is bound up with many trends in other disciplines, as well as the changing intellectual climate at the turn of the millennium, some of which we must examine, even though they are complex.

Toward a "Secular History" of Ancient Israel?

One reason for the declining interest in traditional histories of ancient Israel is that most seemed, in the scathing critique of Giovanni Garbini, little more than "paraphrases of the biblical texts."[1] In that case, who needed them?

Already in 1987, Thomas L. Thompson, one of the European revisionists, had become disillusioned with text-based histories of ancient Israel and thus declared: "It is . . . the independence of Syro-Palestinian archaeology that now makes it possible for the first time to begin to write a history of Israel's origins. Rather than the Bible, it is in the field of Syro-Palestinian archaeology, and the adjunct field of ancient Near Eastern studies, that we find our primary source for Israel's earliest history."[2]

---

1. Garbini 1998, 2.
2. See Thompson 1987, 39. Cf. the scathing review of Thompson 1992 in Rainey 1995.

I couldn't have said it better myself. In fact, I had been saying precisely these same things for a decade or more — using the very terms "Syro-Palestinian archaeology" and "independent discipline" (as far back as 1973).[3] A few years later Thompson produced his own effort at an archaeologically based history, but it was far from successful.

Can a "History of Israel" Be Written?

To most readers this would seem to be a nonquestion. But it is not that easy. In fact, most scholars of the Hebrew Bible today are skeptical. Obviously I do not agree, or else a work like the present one could never have been conceived. Yet the current historical malaise must be taken seriously at the outset of our task, as a sort of prolegomenon.

The discussion of ancient Near Eastern historiography (or history writing) goes back to fundamental works of American biblical scholars John Van Seters (1983) and Baruch Halpern (1985). Papers published in 1991 from a symposium broached the issue of ancient Israel more directly and reflected the views of several scholars who would soon be protagonists, including myself. Significantly, it introduced archaeology as a factor for the first time.[4]

Then in 1992 there appeared from the pen of Thomas L. Thompson the massive *Early History of the Israelite People from the Written and Archaeological Sources*, which despite its title made only scant and amateurish use of archaeology.[5]

The following year Gösta Ahlström published another, even more ambitious "secular history," *The History of Ancient Palestine from the Paleolithic Period to Alexander's Conquest*. Ahlström was a far better scholar, with few of the obvious ideological biases of Thompson (later one of the prominent revisionists; below). But he also had no firsthand acquaintance with archaeological data. These early histories attracted little

3. Cf. Dever 1981, 1985, 1988, 1997a, 1997b, 1998, 2000, 2001a, 2004.
4. Cf. Van Seters 1983; Halpern 1985; Dever 1991.
5. Cf. Thompson 1992. Actual archaeological input is rare; and there is no documentation whatsoever. Ironically, even *this*, his own "history," Thompson soon repudiated — "what was after all hardly history, critically speaking"; see Thompson 1997, 178. There is no clearer giveaway of the ideologue than an about-face that depends not on new data but on a "change of mind" — never acknowledging, of course, such an about-face. Lemche also takes a 180-degree turn away from his 1988 history; see Lemche 1998a, 146-48.

attention at the time, and today they are only curiosities in the history of scholarship.

The real debate had already begun the year before Ahlström's *History*, with the deliberately provocative work of Sheffield University's Philip R. Davies, *In Search of "Ancient Israel."* Davies distinguished three "Israels": "biblical" and "ancient Israel," which were simply social constructs of biblical scholars ancient and modern, mostly Jewish and Christian, that is, literary fictions designed to enhance these scholars' own self-identity. To be sure, there was then a "historical Israel," which may have existed in Iron Age Palestine. But it is unrecoverable because all the biblical texts are Persian (or Hellenistic) in date and therefore irrelevant (below); and archaeology, while theoretically useful, is "mute." The argument that the texts of the Hebrew Bible are "too late" to contain any real history of an earlier era came to be a key issue.[6]

The next year, 1993, another scholar of the revisionist Copenhagen school, Niels Peter Lemche, argued for a later and more deliberate date for the composition of all the texts of the Hebrew Bible, that is, the Hellenistic era (3rd-2nd centuries B.C.E.). The Hebrew Bible would thus be a free literary composition, fictitious throughout, and little more than the original Zionist myth, as Lemche argued in his 1998 book, *The Israelites in History and Tradition*. The Hebrew Bible is thus a late Hellenistic phantasmagoria, the product of the imagination of a beleaguered Jewish community; in effect, it is a literary hoax that has misled countless generations until it was unmasked by the intrepid revisionists. It therefore has no real-life historical context, except in the Hellenistic era in Palestine.[7]

"Maximalists" versus "Minimalists"

In 1996 there appeared two books that sharpened the growing historiographical controversy about an ancient Israel. The first, coedited by Fritz

---

6. Davies' "search for ancient Israel" (1992) cites as archaeological evidence *only* Amihai Mazar's *Archaeology of the Land of the Bible, 10,000-586 BCE,* in a single footnote — and that to dismiss the entire Iron Age database as "irrelevant" for his (Davies') "Persian period Bible"; see Davies 1992, 24 n. 4. Cf. the review of Zevit 1999.

7. Lemche's original "evidence" for a Hellenistic date for the Hebrew Bible consists of a single footnote, asserting that the Hebrew Bible's historiography most "resembles that of Herodotus"; see Lemche 1993, 183 n. 39. For a critical review of Lemche 1998a, see Hendel 1999.

and Davies, focused the discussion on a more specific issue that would soon come to dominate the discussion: the formation of the Israelite state. The tendency to down-date everything to the 9th century B.C.E. or even later — and thus to deny the united monarchy or Saul, David, and Solomon any historicity — would soon become the mark of a major division between the so-called maximalists and minimalists. And here, finally, the voice of archaeology began to be heard, although again with divided opinions.[8]

The other 1996 volume was by far the more ideological, taking the discussion to the extreme of denying the existence of a historical Israel altogether. Keith Whitelam (now at Sheffield University) gives away his political agenda in the title: *The Invention of Ancient Israel: The Silencing of Palestinian History*. Not only is there no "ancient Israel," the *search* for such an Israel has been illegitimate all along. It is the history of the "Palestinian people" that should have been our concern. Biblical scholars (and now archaeologists as well), mostly Israelis and American sympathizers, have systematically robbed the Palestinians of their cultural heritage. Here ad hominem attacks, distortions of the data, and caricatures abound on almost every page. Even Whitelam's coconspirator Lemche seemed taken back at Whitelam's ideological extremes, as did other reviewers.[9]

While Whitelam agreed with my earlier call for the liberation of the discipline of archaeology from theology, it was the only point on which we agreed. On several occasions I have sharply criticized his not-so-covert political agenda. From then on ideology and escalated rhetoric would increasingly characterize what had been largely a discussion on historiography.[10]

The next year (1997) another pivotal work appeared, a collection of essays edited by the University of Hull's Lester L. Grabbe, *Can a "History of*

---

8. The terms "minimalist" and "maximalist," which have become so prominent, derive from Hallo 1990. Along with many other scholars, I do not find them very useful, and I usually avoid them. *Good* scholars are "maximalist" on some topics, "minimalist" on others. The literature on the origins of the Israelite state (the biblical united monarchy) is vast; but see, most recently, with references, Dever 2000a; 2001a, 124-57; 2004; Master 2001; E. Mazar 2002; Finkelstein 2003; Lehmann 2003; Ortiz 2004; Faust 2007; E. Mazar 2007.

9. See Lemche 1998a. He concludes that Whitelam's book is "very politically correct"; p. 149. Precisely. Furthermore, his "Palestinians" in the Bronze Age are "invented"; p. 151. *No one* has "silenced Palestinian history"; we archaeologists have been writing their history for more than a century. Where has Whitelam been? And can he do better? See further the review of Zevit 2002.

10. Cf. especially Dever 1998; Whitelam is the most resolutely ideological of all the revisionists. For ideology generally, see Chapter I.

Israel" Be Written? While Grabbe himself was moderately optimistic, many of the other contributors were skeptical. Among the contributors were Davies, Lemche, and Thompson. Thompson's chapter was little more than a vicious personal attack on me for my attempts to reconstruct an early Israel. Thompson insisted that "Not only is the Bible not written from the perspective of ancient Israel, but even the New Israel — which is the Bible's perspective — does not have *any such historical context* except within the literature in which it exists" (emphasis mine). At this point I began to characterize the revisionists (mostly at Copenhagen and Sheffield) as nihilists. If they continue to insist that there is *no* historical ancient Israel, what else could one conclude?[11]

Robert Carroll's chapter cuts right to the chase. The Hebrew Bible is "sacred fiction," "verified falsehood," "propaganda." Further, "To the question 'can a history of ancient Israel be written,' I am inclined to answer 'No,' unless it is allowed that a bonus or unreliable history is still an adequate account of history." Carroll's concept of history in general is nihilist. He excoriates me for "name-calling," an exercise in which he is a master throughout his chapter. He puts me (and numerous other archaeologists) in the category of a "happy group of optimists" who suppose that archaeology can supply real data. His text-bias is clear: "Shards lacking writing are harder to interpret and less interesting than shards with writing on them." Less interesting to *whom?* Again, archaeology is mute.[12]

Just two years later (1999), Thomas L. Thompson published a work that almost defies description: *The Mythic Past: Biblical Archaeology and the Myth of Israel.* Again, the title is a giveaway. The book virtually repudiates history and scarcely refers to any archaeological data. "Archaeology" here simply means the supposed American-style Albrightianism that so preoccupies Thompson. This and other schools are simply Thompson's

---

11. For Thompson's nihilism, cf. "We are trying to create a past reality that does not and cannot exist"; 1997, 180. "We have already identified 'ancient Israel' as a literary construct, and we are in the course of identifying ancient Judaism as a religious one"; 1997, 185. "Old Israel is the lost Israel: the human Israel of an unknown past"; 1997, 187. Elsewhere, Thompson concedes that there *may* have been some such Israel; but his actual treatment is nihilist. Barr remarks of my designation "nihilist," that it has occurred to several other observers (Barr 2000, 71).

12. See Carroll 1997, 99. Carroll knows even less about archaeology than the other revisionists. He says attempts to write *any* "history of ancient Israel" are all "bogus history"; p. 93. Like Thompson, Carroll is a nihilist if that term has any meaning (n. 11 above). Only Lemche among the principal revisionists is somewhat more positive.

whipping boys for what is the most ideologically driven work in the entire history of the historiographical controversy. Grabbe, his colleague and founder of the European Seminar on Methodology in Israel's History, in which the revisionists are prominent, wrote a sharply critical review.[13]

A few of Thompson's often inscrutable assertions (there is no documentation whatsoever) will suffice. (1) "It is only a Hellenistic Bible that we know; namely the one that we first begin to read in the texts found among the Dead Sea scrolls." (2) "The Bible's 'Israel' (is) a literary fiction . . . the Bible is not a history of anyone's past." (3) "It is surprising that so much of the Bible deals with the origin tradition of a people that never existed as such." And on archaeology, "biblical archaeology's Iron Age became a rationalized paraphrase of the Old Testament: a secular Bible if you will." There is no other way to put it: Thompson is either ignorant or deceitful.

Thompson's fundamental ideology may best be seen in statements like these: "There is no more 'ancient Israel.' History no longer has room for it. This we do know. And now, as one of the first conclusions of this new knowledge, 'biblical Israel' was in its origin a Jewish concept."[14]

An Archaeological Critique

Already by the time Thompson's *Mythic Past* appeared, I had published several articles opposing the revisionists (as they had by then been styled). I accepted their challenge to traditional historiography, but I rejected their use (or misuse) of archaeology, pointing out how problematic their half-concealed ideology was.[15]

Two of my articles (in 1996) were direct personal responses to Lemche and Whitelam, whose abuses of archaeology were the most egregious, demonstrating both their incompetence and an astonishing presumptuousness. A 1998 article entitled "Archaeology, Ideology, and the Quest for an 'Ancient' or 'Biblical' Israel" began to engage the broader issues, and I was also able to confront Whitelam's recently published *Invention of Ancient Israel* (1996).[16]

13. See Grabbe 2000.

14. See Thompson 1995, 97. For a sampling of Thompson's other claims, no less nihilistic, see Dever 1998, 43-44; 2001a, 31-34.

15. My 1998 article on revisionism was written before the appearance of Thompson's 1999 *Mythic Past*. For a later critique, see Dever 2004.

16. See Dever 1998, 2000, 2004.

It was obvious by that time that the European revisionists — principally at Sheffield and Copenhagen — constituted a self-conscious school, one that impacted not only biblical (Old Testament) studies but also Syro-Palestinian or biblical archaeology.[17] Yet surprisingly, despite a decade-old discussion, no archaeologist other than me had written to address the revisionists at all.

The reason is probably that the Israelis, for their part, rarely pay much attention to what they regard as archaeological theory in the rest of the world. And despite popular opinion, Israelis do not really do what we call biblical archaeology, nor would most call themselves biblical historians. Thus Israelis were largely oblivious to the growing storm, with the exception of some inner quarrels about biblical archaeology and chronology, and one major work with broader concerns.[18]

In 2001 Israel Finkelstein teamed up with the well-known journalist Neil Asher Silberman to publish *The Bible Unearthed: Archaeology's New Vision of Ancient Israel and the Origin of Its Sacred Texts*. Although I have been critical of this work,[19] a semipopular book with no documentation, one must credit Finkelstein with being perceptive about changes in the larger disciplines, coming from abroad as it were.

Finkelstein did not challenge the revisionists directly, and he even sympathized to some degree with their low chronology (because of his own low chronology for the Iron Age). He did, however, stake out a more moderate position that he would come to characterize as centrist. Some of the revisionists, like Lemche and Thompson, soon tried to co-opt Finkel-

17. In response to my critiques of the revisionist school, they have protested that the Copenhagen and Sheffield group do not constitute a "school," that I have unfairly lumped them together. See, for instance, Thompson 1995, 693-94; cf. also Carroll 1997, 97. Yet Whitelam's response is unique: he says he cannot belong to a minimalist "school," since there is no such thing; Whitelam 2002. See (1) Lemche's summation of the "Copenhagen perspective" (Lemche 1998b); (2) Thompson's caricature of a "Harvard school" to which I supposedly belong (1993); and (3) the fact that in all my critiques I have discussed them separately, noting only their common skepticism regarding the biblical texts or that they are all agreed, "school" or not. It is worth noting that virtually all recent discussions treat Davies, Lemche, Thompson, and Whitelam (occasionally also Carroll) as a group; cf. Barr 2000, passim, who treats all these scholars as revisionists, precisely as I do. See also Kofoed 2005, lx, x, and especially Brettler 2003.

18. Thus Finkelstein 2007; A. Mazar 2007b, 2008, the latest (and best) treatments. Cf. also Faust 2007. The first full-scale "social history," based on the archaeological data, is Faust 2011. On the biblical texts, see Albertz 2007, with bibliography.

19. See Dever 2001c.

stein (the only archaeologist they ever approved of), but in all fairness he was never as extreme left wing as they are.

Quite by coincidence, I had been working independently on a much larger, full-scale response to the revisionists, which was published the same year (2001), *What Did the Biblical Writers Know and When Did They Know It? What Archaeology Can Tell Us about the Reality of Ancient Israel.* Unlike Finkelstein and Silberman's book, which had no footnotes, my frontal attack was fully documented. It was also admittedly more rhetorical, since the revisionists had already singled me out for increasingly ad hominem attacks. I was a "credulist"; "a crypto-fundamentalist"; my "methods . . . [had] little to do with archaeology"; I had "never recognized the methodological and historiographical issues that were involved."[20] Largely alone as a representative of a school that was coming to be caricatured as "maximalist" (versus "minimalist"), I was an easy target.

Other Responses to Revisionism

Among American biblical scholars who were willing to make forays into the revisionist literature, I can note only a few brave souls. Most outspoken (and earliest on) was Baruch Halpern, himself a distinguished biblical historian. In a 1995 article entitled "Erasing History: The Minimalist Assault on Ancient Israel," Halpern observed that none of the revisionists is trained as a "real historian"; "their exposure to history as it is practiced with respect to other times and places is almost always marginal." Furthermore: "The most extreme forms of this new historiography do not even engage archaeology in an intellectually honest fashion. They appeal to archaeology, instead, to subvert the validity of the textual (biblical) presentation."

Halpern's most astute observation is this: "The views of these critics would seem to be an expression of despair over the supposed impossibility of recovering the past from works written in a more recent present — ex-

---

20. For some of Thompson's caricatures, see the references in n. 14 above. Lemche has labeled me as almost a "Nazi" on the one hand (Lemche 2000, 173) but a virtual "Zionist" on the other hand, as well as a "Triumphalist." Elsewhere he dismisses me as a "rustic" (an unsophisticated non-European, I suppose; Lemche 1998b, 176), although Barr's identical charge of "postmodernism" he takes somewhat seriously. Whitelam outdoes them all in rhetoric (since he has no facts), accusing me of "facticity." I confess. I'm also guilty of "intellectual imperialism." See Whitelam's unpublished paper from a closed symposium of the Society of Biblical Literature meetings.

cept, of course, that they pretend to provide access to a 'real' past in their own written works in the contemporary present."[21]

Halpern puts his finger on a key issue: *ideology*. And the hypocrisy of the revisionists lies in the fact that while scurrying about like beavers to ferret out their opponents' ideology, they are oblivious to their own. None is more guilty of such hypocrisy than Whitelam. His response to me, for instance, when I have cited archaeological evidence he has ignored, has seized immediately on ideology (mine, of course), oblivious to facts.[22] That is the hallmark of the ideologue, the difference between ideology and honest scholarship.

Ideology Rears Its Ugly Head

The revisionists have charged directly or indirectly (1) that I am an older white male who represents the establishment; (2) that I identify more with American scholarship than with Continental; (3) that I still cling to the Enlightenment tradition and have characterized postmodernism as both absurd and morally offensive; (4) that I reject cultural relativism and sometimes engage in rhetoric in opposing it; (5) that I believe that one can be at least partially objective; (6) that I have worked for more than forty years in Israel by choice; (7) that I think those who caricature archaeology as "mute" are ignorant; (8) that I hold strongly that sometimes a direct connection can be made between an archaeological artifact and a biblical text; and finally (9) that I believe that we can identify an "ancient" or "historical Israel" in the Iron Age. These are strong charges; but I plead guilty.[23]

I have also made certain charges against the major revisionists, principally that (1) their frequent one-sided arguments obscuring contrary evidence constitute dishonest scholarship; (2) their portraits of archaeology and archaeologists are often caricatures; and (3) many of their publications are thinly disguised ideological manifestoes.

I stand prepared to document these (and other) charges, and that no

21. Halpern 1995.
22. Whitelam's response to my citing archaeological data that he should have known and cited is instructive. He never consults the data, but turns immediately to ad hominem arguments — always the proof that it is only ideology at work (but never *theirs*).
23. My ideology is right up front. Cf. the foreword in my 2001a, 2003b, and 2005c semipopular books. See also Chapter I above. Even so, you can't win. I've written to Davies to say that I'm not a theist, but he says I am anyway; Davies 1997, 117 n. 19.

doubt explains the hostility of the revisionists against me, which goes far beyond legitimate scholarly differences. In particular, the revisionists take umbrage at my characterization of them as "nihilists." But they *are*, when again and again they assert in one way or another that "there was no ancient Israel." They may attempt to rationalize such statements by claiming that what they meant was that the historical Israel that we might reconstruct is not the same as the idealistic one portrayed in the Hebrew Bible (a platitude). But that is not what they said. Nor have any of them made an honest effort to reconstruct some historical Israel — all the while demonizing us archaeologists for our efforts. That is what I mean by nihilism; and I am not alone in this charge.[24]

Ziony Zevit, an American biblical scholar who knows archaeology perhaps better than any other, attacked some of Davies' presuppositions in *In Search of "Ancient Israel."*[25] In 1998 Whitelam's *Invention of Ancient Israel* was reviewed by Benjamin Sommers, who documented its inflammatory anti-Israel ideology.[26]

In a symposium at Northwestern University in 1999, most of the protagonists of the revisionist controversy read papers, including Thompson and me (Davies declined to appear). Marc Brettler, of Brandeis University, read a paper entitled "The Copenhagen School: The Historiographical Issues." Brettler had published in 1995 a perceptive review of the issues in *The Creation of History in Ancient Israel*. His 1999 paper was an exceptionally fair and balanced critique. He easily refuted Lemche's "Hellenistic date" for the composition of the Hebrew Bible. He noted, precisely as I had, that despite a lack of the typical jargon of postmodernism, the revisionists' creeping skepticism pushed them in that direction. And, most perceptively, Brettler observed that Thompson's curious preoccupation with various archaeologies, theology, and all sorts of ancient Near Eastern comparisons, as well as his metaphorical treatment

---

24. The revisionists nearly all reply to my critique of their "non-histories" (Dever 1998) that they deny only "biblical" and modern scholarly "ancient Israels." But their language is ambivalent. And if they do concede that there may have been *some* "historical Israel," they do nothing to illustrate it. Barr has made the same point: "Again, in spite of the historical zeal of Davies and others, which some see, in any case, to end up in a nihilistic destruction of history": Barr 2000, 165. They *cannot* write history, since they dismiss the texts as fiction, and now that archaeology is a primary source, they are incompetent to deal with it.

25. Levine and Malamat 1996.

26. Sommers 1998.

of the biblical text, was because he "cannot engage in close reading of the text in Hebrew."[27]

If American responses to revisionism were scant, those of Israelis were almost nonexistent. The archaeologists simply quoted my works in an occasional footnote. Only Finkelstein seemed to take all this as a threat (perhaps because he thought, as I did, that revisionist use of archaeology was amateurish). The editor of the *Israel Exploration Journal,* Jonas Greenfield, published (with Baruch Levine and Avraham Malamat) a review of Whitelam's *Invention of Ancient Israel* that came close to calling it anti-Semitic (as I had done).[28] Sara Japhet, an Israeli Judaic studies scholar, deftly describes the biases of the revisionists in her "In Search of Ancient Israel: Revisionism at All Costs."[29]

So much of the revisionist denial of any historicity to ancient Israel depended all along on their Hellenistic date for the biblical texts. Particularly devastating to their position was a series of articles by the distinguished Israeli Hebraist Avi Hurvitz, who completely demolished their claims (since none of them were expert linguists or philologians, as Brettler had already showed). I had cited Hurvitz's works several times; but of course the revisionists simply ignored this evidence, as they did all the data adduced against their position.[30]

27. Brettler 2003, 18.

28. Cf. nn. 25, 26 above. My reference to "anti-Semitism" (Dever 2001a, 35-37) is based on Whitelam's *blanket* condemnation of Israeli scholars and American scholars aligned with them, with little or no documentation. This is a caricature, and it is based on an obvious ideological bias. In October of 2001 (!), Thompson convened an "international" symposium on the history of Jerusalem in Amman, Jordan, to which no Israeli or American scholars were invited. It was funded by and published by an Arab agency in Damascus, and Thompson was invited to Arab capitals to celebrate the appearance of the volume. His remarks, as published in the foreword, are a dead giveaway to his political agenda. See Thompson 2003, vii-xi. Similarly, Whitelam's *Invention of Ancient Israel* is a best seller in East Jerusalem; and in Arabic translation (Beirut) it is a popular textbook. Whitelam claims to have had nothing to do with the Arabic translation. Lemche rises above all this. Cf. nn. 25, 26. Cf. further Barr 2000, 82-89.

29. Japhet 1998.

30. Cf. Hurvitz 1997, 1999. For further discussion of the fallacy of "late date = nonhistorical," see Kofoed 2005, 33-112, and references there. The revisionists have all ignored the detailed linguistic arguments that date biblical Hebrew relatively early, and disprove the notion that it is a late, artificial "scribal argot" (contra Knauf and Davies). In his 2000 article Lemche returns to his Hellenistic date, but does not refer anywhere to Hurvitz 1997. As far as I can see, Thompson similarly ignores Hurvitz's linguistic data. Davies has responded in a "white paper" that I have seen.

"Faith and History": Evangelical Responses

I have noted the rather dispirited response of mainstream biblical scholars to the challenge posed by revisionism. This is largely because a generation or more ago the focus had already shifted from the Bible as history to the "Bible as literature" — a trend easily documented.[31] In short, if the Hebrew Bible had turned out to be unhistorical, many biblicists simply no longer cared much. But that was not true for more conservative scholars who represented faith communities, many evangelical Christians of course (Orthodox Jews were oblivious).

Already in 1994, as early as the first archaeological confrontations, more conservative American scholars had entered the fray with the publication of V. Philips Long's *Art of Biblical History* (and later, in 1999, *Israel's Past in Present Research*). The attempt here to refute revisionism did not, however, involve archaeology. At the same time (1994), however, there appeared a work edited by well-known evangelical scholars Alan R. Millard, James K. Hoffmeier, and David W. Baker, *Faith, Tradition, and History: Old Testament Historiography in Its Near Eastern Context*. Although the essays did not include contributions by any professional archaeologists, several authors did refer to the recent work of professionals (including myself), and they invoked Syro-Palestinian and biblical archaeology as a possible independent witness alongside texts. A few revisionist scholars were addressed as "minimalists," even though the discussion was then still in its infancy.

By 1999, David W. Baker had teamed up with Bill T. Arnold to edit a volume that dealt more specifically with the possible contribution of archaeology to the growing historiographical controversy, *The Face of Old Testament Studies: A Survey of Contemporary Approaches*. The indices indicate, however, how few archaeologists there were to include in the discussion, their scarcity as participants already noted.

In 2002 V. Philips Long, David W. Baker, and Gordon J. Wenham published a series of evangelical essays under the title *Windows into Old Testament History: Evidence, Argument, and the Crisis of "Biblical Israel."* Now revisionism and minimalism were confronted more directly, and some chapters did adduce archaeological data (as that of Richard Hess).

31. This scholarly shift is sometimes called the "literary turn" — the same phrase used to describe postmodernism. A coincidence? Virtually every recent survey of Hebrew Bible (and Old Testament) studies begins with the literary turn, as Barr 2000, 16ff.; Collins 2005, 30-42, show. Earlier evangelical surveys do the same; cf. Long 1999.

American evangelical scholars soon produced a volume of essays devoted specifically to archaeology's role, and especially the future of biblical archaeology, *The Future of Biblical Archaeology: Reassessing Methodologies and Assumptions* (2004), edited by James K. Hoffmeier and Alan Millard.[32] Particularly cogent was the lead chapter by Ziony Zevit. Most contributors were conservative, although not necessarily evangelical, and several were well known in larger circles.

A decidedly polemical work by Kenneth A. Kitchen, a British evangelical scholar and distinguished Egyptologist, took the revisionists to task at every turn: *On the Reliability of the Old Testament* (2003).[33]

American evangelical scholars also distinguished themselves by producing the only new histories of Israel of this era: Walter Kaiser's *History of Israel* (1998) and Ian Provan, V. Philips Long, and Tremper Longman's *Biblical History of Israel* (2003).[34]

A few of the above evangelical scholars had confronted the revisionists head-on, and they had triggered a scathing response, obviously ideological, I would say. There cannot have *been* an ancient Israel, because that would prove inconvenient.[35] Why the heat, one may ask — or why was the issue of historiography perceived as so crucial by conservative scholars?

The answer is obvious: history is the "ground of faith." Indeed, in Protestant circles generally, this is the typical theological position. "Salvation history," as it is termed, asserts that God reveals himself in specific historical events, to which the believer responds and in which he or she finds the ultimate meaning of life. Thus everything depends upon whether or

32. See Hoffmeier and Millard 2004. Many of the chapters engage my work in dialogue. I was invited to the symposium, but at the time a personal tragedy occupied all my attention.

33. I have sometimes characterized Kitchen, a colleague and friend, as a fundamentalist. He insists, however, in correspondence with me that he is a "factualist." Cf. Kitchen 2003, xiv.

34. These are old-fashioned "positivist" works, which I agree are passé. Even though I wrote for the dust jacket of Provan, Long, and Longman, in the final analysis one cannot have a real "biblical" *history,* only an ideal portrait based on the accounts of the biblical writers, which are obviously biased.

35. The revisionists reject *all* previous histories of ancient Israel, those to the right with scorn. Theirs is the view of Thompson, who insists that there cannot have *been* a history, since "Israel" is a literary construct. As he puts it: "We cannot speak of the tradition as historical at all. The Bible isn't interested in telling us anything about the past"; Thompson 1999, 189. Cf. n. 24 above.

not these salvific events actually *happened.* So every attempt to liberate faith from history has been stoutly resisted, even in some liberal Protestant communities.[36]

In Roman Catholic theology, biblical history is less critically important, because Scripture is subservient to the authority of the bishops and popes — to the dogma of tradition. The same is true of Judaism (except for Orthodoxy), where later tradition also dominates. Nevertheless, even here it could hardly be welcome news that biblical Israel was simply a "pious fiction."

The strongest counterattack against the revisionists has come, ironically, from Copenhagen, in Jens Bruun Kofoed's *Text and History: Historiography and the Study of the Biblical Text* (2005). In a carefully reasoned and exhaustively documented analysis, Kofoed attempts to stake out a balanced but truly conservative counterposition. Yet even here, the contribution of archaeology, which so many studies have shown can be positive, receives scant attention. Several of my publications, for instance, are mentioned in a footnote, but with scarcely any appreciation of the potential contribution of the data. Israeli archaeologists are not referenced at all. Nor is there more than passing reference to postmodernism.[37] So much for dialogue (but cf. below).

End-of-the-Millennium Assessments

I have documented the growth of a historiographical crisis that began some twenty-five years ago and has come to dominate much of biblical studies and even some aspects of Syro-Palestinian archaeology. However, some scholars have still not grasped the significance. Happily, two excellent state-of-the-art analyses have been published recently that help put things in context. The first is by the late James Barr of Oxford University, one of the leading Old Testament scholars of our time. Delivered as lectures in 1997, the work was published in 2000 and is entitled *History and Ideology in the Old Testament: Biblical Studies at the End of a Millennium.*

36. The "faith and history" movement came to fruition chiefly in the revival of "biblical theology" in the 1950s. See Barr 2000 and references; cf. a typical evangelical statement in Moberly 1999. I have offered a critique of biblical theology from an archaeological perspective in Dever 1985, 1997a. See further the Conclusion here.

37. See Kofoed 2005, 2-6, for passing notice. In the index there is only one reference to "biblical archaeology" (p. 6). Surprisingly, "postmodernism" gets five references.

The title itself captures the current mood, and much of the discussion is indeed about ideology and its impact on history writing.

Chapter IV is entitled "History of Israel"; chapter V, "Ideology"; chapter VI, "Postmodernism"; and chapter VII, "Postmodernism and Theology." Chapter I sets the tone of the discussion: "Bible, History, and Apologetics" (the latter meaning, of course, the defense of).

Early on Barr describes the decline of traditional historical-critical methods, as he remarks somewhat ruefully on how "a new generation of theory-driven scholars emerged after the 1960s determined to read themselves into the text." And in that connection he introduces almost immediately a term that will characterize his discussion throughout: "postmodernism."[38]

Postmodernism and Revisionism

Elsewhere I had argued that the biblical revisionists are best understood as thinly disguised postmodernists, especially in my *What Did the Biblical Writers Know and When Did They Know It?* (2001), so I am pleased that Barr, writing before my book appeared, had reached the same conclusion independently. Indeed, much of his book is devoted to discussing the connection. But what do we mean by the slippery term "postmodernism"? (Back to Barr momentarily, but see his definition.)[39]

The term defines not so much any discernible movement as it does an attitude — one of extreme skepticism toward everything deemed "modern," that is, in effect, the entire Western cultural tradition.

The revisionists have ridiculed my invoking the Western cultural tradition as involved in and threatened by postmodernism, as though I had somehow upped the ante.[40] They obscure the fact that the "modern" over

38. Cf. Barr 2000, 139. Barr defines many aspects of postmodernism throughout his analysis, coupling it with revisionism, as I do.

39. See n. 38 above. For Barr's favorable review of my earlier publications, see Barr 2000, 71-74.

40. See especially Davies' review of my 2001 book in the magazine *Shofar*. In addition, Whitelam has characterized me as attempting to dominate the discourse (a favorite postmodern term), as something like an agent of American "intellectual imperialism." (This in a paper read in a closed session at a national professional meeting.) This outright rejection of the Western cultural tradition (read "American") is, of course, the principal hallmark of postmodernism. See n. 41 below.

against which postmodernism has set itself in a life-and-death struggle is precisely that tradition. *This* is the Great Story — the "metanarrative" about which postmodernists say we must be skeptical, must reject.

The values of the Western cultural tradition — those at stake in my judgment — are often summarized as a triad: reason, liberty, and economic growth. Not by coincidence, these are precisely the values that postmodernism rejects. (1) Reason, the Enlightenment heritage, is caricatured as a sort of hubris about scientific modes of explanation, a promise of dominance over nature that could not be realized. (2) Liberty is taken to mean unbridled self-gratification, typical of the macro Western-style democracy, which is simply another tool of cultural imperialism. (3) Economic growth, of course, is identified with capitalism, the free-market system that is the hallmark of democratic nation-states, in short with greed.

And what did postmodernism offer in place of these decadent Western values? In place of reason, it offered simply an assertion that there were no truths to be known, only conflicting interpretations. In place of democracy, it offered anarchy. In place of economic growth, it offered endless class struggle. Is it any wonder that many observers have pointed out that all this amounts to nihilism? It appeals only to some vague utopian universalism.

In my view, postmodernism is essentially a theory of knowledge according to which there *is* no knowledge. It all began among left-wing intellectuals in Europe in the 1960s, especially in France, with a wholesale rebellion against the traditions of the Enlightenment. Its thrust was anti-everything, it seems, and especially the notion of *reason,* of rationality. Now the irrational was celebrated: the "other"; the novel; the absurd. And the principal targets became *texts* that enshrined the notion of modernity, of progress.[41]

Some quotations from leading gurus may suffice.

There is nothing outside the texts; texts refer only to other texts.

— *Jacques Derrida*

---

41. For my discussion of postmodernism, see Dever 1998; 2001a, passim; 2005a. The quotations from Derrida, Foucault, Lyotard, and many more will be found conveniently in one of the best introductions to postmodernism, Lemert 1997, defending the movement in its more modest (!) forms. To the contrary, see the devastating critique in Windschuttle 1996; cf. also, more generally, Gress 1998; Tarnas 1991.

> All readings are political, i.e., not about Truth, but about gender, class, race, power — ideology. I have never written anything but fiction.
>
> — *Jean Michel Foucault*

> All claims to knowledge are only social constructs. One must have incredulity toward all Metanarratives.
>
> — *Jean François Lyotard*

The latter phrase — "social construct" — has sometimes been used to characterize postmodernism as constructivism: there are no realities, only inventions, that is, subjective interpretations, illusions. If then a text, a truth claim, is only a "construct," what is one to do with it except *"deconstruct"* it? There is no such thing as authorial intention, or even, for that matter, an author. So the text can be stood on its head; turned inside out; manipulated so as to make it contradict itself; in the end interpreted to mean anything one wants it to mean.

Thus was born the principal method of postmodernism, and the only term most people have heard of: "deconstruction." The only criterion is "political correctness," that is, according to *our* political agenda. The irony of the latter — the other popular slogan that ordinary folk have heard of — is that postmodernism begins with the denial that there *is* any absolute, anything correct.

But that is only one of postmodernism's many contradictions, its absurdities. More significant (and, one would think, more damaging) is the fundamental notion that one cannot know *anything*. But if so, how can we know *that?* However, that is rational thinking, and postmodernism is nothing if not proudly irrational.

Trying to reason with those who claim to be postmodernists is obviously a waste of time. Ridicule may be the best weapon of those who, like me, are unreconstructed modernists. In any case, I have found a number of spoofs and semiserious portraits helpful.[42]

One of the most trenchant analyses of postmodernism is David Gress's *From Plato to NATO: The Idea of the West and Its Opponents.* Gress observes:

> If postmodernism was merely nihilism, it offered nothing other than a new name to distinguish itself from the more serious and better-defined

---

42. See especially Windschuttle 1996; Gress 1998; Tarnas 1991. Also, Barton deftly skewers some of postmodernism's absurdity; see, for instance, Barton 1996, 161.

nihilism analyzed by Nietzsche and Spengler, and feared by the interwar revivalists. And if postmodernism concealed, under a façade of nihilism, yet another version of the radical attack on the legitimacy of the West, that again was nothing new, merely a tedious and repetitive recital of the same alleged grievances and errors denounced by Rousseau, Marx, and their followers for two centuries. The sole contribution of postmodernism as a label or a movement was to sow further confusion by combining anti-capitalist and anti-modern sentiments.[43]

Even more devastating is Keith Windschuttle, *The Killing of History: How Literary Critics and Social Theorists Are Murdering Our Past*. He documents in detail how postmodernism's unsupported propositions make any writing of history impossible.[44]

But all our efforts are useless unless postmodernism is the enemy, that is, unless the revisionism, the nihilism, we hope to counter is really to be identified with postmodernism.

That is the issue, one that I addressed already in the mid-1990s, first in several preliminary articles, then in a full-length book much of which was devoted to an exposé of the ideology of the principal revisionists.[45] Here I need only note how close their basic assertions are to those of the classic postmodern slogans noted above.

Postmodernism	Revisionism
"There is nothing outside the text"; it corresponds to no external reality.	The biblical texts do not refer to any "historical Israel."
"All readings are political"; there is no objectivity, only ideology.	The "ancient Israel" of the Bible and of scholars is an ideological construct.
"All claims to knowledge are social constructs," inventions.	"Ancient Israel" is invented.

To me, revisionism's dependence on postmodern epistemology (theories of knowledge) was obvious early on. I was temporarily deterred from making a connection only because of the relative lack of typical post-

43. Gress 1998, 477; see further 475-80.
44. See nn. 41, 42 above.
45. Dever 2001a, 23-52.

modern jargon, as well as direct references to postmodernist literature, in most revisionist discourse. And that is still true. Furthermore, as my charge began to surface, the revisionists issued stout denials (with no evidence, of course).[46]

I would have had more respect for them had they candidly admitted their indebtedness to postmodernism and defended it. After all, insofar as postmodernism is a philosophy, it can be defended, even if not to my personal satisfaction.[47] One might even mount a defense of classical nihilism — although how one uses nothing to defend nothing is a mystery to me.

I confess that when I first began to oppose revisionism and to see the connections between it and postmodernism, I expected that the connection would help to discredit revisionists. That was because I had already come to reject postmodernism as a failed value-system. I found it repugnant because of its arrogance, its cynicism, its moral relativism, and ultimately its nihilism. In addition, I regarded postmodernism as passé in real intellectual circles.[48] Not to worry; the revisionists insisted that all that had had no influence on them. They had not, as I charged, belatedly adopted postmodernism. I persisted, however; and in time a few other scholars came to see the connection.[49]

James Barr, to whom I return now, had not seen much of my critique of the revisionists when he gave his 1997 lectures, published in 2000 as *History and Ideology in the Old Testament: Biblical Studies at the End of a Mil-*

46. Lemche's response to Barr's identification of him and the other revisionists with postmodernism, despite the lack of the typical language, is that they should have read the gurus earlier, but they came to the literature only later, an ideological about-face. Cf. n. 47 below.

47. It is part of revisionist hypocrisy that while denying that they are postmodernists (as nearly all critics now recognize), they adopt nearly all the basic presuppositions. Cf. n. 46 above. Nevertheless, they do avoid the typical jargon as others have observed; see Brettler 2003. I have more respect for those who offer a candid defense of postmodernism, such as Lemert 1997 in his light-handed treatment.

48. I have characterized postmodernism as worth considering, but in fact a passing fad; Dever 2001a, 249-54, 60. Already in his classic work *The Closing of the American Mind* in 1987, Allan Bloom had observed that in Paris circles where it originated postmodernism was a fad that would soon pass; Bloom 1987, 379. This in 1987! See recently the remark of Prof. Terry Castle, professor of literature at Stanford University, when asked if postmodernism was dead yet: "It carries on in its zombie-like, jargon-ridden way here and there. But it's on the wane"; *New York Times Magazine,* January 17, 2010, 16. Brettler says revisionism has become "tiresome"; Brettler 2003, 21. Finally, note that Terry Eagleton, one of the early gurus of postmodernism, has now written a book entitled *The Illusions of Postmodernism* (1996); cf. Ellis 1989.

49. See, in particular, Barr 2000, passim; Collins 2005; Kofoed 2005, 10-11.

lennium. Nevertheless, he devoted most of the 180-page book to an exhaustive documentation of just the charge that I had made (in more detail, of course).

Of Whitelam's *Invention of Ancient Israel*, Barr says it is "incredibly naïve"; that its theories of knowledge are "obviously absurd"; that there is "no factual evidence" for its claims. Overall Barr concludes, "I find the revisionist views unconvincing. The main reason for this lies in the excessive weight placed upon the concept of *ideology*." And even though he was drawing only on one early publication of mine (1998), Barr states that "Dever's position deeply damages the assurance of Philip Davies that basic historical methodology must support his (Davies') position."[50]

As for my concern that all this means "the end of history," Barr saw it as the end of theology as well (although not my concern here). He ended his book with the observation, "The wise saying should be heeded: that revolution devours her children."[51]

We are fortunate to have another recent state-of-the-art analysis in John Collins's *Bible after Babel: Historical Criticism in a Postmodern Age* (2005). Note the title again — *Postmodern* — with the same emphasis as mine. Collins notes my work in some detail, but he thinks my position somewhat closer to that of the revisionists, because on some issues such as the historicity of the biblical patriarchs, or the exodus-conquest, my views are also somewhat minimalist. But all good scholars are minimalist on some topics, maximalist on others. Collins notes what he calls Thompson's "obvious delight in undermining the tradition wherever possible" (postmodernists *always* delight in that). Davies, he says, is an "ideologue," as I had said. Whitelam he regards, correctly, as the most postmodern.[52]

The Real Issue: What Can We Really Know?

The underlying theme running through all the above topics is epistemology, which has to do with theories of knowledge. What do we know (or think we know), and how do we know it? That was the deliberate focus of

---

50. Barr 2000, 70-74. When he wrote, Barr had not seen my 2001 work.

51. Barr 2000, 180. The "end-of-history" notion is indebted to Francis Fukuyama's 1992 work *The End of History and the Last Man*. See Windschuttle 1996, 159-73, 178. Certainly postmodernism and biblical revisionism mean the end of history *writing*, since it is all fiction. My guess, however, is that man will survive.

52. Collins 2005, 32.

my 2001 book, *What Did the Biblical Writers Know and When Did They Know It?* It may be no coincidence that by 2007 one member of the European Seminar, and a leading biblical scholar, Lester L. Grabbe, had published a book entitled *Ancient Israel: What Do We Know and How Do We Know It?* (see Chapter I above). Again, the focus is on epistemology. And where so many other members of the European Seminar are skeptics (if not nihilists), Grabbe is surprisingly optimistic — I say surprisingly, because although a colleague of the European revisionists, Grabbe completely repudiates their postmodernist notion of "the end of history." In fact, he scarcely refers to any of the revisionists (specifically repudiating my technique of direct confrontation).[53]

Grabbe's central contention is that the only way out of the current historiographical impasse is to recognize that *archaeology* is now our primary source in writing any history of ancient Israel. That is welcome confirmation of a view that I have championed for many years, usually against mainstream biblicists. In a rave review of Grabbe's book, I hailed it as a breakthrough in the long-stalled attempts at a dialogue between archaeology and biblical studies.[54]

Grabbe's tactic is to compare the textual and the archaeological data, then rank the results along a continuum of knowledge from left to right — from proven wrong to proven correct — the middle ground being the most reliable. This is very similar to my *convergences* between the two classes of data, and the attempt then to isolate and defend a historical core.

The State of the Art

At about the same time that Grabbe's self-described prolegomenon was taking shape, several other programmatic works were appearing, all addressed specifically to the question of writing new histories of ancient Israel. A series of papers at an Oxford University seminar appeared under John Day's editorship in 2004, entitled *In Search of Pre-exilic Israel* — obviously an answer to Davies' pessimistic *In Search of "Ancient Israel"* (1992). The papers, all by mainstream scholars, not evangelical or conservative scholars, offered an alternative to the minimalist's approach.[55]

53. Dever 2010.
54. Dever 2010.
55. (London: T. & T. Clark, 2004). I was the only archaeologist invited. My paper was

A survey of the scene at about the same time by Diane Banks, entitled *Writing the History of Israel* (2006), traced the development of Israelite historiography from its beginnings in the mid–eighteenth century to the present. This work, however, by a beginning scholar, is generally noncommittal and is often disappointing, especially in its lack of understanding of the possibilities of archaeological data.[56]

In 2007 Oxford's Regius Professor, H. G. M. Williamson, published under his editorship a series of papers entitled *Understanding the History of Ancient Israel*. Here, for the first time, several archaeologists were included (Israel's Amihai Mazar and David Ussishkin), alongside two European revisionists (Davies and Whitelam) and a number of mainstream biblicists, historians, epigraphers, and art historians. This exceptionally varied volume was surprisingly positive, especially in the thoughtful paper of Hans Barstad of Edinburgh, "The History of Ancient Israel: What Directions Should We Take?"[57]

A year after Grabbe's own *Ancient Israel*, he issued in 2008 another of the series of volumes of the European Seminar in Historical Methodology under his editorship, *Israel in Transition: From Late Bronze II to Iron IIA (c. 1250-850 B.C.E.)*, volume 1, *The Archaeology*. Obviously most of the papers were by archaeologists, both Israeli and American. Although the book extended only down to the 9th century B.C.E. (i.e., principally the beginning of the biblical united monarchy), several of the papers addressed the intersection of archaeology and the history of ancient Israel.[58]

---

entitled "Histories and Non-histories of Ancient Israel: The Question of the United Monarchy" (pp. 65-94).

56. For her understanding of archaeology Banks quotes me, but rarely any other specialist, and she really doesn't catch on. Nonetheless, she concludes that a history "without reference to the Bible" would be desirable, and "should such a history be written, it would have significant implications for the study of the Hebrew Bible." See Banks 2006, 233-34. This work came to hand after my manuscript was completed, but perhaps I have fulfilled her prediction.

57. A. Mazar's 2007 paper, entitled "The Spade and the Text: The Interaction between Archaeology and Israelite History Relating to the Tenth-Ninth Centuries B.C.E." (pp. 145-71), is superb, one of the best statements of any archaeologist to date. Cf. A. Mazar 2007b, very similar, debating Finkelstein 2007.

58. Again, Mazar's paper was excellent. Grabbe's introduction (pp. 3-18) and "Reflections on the Discussion" (pp. 219-32) demonstrated that his grasp of the issues is unparalleled for a nonspecialist (as is his 2007 work).

On the "Limits of Skepticism" — and Beyond?

Ideology; revisionism and postmodernism; "minimalists" versus "maximalists"; what we can and cannot know; archaeology as a "primary source"; nihilism; faith and history. All the issues addressed in this chapter have to do with the prevailing attitude of *skepticism,* presumably now the antidote to "credulity." It is not unfair to say that postmodernism and biblical revisionism represent precisely extreme skepticism — a charge the protagonists would likely not deny. But such skepticism is not a method; it is not an alternative if our goal is to write *any* history of ancient Israel.

One of the most sensible and constructive observations on the issues raised here is found in the 1990 presidential address before the American Oriental Society by the distinguished Yale Assyriologist William W. Hallo, entitled "The Limits of Skepticism." It is a penetrating critique of ancient Near Eastern historiography, but also of current biblical studies, advocating an avoidance of extremes, concentrating instead on a broad, critical, comparative approach to *all* the available data.[59]

This attitude of balanced, fair-minded "sweet reasonableness" is refreshing and hopeful, especially in the light of the all-too-familiar flights of rhetoric (in which I myself have sometimes indulged). I want now to conclude this chapter by suggesting that Hallo's "limits of skepticism" might be taken as the "beginnings of optimism" — the prolegomenon to any new histories of Israel, such as the one attempted here. It's either that or give up.

It is obvious that Thompson and Lemche will not or cannot write any new histories; they already have failed histories on their hands (or so I have argued). Davies has rejected out-of-hand all the Iron Age data; and he is not competent alone to write his "Persian period" history of Israel. And Whitelam is stuck with his "history of the Palestinian people," for which he is not competent, and which, in any case, we archaeologists have been doing without him for a century or more.

Other postmodernists fare no better. Alberto Soggin's *Israel in the Biblical Period: Institutions, Festivals, Ceremonies, Rituals* (2001) is no history, only a series of topical articles. The most extreme of all is Mario Liverani's *Israel's History and the History of Israel* (2007), which, while novel, rests on an outdated Marxist paradigm.[60]

---

59. See Hallo 1990. On Hallo's "comparative method," see further Evans, Hallo, and White 1986.

60. Soggin 2001 is further to the left than his earlier history (1999) and much less ho-

Perhaps another metaphor would be to speak of different dimensions than the above boundaries, or "widening circles." (1) The inner circle would pose the challenge of understanding the Hebrew Bible and writing any history of Israel. (2) The next circle would be the radical crisis of representation that plagues all the humanistic disciplines as they search for new paradigms.[61] (3) The widest circle would be the clash of postmodernism and the Western cultural tradition within the West itself, as well as the external threat to the West posed by the only competing worldview, strident Islam.

In all these circles, the issue today is: What is "true"? Is there anything beyond "post"-modernism? To some it seems that the next era might be "pre-apocalyptic." In the following chapters, I shall offer my own very modest contribution to history writing in an axial age. Even though it has to do only with the small inner circle, I believe that it also has implications for the wider circles. We in the West (most of us, at least) have defined our destiny in part by our understanding of the biblical world and what happened there.[62]

The revisionists are on the wrong side of history — the wrong side because they cannot write any persuasive histories, and also the wrong side because history is moving on without them. Where they leave off, I shall begin.

---

mogeneous. The influence of postmodernism is clear, even though direct references are missing. Liverani's 2007 history is unique in being as far left as one can get, since he is a committed Marxist. Nevertheless, this is a brilliant and imaginative work, paralleling a real "Hellenistic Israel" with a fictitious "biblical" (and archaeological) Israel.

61. For the "crisis of representation," see Marcus and Fischer 1986.

62. Spirited defenses of the Western cultural tradition will be found in the works cited in nn. 40, 43, 44, 48 above. In Dever 2001a, 190-94, I offer my own modest defense, noting that for all its faults this tradition has proven superior to any other yet known in providing freedom, equality, prosperity, and hope to countless millions. The only viable alternative to this, our tradition, our worldview, would be Marxism (now defunct everywhere) or Islam, which doesn't even pretend to the above values. See further the positive conclusion of Gress 1998, 552-59.

CHAPTER III

The Natural Setting

All human societies are shaped in part by the natural environment in which they develop over time. If one compares the Anasazi of the American Southwest with the Eskimos of Alaska, it will be obvious that these peoples have developed their distinctive traits by adapting to very different natural conditions. Had Israel originated and pursued its destiny in Switzerland rather than the Holy Land, it would certainly have been different (and so would our world).

All this does not mean that we fall prey to what is called geographical determinism, because the natural environment is not the only factor that shapes culture. Ideology also matters, and in exceptional cases it may even trump everything else.

PART I: THE PHYSICAL DATA

Historical Geography

The Israeli historical geographer Yohanan Aharoni began his classic work *The Land of the Bible* (1967) with the following observation: "The history of any land and people is influenced to a considerable degree by their geographical environment. This includes not only the natural features such as climate, soil, topography, etc., but also the geopolitical relationships with neighboring areas. This is especially true for Palestine, a small and relatively poor country, which derives its main importance from its unique centralized location at a juncture of continents and a crossroads for the nations."[1]

The present work asks the question, What was it *really* like in ancient Israel and Judah in the 8th century B.C.E.? Thus we must begin by looking at the context — the unique physical setting — that constituted the basic facts of life for the people we seek to understand. First we will consider nature itself, then the physiological responses that it triggered. In the latter task we shall see what the biblical writers thought, and then we will resort to our imagination to reconstruct what ordinary people might have felt about their environment.

The Levant

By the term "Levant" (from the French verb "to rise"), I shall mean here the eastern Mediterranean shores, seen by the West of course as the lands of the rising sun, but also as the part of the world where civilization arose.[2] The area extends from the southern shores of Turkey (ancient Anatolia) down the coast of Syria, Lebanon, and Israel, to the delta of Egypt. The extension to the east, farther inland, is blocked by the Great Syrian/Arabian Desert (the "Nafud"). The resultant semicircular landmass has often been called the Fertile Crescent, an arc skirting the desert from the Arabian Gulf, up the Tigris and Euphrates Rivers, westward across the foothills of the Anatolian Plateau, and down the Orontes and Jordan Valleys to the Sinai.

The Great Rift Valley

Our attention here will be focused on a portion of the narrow littoral along the Mediterranean coast, the southwestern portion of the Fertile

---

1. Yohanan Aharoni was Israel's leading historical geographer. His classic Hebrew work *The Land of the Bible* (1962) was translated into English under that title by Anson Rainey (1967; revised and enlarged edition 1979). Rainey, an excellent historical geographer himself, has now collaborated with R. Steven Notley to produce the current standard work, *The Sacred Bridge: Carta's Atlas of the Biblical World* (2006). For an overview of the discipline of historical geography, see pp. 9-24.

2. Throughout this work I will cite *The Sacred Bridge* (above, n. 1) as Rainey 2006, since his part of the volume is the only one relevant here. On the geographical setting discussed here, see pp. 25-42. There are a number of other biblical atlases, but none compares with Rainey and Notley.

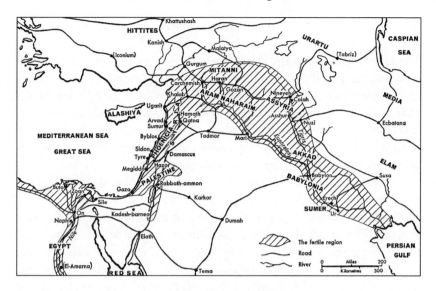

Fig. III.1. The Fertile Crescent.
Aharoni 1967, map 1

Crescent, or what is today modern Israel and the West Bank. Here the Rift Valley is the dominant feature of the landscape. This is a deep valley formed long ago by tectonic activities, extending some 3,700 miles from southern Turkey all the way to the Zambezi River in Mozambique. In the middle portion the Rift Valley is drained by the Orontes River in Syria, and in Israel by the Jordan Valley (including the Sea of Galilee and the Dead Sea). At the shores of the Dead Sea, the elevation is some 1,230 feet below sea level.

On both sides of the rift there arise mountain ranges or cliffs as high as 6,500 feet. The western heights in Syria (and in upper Galilee in Israel) are called the Lebanon Range, while those opposite the valley are called the Anti-Lebanon Range (in Syria and Jordan). Beyond the latter the vast desert begins. Thus we have a relatively narrow strip of land running through the Rift Valley and its surrounding ravines, linking Africa with Asia. It is often termed a "land bridge," or as Carta's monumental atlas of the biblical world (2006) has it, the "Sacred Bridge."[3]

3. See n. 1 above.

Bridge to Nowhere?

The valley itself is deep and treacherous (the Jordan Valley), but in Syria it broadens out into the Beqʻa Valley (from the verb "to split"). The alternate north-south route — the "Way of the Sea" (Heb. *dĕrĕk hā-yām*) or the "King's Highway" — had shifting sand dunes or was marshy along the narrow coast, so the route often hugged the foothills or turned inland through narrow passes. In any case, all the major corridors between two great empires, Egypt and Mesopotamia, ran this gauntlet.

This land bridge through Israel (and Transjordan) carried major trade routes for millennia, as well as successive invading armies. A bridge facilitates traffic; but it may easily be blown up. The frequent clashes of great empires in large part determined ancient Israel's destiny, a small and vulnerable people caught in the middle of events far beyond their control.

The precarious geopolitical situation of ancient Israel and Judah was worsened by its small and isolated location; mountainous and fragmented terrain; thin, rocky soils; vast arid regions; and sparse, unpredictable rainfall (below). This was truly a marginal area, blessed with few natural resources. If geography had indeed been decisive, Israel and Judah would have disappeared and been forgotten long ago.

Fractured Topography, Fractured History

The country is small — about 250 miles from north to south. At its widest point (near the southern end of the Dead Sea) it is only some 90 miles across. But the southern third of the country comprises the barren Negev Desert, uninhabitable for the most part. The coastal plain north of Tel Aviv is only 25 miles wide, further constricted here and there by marshes to the west and the Samaria hills to the east. The central part of the hill country — Judea, Samaria, and the hills of Galilee — is the heartland, but it is mountainous and broken up by deep ravines that make travel and communication difficult. The only east-west feature in the country, the Jezreel Valley, in the north, was too marshy and malarial in antiquity to be occupied. The subtropical Jordan Valley is flanked by steep banks, and the river could not be exploited with primitive technology. The broken topography and starkly differing regional conditions of the country meant that it was scarcely ever really united, with regional factions constantly vying throughout history for the scarce resources.

The Natural Setting

A "Land of Milk and Honey"?[4]

All ancient economies were agricultural, so arable lands with good soils and adequate rainfall were essential. But in the southern Levant very few regions were ideal. The coastal plain to the south was poorly drained and marshy, the northern portion almost nonexistent because of the mountains verging almost to the sea. We have noted the inhospitality of the Jezreel and Jordan Valleys. The central mountainous regions had good soils in the intermontane valleys, but the shallow rocky soils of the hillsides were difficult to till and plant without laboriously built terraces. Here and there, however, deep rich *terra rosa* soils did exist, particularly in the Shephelah or western foothills.

The fractured topography is also reflected in the extremes in elevation. The Dead Sea is almost 1,300 feet below sea level, the Sea of Galilee 700 feet below sea level. Yet the highest points in the Central Hills rise to more than 3,000 feet above sea level; the hills of upper Galilee to some 4,000 feet; the heights of Mount Hermon to more than 9,000 feet. (The hills of Transjordan are similar in height.)

Much of the southern Levant was arid or semiarid, suitable only for pastoral nomadism, with annual rainfall of circa four to eight inches. In Israel and Judah there were no significant rivers or perennial streams (except for the Jordan; above). Most riverbeds were wadis, dry much of the year; they flooded and were unusable during the rainy seasons. The annual rains varied greatly, and there was often too little water or too much. In any case, all the rain fell from mid-October to late April, and the long summer months were entirely dry. Temperatures could rise to 130 degrees in the Negev and the Jordan Valley; to 100 degrees along the coast; and even to 90-95 degrees in the hill country. In drought years — perhaps one in five — even the winter rains failed.

In areas with more than eight inches of annual rainfall, dry farming of grains and cereals, as well as cultivation of fruits and vegetables, was possible in good years. Such regions were:

The southern/Philistine Plain	15-25"
The northern coastal plain	25-30"
The Judean Shephelah (foothills)	25-30"

4. The stock biblical phrase "the land of milk and honey" is obviously rhetorical; cf. N. MacDonald 2008, 3-9.

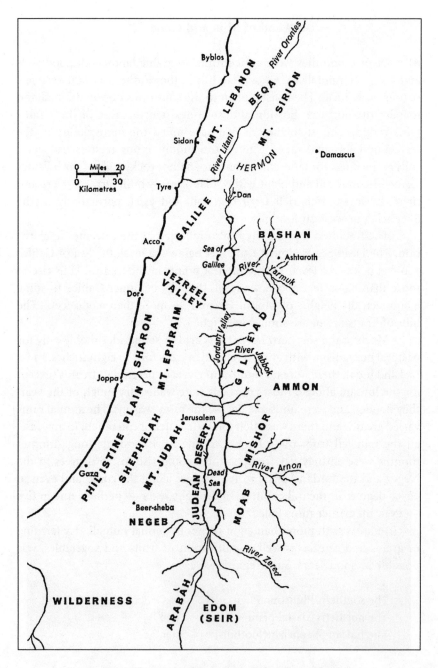

Fig. III.2. The geographical regions of ancient Palestine.
Aharoni 1967, map 2

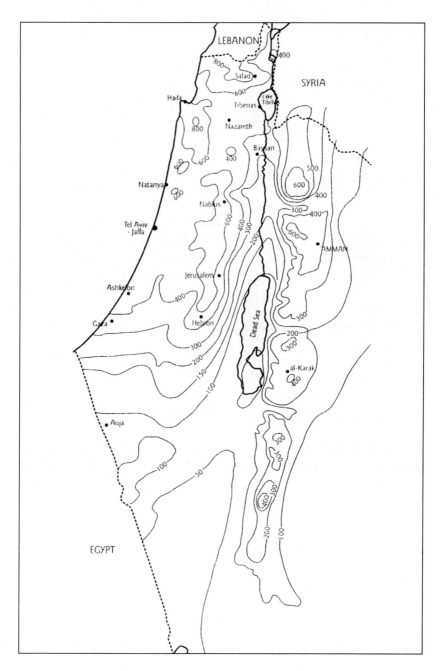

Fig. III.3. Rainfall map showing isohyets (in mm.).
B. MacDonald 2000, fig. 4

The Jerusalem hills	20-25″
The Samaria hills	25-30″
The lower Galilee	25-30″
The upper Galilee	30-40″

The major geographical designations of the land were determined to a large extent by the conditions described above. They were from west to east generally:

(1) The Coastal Plain:	Philistine Plain to the south
	Sharon Plain in the center
	Plain of Acco to the north
(2) The Judean Shephelah:	Foothills of the Central Ridge
(3) The Central Ridge:	Judea to the south
(Lebanon Range)	Samaria in the center
	Lower and upper Galilee to the north

(4) The Jordan Valley and the southern Arabah
(5) The Transjordanian Plateau: Bashan, Gilead, Ammon, Moab, Edom
(6) The Jezreel Valley: separating Samaria and lower Galilee

"Landscape" as a Mental Template

Most of the names above are known from extrabiblical texts, and of course the distinctions themselves are based on natural features. Nevertheless, archaeologists today understand "landscape" as consisting of both nature and the human perception of the natural world.[5] Thus we turn now to the biblical terminology and what it reflects of the psychology of the writers and other folks in ancient Israel and Judah.

PART II: THE BIBLICAL DATA

The inhabitants of ancient Israel and Judah were acutely aware of their environment, more so than we moderns, because their very lives depended

5. Landscape archaeology is now a well-recognized subdiscipline, one that sees landscape as perception — "state of mind" — as well as physical setting. See further Dever 2003d.

upon practical knowledge of the way nature works. And although they lacked our scientific understanding and terminology, they were sophisticated in their own intuitive and experiential way. Happily some of their popular worldview finds its way into the Hebrew Bible despite the elitist outlook of its writers and editors.

The Land Itself

The ancients did not know that their land was unique, since they had no basis for comparison (except perhaps for Egypt).[6] Nevertheless, they appreciated it for its own qualities, which they knew well indeed. This good land — "Land of Promise" — was a gift, and therefore precious.

That theme resonates throughout the Hebrew Bible. Moses pleads with Yahweh: "Let me cross over to see the good land beyond the Jordan" (Deut. 3:25). He assumes that Yahweh had promised the land, for he says to the people: "God has brought you into the land that he swore to your ancestors, to Abraham, to Isaac, and to Jacob, to give you — a land with fine, large cities that you did not build" (Deut. 6:10). It is a land "flowing with milk and honey" (Deut. 11:9). Deuteronomy 8:7-10 is worth quoting in full:

> For the LORD your God is bringing you into a good land, a land with flowing streams, with springs and underground waters welling up in valleys and hills, a land of wheat and barley, of vines and fig trees and pomegranates, a land of olive trees and honey, a land where you may eat bread without scarcity, where you will lack nothing, a land whose stones are iron and from whose hills you may mine copper. You shall eat your fill and bless the LORD your God for the good land that he has given you.

Several passages that contain the Promised Land theme describe the intended territory of the Israelite people in some detail. Thus Deuteronomy 1:6-8:

> The LORD our God spoke to us at Horeb, saying, "You have stayed long enough at this mountain. Resume your journey, and go into the hill country of the Amorites as well as into the neighboring regions — the

---

6. The biblical worldview is reflected in the Table of Nations in Gen. 10, together with its parallel in 1 Chron. 1:4-23.

Arabah, the hill country, the Shephelah, the Negeb, and the seacoast —
the land of the Canaanites and the Lebanon, as far as the great river, the
river Euphrates. See, I have set the land before you; go in and take possession of the land that I swore to your ancestors, to Abraham, to Isaac,
and to Jacob, to give to them and to their descendants after them."

One should also note the summaries in Joshua 10:16-17 and 12:8-24 (the
latter a list of Canaanite kings and their cities).

The Hebrew Bible is aware of the natural and cultural boundaries of
ancient Israel and Judah. Numbers 34 is the classic text. Yahweh specifies to
Moses what their "inheritance" in Canaan shall be: it stretches from Egypt
to the borders of Lebanon ("Lebo-hamath").

Other texts mention several more specific regions of the land, although they cannot conceive of the modern, empirical classification that
we have offered.

Region	Text
The Mediterranean ("Great Sea")	Josh. 9:1
The "Land west of the Jordan"	Josh. 12:7
The Sharon Plain	1 Chron. 5:16; 27:29
The "Way of the Sea"; "King's Highway"	Isa. 8:23 (9:1); Num. 20:17
The Shephelah (foothills of Judah)	Josh. 11:16; 15:33-42; 1 Kings 10:27
The hill country	Josh. 11:16
The Jordan Valley	Josh. 11:21
Galilee	Josh. 11:2; 19:35-38
The Jezreel Valley	Josh. 17:16; Judg. 1:27
The Dead Sea	Gen. 19:28; Deut. 3:17; Josh. 3:16
The Arabah (southern Jordan Valley)	Deut. 2:8; 3:8
The "Land east of the Jordan"	Josh. 13:27
The Eastern desert	Judg. 6:1-3
Bashan	1 Kings 4:13; Amos 4:1
Gilead	Deut. 3:10; 4:43
Moab	2 Kings 3:4
Ammon	Num. 21:24
Edom	Ezek. 27:16

Natural conditions of the land are also alluded to in many texts. The
unique weather pattern is attributed to Yahweh, who "will open for you his

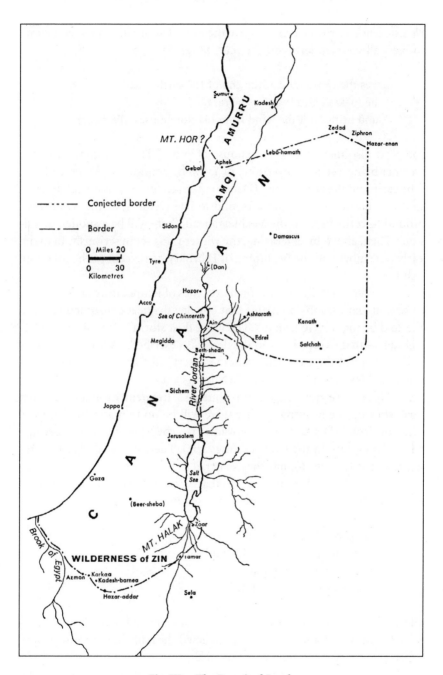

Fig. III.4. The Promised Land.
Aharoni 1967, map 4

rich storehouse, the heavens, to give the rain of your land in its season and to bless all your undertakings" (Deut. 28:12). Yahweh

> makes the clouds rise at the end of the earth;
>> he makes lightnings for the rain
>> and brings out the wind from his storehouses. (Ps. 135:7)

Job 38:22 also mentions a "storehouse of snow." Thus the concept of the weather being a sort of "overflow" of Yahweh's abundance. And the phrase "the early and the latter rains" (Deut. 11:13-17; cf. Jer. 5:24) is an apt description of what usually happens. In mid to late October, as the wind shifts around to come in from the Mediterranean, there will be a sudden downpour. Then, after a brief clearing, the winter rains set in seriously. Between early December and the beginning of February, 75 percent of the total rain will fall.

The typical daily and seasonal extremes of temperature are described in several texts. Jacob complains that "by day the heat consumed me, and the cold by night" (Gen. 31:40). The fierce dust storm — the sirocco (Heb. *shārāv*) — that sweeps in from the desert is described: "A hot wind comes from me out of the bare heights in the desert" (Jer. 4:11). Thus the land is one that "devours its inhabitants" (Num. 13:32).

There were not only storms, but also frequent droughts. Yahweh "will shut up the heavens, so that there will be no rain and the land will yield no fruit" (Deut. 11:17). The wadis (riverbeds) will dry up "because there [is] no rain in the land" (1 Kings 17:7). There are wells (Num. 21:16) and cisterns (Isa. 36:16), but they may fail.

The eternal cycle of the seasons that we have described in some detail is alluded to, but only to recognize two seasons:

> "As long as the earth endures,
>> seedtime and harvest, cold and heat,
> summer and winter, day and night
>> shall not cease." (Gen. 8:22)

In Chapter VI, on village agriculture, we shall pursue further how the natural conditions of ancient Canaan impacted the daily life of most people, especially the peasants who constituted the bulk of the population. There we will indulge in speculation about how ordinary people, not those who wrote the Bible, felt about their environment, its dangers and its promise.

CHAPTER IV

The Database: Sites and Hierarchies

In Chapter III, I described the overall geology and geography of ancient Palestine, the larger context within which Israel and Judah emerged and had reached a certain evolutionary stage by the 8th century B.C.E. Let us now turn to the more specific historical, cultural, and political context within which individual sites took shape. In particular, we want to ask *why*. It is this deliberate, systematic focus on explanation — cause and effect — that will make our inquiry truly *historical*. Instead of a merely descriptive or synchronic approach, treating the archaeological data topically, we shall take a diachronic approach, charting change through time.

To do this, however, we will need to develop a multitier hierarchy of sites, grouping and characterizing them by means of appropriate criteria.

The result will be detailed maps of virtually all excavated 8th century B.C.E. sites in Israel and Judah (since archaeological data are primary for our purposes), which will provide us with the essential database for all subsequent discussions here. We shall also include survey data where possible, even though we cannot illustrate or quantify it; few, if any, of these sites can be identified. Thus we may list some sites but will not add them to our maps. True to our principle of archaeological data first, the chart in figure 1 uses mostly Arabic place-names (some Hebrew) initially because the other names are often based on biblical or other texts (although the maps and the discussion may use either name).

We may then supplement this list with a few other contemporary names, known to us mainly from biblical or Neo-Assyrian texts, but more or less plausibly identified with archaeological sites.

Fig. IV.1. Hierarchy of 8th Century B.C.E. Sites

I. Tier 1: Capitals

Site (Arabic/Hebrew Name)	Biblical Name; Stratum	Acres	Population
N: Sebastiyah	(Samaria, PP IV-VI)	18 *(upper)*	2,000
S: el-Quds	(Jerusalem, 12)	10-15	12,000?
			(7th cent.)

II. Tier 1: Other (Administrative Centers/District Capitals)

Site (Arabic/Hebrew Name)	Biblical Name; Stratum	Acres	Population
Tell el-Qadi	(Dan II)	50	5,000?
Tell el-Qedaḥ	(Hazor, VI-V)	15	1,000
Tell et-Mutesellim	(Megiddo, IVA)	15	1,500
Tell el-Jezer	(Gezer, VI)	31	3,000
Tell el-Rumeileh	(Beth-Shemesh, 3-2 [IIb, c])	7	700
Tell ed-Duweir	(Lachish, III)	31	3,000
Tell es-Sebaʿ	(Beersheba, III)	3	300

III. Tier 2: Cities/Urban Centers (1,000-)

Site (Arabic/Hebrew Name)	Biblical Name; Stratum	Acres	Population
Tel Reḥov	(III-II)	12	1,200
Tell Dothan	(Dothan, Level 2)	15	1,500
Tell Tiʿinnik	(Taʿanach, IV?)	18	1,800
Tell el-Ḥusn	(Beth-Shean, IV)	10	1,000
Tell Balâṭah	(Shechem, VIII-VII)	15	1,500
Tell en-Naṣbeh	(Mizpah, 3A)	7-8	800
Kh. Rabûd	(Debir, B-II)	15	1,500
Tell el-Khalil; Kh. ʿArbʿa	(Hebron)	7.5	750
Tell Jemmeh	(Yurza?, C-D)	12	1,200
Tell el-Ḥesi	(Eglon?)	25	2,500
Tell Abū Hureireh	(Gerar)	50	3,000?

IV. Tier 3: Towns (300-1,000)

Site (Arabic/Hebrew Name)	Biblical Name; Stratum	Acres	Population
Tell el-Farʿah (N.)	(Tirzah?, VIId, e)	10?	1,000?
Tell Yoqneʿam	(Jokneam, XII)	10	1,000
Tell el-Ifshar	(Hepher?)	10	1,000
Kh. et-Tell Dhurur	(Zeror)	?	500
Kh. Jemain	(?)	3	300
Tel Michal	(Makmish)	10	1,000
Tell el-Hammeh	(Hamath)	7	700
Kh. Banat Barr	(?)	7	700
Marjameh	(Baʿal Shaʿlishah?)	7	700

Beitin	(Bethel)	4	400
Tell el-Jîb	(Gibeon)	5	500
Tel Batash	(Timnah, III)	7	700
Ras Abū-Hamîd	(Gibbethon?)	10?	1,000?
Kh. el-Qôm	(Makkedah)	?	500?
Minet Rubin	(Yavneh Yam, X)		
Tell el-Judeideh	(Moresheth-gath)	?	500
Kh. et-Ṭubeiqah	(Beth-Zur)	4	400
Tel Zayit	(Libnah?)	6	600
Tell Ḥalif	(Jahneel, VIB)	3	300
Tell es-Shārîyeh	(Ziklag)	4	400
Tell Beit Mirsim	(unknown, A$_2$)	10	1,000
Tel Masos	(?, IIA)	8	800
Kh. ʿArʿarah	(ʿArôʿer, II)	?	?
Tel ʿIra	(Ramah?, VII)		

V. Tier 4: Villages (50-300)

Site (Arabic/Hebrew Name)	Biblical Name; Stratum	Acres	Population
Tel Qades	(Kedesh)	?	?
Qaṣrin	(Qasrin VIII)	?	?
Tel Yinʿam	(Jabneel?)		
Tell Chinnereth	(Kinneret, II)	2.5	250
Tel Qiri	(?; VI)	2.5	250
Tel Qashish	(Dabbesheta?)	2.5	250
Kh. Jemein	(?)	2.5	250
Beit Aryeh	(?)	1	100
Kh. Kla	(?)	1.5	150
Naḥal Rephaim	(Naḥal Refaim)	?	?
Tell Kurdâneh	(Aphek, X)	?	200?
Tell es-Ṣandaḥannah	(Mareshah)	?	200?

VI. Forts

Site (Arabic/Hebrew Name)	Biblical Name; Stratum	Acres
Tel Jezreʿel	(Jezreel; ?)	
Tell esh-Shûni	(Kudadi)	
Kh. el-Maḥrûq	(?)	
Qumran	(ʿIr-ha Melaḥ?)	
el-Khirbeh	(?)	
el-Buqeiʿa	(Valley of Achor?)	
Risbon le-Zïyyon		
Ramat Raḥel	(Beth-Haccherem VB)	
Tel Arad	(Arad, IX-VIII)	
Kh. Abu Tuwein	(?)	
Tel Malḥata	(?, IV)	4
Ḥorvat Radum	(?)	

PART I: THE ARCHAEOLOGICAL DATA

Developing a Multitier Hierarchy: Tier 1

The essential criteria for arranging all the known sites in a hierarchy would include the following: (1) strategic location, with particular respect to the potential for regional domination; (2) relative size; (3) the presence or absence of monumental architecture; (4) evidence of cultic remains; and (5) socioeconomic aspects as evidence of elites. Using these strictly archaeological criteria in our initial analysis, we should be able to recognize the following hierarchical distinctions:[1]

> The capital cities of each kingdom; Tier 1; fig. IV.2
> District administrative centers; also Tier 1; fig. IV.2
> Urban centers, or true cities (population of ca. 1,000 and upward);
>   Tier 2; fig. IV.18
> Towns (ca. 300-1,000); Tier 3; fig. IV.23
> Villages (ca. 50-300); Tier 4; fig. IV.25
> Hamlets, farmsteads (below 50); Tier 5 (not mapped)
> Forts; unique, so not ranked; fig. IV.29

Tier 1 Sites: Capitals

1. The first criterion for distinguishing Tier 1 sites — location — is satisfied by situating a presumptive site in what may be called first its environmental niche, looking at its physical setting (Chapter III). Why is this particular site where it is, given the usual environmental constraints? And why not somewhere else, especially if the location seems to pose problems? At the next level of analysis, we need to look at the cultural context. This is what urban geographers call a "central place," capable of dominating its immediate region, not only by its location but also by its potential political influence.[2]

If the first criterion is met, we may then distinguish a Tier 1 site — a state capital or a district administrative center. There can of course be only

---

1. For orientation, see Hodder and Orton 1976. Obvious as a hierarchy of sites would seem to be, most standard archaeological works do not do such analyses.
2. Cf. Renfrew and Bahn 1991, 154-62. Cf. n. 30 below.

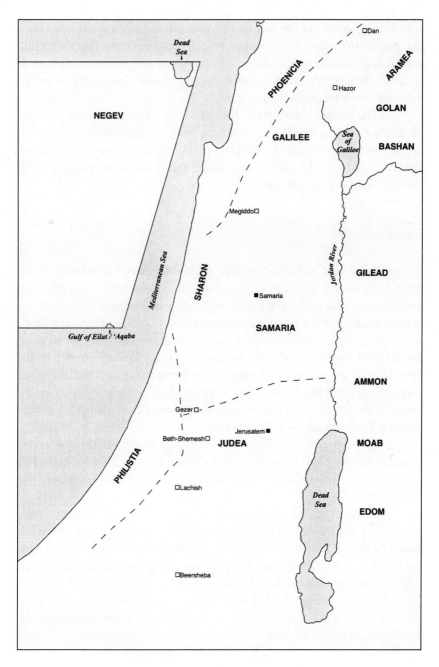

Fig. IV.2. Tier 1: Capitals and administrative centers

one Tier 1 capital site for each state (or one successive capital at a time). But there can and probably will be several contemporary Tier 1 sites that served as regional centers. And in both cases, size may be a secondary qualification. A relatively small site may nevertheless dominate a region politically and even socioeconomically.

2. The second criterion for distinguishing a Tier 1 site is the presence or absence of monumental architecture. This would include not only defenses but also evidence of deliberate planning, separation of public and private areas with the former dominant, and evidence of palaces, storehouses, and possibly cult centers.

Samaria

Let us look first at Samaria. Samaria was the northern kingdom's unchallenged capital for a century and a half, but it extended over less than twenty acres and may have had a population of no more than 2,500 — mostly royalty, nobles, administrators, garrison troops, and their families.

The archaeological evidence (leaving aside for now the biblical data) begins with the choice of a site for the capital. Samaria is situated in the heartland of the Samaria hills on a hilltop rising some 1,450 feet above sea level, dominating the surrounding countryside (the name means "watchtower"). Samaria also lies at a major north-south crossroad. The ancient name is known from Neo-Assyrian texts.

Before the structures that make it a capital were built, the site was essentially unoccupied. It was probably chosen so as to found a capital *de novo*, that is, without any complicated prior history or tradition (like Washington, D.C.).

American excavations, among the earliest anywhere in the Holy Land, were carried out by Harvard University in 1908-10. These were followed by the joint British-Palestinian (Jewish) excavations in 1931-35. One member of the staff, Kathleen Kenyon, was later to become one of the giants of Palestinian and biblical archaeology.[3]

The excavations revealed a lower city, covering perhaps fifteen acres or more, which has not been excavated. There are a few remains of the royal quarter on the summit of the hill, crowned by an impressive acropolis. There the rectangular palace compound comprises about 2,400 square

3. M. C. Davis 2008.

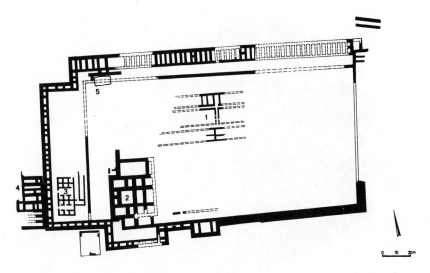

**Fig. IV.3. Major structures on the Israelite acropolis at Samaria, Period II.
The numbers on the illustration refer to the following: 1. residence,
2. first palace, 3. ostraca house, 4. later palace, 5. reservoir.**
Herzog 1997, fig. 5:22

feet, the whole area surrounded by a lower solid wall and an upper case-mate (double) wall founded on bedrock that may have had dozens of chambers. Most of the upper compound remains unexcavated, except for three structures. One was a multiroom palace with a courtyard, constructed of superb Phoenician-style chisel-dressed masonry (ashlar), the finest found anywhere in the country.

Nearby was a smaller multiroom building, in which was found part of a hoard of beautifully carved ivory decorative panels in Phoenician style. When taken together with other fragments found scattered elsewhere, they number in the hundreds. All these ivories were burnt when the palace was looted and destroyed by the Assyrians in 721 B.C.E. We will look further at these in Chapter VII.

In the poorly preserved ruins of a building in the center of the compound were found sixty-three ostraca, or inscriptions in ink on potsherds. Dating to the 8th century, these ostraca are mostly dockets recording shipments of commodities like oil and wine sent to the palace as payment for taxes. The personal names and place-names on the ostraca enable us to reconstruct an elaborate network of wealthy landowners in the region. A number of sites in this region of Mount Ephraim are unknown otherwise

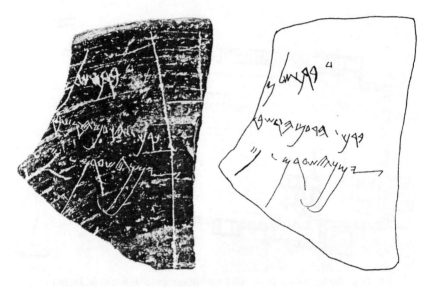

Fig. IV.4. Samaria ostracon: the "Barley checque."
Aḥituv 2006, p. 311

(even in the biblical texts). Again we shall look at the full implications of these sites below (Chapter VII).

The archaeological data alone would identify Samaria as a royal construction, unparalleled anywhere else in the country. There is a separate palace compound with massive fortifications; a large and luxurious residence built in Phoenician style; a subsidiary residence embellished with Phoenician-style, ivory-inlaid furniture; and a separate archive building for keeping records of tax receipts. These features, plus Samaria's strategic location, make it clear that this was indeed the capital of the northern kingdom from the early 9th to the late 8th century.

Of particular interest to us here are two chronological facts that show change. (1) All the early structures (9th century) continued in use throughout the 8th century, with the addition now of an external building of substantial proportions. (2) The Assyrian destruction in 721 dates the ivories and the ostraca rather closely to the mid to late 8th century, marking further change.[4]

---

4. See the discussion of these ivories in Chapter VII; cf. Tappy 2006.

Jerusalem

Jerusalem, the other capital city, was also relatively small. In the days of David and Solomon, in the 10th century B.C.E., its population was probably no more than 1,000, again mostly ruling elites and their families. They lived in the City of David on the spur of the Ophel below the Temple Mount, near the Gihon Spring in the valley below (perhaps 10 acres in extent). By the late 8th century, however, the city had expanded dramatically to some 150 acres, with a population of up to 15,000, no doubt swollen by refugees fleeing the Assyrian destructions in the north.[5]

The strategic location of Jerusalem is less obvious than that of Samaria. It lies perhaps too near the northern border with Israel. It is perched right on the watershed with the Judean Desert. It has a notoriously inadequate water supply. And it had a very long and troubled past already in pre-Israelite times. Nevertheless, Jerusalem sits atop one of the highest hills in the country, at about 2,600 feet above sea level, with splendid vistas in every direction. Its defensive weaknesses to the north and west, as well as its meager water resources, were compensated by available technology.

Finally, there is ideology. Tradition was reinterpreted to suggest that Israel's claims went back to patriarchal times — Abraham and Isaac's sacrifice on this very "Holy Mountain." And David's miraculous capture of the Jebusite city was a perpetual reminder of Israel's dispossession of the despised Canaanites. In short, Jerusalem became then (and remains now) an eternal symbol, a triumph of man over nature. (Even without the Bible, we know Jerusalem's earlier traditions archaeologically.)

Unfortunately for archaeologists, Jerusalem has always been a vibrant, living city, not an archaeological site open to investigation. Over the past century and a half there have been, however, hundreds of smaller chance discoveries, as well as numerous salvage excavations here and there, notably those of Dame Kathleen Kenyon in 1962-67. After the Six-Day War,

5. The population of Jerusalem in the 10th century may have been no more than circa 1,000, based on an estimated size of some 10 acres. The population by the late 8th century, however, had swollen due to an influx of refugees from the northern kingdom after the Assyrian campaigns in 732-721. Including the newly occupied Western Hill, Jerusalem now extended over about 150 acres, which implies a population of circa 15,000. This would have made Jerusalem the largest city in the land. The literature is extensive but see Lehmann 2003, 130. Geva describes a late-8th-century city of about 150 acres, with a population of some 15,000-20,000; cf. Geva 2003, 206. See Faust 2005a; A. Mazar 2007b, 160.

Fig. IV.5. The Old City of Jerusalem, looking east toward the Mount of Olives.
Photo: W. G. Dever

the Israelis carried out the first large-scale excavations anywhere inside and around the walled Old City, especially those of Benyamin Mazar around the south and west ("Wailing") walls in 1968-78; the extensive excavations of Nahman Avigad in the soon-to-be-rebuilt Jewish Quarter in 1968-82; and Yigal Shiloh's excavations in the "City of David" (1978-85).[6]

Despite the confusing mass of data and the problem of sorting it out, there is a surprising amount of evidence for Jerusalem's continuing to function after its founding in the 10th century as Judea's capital in the 8th century — and even expanding enormously. The Temple, "Citadel of David," other administrative structures all continued, as did the elite residential quarters on the slopes above the Gihon Spring. In addition, a stretch of 400 feet of a heavy stone Iron Age defensive wall is known along the eastern slopes of the Ophel ridge. Above that rise four long stepped terraces, on which rows of multiroomed houses were built, some of them evidently the residences of noble families. (We will return to these below.)

6. A list of publications on Jerusalem would itself fill an entire volume. For up-to-date discoveries and extensive bibliography, see Stern 1993, 698-804; 2008, 1801-37. Very useful syntheses will be found in many of the chapters in Vaughn and Killebrew 2003.

Fig. IV.6. The Ophel ridge, looking north to the Temple Mount.
Photo: W. G. Dever

At the very end of the 8th century, facing the threat of the siege of Sennacherib in 701 (Chapter X), the rulers of Jerusalem undertook several extraordinary defensive measures. To supplement the earlier water systems, they dug a 1,200-foot-long tunnel through the bedrock to conduct the waters of the spring of Gihon at the foot of the eastern slope inside the walled city to reservoirs there. Part of a monumental inscription discovered at the south end of the tunnel in the 19th century c.e. documents how this extraordinary engineering feat was carried out. The name of the king is missing, but the elegant late 8th century b.c.e. Hebrew script suggests that this was a royal inscription.[7]

Another defensive measure was Avigad's "Broad Wall," some 24 feet

7. See Rainey 2006, 253; the translation here is taken from Rainey. For a recent popular explanation of how the tunnel was dug, see Shanks 2008. See further Reich and Shukron 2006. The date is secure, 701, or slightly earlier. But one of the revisionists, Davies, has attempted to down-date the inscription to the 2nd century b.c.e.; cf. the scathing rebuttal by a number of specialists in Shanks, "Defusing Pseudo-scholarship: The Siloam Inscription Ain't Hasmonean," in Shanks 1997, 41-50. This only shows how far ideologues will go to avoid confronting inconvenient data. See further on the tunnel Chapter VII and n. 32; Sneh, Weinberger, and Shalev 2010.

wide, and now exposed for a length of more than 200 feet. This wall, if it extended to the northwestern quarter of the city and a gate there (now Jaffa Gate), would have expanded the city within the walls enormously — perhaps fourfold or more. This major alteration of the city's defenses to take in the entire Western Hill was probably both a defensive measure and an attempt to provide for a massive influx of refugees from the north following the fall of the northern kingdom in 732-721. It is estimated that the city's population had grown to as much as 15,000 by the late 8th century.[8] All this makes Jerusalem an impressive capital city.

Tier 1: Other Centers

Tier 1 also comprises district administrative centers other than capitals, cities whose size was not necessarily a deciding factor. We can distinguish seven of these centers, again on the basis of archaeological criteria: Dan, Hazor, and Megiddo in the north; and Beth-Shemesh, Gezer, Lachish, and Beersheba in the south (there may have been more centers unknown thus far) (see figs. IV.1 and IV.2).

Dan

Dan is the northernmost big city in Israel, situated right on the present-day Lebanese and Syrian borders. It is a very large mound, about fifty acres, its slopes quite steep. Its size and strategic location are augmented by a copious water supply. The springs, which bubble up on the surface all around the site, are part of the headwaters of the upper Jordan River, which come together just at this point, near the Banias waterfalls.

Dan thus possessed all the elements for a district administrative center, which it became almost immediately after the breakup of Israel into two states upon the death of Solomon (Str. IV). In fact, Dan was possibly the real cultural and religious capital in the north early on, before the political capital was established at Tell el-Farʿah (N.) and then moved shortly thereafter to Samaria.

Dan was excavated from 1966 onward by the venerable Israeli archae-

---

8. See Biran in Stern 1993, 323-32; 2008, 1686-89. See also Biran's popular book *Biblical Dan* (1994).

Fig. IV.7. Tel Dan city wall and gate area, from the south.
Photo: W. G. Dever

ologist Avraham Biran. Almost immediately the site, named Tell el-Qadi in Arabic, was identified as ancient Dan by the discovery of a Greek inscription reading "To the God who is in Dan."

The 9th century is characterized by city walls, a triple-entryway city gate with a large outer plaza, and a massive stone-built high place *(bāmāh)* with a large four-horned altar in the forecourt. Use of these structures seems to have continued into the 8th century (Str. II), with certain alterations. The paved roadway leading up from the gate was now partially blocked with the addition of an upper two-entryway gate. The high place may have continued in use, but imprecise excavation and the lack of final reports leave the question open. In any case, Dan probably remained a district administrative as well as a cult center into the 8th century. In particular, it stood as an outpost on the northern border with the Aramean city-states (Chapters VIII, IX). It has even been suggested that small buildings found outside the gate area may have been bazaars allotted to Aramean traders in an attempt to win concessions (below).

Fragments of a monumental Aramaic inscription were found in the Assyrian destruction debris (732 B.C.E.) in the outer gate plaza area. It is ironic that the inscription mentions the destruction of Dan by an Aramean king (probably Hazael), but it also provides us with our only extrabiblical reference to the "House of David" and an Israelite king who is probably Jehoram. The inscription dates to the mid-9th century, not the late 8th-century level in which it was found. It was originally a display inscription in the gate area.[9] Nevertheless, both the 9th-century and the late-8th-century destructions attest to Dan's importance (see further Chapter VII below).

Hazor

Hazor is the most impressive city in northern Israel, comparable even to major contemporary cities in Syria. It is located on the eastern spur of the Naphtali mountains, overlooking the Huleh Valley, guarding the main north-south road. The Canaanite site was huge: over 200 acres, constituting a vast lower city, heavily fortified, with a palace and several temples. By the Iron Age, however, there was only a more modest fortified acropolis of about 15 acres.

Hazor was excavated in 1955-58 by a large team of Israeli archaeologists under the direction of the legendary Yigael Yadin. From 1987 to the present there have been renewed excavations directed by Amnon Ben-Tor.[10]

In the 8th century B.C.E. (Str. VI-V) the city wall was augmented, but an earlier citadel probably continued in use with only minor alterations. Adjacent to the citadel were now constructed several fine houses, perhaps belonging to noble families. This area was approached by a gate with palmette capitals. It has been estimated, however, that as many as three-quarters of the buildings of Hazor VI-V had public functions. That would make Hazor indisputably a district administrative center now, just as it had been earlier (Chapter VII).

The most prominent construction of this era was a marvelously engineered water system, dug in the 9th century, with a square shaft some thirty feet by thirty feet, and descending steps, cut through bedrock down about sixty feet. A long sloping tunnel at the bottom led to the water table another thirty feet down. This water system was constructed as the Assyr-

9. References are too numerous to list, but see principally Biran and Naveh 1993, 1995. Cf. Schniedewind 1996b; Lemaire 1998; Na'aman 2000; Hagelia 2004; Aḥituv 2006, 466-83. Revisionists Lemche and Thompson have declared this inscription a "forgery"; see the rebuttal in Rainey 1994.

10. See Yadin in Stern 1993, 594-606; Ben-Tor in Stern 2008, 1769-85. See also Yadin's popular book *Hazor: The Rediscovery of a Great Citadel of the Bible* (1975).

Fig. IV.8. Plan of the outer and inner gate complex at Tel Dan.
Numbered areas are as follows: 1. paved piazza, 2. outer gate,
3. main gate, 4. paved street, 5. upper gate.
Biran 1994, fig. 206

Fig. IV.9. The water shaft at Hazor.
Photo: W. G. Dever

ian advances westward drew closer in the late 9th century, and then it continued in use in the 8th century.

Megiddo

Megiddo is another large, impressively located mound. It is situated at the northern end of the major pass leading up from the Coastal Plain, through the Carmel Ridge, and out into the Jezreel Valley. The mound, covering fifteen acres, is exceptionally high and steep, with more than twenty strata.

Megiddo was excavated in 1925-38 by a large, well-funded team of American archaeologists, sponsored by the University of Chicago with Rockefeller money. The onset of the Second World War halted fieldwork, and the ambitious scheme of publications was only partially realized.[11]

A major Canaanite city, Megiddo became an Israelite district capital in the 10th century, and then a fortified citadel and chariot city by the 9th

11. See Shiloh in Stern 1993, 1003-24; Finkelstein, Ussishkin, and Halpern in Stern 2008, 1944-50.

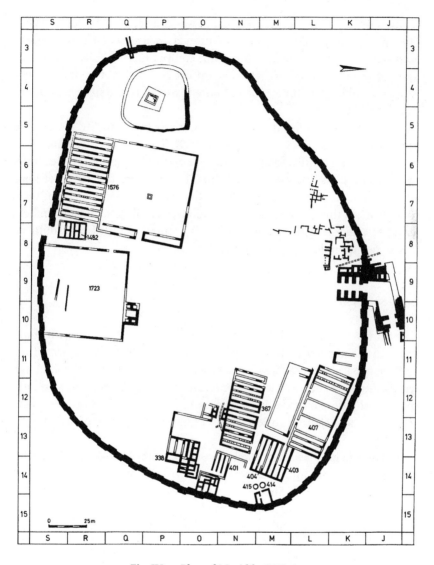

Fig. IV.10. Plan of Megiddo IV B-A.
In this phase the inner gateway is reduced to three entryways.
Herzog 1997, fig. 5.21

THE LIVES OF ORDINARY PEOPLE IN ANCIENT ISRAEL

century. By the late 9th century Megiddo was completely rebuilt (Str. IVA). The solid offsets-insets city wall continued in use, as well as a three-entryway gate. The stable (or storeroom) compounds were also still in use. Most of the interior of the city was not excavated, but it is nevertheless clear that public structures took up more than half of the space within the city walls (Chapter VII).

Another magnificent water system is attributed to Str. VA-IVB at Megiddo but continued in use into Str. IVA. The "gallery" building provided an entrance into a square, vertical shaft descending some 20 feet into bedrock. Then, as at Hazor, a horizontal tunnel more than 225 feet long and extending under the city wall led to the spring outside, which was then concealed. All things considered, Megiddo was ideally situated and embellished to make it a district administrative center, the next one south of Hazor, twenty miles distant (see fig. IV.2).

Beth-Shemesh

To turn now to Judah, the site of Beth-Shemesh is relatively small compared to the northern administrative centers, only about seven acres (but cf. Beersheba, at a mere three acres; below). Yet its location and distinctive features make it such a center beyond reasonable doubt. It is situated on a prominent hilltop overlooking the Sorek Valley that carries the main roads from the Shephelah up to Jerusalem, right on the border of Judah with Philistia.

The site has been excavated since 1990 by Tel Aviv University under the direction of Shlomo Bunimovitz and Zvi Lederman.[12] The features of Str. 3-2 that define Beth-Shemesh as an administrative center are a massive city wall, a large public building, open plazas and courtyards, a huge storage silo, an iron-working facility, and above all an impressive water reservoir.

Gezer

Gezer lies right on the southern border of Israel with Judah. It is a large mound (circa thirty-three acres), magnificently situated on the western flank of the Central Ridge where it joins the Shephelah, overlooking the

---

12. See Bahat in Stern 2008, 249-53; Bunimovitz and Lederman in Stern 2008, 1644-48.

Fig. IV.11. The tell of Gezer, seen from the north.
Photo W. G. Dever

Coastal Plain beyond. It guards the main road leading through a narrow pass up to Jerusalem.

The site was one of the first to be excavated in the Holy Land, dug in 1902-8 by an Irish archaeologist, R. A. S. Macalister. The Harvard Semitic Museum–Hebrew Union College excavations in 1964-73 were directed by G. E. Wright, this writer, and J. D. Seger. The ancient name is known from the Arabic name Tell el-Jezer, as well as bilingual inscriptions.[13]

Gezer, as excavated, has twenty-six strata, stretching from the mid–4th millennium B.C.E. to the Roman era. It became a prominent Iron Age site in the 10th century B.C.E. (Str. VIII), when a monumental four-entryway gate and casemate (double) wall were built. These constructions are almost identical to the 10th-century defenses at Hazor and Megiddo (above), and they may best be interpreted as evidence of the emergence of the early Israelite state and its ability to command men and matériel.[14]

13. See Dever in Stern 1993, 490-506.

14. The literature is vast, but see Dever 2001a, 124-31, and references there. Add now Master 2001; Finkelstein 2003, 2007; A. Mazar 2007a, 2007b; and on chronology Levy and Higham 2005; Sharon et al. 2007. Cf. n. 23.

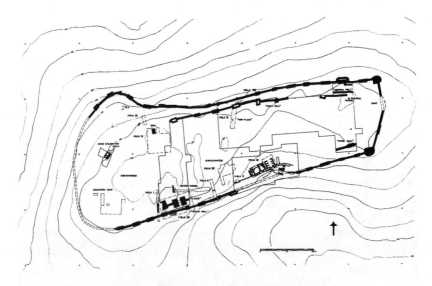

Fig. IV.12. Plan of major structures at Gezer.
W. G. Dever. Dever et al. 1986, plan I

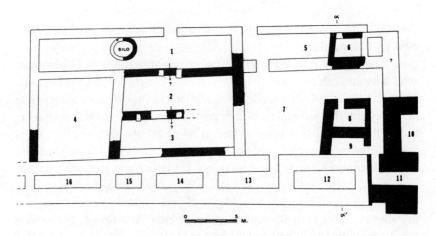

Fig. IV.13. Structures of Str. VII-VI in Field III at Gezer.
Dever 1984, fig. 4

Str. VI, belonging to the 8th century, still uses the three-entryway gate of Str. VII (reduced after the Shishak raid, ca. 918), as well as the older casemate city wall. Palace 10,000, adjoining the gate to the west, is replaced by Palace 8,000, a courtyard and cluster of rooms resembling the plan of the Assyrian-style *bit ḫilani* palaces. This large complex is likely to have been the residence of the governor of Gezer and/or administrative buildings. This, plus Gezer's superb border location, makes it one of our local administrative centers. Str. VI came to a violent destruction in the Assyrian campaigns of 732 (Chapter X).

Lachish

Lachish, farther south in Judah, is clearly another administrative center of the 8th century (Str. III). The mound is magnificent: large (thirty-one acres), very steep, visible from a great distance. It stands astride the main road from the coast, up from the Shephelah on which Lachish borders, into the southern Central Hills, and on to Hebron.

Lachish was excavated on a large scale by British archaeologist John Starky in 1932-38, then even more thoroughly exposed by Israeli excavations in 1969-76 directed by David Ussishkin. It is by far the best-known and best-published site in all of Judah.[15] After the destruction of Str. IV (perhaps by earthquake?), the lower and upper stone city walls, the triple-entryway gate, and the massive palace-fort on the acropolis were rebuilt. The latter ("Podium C") is the largest pre-Roman structure ever found in ancient Palestine, the massive ruined foundations still visible from miles away.

Added to the rebuilt and expanded palace-fort was a series of buildings to the north and east. The northern unit may have been partly residential, or used for archives. Connecting this area to the southeastern complex is a large courtyard measuring circa 325 by 235 feet, perhaps a parade ground for chariots. Built into the latter complex are several long triple-colonnaded structures, which when found at several other sites have been regarded as stables, but are more likely storerooms.[16] In this case they would have been used to store commodities such as grain, oil, and wine, taxes paid in kind.

A large square shaft dug into bedrock (the Great Shaft) continued in

---

15. See Ussishkin in Stern 1993, 897-911.

16. See the references to these tripartite buildings in A. Mazar 1990, 496-78; cf. Herzog 1992, 223-28. Cf. Chapter V, nn. 24, 29, 30 below.

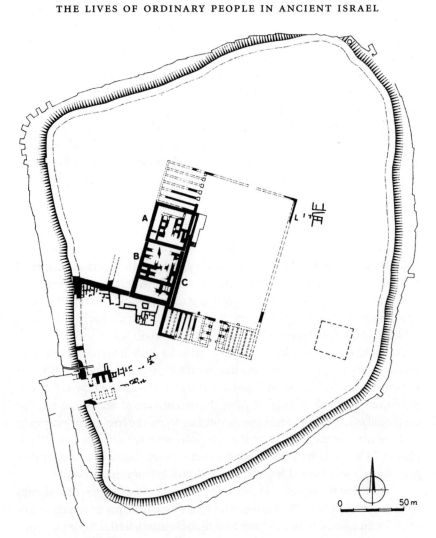

Fig. IV.14. Plan of Str. III at Lachish, with Palaces A-C.
Herzog 1997, fig. 5.27

use, but whether it served as a water system is unclear. Lachish III ended in a fierce conflagration during the campaign of Sennacherib in 701 (see Chapter X). This great battle, its memory preserved both in Neo-Assyrian annals and on large stone pictorial reliefs found lining the walls of the palace of Sennacherib in Iraq, testifies to the importance of Lachish. It was the principal target of the entire campaign.

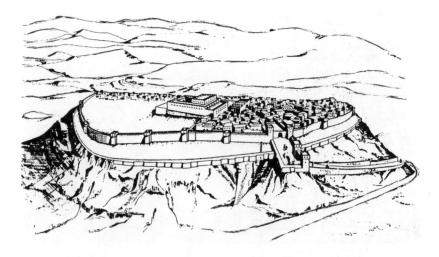

Fig. IV.15. An artist's reconstruction of 8th-century Lachish.
Fritz 1995, fig. 38

Beersheba

Beersheba (Tell es-Sebaʿ) provides us with our most fully excavated and best-preserved district administrative center of any period. The site is atop a small hill overlooking a deep wadi, with a view for miles in all directions, especially to the south into the Negev. Beersheba is thus the farthest south of any major town or city in Judah.

Beersheba was excavated by the Israeli archaeologist Yohanan Aharoni in 1969-76. Due to his premature death, only preliminary reports have appeared, and the stratigraphy is still debated.[17] Str. II continues and builds upon the well-laid-out Str. III city of the 9th to mid–8th century, but it exhibits an even greater degree of uniform town-planning. The oval-shaped casemate city wall crowns the contours of the steep mound. Following the wall line exactly, about ten feet inside, is a ring road. Between these parallel constructions is a compact series of identical pillar-courtyards, as many as forty of them.

Farther into the core of the town is another double row of houses, perhaps thirty more, as well as a few more monumental buildings, probably shops and the like. There is then a third inner sector. To the southeast a typical triple-entryway city gate is flanked by three of the triple-colonnaded

---

17. See Aharoni in Stern 1993, 167-73; Herzog in Stern 1993, 1594-97.

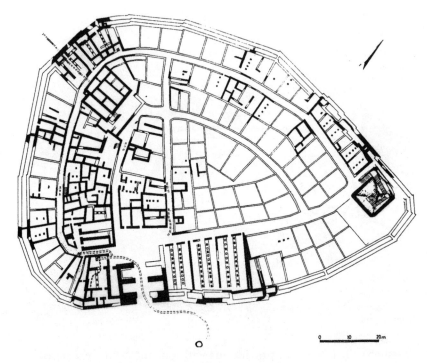

Fig. IV.16. Plan of Str. II at Beersheba.
Herzog 1997, fig. 5.4

storehouses that we have seen at Lachish (also at Hazor and elsewhere). Inside the gate is a large public plaza. Finally, a large water reservoir is situated to the north, into which drained water collected from all over the site. A temple or sanctuary may have existed at the site, but only the basement of any such structure remains.

The plan of Beersheba III-II is unique, obviously deliberately reflecting a city built, as it were, *de novo*, no doubt as a district administrative center. In particular the houses, actually built into the city walls, cannot have been designed for any other than barracks troops (and perhaps some of their families). And the storehouses — found chock-full of ceramic vessels — surely served as receptacles for taxes paid in commodities to the administrative center here.[18]

18. See n. 16 above.

Fig. IV.17. Casement wall and houses, Beersheba.
Photo: W. G. Dever

Tier 2: Demography and the City

Up to this point, in considering Tier 1 centers, I have been using the criterion of size selectively and even then secondarily. We have assumed that Tier 1-2 centers had a relatively large population, but the numbers given in figure IV.1 are obviously estimates.

However, from where do we derive these population figures? Are they simply guestimates? For some time now, archaeologists have been paying more attention to demographic issues, and they have developed several yardsticks by which to measure population and population growth. The overall model is often called "settlement archaeology," or the attempt to quantify settlement size, type, density, and population. This and other models come mainly from ethnography, where we can calculate the average amount of living (floor) space required by each individual, ten square meters being the average figure.[19] One can then estimate the number of houses per acre, up to twenty, with an average family

19. For orientation to demographic estimates, see Shiloh 1980, and more recently Zorn 1994; Lehmann 2003, 130-36. Cf. nn. 21, 23.

size of five per household. That yields a population average of circa 100 per acre.

The number, size, and distribution of all settlements in a region are then determined, largely from surface surveys. The number of excavated and surveyed sites can then be used to calculate the total built-up living area in a region, which when multiplied by the coefficient of 100 per acre yields an overall population estimate.

The population estimates for the 75 sites listed in figure IV.1 are based on the above model. And while the precise population remains only an estimate, the *relative* figures are quite useful and adequate for our purposes here. We must caution, however, that while we may have succeeded in mapping most sites in a given region, a certain number of others will remain unknown or will have been lost to erosion, will have disappeared under alluvial deposits, or will have been destroyed by extensive modern development. Nevertheless, intensive surface surveys can indeed supplement the 75 excavated sites used as our database here, often to a surprising degree. Thus the recent surveys done by Israeli archaeologists in the Samaria region (biblical Ephraim and Manasseh) have revealed more than 400 Iron II sites (ca. 900-600 B.C.E.).[20] Most cannot be identified with biblical or other names, of course. But they can give us an independent source of information. For instance, if all these sites were occupied in the 8th century and each had a population of circa 500, that would swell our estimates for the Samaria region to 20,000.

Nevertheless, the population of Israel and Judah in the 8th century cannot be known precisely. There is, however, a consensus among authorities that the total population would have been circa 150,000 by the end of the monarchy — in contrast, for instance, to circa 100,000 in the period of the united monarchy two centuries earlier.[21]

Tier 2: Sites as Cities

We distinguish here eleven Tier 2 sites, that is, urban centers or true cities. We may now begin to use population size as a fundamental criterion, again figuring about 100 people per acre. So the term "city" here will designate a site of ten or more acres, or a population aggregate of 1,000 or more, using the coefficient of 100 per acre described above.

20. See Zertal in Stern 1993, 1311-12; Finkelstein in Stern 1993, 1313-14.
21. For basic methodology, see n. 19 above.

But is the threshold of circa 1,000 too small? And could we not break down this category of city further, since the population estimates range from circa 1,000 to circa 5,000?

In other areas of the ancient Near East, and among scholars in different disciplines, the definition of city differs considerably. If size alone is taken as the most significant criterion, the presumed threshold for distinguishing a city from a town may be much higher than our figure for Palestine.

In ancient Mesopotamia, for instance, where all authorities agree that the first true cities arose in the 4th millennium B.C.E., only population aggregates of about 20,000 to 40,000 are thought to be properly designated cities. A recent Ph.D. dissertation at the University of Arizona sought to be more precise by developing another model: the relation of population size to food production, or the "carrying capacity" of the immediate region. The proposition is that a town must develop into a city when the growth of population outstrips the means of production. That is, the city must now organize the countryside — the outlying towns, villages, and agricultural areas — in order to feed itself. It thus becomes a center, in effect a complex, specialized, and highly stratified market town.[22]

By analyzing the capacity of southern Mesopotamia's rich alluvial, irrigated plains, one reaches the conclusion that at about 40,000 a population reaches the limits of self-sufficiency, and it becomes a city.

This model has its attractions, not least that of providing an objective way of defining the city. But it simply will not work for ancient Palestine, for reasons that soon become clear. There is, to be sure, one constant for both areas; but there is also a fundamental difference.

Let us look first at the constant factor, a fact of life. In all preindustrial eras, agricultural production was limited by the fact that people in settled areas could scarcely commute more than about two miles from their domiciles to the fields. The practical difficulties of transporting tools and supplies to the field by hand or on donkey back, of protecting the ripe crops, and of carrying the harvest home made venturing farther into the hinterland impractical or impossible.

In Mesopotamia, with its flat, rich fields, some producing two crops a year, a town of 20,000 (or more) could still feed itself, and thus did not need to transform itself into a city. So the above model may work, with a threshold of circa 40,000. A two-mile radius beyond a settlement would yield a total food production area of up to four to six square miles.

22. See Falconer and Savage 1995.

In ancient Palestine, however, the same distance constraints were no doubt also operative, due to human nature. But the difference is that the capacity for food production of the area surrounding a village or town in Palestine was *much* lower. That is because of the difference in geography and climate (see Chapter III).

In Palestine the rough hilly countryside, thin rocky soils, and scant and unpredictable rainfall (with no possibility of gravity-fed irrigation) all conspired to severely limit agricultural production. As a result, a radius of circa four to six miles surrounding a site could produce only enough to feed about 1,000 people, rather than 40,000. A scalar difference is what distinguishes Palestine. Thus much *smaller* sites become, properly speaking, cities.

That is how we define city here: a site of ten acres or more, with a population of 1,000 or more. The upper limit — perhaps 5,000 or more — does not seem to matter. In any case, there were no megalopolises in ancient Palestine before the Roman period. As we shall see, however, states can be quite small, and ancient Israel and Judah were by any reasonable criteria true states by the 8th century B.C.E. (and even before).[23]

The Northern Cities

It is not only size that defines a city, however, but also location and to some degree the functions governed by location. All the eleven Tier 2 cities we presume to have existed in the 8th century — on archaeological grounds — are located in prime areas, areas either rich in resources or of strategic

23. Finkelstein maintained until recently that Judah did not reach full statehood until the late 8th century, that is, after the fall of the northern kingdom. Conventional scholarship, however, still sees the emergence of a Judean state either in the late 10th or early 9th centuries. Cf. A. Mazar 2007b. The recent excavations at Kh. Qeiyafa, on the border of Judah and the Philistine Shephelah, reveal a one-period fortified outpost, dated securely to the 10th century. This is surely evidence for an early Judean state with a highly centralized government. See Garfinkel and Ganor 2009; cf. n. 14 above.

For a useful comparison of views on the question of Israelite statehood, see the articles by Faust, Grabbe, Herzog, and Silberman in *Near Eastern Archaeology* 70/1 (2007): 4-25, with full references to wider literature. Most of this discussion, however, pertains to the rise of the state in the 10th or 9th century. By the 8th century Judah had been a true state for at least a century, if not more. Cf. Bunimovitz and Lederman 2009, who demonstrate that the early-9th-century, if not the 10th-century, Beth-Shemesh reflects state-level organization (12).

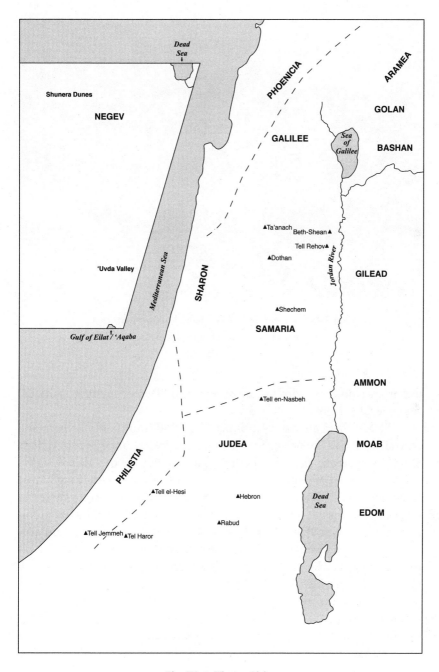

Fig. IV.18. Tier 2: Cities

Fig. IV.19. The mound of Shechem, looking southeast
toward the Bronze Age defenses.
Photo: W. G. Dever

importance, like the administrative centers of Tier 1 (for further discussion, see Chapter V).

Five of them are closely grouped in the hill country of northern and central Samaria, extending into the eastern Jezreel and Jordan Valleys: Shechem, Dothan, Taʿanach, Beth-Shean, and Tel Reḥov. All are within twenty-five miles of one another.[24] This is the heartland of the kingdom of Israel, Samaria itself located within the rough triangle formed by these five large cities. All are in the region receiving twelve to sixteen inches of annual rainfall where there are rich *terra rosa* soils, good drainage, and adequate springs and wells. The densely terraced hillsides are covered with olives and grapes, the small intermontane valleys cultivated with wheat, barley, and vegetables of many kinds.

Shechem, for instance (Heb. "shoulder"), is a prominent mound extending from the slopes of Mount Gerizim, guarding the crucial pass between that mountain and Mount Ebal, through which runs the main road north from Jerusalem to Samaria and beyond. Shechem had a long Bronze

24. See Campbell in Stern 1993, 1345-54. Cf. also G. E. Wright 1965.

Fig. IV.20. Israelite Beth-Shean, seen from the classical period lower city.
Photo: W. G. Dever

Age/Canaanite history, and it was a traditional center long before Israelite times.[25]

Dothan is a steep, impressive mound of twenty-five acres, rising abruptly from the Plain of Dothan, visible for miles around. Dothan had a long Bronze Age tradition and a history that was well known by Israelite times.[26]

Ta'anach, another large, steep tell, forms part of the chain of the Gilboa Mountains guarding the southern reaches of the Jezreel Valley. The pass through the hills into the valley here is second in importance only to the crucial pass at the sister city of Megiddo, a district administrative center, only five miles distant (above). Ta'anach had been a major city throughout the Canaanite era.[27]

Beth-Shean is arguably the most impressive tell in the country, rising an incredible eighty feet above the small flood plain of the Jalud River, which empties into the Jordan just to the east. Beth-Shean stands sentinel

25. See Cooley and Pratico in Stern 1993, 372-74.
26. See Glock in Stern 1993, 1428-33.
27. See Mazar in Stern 1993, 214-23; Stern 2008, 1616-22.

to one of the two or three great crossroads of ancient Palestine, guarding all the routes that funnel from central Palestine across into Transjordan and thus to Damascus and beyond. The site was already a major urban site in the Middle and Late Bronze Ages, and it had been an Israelite stronghold since the early days of the monarchy.[28]

A few miles south of Beth-Shean is another impressive mound, Tel Reḥov, a twelve-acre site overlooking the Jordan Valley. Excavations still in progress there have revealed a large, densely built-up domestic area, destroyed circa 840 (Str. IV), then rebuilt in the 8th century (Str. III-II). The material culture differs somewhat from that of other Israelite sites, and it shows some affinities with Transjordan and with Aramean sites farther north.[29]

It may be significant that the area dominated by these five northern cities, together with Samaria, does not extend westward to the Sharon Plain, or northward into Galilee. That may be explained by the fact that the southern Sharon Plain was narrow and marshy in antiquity and difficult to exploit (Chapter III), while the northern Sharon Plain was dominated by Phoenician settlements. Taʿanach and Megiddo, both close to the plain and fortified, marked the western borders of the territories under effective Israelite control.

To the north, the hill country of lower and upper Galilee, while fertile and well watered, was regarded as somewhat remote and remained so even in much later times (and is still today). Here the Tier 1 sites of Dan and Hazor were the main Israelite outposts, especially Hazor, with its acropolis, citadel, and heavy fortifications. Still farther north and east, in the upper Jordan Valley, Aramean influence extended south from Damascus and is seen in northern Israel sites like Beth-Saida, Tel Hadar, and ʿEn-Gev around the shores of the Sea of Galilee (Chapter IX).

These five Tier 2 sites form a sort of triangle (fig. IV.18). That is probably not fortuitous. Archaeologists working recently in Europe and dealing with the analysis of settlement patterns (landscape archaeology) have come up with a model called central place theory. Pioneered by the German geographer Walter Christwaller, this model maps all the sites in a given region, arranges them in a multitiered hierarchy, then plots their geographical distribution by drawing "Thiessen polygons."[30]

---

28. See Mazar in Stern 2008, 2013-18.

29. See n. 2 above.

30. See Renfrew and Bahn 1991, 159-61, on the application of central place theory on the alluvial plains of southern Iraq.

On a flat landscape, with no rivers or other barriers, and no variations in resources, a central place will tend to dominate the region, with
secondary villages or hamlets surrounding it at regular, predictable inter-
vals. A classic Thiessen polygon would look like this.

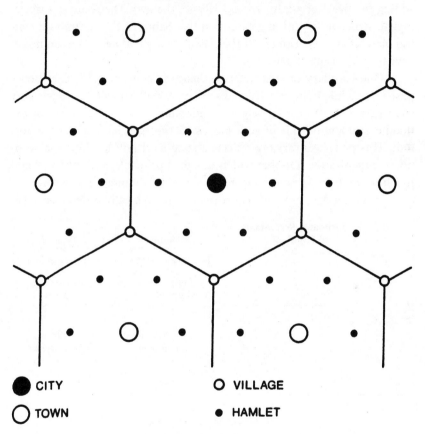

CITY   O VILLAGE

O TOWN   • HAMLET

Fig. IV.21. Thiessen polygons

Central place theory has been applied with some success to the analysis of settlement patterns in Iraq (Mesopotamia), notably in the Diyala
region east of Baghdad.[31] But that area is a flat alluvial plain — precisely
the kind of landscape for which central place theory was devised (it
worked best in the Netherlands).

31. See Kochavi in Stern 1993, 1252.

The landscape of Palestine is vastly different, as we have already shown. Therefore, central place theory has rarely been invoked by any archaeologist working in Israel (or Jordan). Nevertheless, a rough Thiessen polygon can be drawn up for the five Tier 1-2 urban centers discussed here, adding the five Tier 3-4 towns and villages (below). The result is surprisingly instructive — with the exception that Samaria, the paramount central place, is at the periphery. If the classic theory had held, Dothan might have been the central place.

One corollary of central place theory is relevant here. The theory posits that a hierarchically ordered settlement pattern will have a few very large sites at the top, relatively more medium-sized sites (towns) in the middle, and a multitude of very small sites (villages, hamlets) at the bottom. This pattern invariably reflects a state-level political and socioeconomic organization. On that widely accepted principle, ancient Israel and Judah in the Iron Age did constitute true states, despite some skeptics.

A typical diagram will reflect such a hierarchically ordered society.

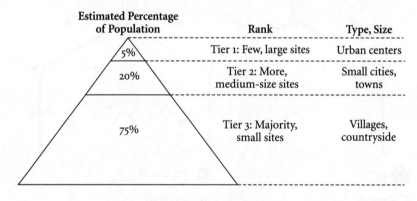

Fig. IV.22. Diagram showing "rank-size" hierarchy
of settlements and population estimates

The Southern Cities

The picture presented by Tier 2 sites (cities) in the southern kingdom of Judah is somewhat different. There we have six Tier 2 cities. But there seems to be no discernible pattern in their distribution. The sites range from Tel Jemmeh to the southwest, on the Philistine border, to Tell en-Naṣbeh on the border with the northern kingdom. Jerusalem, the capital, is located in the northeastern corner of the region. Nevertheless, most of the Tier 2 sites are closely clustered in the central Judean hill country — clearly the heartland of Judah. This is what we should expect. Philistia lies to the west; Israel consists of the northern border; the Judean Desert stretches eastward; and the Negev Desert stretches south from Beersheba to the Gulf of Eilat on the Red Sea (some 150 miles).

The implications seem clear, and they probably reflect the practical logic of the ancient Judeans. Judah is much smaller than Israel in land area but at the same time much more homogeneous geographically and, we should add, culturally. The north was perennially open to Aramean and especially Phoenician influences — larger and more prosperous in the 8th century, but less homogeneous and less secure. Judah was more isolated but less volatile; and it outlived northern Israel by more than a century (see Chapter X).

A closer look at individual Tier 2 cities in the south (Fig. IV.18) is revealing. Here location, as well as size (ca. 1,000 population), seems pertinent. Tell en-Naṣbeh (biblical Mizpeh; below) crowns a prominent hilltop on the main road seven miles north of Jerusalem.

Gezer, to the northwest, seems to have been reckoned with Israel before the late-8th-century Assyrian destructions but with Judah thereafter. It is situated on the last hill of the central ridge as it slopes westward down to the Shephelah and the Coastal Plain. It is located on a spur, overlooking the Aijalon Valley and the road up to Jerusalem to the east and the entire coastal region to the west. It has a nearly 360-degree view, and on a clear day one can see all the way to Ashdod on the coast. No site in ancient Palestine is more strategically located (for the monumental remains, see above).

Kh. Rabûd to the south (probably biblical Debir) is situated on a high rocky hilltop in the Hebron hills — the only large mound in the region.[32] Furthermore, it has good water resources, especially important since Rabûd is one of the southernmost Judean sites before one comes to Beersheba (some twelve miles south) and the northern Negev Desert. Hebron, to the northeast, only a few miles away, was probably a major city in the 8th century, and it is similarly well located (Ar. *Kh. 'Arba;* "four hills"); but the lack of systematic excavation precludes us from saying more.[33]

The three sites to the extreme southwest form a closely spaced trian-

---

32. See Ofer in Stern 1993, 606-9.
33. See Fargo in Stern 1993, 630-34; Oren in Stern 1993, 580-84.

gle and are clearly situated to guard the border with southern Philistia, situated in the low, rolling loessial dunes of the northwestern Negev. These sites have fewer natural advantages, but there is nevertheless a logic to their location. Two of the three are quite large: Tell el-Ḥesi (biblical Eglon?) at twenty-five acres, and Tell Abu Hureireh/Tel Haror (biblical Gerar) at fifty acres.[34]

Tier 3: Towns

We have identified twenty-four sites in Israel as towns (300-1,000 population; fig. IV.23). The twelve in Judah are of fairly consistent size, with most sites in the range of 500-1,000 population. Two of the largest towns face the border with Philistia: Tel Batash (biblical Timnah; seven acres) and Beth-Shemesh (seven acres).

Several towns in the central Judean hill country (Beth-Zur and Gibeon) are well situated in regions with good arable soils and twelve to sixteen inches of annual rainfall.[35]

The southern border is obviously defined by the northern Negev Desert: Tel 'Ira (Ramah of the Negev) and 'Arô'er. The overall distribution of Tier 3 towns in Judah suggests the same homogeneous geopolitical and socioeconomic character of the Judean state as we saw for Tier 2 cities.

The twelve Tier 2 towns that we know archaeologically in the northern kingdom are widely but logically distributed. Six are located along the Philistine and Phoenician borders. One (Bethel) is right on the southern border with Judah. One (Tell el-Hammeh; biblical Hamath) is in the Jordan Valley, small (seven acres) but very impressive in height.[36]

Interestingly enough, we know of few if any 8th-century Tier 3 towns in Galilee. That may be, however, because far fewer archaeological investigations have been carried out there. And many of the small tells there may have been obscured over the centuries. Even so, survey data would add dozens of sites (below).[37] In Chapter V we shall look at some of these towns, north and south, in more detail.

34. Funk in Stern 1993, 259-61; Pritchard in Stern 1993, 511-14.
35. See Kelso in Stern 1993, 192-94; Cahill and Tarler in Stern 1993, 561-62.
36. See Ofer in Stern 1993, 815-16.
37. Other scholars speak of villages, but rarely is a definition of the term offered. Faust, who has discussed social factors more than anyone else, does define an Israelite village as having the following features: (1) a nucleated site, usually on a hilltop or hillside; (2) an

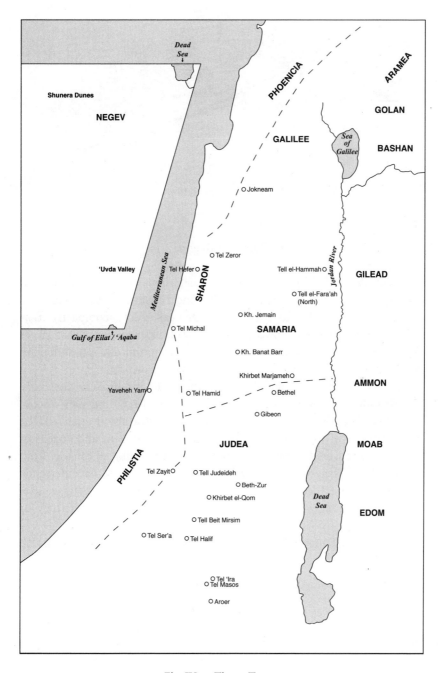

Fig. IV.23. Tier 3: Towns

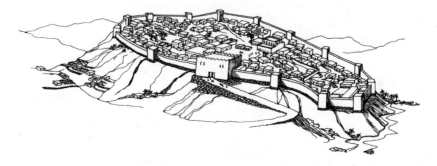

Fig. IV.24. A walled town.
Reconstruction based on Kh. Marjameh, after Mazar 1982.

Tier 4: Villages

Just as we developed working criteria for defining a city, we must do so in distinguishing a village. I suggest, following Faust, that our villages are (1) quite small (here five to three acres), often isolated; (2) compactly organized; (3) often enclosed by a boundary wall; (4) with somewhat larger houses but no monumental architecture; (5) economically self-sufficient. By these criteria, we have thirteen villages to consider here.[38]

We have isolated some of these in the north and three in the south. To this number, however, we must add the several hundred sites discovered in surface surveys (even though we can say little about them). In the Israeli surveys of the 1970s and onward in Galilee, dozens and dozens of sites were discovered, in an elaborate network extending all the way from hamlets and villages to some fortified towns. All seem to have persisted throughout the 8th century until the Assyrian conquests in 733-732, after which the region was almost completely abandoned for a century or more.[39]

The Israeli surveys in the more open region of Judah were much

---

occupied area from one to three acres; (3) usually surrounded by a perimeter wall; (4) characterized by four-room houses, often much larger than usual; (5) self-sufficient, based on concentrated production (usually oil and wine processing). Faust discusses more than a dozen such villages in the Iron II period, but few have been sufficiently excavated. Others are 7th century in date and thus fall outside our purview here. See Faust 2011, 126-72.

38. See Zertal in Stern 1993, 1311-12; Finkelstein in Stern 1993, 1313-14; Dar in Stern 1993, 1314, 16; Borowski 2003, 13-25. See also n. 37 above.

39. See n. 38 above.

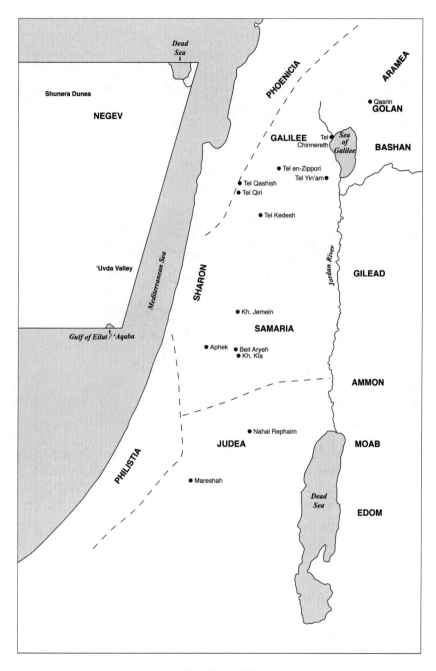

Fig. IV.25. Tier 4: Villages

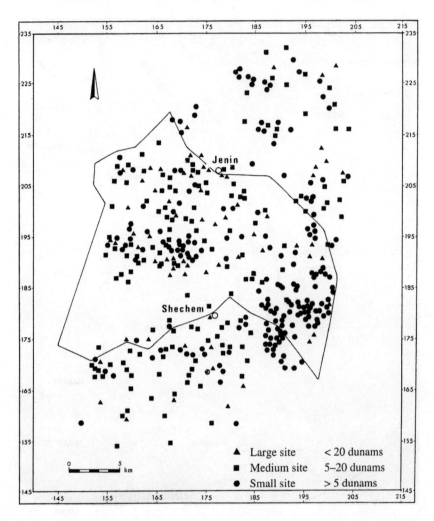

Fig. IV.26. Survey map of the central Samaria hill country.
One dunam = ¼ acre
Zertal 2001, fig. 2.1

more extensive, so it is likely nothing of importance was missed. Here some eighty-eight 8th-century sites were located, totaling 225 acres of built-up area, with an estimated population of 2,300 (using the same acre/ population coefficient explained earlier).

The northern villages discussed here, ranging in population from 150 to perhaps 500, are distributed about as we should expect. Several are lo-

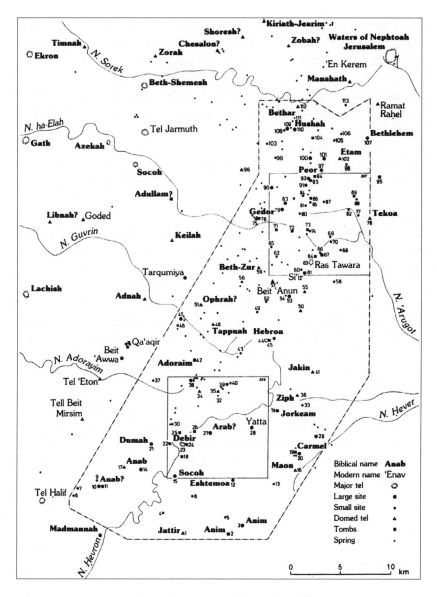

Fig. IV.27. Survey map of the Judean hills.
Ofer, in Stern 1993, 815

cated in the Samaria hills, but more are in more remote Galilee: Tel Yin'am (biblical Jabneel?) and Tel Qades (biblical Kedesh).[40] One site, a bit surprisingly, is on the Golan Heights, in an area of Aramean influence (Qaṣrin), but it consists only of sherd scatters. The others we know are very closely clustered in the western end of the Gilboa range along the southern reaches of the Jezreel Valley, including the best excavated and published sites (Tel Qashish and Tel Qiri).[41]

The relative lack of villages in the Samaria hill country is probably due to the fact that hundreds of village sites have been surveyed but few have been excavated. Adding these sites to our archaeological map would no doubt fill the lacuna quite well, as would the nine that we know from the Samaria ostraca (above).

Here we may add a few villages in the Samaria foothills that have been surveyed and at least partially excavated by Israeli archaeologists. There are three significant sites some fifteen miles southwest of Samaria, where we have some semblance of a village plan. The best known is Beit Aryeh, a small (one acre) rectangular walled site with ten to fifteen typical Israelite four-room houses and dozens of agricultural installations (mostly for olive oil processing). There were no public structures, but one pillared building may be a storehouse. The village seems to have been capable of producing an agricultural surplus. The population was probably about 100.

Two other villages are Kh. Banat Barr and Kh. Kla. Kh. Banat Barr is an approximately two-acre site spread out over several hundred yards along a cliff. Surveys have revealed the remains of several buildings (some four-room houses), cisterns and pools, caves, and terraces. There may be as many as several dozen houses, with a population of 150 or more.

Kh. Kla is a fortified site of about one acre, protected by a wall and a gatehouse with towers. Several "industrial" installations surround the cluster of buildings. One of the buildings was a large, eight-roomed structure that suggests some sort of public initiative (see further Chapter VI).

40. For more detailed discussion of Tel Qiri, see Chapter VI.
41. See Ben-Tor in Stern 1993, 1200-1203.

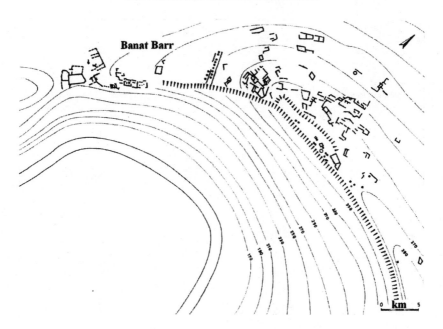

Fig. IV.28. Plan of the village of Kh. Banat Barr.
Faust 2010, fig. 24

Forts

We can identify at least a dozen sites as forts.[42] But it is difficult to rank them anywhere in our multilevel hierarchy of sites because they differ so much from each other. The common characteristics, however, that enable us to classify these sites as "forts" include the following: (1) their small size, with few domestic features; (2) their location on strategic borders; and (3) the presence of impressive defensive elements, such as fortifications and citadels.

Four of these fortresses face the Negev Desert south of Beersheba. Tel Malḥata IV (four acres) exhibits massive fortifications, but little else.[43] Ḥorvat Radum, nearby, has only a fortress and probably was intended as an outpost of Ḥorvat ʿUza, four miles due east.[44]

The most impressive fortress in the south — perhaps in the whole

42. Like villages, sites designated as forts are poorly defined. The criteria are mostly commonsensical, as ours here are.

43. See Kochavi in Stern 1993, 934-36; Beit-Arieh in Stern 1993, 1254-55.

44. See Aharoni in Stern 1993, 82-87.

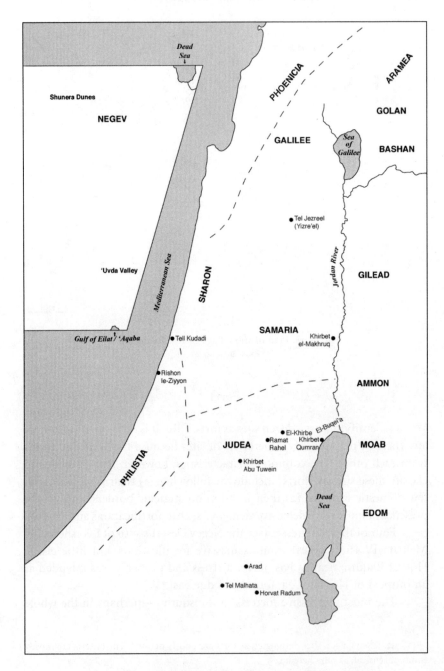

Fig. IV.29. Map of 8th century B.C.E. forts

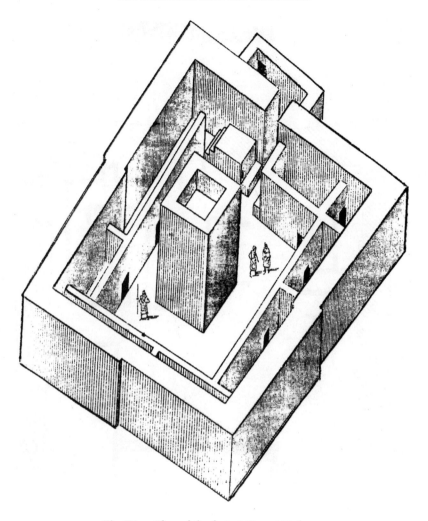

Fig. IV.30. Plan of the fort at Ḥorvat Radum.
Stern 2001, 153

country — is Arad. Due to faulty excavation and scanty publication, how-ever, the stratigraphy of Arad has been hotly debated. Here we follow Ze'ev Herzog's reworking of the material, thus dating IX-VIII to the 8th cen-tury.[45] Much of the acropolis was taken up by a large square fortress, with

45. It is essential to consult Herzog's reworking of the confused stratification of Arad. Herzog et al. 1984; cf. also Herzog 2001, 156-78.

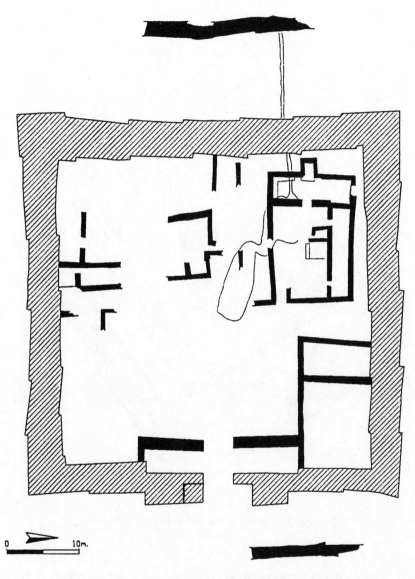

Fig. IV.31. Plan of the Arad fort and temple (Str. IX-VIII).
Herzog 2001, fig. 6.5

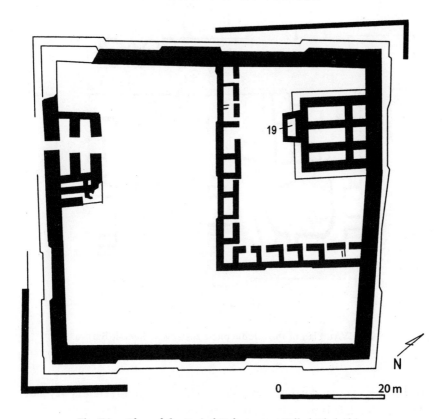

Fig. IV.32. Plan of the Period II fortress at Tell el-Kheleifeh.
After Barkay 1992, fig. 9.29

thick solid walls and corner buttressed towers, replacing the smaller 9th-century structure. This fortress appears to have been destroyed in the campaign of Sennacherib in 701.

There may well have been several other 8th-century forts in the Negev. But most scholars date the numerous Negev forts earlier, to the 10th century.[46]

Much farther south are three remarkable Judean forts. First is at Tell el-Kheleifeh, just north of the Gulf of Eilat on the Red Sea (possibly biblical Ezion-Geber). Although badly excavated and published, Period II re-

---

46. On the disputed date of the Negev forts, see most recently Faust 2006c; Gilboa 2009. There is a growing consensus that these forts should be dated to the 10th century or at latest to the 9th century. In any case, they are outside our purview here.

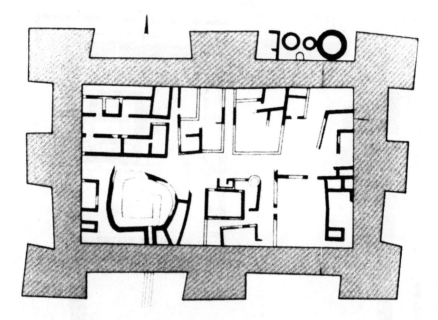

Fig. IV.33. Plan of the middle phase fortress at Kadesh-Barnea.
Barkay 1992, fig. 9.32

veals a large square fortress compound, with its own three-entryway gate. The precise date is uncertain, but there is some 8th-century pottery.[47]

Still farther afield is the small Judean fort at Tell el-Qudeirat in the eastern Sinai Desert, almost certainly biblical Kadesh-Barnea. Here, at a small but steep mound near the spring, three superimposed fortresses have come to light. The "middle" fort belongs to the 8th century. It features exceptionally thick, solid walls, incorporating eight towers, surrounded by a deep fosse. In one of the three phases a large cistern was constructed.[48]

Even more remote is the fort sanctuary at Kuntillet ʿAjrûd (now named Ḥorvat Teman), in an isolated area in the eastern Sinai Desert. On a hilltop overlooking a spring and several wells, and the ancient trade routes through the Sinai, there is a one-period structure that appears to have functioned like a caravanseray — a stopover site, with shelter and provisions. The main structure is, however, a rather typical rectangular Negev fort, with solid walls about one meter wide (one a double wall) and four

47. See Pratico in Stern 1993, 867-70.
48. See Cohen in Stern 1993, 843-47.

Fig. IV.34. Aerial view of Kuntillet ʿAjrûd.
Photo courtesy of Zeev Meshel

corner towers. The inner courtyard measures some sixty by thirty feet. Steps in one corner suggest an upper story above the walls and towers.[49] At the east end is an offset, double-entryway gate between towers, with two flanking chambers that are like *favissas,* or cult repositories.

We will discuss the fort's function as a shrine that included many cult objects and numerous enigmatic Hebrew graffiti in Chapter VIII. But here we stress the function of the site as a fort, with a date from the late 9th century well into the 8th century. It is thus the most remote Judean fort that we know.

Turning back to the north, there is a small fort at Rishon le-Zīyyon, near modern Tel Aviv, close to the border with the northern Philistine plain.[50]

To the east, only twelve miles southwest of Jerusalem, is Kh. Abu Tuwein. Here a large fortress is the only structure on the site. Located where it is, the function of this fort is unclear.[51]

49. See Meshel in Stern 1993, 1458-64.
50. See Levy in Stern 2008, 2018-20.
51. See Mazar in Stern 1993, 15-16.

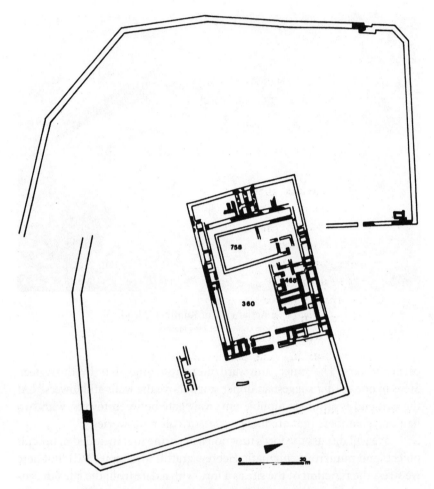

Fig. IV.35. Plan of Str. VA at Ramat Raḥel.
Fritz 1995, fig. 47

There are several forts to the east, at Qumran ("City of Salt"?), and on the northwest shore of the Dead Sea, and in the Buqeiah wilderness stretching north and northwest. These forts make good sense, defending as they do the eastern borders of the Jerusalem district, going down to the Jordan Valley.[52]

Kh. Maḥrûq, about fifteen miles to the northeast, is right down in the

52. See Cross in Stern 1993, 267-69.

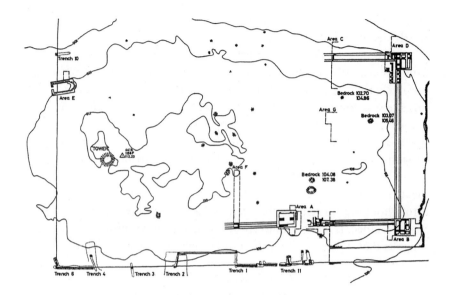

Fig. IV.36. Plan of Jezreel.
Ussishkin, in Stern 1993, 1838

valley, overlooking the north-south Jordan Valley road (still today). The site features little but two large towers, one rectangular, the other round. Here, a fort makes very good sense, looking directly across to Transjordan.[53]

One final Judean site that might be considered a fort is the hilltop site of Ramat Raḥel, on the southern outskirts of Jerusalem today. Founded in the 9th century and continuing in use into the 8th century, it was initially (Str. VB) a royal stronghold, surrounded by gardens — a sort of retreat from the capital. Then in the 8th century a casemate fortress with a magnificent palace at its center was established (Str. VA). The impressive plan, the fine ashlar masonry, the proto-Aeolic capitals, the magnificent furnishing, the seal impressions — all these make it clear that at this stage Ramat Raḥel did indeed function as a stronghold. It was unique in being also a royal establishment, connected directly to the capital.[54]

The only other 8th-century fortresses we know are in the northern kingdom, where security was undoubtedly a more pressing concern. Kudadi, on the Mediterranean coast near Tel Michal, obviously guards the

53. See Levy and Peilstöcker in Stern 2008, 2021-22.
54. See Aharoni in Stern 1993, 1261-67. Excavations at the site are ongoing.

border with Philistia. Here there are two successive fortresses, the second clearly belonging to the 8th century.[55]

A unique fortress in the north is that at Jezreel, guarding the roads from the Samaria hill country down into the Jezreel Valley. Perched impressively right at the edge of the valley, and overlooking it from a height, this site was constructed in the 9th century as a royal stronghold but also as a sort of retreat from Samaria,[56] some twenty miles southwest. However, it was destroyed in all probability in the late 9th century by Aramean incursions, so it was probably abandoned during the period surveyed here.

Oddly enough, we know of no forts along the borders with the Aramean kingdoms to the north, despite the obvious threat they posed throughout the 8th century. Tel Soreg, inland from the eastern shore of the Sea of Galilee, is a small 8th-century fort. But its location near 'En-Gev suggests that it was an Aramean, rather than an Israelite, outpost.

PART II: THE BIBLICAL DATA

What Does the Bible Add?

True to our fundamental principle of giving priority to the archaeological data, we have attempted thus far to create a database, that is, a hierarchy of all excavated sites (factoring in survey data where possible). Thus we have summarized what we can now know of what life was like in the 8th century B.C.E., on the basis of archaeological excavation and (some) surveys. But now we must interlace the sites named in the biblical texts, our most extensive textual data.[57] To do otherwise would be methodologically and historiographically indefensible. Yet, the inquiry may be of limited value.

Biblical scholars since Martin Noth in the 1950s have opined that archaeology is "mute" (Ger. *dumm*), apparently because it is anonymous, that is, it can describe events but usually cannot attach individual names to them. True; but does it really matter? The answer may be "Not much."

First, the Hebrew Bible's pertinent data for place-names in the 8th

---

55. See Avigad in Stern 1993, 882.
56. See Ussishkin and Woodhead in Stern 2008, 1837-39.
57. Because I am postponing the biblical texts until Part II of each chapter and therefore forgoing biblical names, I have used Arabic names for most of the sites in Chapter IV.

century, which is what we are considering here, may be found in 2 Kings 14–20, supplemented here and there by a few references in the books of Isaiah, Amos, and Micah (prophets of the 8th century). But are these few textual sources, presumably authentically set in an 8th-century context, reliable? The accounts in 2 Kings constitute part of the epic Deuteronomistic History (Deuteronomy, plus Joshua–Kings) that cannot have been compiled before the late 7th century, and may date much later (the period of the exile).[58] The book of Chronicles, a roughly parallel account of the monarchy, is probably even later, but it may add some possible information. And there is unanimous agreement that the prophetic books above were produced not by the 8th-century individuals (?) whose names they now bear but by later prophetic schools. Where does that leave us — unless these accounts preserve here and there older traditions both written and oral? (See further Chapter I, on sources.)

First, a few extrabiblical texts provide some controls, at least for some place-names. For instance, the cuneiform Neo-Assyrian annals concerning the campaigns of Tiglath-Pileser III in 745-727 contain a reference to the first three cities the Assyrians encountered on the northern borders of Israel: Ijon, Abel-Beth-Maacah, and Janoah, obviously in geographical order.[59] It happens that our presumed historical sources in 2 Kings list precisely these three sites, in the same order (15:29), and they attribute their destruction to Tiglath-Pileser (III).

That convergence cannot be coincidental. Furthermore, the precise

58. The literature on the Deuteronomistic History (Dtr) is vast, but for orientation see Chapter I. In this work I regard the Deuteronomistic History (Deuteronomy, Joshua, Judges, 1-2 Samuel, 1-2 Kings) as a composition originating in Judah in the 7th century, with the final edition belonging to the exilic and postexilic periods. Along with many scholars, I hold that this work contains some reliable information about the divided monarchy, but it must be used carefully and preferably when the archaeological data are congruent. For an example of how this history impinges upon archaeology at the moment, compare the treatments of A. Mazar 2007a; Finkelstein 2007.

59. The books in the Hebrew Bible that bear a particular prophet's name were written by later schools that collected earlier prophetic traditions and attached a name to them. However, the fact that these works as we have them are later than, for instance, the 8th century does not mean that they are devoid of any historical merit. Thus where information from Isaiah, Amos, and Micah "fits" with what we know from other sources, we have employed it. On the phenomenon of Israelite prophecy in general, see Ben Zvi and Floyd 2000; cf. Toorn 2007. Grabbe concludes that there are some historical data in the prophetic literature, especially where these data can be compared with extrabiblical evidence. For his positivist view of Jeremiah, for instance, see Grabbe 2007.

late-8th-century date it gives us effectively disposes of the revisionist notion of some biblicists that these sources are late (Persian, or even Hellenistic) and therefore cannot be historical (Chapter II). Here, at least, they are.[60] But does that mean that all the other place-names in 2 Kings are reliably historical and thus pertinent to our inquiry? And what about Chronicles?

Then there is the problem of dating the many other biblical texts that contain dozens, even hundreds, of place-names. A classical example of our dilemma is the list of administrative districts in Judah in Joshua 15:21-63 (plus chapters 13–19 generally), which some biblical scholars would date to the reign of Jehoshaphat, 867-851 (cf. 2 Chron. 17:2). This list alone would provide us dozens more place-names of biblical sites that we might actually locate and identify, even if most are known only by surface surveys.[61]

Yet there are problems. (1) Are these towns genuine and not simply the invention of the biblical writers? (2) If so, are they reliably 9th century in date? That would assume that the text of Joshua 15, although not earlier than the 7th century (above), preserves authentic information about a period 200 years earlier. (3) Finally, if we knew that these 125 or so towns were established already by the 9th century, did they continue to be occupied in the 8th century (probably, but we do not always know that)?

Apart from the possible sources in 2 Kings, we have noted references to some sites in Isaiah, Amos, and Micah, which seem to have an 8th-century setting (i.e., original context). We shall treat these in detail below, but here we note that the towns mentioned in these texts, even if authentically 8th century in date, cannot be presumed to be the only ones known to

60. 2 Kings 15:29 mentions "all the land of Naphtali," exactly parallel to Tiglath-Pileser III's "wide land of Naphtali." Cf. *Ancient Near Eastern Texts Relating to the Old Testament,* ed. J. B. Pritchard, 3rd ed. (Princeton: Princeton University Press, 1969), 284.

61. Josh. 15–19 contains a detailed boundary list, which if taken literally as a historical witness would provide us with a map of Israel and Judah, plus information that would locate dozens of biblical towns and cities. This text has been hotly debated, however, because it purports to describe the tribal boundaries in the 12th century (as we now know), but in its present form it cannot be earlier than the 7th century, and perhaps later (cf. 1 Chron. 2; 4). Aharoni's classic *Land of the Bible* simply assumes the validity of this text; cf. Aharoni 1979, 348-62. Rainey's *Carta Atlas* similarly takes the boundary lists as authentic; cf. Rainey 2006, 151-54, 181-85. Rainey notes the problem but says simply that "It is likely that the pericopes (passages) discussed above derive from the same archival sources that preserve the list of Solomon's commissioners' district" (185). The "Solomonic district list" is contained in 1 Kings 4:7-19; but this, too, is of dubious value, just as the boundary list above is. On the value of these lists potentially, see n. 58 above. Here I shall make little or no use of these texts, because in my opinion they add nothing to our portrait of the 8th century.

the authors and redactors. These are the only ones that happen to be mentioned. There would have been many more (below).

Finally, there are many problems with identifying and locating sites, even if they have names. The fact is that many of the sites discussed above have already been positively identified entirely on the basis of nonbiblical data. These would include most of the major sites, such as Dan, Hazor, Megiddo, Ta'anach, Kinneret, Beth-Shean, Gezer, Gerar, and several others. Here either the Arabic name (Ar. "Jezer" = Heb. "Gezer"), textual data found at the site (Dan), or extrabiblical texts that make the name clear (Samaria and others) are decisive. In these cases, the references in the Hebrew Bible are irrelevant.

Furthermore, having a definite name for a site would not change our description of the site and its function in any of the above cases in any significant way. Such data are, simply speaking, a luxury: nice, but not necessary.

The Macro Environment

Apart from individual place-names, are there any clues in the Hebrew Bible as to the hierarchy of sites we have developed here? The best guide is Ferdinand Deist's *Material Culture of the Bible: An Introduction* (2000), although it is only a discussion of the texts, not *real* material culture (i.e., archaeological data).[62]

The Hebrew Bible appears to recognize only some of the distinctions we have made. There are said to be only:

1. Fortified cities *('îr; qiryâ)*
2. Villages *(ḥāṣērîm)*

In short, the Hebrew Bible recognizes essentially only a sort of two-tier hierarchy.

62. Deist's work on "material culture" is a great disappointment. He makes almost no use of the *real* material culture, that is, the archaeological data. He does not even list standard handbooks such as the textbooks of Ben-Tor and Levy. He opines that "the archaeological evidence is partial and, above all, dumb" (Deist 2000, 55). Apart from a sort of lexicon for biblical texts that refer to various ideas and things, this work is of very little value. The only scholars competent to discuss "material culture" are obviously archaeologists, or archaeologists in collaboration with biblicists.

Despite this niggardly data, several scholars have tried to expand and quantify the biblical evidence. The Israeli archaeologist Ze'ev Herzog distinguishes seven settlement patterns in Iron Age Israel.[63] Biblical scholar (and archaeologist) Volkmar Fritz recognizes only capital cities, administrative or military cities, and residential cities (surprisingly, no towns or villages).[64]

In any case, the biblical texts add no significant data to our development of a hierarchy of sites. In fact, their simplistic portrait of reality in biblical times is contradicted by the more objective archaeological data.

Supplementary Place-Names from the Hebrew Bible

If the biblical texts do not help us to draw a larger portrait of the hierarchy that we seek to develop here, what about a more modest contribution, that is, identifying individual sites that might be used to fill in the categories we are using? After all, we know that maps based exclusively on excavated sites represent only a minority of the population. Such sites are mostly larger, more visible tells that yield information on cities and towns. But the bulk of the population lived in rural areas in small villages and hamlets (cf. fig. IV.22), most of which remain undiscovered, and of course unexcavated.

The lacuna on our map might be filled theoretically by incorporating survey data. As we have already seen, at least 400-500 sites in Israel and Judah have been found in intensive surface surveys carried out recently by Israeli archaeologists. Most are not tells, but sites so small that they have escaped attention until recently. Many sites consist only of sherd scatters. And of course, many ancient sites have simply been lost due to erosion, alluvial deposits, or modern construction. Thus we will never have a complete, or even representative, map of Israel and Judah in the 8th century.

63. Cf. Herzog 1997. Zertal distinguishes several types of settlements: (1) towns and cities, (2) villages, (3) farms, (4) enclosures and seasonal sites, (5) fortresses. See Zertal 2001.

64. A widely used work by the late Volkmar Fritz, devoted to an analysis of cities, defines a "city" (in the Early Bronze Age!) as (1) a large site, fifteen to twenty-five acres; (2) protected by a ring of walls; (3) exhibiting monumental architecture; (4) exhibiting evidence of planning; and (5) showing evidence of social stratification. See Fritz 1995. He applies this site hierarchy to the Iron Age without further differentiation. He does not deal at all with our towns, villages, and farmsteads. See also de Geus 2003. This work is somewhat more comprehensive, but it is less authoritative since the author is not an archaeologist.

Despite these constraints, we might be able to utilize the biblical data, however limited, to add the names of some sites — especially if the biblical names can be positively identified with known archaeological sites. All the names on the maps of excavated sites here are biblical, even though we have derived nearly all of them from nonbiblical sources. But could we add a few more that are based on unexcavated sites mentioned in biblical texts?

A perusal of all the above-mentioned texts (2 Kings 14–21; Isaiah; Amos; Micah) reveals an interesting picture. The twenty-two extra sites derived from the Hebrew Bible can be summarized as follows (* = also known from Neo-Assyrian texts):

Fig. IV.37. Biblical Place-Names of the 8th Century B.C.E.

ISRAEL	*2 Kings 14–21*	*Isaiah*	
	*'Ijon (Tell ed-Dibbîn)	Rimmon	
	*Abel-beth Maacah	(Rumâneh)	
	*Janoah (Yānûḥ)		
	Gath-hefer		
	(Kh. ez-Zuvr'a)		

JUDAH	*Isaiah*	*Micah*	*Amos*
	Aiath (Kh. Haiyan)	Adullam (esh-Sheikh Madkhor)	Tekoa
	Michmash (Mukhmâs)	Moresheth-gath	(Tell el-Judeideh)
	Ramah (er-Ram)	Beth-leaphrah	(et-Taiyibeh)
	Anathoth ('Anata)	Maroth (?)	
	Gallin (?)	Iaanan (?)	
	Gebin (?)		
	Laishah (?)		
	Madmenah (?)		
	Migron (?)		

The book of Chronicles is considerably later and is regarded with a good deal of skepticism except where it agrees with Kings (above). It is of little or no value for place-names, except for specifying several "cities in the Shephelah and Judah" (2 Chron. 28:18):

Beth-Shemesh
Gederoth (unknown; = Gedor?)
Soco (and its villages; Kh. 'Abbâd)

Timnah (Tel Batash)
Gimzo (Jimzū, north of Gezer)

Chronicles also adds to the few place-names in Kings — Dan, Beersheba (the traditional boundaries of Israel), and Elath (Ezion-Geber).

There are several implications of these biblical data. (1) 2 Kings lists no presumptive 8th-century sites from Judah (only five from Israel), even though it is a southern source. Is that because the book of Kings simply presumes its readers' knowledge of the south?

(2) In any case, of the twenty-some sites gleaned from these particular biblical texts, only thirteen can be plausibly identified and thus located: five in Israel, and eight in Judah (those in fig. IV.1 giving the Arabic equivalent). And even in these cases, the identification depends either on the Arabic name, supposing that it preserves the ancient name, or on topographical indicators in the biblical texts (i.e., extrapolating from sites closely grouped, near known biblical sites).

(3) Even if the identification seems assured beyond reasonable doubt, none of these sites have been excavated, so apart from pottery dates based on surface surveys, we cannot be sure that any actually were occupied in the 8th century.

(4) Finally, the chief reason for attributing these sites to the 8th century at all is that they are mentioned in biblical texts presumed to be 8th century in date. The only indisputably contemporary textual evidence comes from nonbiblical texts, in this case the Neo-Assyrian annals. There the topographical knowledge of the authors and editors of 2 Kings (part of the Deuteronomistic History; above) can be confirmed by extrabiblical evidence.[65] But even so, these three 8th-century sites — Ijon, Abel-Beth-Maacah, and Janoah — have not been excavated. Thus we can say little about them, except to cite their location and size, and that does not seem to warrant placing them on our maps here.

In conclusion, this exhaustive survey of the biblical data on site distribution as well as place-names adds little or no genuine historical information to our archaeologically based history. That is the principal reason we may consider archaeological evidence as the primary data.

---

65. I have developed the idea of "convergences" between texts and artifacts as historical confirmation in Dever 2001a.

How Many Cities? How Many People?

Having surveyed the distribution of cities, towns, villages, and forts over the 8th-century landscape of Israel and Judah, what can we say finally about the total population of the area?

Using the above coefficient of 100 people per acre, a consensus figure, the seventy-five sites on the chart and maps here in Chapter IV would yield a figure of some 80,000. Adding the 500 or so known from surveys, assuming an average (or median) of 10 acres, we could add, at least theoretically, another 50,000, for a total of about 130,000. Including the neo-Philistine, Phoenician, and Aramean sites that we have deliberately excluded in our history of Israel would increase the total to roughly 150,000. That comports well with the figure of 150,000 often given for Iron II Palestine (ca. 900-586 B.C.E.) west of the Jordan.

That represents a substantial increase from an estimated 100,000 in the 10th century, that is, the supposed united monarchy. It is smaller, however, than some estimates of as much as 400,000 for Israel and Judah by the 7th century (which is doubtful).[66] Yet it is significant that by the 8th century the population had grown (and perhaps peaked), a sign of historical change and development that the archaeological data brought forward here would fully support.

66. Population estimates for Israel and Judah in the 8th century range from circa 150,000 to 400,000. Cf. Broshi and Finkelstein 1992.

CHAPTER V

❧

Cities and Towns

I have already discussed certain large cities (Chapter IV), Tier 1 capitals and district administrative centers. We now turn to Tier 2 and 3 sites that we have defined as cities and towns. The latter are distinguished partly by size; that is, cities are larger than villages, with populations from 1,000 up to several thousand (Chapter IV). But towns and cities are also distinguished by greater complexity. That is particularly true of cities, which we have designated as population agglomerates that are now too large to be self-sustaining. Thus cities will require an administrative apparatus, various social and economic specialists, suppliers of food and services, and the like. Such a highly stratified society and a diversified economy represent a major transformation of village life, and the town plan can be expected to reflect this change.

PART I: THE ARCHAEOLOGICAL DATA

Urban and Town Planning

In this category we are considering cities and towns with populations assumed to have been from about 300 to as much as 3,000. We have thirty-five such Tier 2 and 3 sites that are archaeologically attested (figs. IV.2, IV.18, IV.23).

One cannot analyze the phenomenon of cities and towns as we have defined them (not self-supporting) without addressing the issue of urban planning. Such cities, with their regular layout and designated area, do not simply happen. Someone with foresight must have come up with a reasonable plan to make the most efficient use of the available space, and especially to accommodate the needs of a more stratified society. Here we can simplify matters by distinguishing only two general types of urban plans: (1) ad hoc plans dictated largely by the topography of the site; and (2) orthogonal plans, which impose a more or less rigorous grid upon the area within the city walls.[1] The latter originated in full form long after the Iron Age with Hippodamus, a 5th century B.C.E. Greek architect and engineer. Thus it is relatively rare to find such a plan in ancient Israel and Judah.

Our best example of a planned 8th century B.C.E. site (apart from the Tier 1 administrative centers above) is Tell en-Naṣbeh (biblical Mizpah). Some two-thirds of this seven- to eight-acre site were cleared by American excavators in the 1920s, an unusually large (and today unconscionable) exposure.[2] The thin, poorly preserved remains, some founded directly on bedrock, made stratigraphy difficult. And the death of the director immediately upon the cessation of the excavation left the publication to others. For better or worse, however, we have an almost complete plan of an Iron II city. It was founded in the 9th century as a provincial town (Str. 3C) but transformed in the 8th century (Str. 3B-A) into a well-planned administrative center. (We would have listed it as such had the details been more reliable, especially the chronological phasing.)[3]

The original town had a cluster of small, fairly uniform three- or four-room houses, sharing common walls and roughly following the contours of the natural hilltop. A casemate (double) wall about six or seven feet wide followed the periphery of the houses and probably enclosed the entire site. No gate was found. A sort of "ring road" is situated between this wall and the houses.

By the early 8th century (Str. 3B) the town had been enlarged and was now encircled by a heavier masonry wall some fifteen feet wide, incorporating a dozen or so towers augmented by semicircular bastions. A city gate in the northeastern quadrant featured an outer gate with an offset entrance, guarded by two towers, one a large external bastion. There was also an inner two-entryway gate.

Several new houses, more elaborate than the usual four-room

1. On town planning, see Shiloh 1978, 1987; McClellan 1984; Herzog 1992, 1997; Kempinski and Reich 1992; Zorn 1994; and especially Faust 2002, 2003b.
2. See the reworking of McCown 1947 in McClellan 1984; and especially Zorn 1997.
3. See n. 2 above.

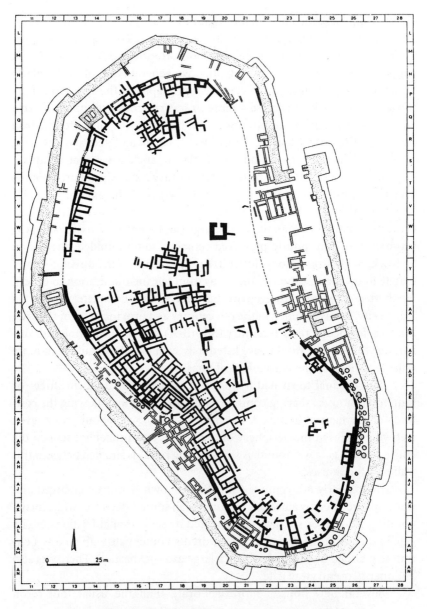

Fig. V.1. Plan of Tell en-Naṣbeh. Str. 3C structures in solid lines;
Str. 3B-A additions in lighter lines.

Herzog 1997, fig. 5.26

houses, were now constructed, together with a large open-air terrace immediately inside the gate, probably as a residence for new officials. Finally, some forty stone-lined silos were dug in other open areas, providing large-scale storage facilities.

These changes resulted in a very sophisticated city plan, which incorporated earlier elements cleverly, but elaborated them into a city well suited to be a major administrative center. The population probably did not increase greatly within the city walls, but the function of the city was transformed (see Chapter VII).[4]

To write real history, as we are attempting to do here, is difficult if we cover only a century or so, and if one is also deliberately restricted to archaeological data. We must deal with (1) changes over time and (2) an explanation for the changes. With Tell en-Naṣbeh we can actually chart significant changes, and the reason no doubt has to do with the need for additional administrative centers as the Judean monarchy reached its zenith in the 8th century. Beersheba Str. II (Chapter IV) exhibits many of the same features, especially in the ring road and abutting houses, but we have already treated that as a planned administrative center.

Two other 8th-century sites, although less extensively excavated, exhibit some degree of urban planning. At Tell el-Farʿah (N.; biblical Tirzah?), Str. VIId remains in the northwest quadrant reveal a new, well-planned city.[5] The old four-room houses have been replaced with more elaborate courtyard houses, although again earlier elements are utilized. The reasons for these changes are not entirely clear. But it is not unreasonable to suggest that Tell el-Farʿah now becomes more of a planned city than a rural town. Even so, it does not seem to have had more than a rather flimsy city wall, although with a single-entryway offset gate.

We have classified Tell Beit Mirsim in the Judean Shephelah as a town, but its estimated population of around 1,000 would possibly classify it as a city. It was excavated in 1926-32 by the legendary American biblical archaeologist W. F. Albright. But much of his stratigraphic phasing has now been reworked.[6] Here the exposure of Str. A$_2$ in the northwest quadrant is pertinent. The plan reveals a tightly compacted group of four-room houses in-

---

4. On the notion of a relatively fixed population but increased complexity, see Herzog 1992, 263.

5. Chambon in Stern 1993, 432-40. Cf. fig VII.10 below.

6. Despite the legendary status of Albright's excavations at Tell Beit Mirsim, virtually all his stratigraphy has had to be reworked. For the most recent summary see Greenberg in Stern 1993, 177-80; cf. earlier Greenberg 1987 on the Iron Age.

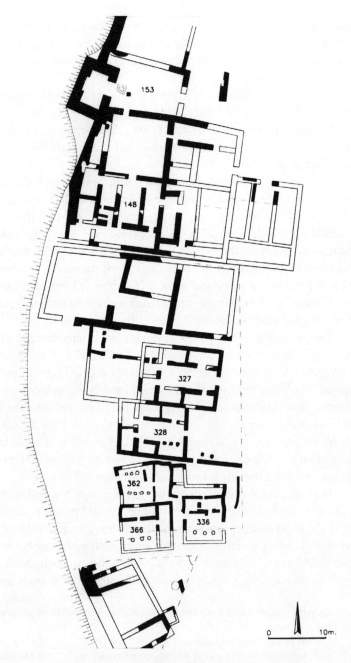

Fig. V.2. Plan of Tell el-Farʿah (N.); the living quarters near the gate in Str. VIId.
Herzog 1997, fig. 5.23

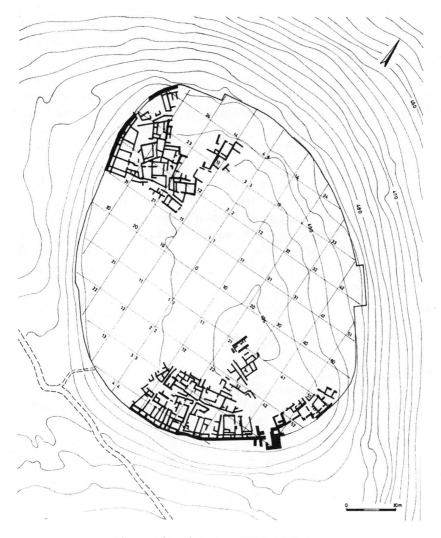

Fig. V.3. Plan of Str. A₂ at Tell Beit Mirsim.
Herzog 1997, fig. 5.29

side the casemate (double) city wall with a large citadel-like structure incorporated into it. Here, however, the street plan is irregular, and there is no ring road. The layout is thus more agglutinative than deliberate.

The other city and town sites in figure IV.2 have not been extensively excavated, so we cannot say anything in particular about the plans. However, one older site now being reexcavated is promising. American excavations in the 1920s-1930s at Tell el-Rumeileh (biblical Beth-Shemesh) cleared some three-quarters of the small mound (seven acres) down to bedrock. Renewed excavations directed by Israeli archaeologists Shlomo Bunimovitz and Zvi Lederman have now corrected the faulty stratigraphy and have added relatively large excavation areas. As a result we now have another extensive town plan. I had originally classified Beth-Shemesh as a provincial town (figs. IV.1, IV.2), partly on the basis of its small size. But the current excavators regard it as a Judean district administrative center, and I concur.[7]

Str. 3 (IIb of the older excavations) belongs to the early 8th century. It was characterized by a massive city wall, still preserved some six feet high, with several towers; an exceptionally large public building; several plazas and common areas; storehouses and a huge silo; and in particular a massive reservoir for collecting water.[8] Succeeding Str. 2 (IIc) continued after a partial destruction, then was destroyed in the Neo-Assyrian campaigns of 701.

Defenses

In an earlier phase of archaeological interpretation, scholars often defined a city largely by the presence or absence of a city wall, the assumption being that a true city must have defenses. That is indeed usually the case; but as we have seen, the degree of size and complexity is a better criterion.[9]

To create a database before we embark on an analysis of social complexity and political history, let us list the relevant 8th-century sites. The city walls can be divided into (1) solid walls (often offsets-insets) and (2) casemate walls, or chambered double walls. City gates in this period (and in Iron II A-C generally) may be three-entryway or two-entryway

7. Beth-Shemesh is currently being extensively reexcavated; see Bunimovitz and Lederman 2009, especially on the site's significant role as a "border fortress" (with Philistia) in the 10th/9th-8th centuries (here cf. level 2).

8. Cf. n. 7 above. Level 2 shows a major destruction in 701 and sinks into decline thereafter.

9. Definitions of what constitutes a city are rare. See, however, Shiloh 1980; Herzog 1992. A city is usually planned, is diversified in function, and is usually fortified. Fritz's criteria are more definitive. A city (1) is larger than circa three acres in size; (2) is planned; reflects the self-confidence of the state; (3) possesses monumental architecture; and (4) is fortified; cf. Fritz 1995, 11-19. Cf. also pp. 72-74 above.

(sometimes called respectively "two-chambered" and "one-chambered"). And while this chart covers known cities, it also embraces some towns.

Fig. V.4. City Fortifications of the 8th Century B.C.E.

Site and Stratum	Walls	Gates
Dan II	Solid, towers	Lower = three-entryway Upper = two-entryway
Hazor VI-V	Casemate (reused)	Four-entryway (reused)
Megiddo IVA	Solid, offsets-insets	Three-entryway
Gezer VI	Solid, plus casemate	Three-entryway
Tell en-Naṣbeh 3A	Solid, towers	Three- and two-entryway
*Tel Batash III	Solid	Four-entryway
*Beth-Shemesh 3, 2	Solid, towers	?
Lachish III	Solid, double	Three-entryway
*Tell Beit Mirsim A₂	Solid	Two-entryway
*Beersheba II	Casemate	Three-entryway
*Tell Ḥalif VIB	Casemate, *glacis*	?
*Tel 'Ira VII	Solid and casemate	Four-entryway

*town rather than city.

What can we learn from these data? First, with regard to the construction of the fortifications, it is significant that most are not original constructions of the 8th century but are reused with some alterations from the 9th (and even the 10th) century. That is not surprising, of course, since these earlier city walls and gates had been monumental structures representing an enormous commitment of resources, engineering skills, and manual labor. Not only had they tended to survive destructions or disturbances such as the Aramean incursions of the 9th century (Chapter X), but they had been proven remarkably effective as defensive installations in any case.

It is the alterations in the 8th century that are most significant. At Hazor the monumental Str. VIII four-entryway gate and casemate wall of the upper city, originally built in the 10th century, seem to continue without major changes.[10] The similar Megiddo Str. VA/IVB gate and solid

10. See Yadin in Stern 1993, 601. The 10th-century gate (Str. X) is not destroyed until the end of Str. V (ca. 732 B.C.E.).

offsets-insets wall, constructed in the late 10th or early 9th century, were also reused, but with a three-entryway gate superimposed on the old four-entryway gate in Str. IVA.[11] The same phenomenon is seen at Gezer in Str. VIII-VI, where again the gate is reused, somewhat smaller in size.[12]

At Dan, the city wall is reused, but the lower three-entryway gate is now supplemented by a two-entryway gate constructed well up the cobbled main street, on a higher terrace.[13]

At Beersheba, the fundamental character of a well-planned administrative center assures that the main defenses will show continuity. The three-entryway gate is reused into Str. III and II. But the Str. IV solid wall is superseded in Str. III-II by a casemate wall. (See fig. IV.16.)[14]

Finally, at Lachish the Str. IV double wall, *glacis,* and three-way gate are rebuilt in Str. III on the earlier foundations, after a destruction possibly by an earthquake.[15]

All these city and town defense systems have a clear *terminus ante quem* (a date before a fixed time), since they all were destroyed in the Assyrian destructions either in 732-721 or 701 B.C.E. Thus these defense systems all have a rationale: the Neo-Assyrian threat beginning in the mid–9th century (Chapter X). Yet in the end, all failed.

Given the delicate balance between preserving the past and preparing for new contingencies, what were the considerations of the administrators and engineers who oversaw these defense systems? Can we learn anything from the archaeological evidence alone? (We know that the Assyrian advance was the problem from nonbiblical texts.)

There perhaps are clues in certain trends that are visible in the archaeological record extending over the 9th and into the early to mid–8th centuries. (1) The city's basic defense systems are reused wherever possible. (2) The original constructions are rebuilt or simply repaired, as necessary. (3) Some new elements are added, such as inner gates (Dan, Tell en-Naṣbeh). (4) There is, however, a trend toward simplification in reducing several three-entryway gates to two-entryway gates (Megiddo, Gezer).

11. See n. 10 above.

12. The Str. VIII four-entryway gate of the 10th century was reduced to three-entryway in Str. VII of the 9th century, to a two-entryway gate in Str. VI of the 8th century. See Dever in Stern 1993, 505.

13. For the addition of the upper gate, see Biran in Stern 2008, 1689.

14. For the addition of the Str. III casemate wall, supplanting the solid wall of Str. IV, see Herzog in Stern 1993, 171.

15. For the possibility of 9th-century Str. IV, see Ussishkin in Stern 1993, 907.

(5) Finally, there is sometimes a shift from more massive solid walls to simpler (?) casemate walls.

The rationale of the 8th-century city planners is obvious in some cases in terms of practicality (nos. 1, 2). But the need to improve on the older systems is also evident (no. 3). The deliberate reduction in the number of chambers in some gateways (no. 4) — barriers to the city — is more difficult to explain. But since we know from other data (below) that the multiple chambers were more for commercial usage than defensive in nature, the actual number of chambers may not have mattered that much.

Furthermore, a two-entryway gate, if massive enough, would be simpler to construct yet just as effective. Similar considerations may have been in operation in the decision to replace solid walls with a lighter yet efficient casemate or double city wall with hollow chambers. The wall would have looked just as formidable to an attacker. But the roomy inner chambers, which were put into practical use for domestic purposes (as we know from other data)[16] in peaceful times, could easily be filled and reinforced.

Perhaps all we can really say from the archaeological data (supplemented, of course, by the Neo-Assyrian, nonbiblical texts) is that from the 9th well into the 8th century there appears to be a nagging, growing concern about the Assyrian advance throughout the country, particularly in the more vulnerable north. This anxiety was justifiable, as proven by the disaster toward the end of the 8th century (Chapter X).

Built-Up Domestic Areas

Inside the perimeter of the city wall and the ring road (if any), all the towns and cities for which we have some semblance of a plan exhibit the same feature, a dense *cluster* of small private houses, usually sharing common walls or courtyards, often not intersected by real streets (or even lanes). We shall look more closely at these residential dwellings (or Israelite "four-room" houses) in Chapter VI. The only available evidence comes from the few sites where exposures are sufficient: Tell en-Naṣbeh 3A; Beersheba II; and to some extent Megiddo IVA, Tell el-Far'ah (N.) VIId, and Tell Beit Mirsim A$_2$.

16. At Gezer, for instance, a casemate to the west of the city gate of the 8th century (Str. VI), destroyed in the Assyrian campaigns, yielded more than a dozen loomweights (from a burned upright loom); several storejars, one bearing an inscription *yayin* (wine); several small terra-cotta inkwells; and a carved bone "fan-handle." See Dever 1985, 1986.

The plan of 8th-century Tell en-Naṣbeh (fig. V.1) reveals up to thirty such houses, abutting the peripheral ring road and extending toward the center of the site (although this area was largely unexcavated). The plan is too sketchy (and may combine elements of different dates to allow precision), but many of the houses are of the typical Iron I-II "four-room" or pillar-courtyard type (below).[17]

The situation of Megiddo is less clear. The 9th-century Str. IVB (fig. IV.10) is characterized chiefly by large public buildings: the reused palace 1723 compound, and an eastern and a western complex of pillared buildings (stables or storehouses; below); and apparently by large open spaces and a large water system. Nine of the fifteen acres were cleared, but only a few private houses were excavated, west of the gate.

Whether some of these features continued in use into Str. IVA of the 8th century is unclear, but it seems likely. (If not, we have no plan of the 8th century.) In that case the few houses near the gate would be relevant, but they yield no details.[18] Megiddo, however, was a major administrative center (Tier 1) and thus not typical of residential cities.

The same must be said of Beersheba II (above), although here the house plans of the 8th century are numerous and quite clear, because 60 percent of the three-acre site was cleared.[19] One can count as many as twenty houses (fig. IV.16), and the unexcavated areas would easily double that figure. Incidentally, the population estimate made on the basis of the whole three acres — circa 300 — would be about the same if one calculated fifty houses and an average family of five to six per house. These figures may be unreliable, however, because Beersheba, like Megiddo, was an administrative center or barracks town. So the houses, although typical (below), may have been occupied not by families but by groups of soldiers stationed there.

A more typical residential town is Tell Beit Mirsim. About three acres of the ten-acre mound were cleared down to 8th-century levels (Str. A$_2$). The resultant plan reveals two relatively large clusters of private houses.

17. Because of the imprecise stratigraphy at Tell en-Naṣbeh, it is nearly impossible to separate the 9th-century and the 8th-century houses on figure V.1 here. Cf. Zorn in Stern 1993, 1098-1102; Zorn 1997.

18. See Herzog 1992, 251-54; cf. Fritz 1995, 88-95.

19. The site of Beersheba was more extensively excavated than would be desirable in most cases, although that does give us an almost complete plan. Aharoni's methods, however (as also at Arad), have left the stratification debatable. It was Herzog who published *Beersheba II: The Early Iron Age Settlement* (1984), whose reworking is the most reliable. Cf. Herzog in Stern 1993, 167-76.

One is in the southeast quadrant just inside the gate, the other near the large tower or citadel in the northwest quadrant. The remains of as many as thirty houses can be made out in the general plan, most rather amorphous. In the northwest area, however, a more detailed published plan shows as many as fifteen tightly clustered houses of the four-room or Israelite type houses (below).[20]

Finally, Tell el-Farʿah (N.; above) has produced the plans of a dozen or so 8th-century private houses near the northwest gate (Str. VIId). The plans of individual houses are not always clear, but some seem to be of the four-room type. What is more, they continue the plan of private houses from Str. VIIb, of the 10th century, where the four-room plan is even clearer (above).[21]

Administrative Buildings

Given the social stratification that cities inevitably reflect, we should expect to find a few buildings larger and more specialized than the houses described above, probably set off somewhat to distinguish them spatially. In fact, we have several such buildings in the 8th century. We have mentioned a few of them when discussing Tier 1 capitals and district administrative centers in Chapter IV. In fact, seven of the eight capitals and regional administrative centers we have identified (figs. IV.1, IV.2) exhibit just such buildings (all but Dan, insufficiently excavated).

The upper city at Hazor reveals a very large citadel and administrative building at the north end of the walled city. It was first constructed in Str. VII of the late 9th century, but it probably continued in use into at least the early 8th century (Str. VI). In addition, an impressive palace was found in Area B of the citadel. A large tripartite pillared building, probably a government storehouse (below), was built in the 9th century, but it may have continued in use into the 8th century. Finally, two Str. VB buildings built side by side that resemble ordinary four-room houses have been regarded

20. See Greenberg in Stern 1993, 180. Cf. n. 6 above. The so-called Western Tower has been regarded previously as a house by others. Cf. Fritz 1995, 109; Holladay 1992. Herzog regards it as anomalous, added later; Herzog 1992, 261.

21. There is some continuity between house plans from the 10th century (Str. VIIb) into the 9th/8th century (Str. VIId). See conveniently Fritz 1995, 97-98; figs. 33, 34. The Str. VIId houses are larger, but the four-room model is still clear; cf. those south of the gate complex discussed here.

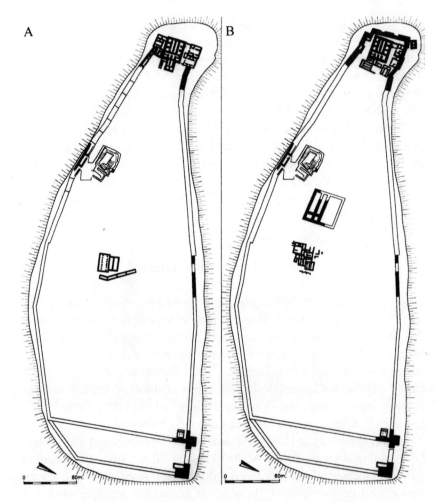

Fig. V.5. Plan of the acropolis at Hazor in Str. VII(A)-VI(B).
Herzog 1997, fig. 5.20

as scribes' houses.[22] All these monumental multiroom structures are located within a walled compound on the acropolis, which further confirms their specialized functions.

The Megiddo IVB monumental structures continued in use into the

---

22. See Reich 1992, 206-7, for this building in Area B, known as a "citadel." It appears to have been constructed in the 9th century, but it continued in use until the Assyrian conquest (Str. VIII-V).

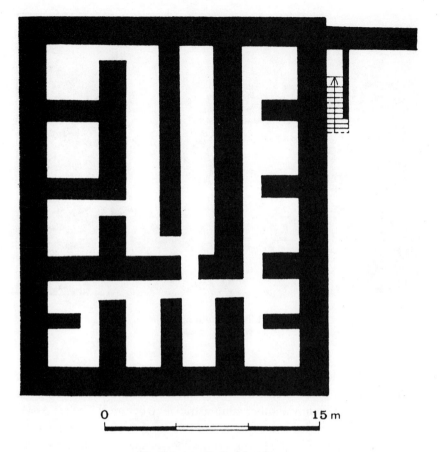

Fig. V.6. Area B citadel at Hazor.
Sharon and Zarzecki-Peleg 2006, fig. 8

8th century (Str. IVA; fig. IV.10), when much of the fifteen-acre site was taken up by what are obviously public and administrative buildings, especially two large complexes of stables or storerooms, a vast open-air plaza with a basin in the center, and a reused palace enclosure (palace 1723; Str. VA/IVB).[23]

I have already noted the royal acropolis at 9th-8th-century Samaria, with its impressive palace, private residence, archive building, and basin for

23. The Str. IVB plan would include the solid wall with a four-entryway gate; the storehouses (the old "stables"); the water system; and Palace 1723 and its compound. In Str. IVA (9th-8th centuries), the plan remains much the same, except that the old palace retains only its perimeter wall; a new southern palace is added (L. 338); and the gate is reduced to a two-entryway gate. Cf. Shiloh in Stern 1993, 1019-21; cf. Fritz 1995, 89-90.

Fig. V.7. Pillared building at Hazor.
Photo: W. G. Dever

water — all enclosed within an area surrounded by a magnificent casemate wall (fig. IV.3). In the 8th century an extramural monumental building was added, almost certainly another administrative structure.[24] The 721 Assyrian destruction produced a collection of ostraca that attested to tax revenues paid to Samaria, as well as luxurious Phoenician-style inlaid furniture that illustrates the lifestyle of the elite officials housed at Samaria.

We have also noted the palace complex of Ramat Raḥel VA, on the outskirts of Jerusalem, probably a royal part-time residence and stronghold (fig. IV.35). Within the spacious walled compound is an inner casemate-walled compound, with a large courtyard flanked by several multiroomed buildings, constructed of fine chisel-dressed masonry (ashlar). Elaborate furnishings, volute capitals, and carved stone balustrades testify to the splendid nature of this palace.[25]

24. For the new 8th-century additions at Samaria, see Herzog 1992, 229 (dubbed the "scribes' house"); cf. Fritz 1995, 129-30.

25. The function of Ramat Raḥel continues to be debated. Fritz regarded it as a "royal, summer residence," not an administrative complex; Fritz 1995, 131-35. Aharoni thought it a "citadel" in Stern 1993, 1263-65.

The plan of Lachish Str. III is particularly instructive. Approximately one-sixth of the thirty-one-acre walled site is taken up by a massive podium designated Palace A-C by the excavators (Ph. C is 8th century). It is the largest Iron Age structure ever found in Israel, visible for miles around. Attached to the palace is a huge open plaza, flanked on the north by several of the tripartite pillared buildings that we have seen elsewhere (below). Another group of such buildings forms the south of the courtyard, along with some large residences. Lachish III is thus clearly an administrative center dominated by monumental buildings, set off by their own enclosure wall (fig. IV.14).[26]

The plan of Beersheba III-II, a well-planned administrative center, has many private houses. But it also produced an elaborate structure four times the size of the typical house, uniquely constructed of ashlar masonry, with a commanding view of the city gate of Str. III-II. Dubbed by the excavators the "Governor's House," this palatial structure is in keeping with Beersheba's role as an administrative center in the 8th century.[27]

Storage Facilities

Seasonal storage of various commodities would have been a necessity in towns or cities of any size, dependent as they were upon the countryside for agricultural produce. One class of 9th-8th-century buildings has attracted widespread attention among scholars because of their unique character.[28] They are all large rectangular, tripartite structures, with two rows of stone columns separating the three long rooms. There is usually a single narrow entrance into the central corridor. In some cases the stone pillars are pierced, presumably for tethering animals; and sometimes there are stone mangers between the pillars. Occasionally these buildings occur in isolation, but more often they are found in multiples, sharing common sidewalls. Most of these buildings have been found empty. But at Beersheba there were hundreds of vessels found in the side chambers, mostly storejars, bowls, and cooking pots.

The table on page 123 lists the specifically 8th-century tripartite

26. See Reich 1992, 206-9; cf. Fritz 1995, 103-7.

27. For the "governor's house," see Reich 1992, 210-11; Fritz 1995, 111-12.

28. On these tripartite buildings as "stables," see Holladay 1986; as "market halls" (Herr 1988); as barracks" (Fritz 1995, 142-43); as "storehouses" (Herzog 1992, 225-82; the view adopted here); cf. de Geus 2003, 63-74. Cf. n. 29 below.

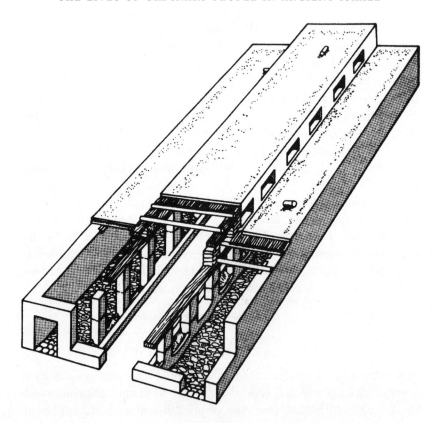

Fig. V.8. Reconstruction of the Str. VIII-V pillared building of Str. II at Beersheba.
de Geus 2003, fig. 19

buildings in question. In interpreting the nature and use of these buildings, several factors should be kept in mind. (1) They are all much larger
than the typical private dwellings, some four to six times as large. (2) They
are all nearly identical in plan. (3) They are constructed on the plan of a
public building, with an entrance corridor and two flanking side chambers. (4) They are all isolated from the residential areas and tend to be located near the city gate or a palace courtyard. (5) While most have been
found nearly empty, the side chambers of the Beersheba buildings were
filled with dozens and dozens of vessels, most of them ideal for storing
foods and liquids. (6) Tether-holes in the columns and some mangers between the columns at some sites (Megiddo) indicate the passage of draft
animals in and out of the central corridor.

The American excavators of Megiddo interpreted these tripartite pil-

Fig. V.9. Tripartite Pillared Buildings of the 9th-8th Centuries B.C.E.

Site	Stratum	Date	Remarks
*Hazor	VII	9th c.	ca. 100 × 65 ft. Columns of dressed stones
Kinneret	II	8th c.	ca. 60 × 33 ft.
*Megiddo	IVA	8th c.	17 units in 4 groups, 5 sq. pillars, mangers. Aver. ca. 75 × 45 ft.
*Beth-shemesh	3 [IIb]	8th c.	ca. 60 × 43 ft.
*Lachish	III		Four, near Palace, ca. 70 × 50 ft.
Tell el-Ḥesi	VIId-c ("City V")	10th/9th c.	ca. 52 × 42 ft.
*Beersheba	III-II	9th-8th c.	Three, adjoining gate, ca. 58 × 34 ft. ea.

*District administrative center

lared buildings, then dated to the 10th century, as stables for horses — probably because of the biblical accounts of Solomon's "chariot cities." Now, however, the buildings are dated to the 9th century (Str. IVA) and regarded elsewhere by most authorities as government storerooms.[29] In that case, either taxes paid in kind, in various foodstuffs, or supplies requisitioned from the populace would have been stored by government officials for trade or later redistribution (below).

A few other kinds of facilities for storage have been found at 8th-century sites, especially stone-lined public silos. The largest one known at Megiddo dates to the late 8th century, during the Assyrian occupation (Str. III). Located in the center of a large plaza, with two descending flights of stone stairs, it had a capacity of more than 4,000 cubic feet.[30] Several such silos were also discovered at Beth-Shemesh in Str. 3-2.[31] At Tell en-Naṣbeh, more than forty smaller silos were found in the expanded city of Str. 3A, near the city gate and several large administrative buildings.[32] Megiddo

29. The so-called stables originally ascribed to "Str. 5A/IVB" and dated to the 10th century are now ascribed to a new Str. IVB of the 9th century. Cf. Fritz 1995, 887-96, and the references there, following in particular Herzog 1992. This arrangement is better, even though it plays into Finkelstein's idiosyncratic "low chronology." Cf. n. 28 above.

30. On the water systems, see Fritz 1995, 151-60. Cf. n. 31 below, adding the water system at Beth-Shemesh. There is also a water system now at Arad.

31. Bunimovitz and Lederman 2009, 128-35.

32. See McClellan 1984; Zorn in Stern 1993, 1101; Zorn 1997.

and Beth-Shemesh have already been designated as district administrative centers on other grounds, and Tell en-Naṣbeh would perhaps qualify as a smaller center.

Industrial Installations

It stands to reason that most larger-scale industrial operations would have been either isolated in peripheral areas within the walled town or city or, more likely, conducted outside the settlement in adjacent areas. However, not many such large open areas have been investigated, so we have little evidence.

It is obvious that olives and grapes would have been processed on a commercial scale, since the large stone presses could not have been easily accommodated within residential areas. At Tel Miqneh, however (biblical Ekron), a Philistine site, olive oil pressing occurred on a monumental scale, almost every house possessing its own beam press.[33] At nearby Tel Batash (Timnah, presumably an Israelite site) we have another beam press from the 8th century. Had we excavated more hamlets and farms, we would undoubtedly have found still more presses.[34]

Pottery, although ubiquitous on all sites, has not left us with any clear archaeological evidence of ceramic manufacture. Ethnographic data suggest that most pottery making was a cottage industry, possibly done by women.[35] Yet we do not have any potters' wheels or kilns dated to the 8th century (or any other phase of the Iron Age).

The fine chisel-dressed (ashlar) masonry attested in a number of monumental buildings implies large-scale quarrying and stone-dressing operations. Yet here again we have no direct archaeological evidence.[36]

Finally the Iron Age is characterized in part by the introduction of

33. On the frequent occurrences of olive oil presses in an "industry," see Gitin in Stern 1993, 1057-58.

34. For Batash III olive oil processing (7th century), see Mazar in Stern 1993, 157-58. See also Bunimovitz and Lederman 2009, 136-37, on Beth-Shemesh and other sites.

35. For pioneering work on women as the ancient potters, see my student London 2008 and references there to her earlier work.

36. Ashlar, or fine chisel-dressed masonry, is commonly thought to be of Phoenician derivation. See the pioneer discussion of Shiloh 1979; cf. now Reich 1992, 211-12. Ashlar masonry is found, however, in Cyprus at sites such as Kalavassos in the late 13th century B.C.E., where it could be of Mycenaean origin.

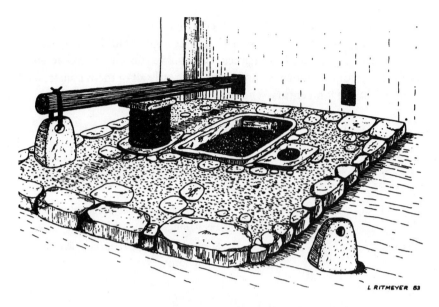

L RITMEYER 83

Fig. V.10. Reconstruction of an oil-processing installation at Tel Miqneh (Ekron),
in a private house (although 7th century).
de Geus 2003, fig. 35

iron tools and other items. Until recently, we had no data here either. But
in recent years a unique iron workshop has been unearthed at Beth-
Shemesh in Str. 3. It was probably constructed in the 9th or even 10th century, then continued in use throughout the 8th century. The smithy was located near some large public buildings and a commercial area, which suggests a managed industry.[37]

The high-quality carved ivory inlays and the numerous inscribed
gemstones that we have (below) were certainly not manufactured at the
level of household production. But we do not have any "factories" where
such luxury goods would have been made.

Water Systems

Ancient Israel and Judah lay mostly within the arid and semiarid zones of
the Levant (Chapter III). Most sites were therefore located near springs,
which were adequate until the population burgeoned by the late Iron Age.

37. Bunimovitz and Lederman 2009, 128-31.

Now — especially with the Assyrian crisis looming on the horizon — it was necessary to employ new technologies to augment and secure the water supply of many sites (cf. Chapter X). We have substantial archaeological evidence for a number of water systems, nearly all of them constructed or in use in the 8th century. The relevant sites can be listed as follows.

Fig. V.11. Water Systems of the 9th-8th Centuries B.C.E.[38]

Site	Stratum	Date	Remarks
Hazor	VII-V	9th-8th c.	Stepped shaft 135 ft. deep; lateral tunnel 135 ft. long
Megiddo	IVA	9th-8th c.	Shaft 130 ft. deep; lateral tunnel 265 ft. long
Gibeon		8th c.?	Stepped shaft 80 ft. deep; supplementary to the spring
Gezer	VII-VI?	9th-8th c.?	Stepped shaft 25 ft. deep; lateral tunnel 125 ft. long
Jerusalem	12	8th c.	Shaft
Beth-Shemesh	3-2	9th-8th c.	Large cistern
Lachish	IV-III?	9th-8th c.	"Great shaft"; large well 79 ft. deep. Unfinished
Arad	IX-VIII?	9th-8th c.	Large well
Beersheba	III	9th-8th c.	Square shaft leading to cisterns
Kadesh-Barnea	"Middle"	9th c.?	Aqueduct from spring

Whatever the differing details, these water systems were technological adaptations to the local facilities, all well engineered, the Jerusalem system as a royal construction exceptionally so. The rationale in each case may be surmised by noting the type of construction chosen. (1) In some systems a vertical shaft was simply dug through bedrock to reach the presumed water table (Gibeon, although it failed). (2) In other systems the vertical shaft was dug deep into the bedrock, at which point a sloping lateral shaft was dug to reach the water table (Hazor; Gezer). (3) In a few systems a similar shaft was dug, but then a long tunnel was excavated to reach a spring outside the city wall (Megiddo; the second Gibeon tunnel; Jerusalem), which was then concealed. (4) In some cases, a deep well sought to

38. See n. 30 above.

Fig. V.12. The Gibeon water system.
Photo: W. G. Dever

reach the water table (Arad). (5) Occasionally a deep cistern was dug to collect runoff water (Beth-Shemesh; the unfinished Lachish "Great Shaft"?). (6) Finally, an aqueduct could be constructed to carry water from a spring into the walled site (as at Kadesh-Barnea, a desert oasis).

Domestic Houses

By far the most conspicuous and important element of ancient Israelite and Judean towns and cities was the ordinary domestic dwelling. We have perhaps several hundred of these houses, many of them securely dated to the 8th century.[39] The first feature that strikes us is the extraordinary continuity of this unique style of house. It is often called the "three-room" or "four-room" house, the "pillar courtyard" house, or even the "Israelite type house" (below). That is because the ground floor exhibits a square or rectangular U-shaped plan, with a central courtyard (counting it, however, as one "room"). On either side of the courtyard are usually two flanking rectangular rooms, often with cobbled floors. Two rows of stone pillars and/or solid walls mark off these side chambers, in any case giving entrance ("rooms" 2, 3). Finally, a separate broad room extends all the way across the back of the structure, sometimes subdivided (the fourth "room"). Most of these houses have a second story. Whether the courtyard was roofed or not is debated.[40]

Despite some variations on this scheme — that is, three or four rooms, and entrances that vary — all these houses obviously reflect a standardized plan, what a typical house should look like. The longevity of this house plan is even more remarkable than its consistency. The earliest such houses appear apparently *de novo* with the emergence of Israel and Israelite culture in the 12th-11th centuries, the settlement horizon. Examples of these Iron I houses are found at Israelite sites like 'Izbet Sarta and Tel Masos, but they also occur at a few early Philistine sites (Tell Qasile XI).[41]

By the 10th century, at the beginning of the Israelite monarchy, these

39. On the "four-room" or "pillar/courtyard" house, see Shiloh 1970; 1978; Stager 1985; G. R. H. Wright 1985; Holladay 1992; Netzer 1992; Fritz 1995, 136-42; King and Stager 2001, 21-35; Clark 2003; Faust and Bunimovitz 2003; de Geus 2003, 74-85; Faust 2003a; 2006a, 71-84; 2011, 208-24; Hardin 2010, 24-60.

40. For this variation from a presumed prototype, see Bunimovitz and Faust, 2003a, 412; Faust 2006a, 77-78. Nevertheless, there is a marked homogeneity in the many examples we have.

41. For early (12th-11th centuries) four-room houses at Izbet Ṣarṭah and Tel Masos, see conveniently Fritz 1995, 57-60, 64-68, and references there.

houses occur at many sites, even extending as far south as the Negev forts (Chapter X). During the divided monarchy they are typical at sites both in the north and in the south. The basic module is now so well suited to mature Israelite and Judean culture that even the houses of patricians are built on the same plan, although larger (Chapter VII).

Scholars have long noted this unique house plan, in particular raising the question of its origins and whether it reflects "ethnicity." It has been thought of as uniquely Israelite, an indigenous house-style that seems to emerge first contemporaneously with the Israelite settlement in Canaan.[42] Now, however, we have a few examples of similar "pillar-courtyard" houses at earlier Late Bronze Age sites, as at Tel Batash in the 14th century (Str. VII).[43] Also, Iron I houses of similar type have been found recently in Transjordan, which is unlikely to have been under Israelite control in the 12th-11th centuries. Especially noteworthy is an example from Tall al-'Umayri in Jordan, a few miles south of Amman, in northern Moab (Chapter VI). Dating to the late 13th/early 12th century (Str. 12), this house ("Building B") was found full of domestic items due to a sudden destruction (perhaps by earthquakes). The plan is indeed similar to the contemporary four-room Israelite houses, as the excavators argue, except for a large stone-paved platform at one end of the central courtyard. Here we seem to have a slight variant of a common Iron I domestic house, probably representing a common *koine* material culture shared by peoples of the new post-Canaanite polities now emerging throughout Canaan.[44]

Whatever the precise ethnic identity of the inhabitants, the structure and contents of this house are very revealing. The excavators have recently published a complete inventory of the finds, nearly 200 objects (Chapter VI). All except for a few storejars in the back room came from the collapsed floors of the second story, thus proving (as we previously thought) that most daily tasks were carried out on the second story or on the roof. The animals, along with stored foodstuffs, occupied the ground floor.

It is significant that here we have an almost complete domestic assemblage of a four-room house. And all of it reflects the typical household activities of the Iron Age, beginning in the 12th century B.C.E. and extending all the way to the end of the Israelite monarchy 600 years later. While

42. See n. 41 above.
43. For the Tel Batash Str. VII house of the 14th century, see Mazar in Stern 1993, 154. For the question of whether it is a "prototype" of the Israelite house, see Faust 2006a, 73-78, denying the connection (as I would).
44. See Dever forthcoming (Ben-Tor).

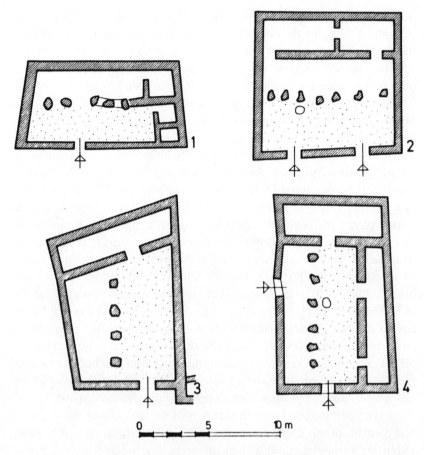

Fig. V.13. Plans of typical Iron Age houses.
Fritz 1995, fig. 24

the 'Umayri house is much earlier than the period we are surveying here, the fundamental continuity of architectural style (and therefore of life-style) assures us that the comparison is apt. Indeed, we now have a similarly well preserved four-room house with all its contents from the 8th century: Tell Ḥalif, in the Judean Shephelah. Here again we have evidence of a two-story, self-contained residence, providing shelter for a sizable family, their food supplies, and their domestic animals.[45] We shall return to this subject in Chapter VI.

45. Cf. Bunimovitz and Lederman 2009; Hardin 2010.

Scholars had long assumed that these unique multiroom, multifunction houses first came into widespread use among the subsistence farmers of the early Iron Age, before the emergence of the Israelite and Transjordanian petty states (10th-8th centuries). They are indeed simple but ideal farmhouses, well adapted to the social and economic factors of farmers (and pastoralists) of the time.[46]

The typical space of these houses ranges from 1,100 to 1,200 square feet (counting both stories), with a few being a bit smaller (ca. 900 square feet). One may compare that with a modest-sized apartment or suburban house today (1,000-1,500 square feet). The ground floor, with its tamped earthen floor and partly-open central courtyard, would have been ideal for carrying in food and various supplies for storage (in the backroom). The small cobble-floored side rooms would have served conveniently as animal stalls, with fodder nearby. The heat from the animals, rising to the living quarters on the second story, would have been welcome in the damp winters. A hearth for cooking is often found on the ground floor, close to the animals being milked, to provisions stored nearby, and to food-processing facilities.

The second story would have been divided into anywhere from four to eight rooms, ample living quarters for a family of a dozen or more members (below). We have evidence of exterior stairs in some cases, or ladders could have been used to reach the upper floor. That the roof was also used for food drying and processing in good weather is indicated by the quantities of domestic artifacts often found above the collapsed second story remains, as well as stone roof rollers (below).

These vernacular houses were relatively simple to construct and maintain, using only local materials and unskilled labor. The foundations were of rough fieldstones, laid carefully but without mortar. The upper courses were of sun-dried mud bricks, plastered periodically with mud plaster. Wooden beams supported the first and second story floors. The roof was made of thatched branches, this too mud plastered. Stone roof rollers found sometimes in the fallen debris indicate that the mud-plastered roof was replastered periodically and rolled flat to waterproof it. Vernacular farmhouses of almost exactly this type are still found in villages all around the Mediterranean, from southern Italy and Greece, through Turkey and Syria, in Jordan, and all the way down to the Egyptian Delta and Nile Valley.[47]

46. Stager 1985.
47. I have seen such houses — complete with roof roller — throughout all these ar-

These four-room houses, so well suited to an early agricultural society and economy in Iron I, were flexible enough not only to survive throughout Iron I but also to come into wide vogue in Iron II (ca. 900-600). They continued to characterize rural sites, of course; but they were also the basic townhouse of the towns, and even of the larger cities, by the 8th century. They were little changed, except when enlarged somewhat and better furnished as elite dwellings (Chapter VI).

Well-dated examples come from larger Tier 1-2 sites like Beth-Shean II, Shechem VII, Tell en-Naṣbeh 3A, Beth-Shemesh 3A, Lachish III, Tell Beit Mirsim A₂, and Beersheba II. Tier 3 towns with such houses would include Tell el-Farʿah (N.) VIId, e; Jokneam VII; Tel Batash III; Tel Ḥalif A, B; and Tel ʿIra VII. There are even a few small Tier 4 villages that boast town walls: Kinneret II (probably because of its fortlike location), and possibly Tel Qiri VI.[48]

One is struck by the homogeneity in all these city and town houses, which is surely significant, as we shall see. How large was the family unit that occupied these typical houses? Previous scholars supposed that the average Israelite and Judean nuclear family had up to ten individuals. Most scholars now reduce that figure to five: two adults and two or three children (most did not survive infancy).[49] In some cases we have a complex of two or three houses linked together, perhaps sharing a common courtyard, constituting a compound that would have housed a multigeneration of up to twenty individuals: the principal parents, perhaps a surviving elderly parent, several younger children, and a married son who had brought his bride to the ancestral home as was the custom. Such large, close-knit stem families are still typical for much of the less developed Middle East. Since those houses were as large as 1,500 square feet, they could easily have accommodated a family of up to fifteen, on the commonly accepted ratio of one person to every 100 square feet of living space (based on ethnographic data). It was Larry Stager who first pointed out twenty-five years ago that this is obviously the biblical *bêt-'āv*, the "house of the father" (more of that below, when we come to integrate the biblical data).

---

eas. In the West Bank there are still such houses, occupied until recently, again with a roof roller. The ʿUmayri house produced a roof roller. See Bunimovitz and Lederman 2009, 88.

48. Ben-Tor and Portugali 1987.

49. Cf. Naroll 1962 for the model; Shiloh 1980 (family size of eight); and Stager 1985, 19 (four-five), for the best application of the model. See Chapter IV, n. 19.

Cult Places

We will cover cult places fully in Chapter VIII. Here, however, we note that it is in large cultural capitals like Dan, and, of course, at the state capitals of Samaria and Jerusalem (Tier 1 sites), that we would expect to find, and do find, cult sites like large sanctuaries and temples. Interestingly enough, at Tier 2 and 3 sites — cities and towns — we do not yet have archaeologically attested sanctuaries, shrines, or temples. Yet we must suppose that they existed. (We have them earlier in the Iron Age, as at Ta'anach; see Chapter VIII.)

We have identified major regional shrines at several of the small forts: at Arad, in the northern Negev Desert, and at Kuntillet 'Ajrûd, in the eastern Sinai Desert. Regional cult places might be expected at such isolated sites.

Almost certainly the most important cult sites that served the masses would have been in the rural areas, that is, in small villages. And indeed, that is where we have identified a number of household shrines (below). With growing attention now being paid to smaller sites, we will no doubt have more such cult places in future.

PART II: THE BIBLICAL DATA

True to our principle of separating our two sources for history writing, we have surveyed nearly all the information we have from archaeology about cities and towns. We turn now to biblical texts to see what we might learn independently, and whether there may be any convergences. We can order the pertinent biblical data in relation to the categories above, under the rubric of cities and towns.

Urban and Town Planning

The writers of the Hebrew Bible may have been aware that orderly cities and towns don't simply happen, that some deliberate human rationale is involved. But we have no biblical terminology that reflects that. We do have, however, some awareness of a few ad hoc distinctions such as we have made about a hierarchy of sites.

The most pertinent passage may be Leviticus 25:29-34, an overall description of the land. Here three distinctions are recognized: (1) walled cities *('îr-ḥōmôt);* (2) unwalled villages *(ḥāṣērîm;* specially said to be unwalled); (3) land surrounding such a city *(sĕdēy migrāš)* and the countryside *(sĕdēy hā-'āreṣ,* "fields of the land"). Elsewhere villages can be called "daughters" of a walled city or town (Judg. 1:27; "Ta'anach and its daughters," *bānôt).* These are presumably unwalled, since this and other passages assume that the villagers would flee to the walled towns and cities in times of danger. Another revealing passage is Joshua 21:12. Here we have mention of (1) a town *('îr),* (2) its villages *(ḥăṣēriāh),* and (3) its fields *(sĕdēy hā-'îr).* If we compare the hierarchy presumed in these two passages, a reasonably coherent picture emerges.

Lev. 25:29-34	Josh. 21:12
1. Walled cities	1. Towns or cities (walls not specified)
2. Unwalled villages	2. Unwalled villages
3. Surrounding fields (and open countryside)	3. Surrounding fields

A problem may lie in the use of the Hebrew term *'îr,* often simply "city," sometimes specified as walled, but also perhaps "town," usually not specified as walled or unwalled. In the comparison above it may seem that our Tier 3 town is missing in the left-hand column but is possibly present in the right column (*'îr,* unspecified; cf. Lev. 25:29, "walled"). Thus *'îr* may be used for what we are calling here a town, rather than a city.

Other terms for a city *('îr)* clearly refer to a walled city. Thus there can be a "fortified city" (*'îr mivsār;* 2 Kings 17:9; 18:8) or a "fortified wall" (i.e., "city"; Isa. 2:15; *hōmāh bĕṣûrāh).*

In the much-discussed boundary lists in Joshua 15 (of uncertain date) a distinction is made between (1) what may be either walled or unwalled towns *(ḥāṣerîm)* and (2) their "daughters" *(bānôt),* evidently hamlets in the countryside.[50]

From these and other biblical references one may conclude the following. (1) The biblical writers recognize only a simple ad hoc two-tier dis-

---

50. Cf. Aharoni 1967, 297-304, who takes the list as originating in the early 9th century but preserving an authentic memory of the 10th century (the united monarchy), or even earlier. See also Rainey 2006, 181-85. I am more skeptical; that is, the text in its present form surely does not antedate the 7th/6th century. But all this is a moot point here.

Cities and Towns

tinction, walled towns/cities and villages. (2) They do not always make clear or consistent distinctions (cf. 'îr = "town" or "city"). (3) In any case, all the biblical passages in question are later than our 8th-century horizon; none in their present form are earlier than the late 7th century (Judges, 2 Kings?); others are postexilic.

Capitals and Kings

The Hebrew Bible does recognize that both the northern and the southern kingdoms had kings, and these kings ruled from capitals that differed from other cities they knew. Many texts, too numerous to cite, acknowledge that a "Samaria" is the capital of the northern kingdom, and that a "Jerusalem" is the capital of the southern kingdom. We even have the names of a series of 8th-century kings.

What of the names of kings? We can extrapolate, on the basis of the archaeological evidence alone, that Israel and Judah in the 8th century were indeed states as defined by universally accepted anthropological criteria. What is called state formation processes are already clearly at work by the late 10th century (or perhaps slightly later, according to recent revisionists). Thus there were kings organizing and centralizing men and material, even if nonbiblical texts happen not to supply their names. But in fact, those texts (mostly Neo-Assyrian) do mention the 8th-century kings that are pertinent here. According to the biblical sources, the relevant kings are as follows (some chronology supplied by other sources).

Fig. V.14. Relevant Kings of Judah and Israel

Israel	Judah
Joash, 805-790	Amaziah, 805/4–776/5
Jeroboam II, 790-750/49	Uzziah, 788/7–736/5
Zechariah, 750/749	Jotham, 758/7–742/1
Shallum, 748	Ahaz, 742/1–726
*Menahem, 749-738	Hezekiah, 726-697/6
Pekahiah, 738-736	
*Pekah, (750?)-732/1	
*Hoshea, 732/1–722	

*Indicates kings known also from Neo-Assyrian sources

135

So what do we learn of any importance from the Hebrew Bible —
even if individual names were deemed essential? Furthermore, the chronological data in the Hebrew Bible are often imprecise and contradictory, so
they must be corrected by extrabiblical data. Even then, such precise inner-
dating is not essential for the sort of long-term settlement history we are
attempting here *(la longue durée)*.

Just as in the analysis of place-names above, we must conclude that
even if some of the biblical evidence is deemed to be truly historical, it
adds nothing essential to the archaeological history presented here. The
anonymous actors in our reconstruction speak just as loudly (and more
objectively) than the biblical kings whose stories have come down to us.

In the *annales* approach we have introduced above, these few kings
and the sketchy accounts of their reigns are simply the *événements* — the
"froth on the surface of the waves." It is the longer-range *conjonctures,* or
structures, and especially the "deeper swells" of the sea over the millennia,
that enable us to take *la longue durée.*[51]

That is what makes the historical reconstruction presented here different. Ours is a history of the masses — of ordinary people and the artifacts they left behind — not accounts of the "public deeds of great men"
that our predecessors presented. In the end, it may be ironically the *biblical
texts* that are "mute," not the artifacts.

Defense Systems

The 8th-century defense systems for which we have archaeological evidence consist of four elements: (1) solid masonry walls, sometimes offsets-
insets; (2) casemate or double and chambered walls; multiple-chamber
city gates, two-, three-, or four-entryway; (3) external towers in some cases;
and (4) sometimes a *glacis,* or sloping outer ramp. If we turn to city walls,
the Hebrew Bible makes no clear distinction in types of defense, but the
writers do refer to city walls themselves many times. The Hebrew term for
such a monumental wall is usually *ḥōmāh,* distinguished from other walls
such as terrace or boundary walls *(gĕdārîm).* Thus there is the wall of Jeru-

---

51. On the "*annales* school" see Dever 1988 and references up to that time. A more recent and convenient introduction is found in Barstad 2007, 25-29. But his estimate that this
approach is common among archaeologists in our field is mistaken. Of course, a practical
longue durée is essential to all archaeology.

salem (Ps. 122:7) or of Tyre (Ezek. 26:4). It is interesting that a few texts use the image of the "wall" for the city itself (Lam. 2:18).

A second term is also used to designate walled cities as "fortified cities" (2 Chron. 19:5, *'îr-habbĕṣûrôth;* Jer. 4:5, *'îr-hāmmibĕṣār*).

The occasional exception we have may be what the biblical writers had in mind in speaking of the "walls *(ḥōmôt)* and bulwarks *(ḥēlîm)*" of a fortified city (Isa. 26:1).

Towers *(migdālîm)* of the city walls or gates, well attested archaeologically, are often mentioned in the Hebrew Bible. We also have a few isolated towers in the Jerusalem area, probably what the biblical writers refer to as "towers" *(migdālîm).*

The city gates that we have seen in the 8th century are not only mentioned several times in the Hebrew Bible, but several functions of these gates are specified. The gate *(ša'ar)* was:

For entering and leaving the city (2 Kings 23:8)
A receiving place for officials (1 Sam. 20:25)
A general gathering area (Ruth 4:1; Ps. 69:12)
A forum for public discussions (2 Chron. 32:6)
A place for juridical actions (Deut. 17:5; Amos 5:10-15)
A marketplace (Job 31:21-22; Prov. 22:22; 24:7; 31:23; Gen. 23:17-18;
    Ruth 4:1-12)
A place for cultic activities (2 Kings 23:8)

As for the construction of the gates, biblical writers note such features as (wooden) doors, nails, the two posts or pivots, iron reinforcing bars, and some sort of clamp. The classic text is the description of Samson's theft of the city gates of Gaza (Judg. 16:3). There are mentioned several of these constructional features: the doors themselves *(dālthôth),* the posts or pivots *(mĕzuzôt),* and the iron bars *(bārîah;* cf. Ps. 147:13). Elsewhere the iron clamps *(ḥēkîn)* are referred to (1 Chron. 22:3). Finally, iron nails for joining the wooden parts are mentioned (1 Chron. 22:3, *maḥbĕrôth).*

In these biblical references we have one of our most detailed convergences with the artifacts. The picture is one of large wooden doors, put together with iron nails and clamps, reinforced with iron bars, and pivoting on two wooden posts. That fits the physical evidence that archaeology now supplies, except for the doors that must have been wooden, which would not have survived; and the iron nails and clamps that are assumed, but similarly would not be expected to be preserved. At the threshold of the 10th-century gate at Gezer, reused into the 8th century, we actually have a stone socket at each jamb, with rust stains showing where an iron shoe allowed two wooden posts to revolve.

What can we say of the interaction of texts and artifacts here? It is interesting to see that the biblical writers did know a great deal about the defenses of the 8th century, especially where the dominant city gates are concerned. For one thing, it means that the radical biblical revisionists who down-date the biblical texts to the Persian (or even Hellenistic) period are simply wrong. Those stories, with their realistic details of the Iron Age, cannot *possibly* have been written much later.

But does the information derived from the biblical accounts, even when generally accurate and reliable, add anything to what we already knew from archaeology? The answer again is: Not much, and nothing crucial.

Some might insist, however, that here the biblical texts corroborate the archaeological evidence. To the contrary; it is the archaeological evidence, now the primary data, that corroborates the biblical texts. The external evidence validates the proposition that the biblical writers knew something about the past, and could report it accurately when they chose to do so. But we no longer need to depend upon the biblical stories, thanks to the wealth of information now available from archaeology.

The biblical texts that we have just adduced add nothing to our knowledge of the 8th-century defense systems in general. Only in the question of the city gates do they tell us something we did not already know, and in the nature of the case could not have known. All the functions of the gates listed above were already self-evident but one. We already knew about the public forum and meeting places from several excavated gate areas, the elaborate thronelike seat where dignitaries met visitors, the trade that went on, and the cultic activities that took place there. We gain only the knowledge of juridical activities that took place there. We knew of benches in the side chambers where people sat, no doubt for discourse. But from the biblical texts we learn why.

Industrial Installations

No material culture remains are more common in all the cities, towns, and villages that we have surveyed than potsherds. We have, however, little archaeological evidence about the ceramic technology that produced the pottery (above). Where and how was pottery made? Who made it? What might biblical texts add to what little we know? The few texts we have are, unfortunately, not very helpful.

Some texts simply mention pottery in passing: Job 10:9 ("clay"); Lamentations 4:2 ("earthen pots"); Isaiah 30:14, Jeremiah 19:11 ("broken pots"); Isaiah 45:9 ("handles"). A few other texts are more specific: Jeremiah 18:1-4 (a "potter's house" with a "wheel") and Isaiah 41:25 ("treading the clay").

But this only means that the biblical writers knew what we know of pot making, all of which is obvious. The only helpful hint here may be the reference to the "potter's house" — obviously a workshop — to which one "goes down." Does that mean that such workshops were extramural (Chapter VII)? They may well have been (in which case we will not have found them). There will have been mounds of clay and materials for inclusions, kneading troughs, wheels, smoky kilns, large drying areas. All this was better done outside the crowded domestic areas. Yet all the ethnographic data converge to suggest that in the ancient world generally there was little large-scale, managed industry. Pottery making was rather a cottage industry, in which women produced most vessels, somewhere in the family compound. But there we must leave the matter. There is much that we do not yet know; and the Hebrew Bible is of no help, nor will it be, since the canon is closed.

Water Systems

We have noted rather elaborate water systems in use in the 8th century, probably government-sponsored at Hazor, Megiddo, Gibeon, Gezer, Beth-Shemesh, Jerusalem, Beersheba, Arad, and Kadesh-Barnea. We have also noted the existence of smaller, local wells and cisterns. A few biblical texts mention cisterns (2 Kings 18:31; Isa. 36:16). But there are specific references to the known major water systems, one at Gibeon (2 Sam. 2:13), and the other at Jerusalem (2 Kings 20:20; 2 Chron. 32:30).

The reference to Gibeon is informative, because we actually have such a "pool" *(běrēkāt)*, that is, a deep shaft that captured water from the water table (plus a supplementary stepped tunnel to reach the external spring). The "upper outlet to the Gihon spring" and a "pool and conduit" in Jerusalem are engineering feats probably to be attributed to Hezekiah in the late 8th century. The latter is a fairly accurate description of what we actually have: the remarkable water tunnel that conveys the waters of the Gihon spring under the city walls and into a collecting reservoir (the "conduit" and "pool"); and the deep vertical shaft ("Warren's shaft") that also leads down to the waters of the spring. We even have part of a monumental royal inscription, dated paleographically to the late 8th century, which describes how this very tunnel was dug. Thus "Hezekiah's tunnel" really is his. It is well dated to the years just before the siege of Sennacherib in 701, a defense mechanism, just as the Hebrew Bible states. Again this is proof that the relevant biblical texts are not late, nor a story made up out of whole cloth. The writers knew what we now know, thanks to archaeology.

Nevertheless, candor requires us to acknowledge that the Hebrew Bible supplies us only the name of a king, one "Hezekiah." That tidbit is not essential to writing a history of the period. As for the description of the actual construction of the tunnel, there is little here that we cannot extrapolate from the physical evidence, which has been carefully analyzed by specialists.

We will survey several cult places in Chapter VIII below. We do have archaeological evidence of religious beliefs and practices in the 8th century. However, we will delay a discussion of the contribution of the biblical texts until we present the archaeological evidence and evaluate its contribution to our knowledge.

PART III: WHAT WAS IT REALLY LIKE?

Here we move beyond all the evidence that we have presented to ask simply: What does it mean? How did ordinary folk *feel* about these realities, and how did they react?

From all that we know about social stratification, about the preference for a rural lifestyle (Chapters VI, VII), I would suggest that many people in Israel and Judah were resentful of what they saw in the rapid urbanization of the two states. If a farmer from a small village in the hinterland went for a visit to a big city, not to mention the capital — a formidable undertaking — I suspect that his first impression would have been awe. Who knew of such things? And what did they portend for a country bumpkin? Monumental city walls, gates, palaces, mansions, streets of shops filled with exotic goods — all this must have made an overwhelming impression.

But then one would have thought almost immediately: What did all this cost? What taxes had ordinary folk had to pay for it? And what kind of political power had it taken to organize and carry out all the projects that made this a real city?

We must not forget that from earliest times in Israel there had been a deep-seated resistance to the rise of the state and the centralization of political power. The biblical accounts are unanimous in reflecting what has come to be known as the "nomadic ideal." In the days of the judges, the prophet Samuel warns that the king and some parties would draft their sons for an army, conscript their daughters as servants, seize their fields and plunder their harvest, and tax them to death (1 Sam. 8:10-18). If that happens, Samuel declares that the people would "cry out" because of their king.

Throughout the monarchy this sort of antistatism remained a popular sentiment. The biblical writers condemn every single king in the north; and in Judah only two kings find their approval, the 8th-century reformer Hezekiah and the 7th-century King Josiah. Countless rebellions and attempted coups had to be put down. And when they failed, the cry was: "To your tents, O Israel."

This persistent nostalgia for simpler times would have fueled resentment from the masses at all times. The development of a highly organized urban society may have been inevitable, but it never met with popular approval. In addition to resentment, a visitor to the big city might have gone away filled with fear. Why these monumental city walls? Who is it that threatens us? And what can we ordinary people do to protect ourselves in the open countryside? I suspect that our poor farmer would have gone home thinking that the rich were getting richer, that the city was a cesspool, and that the world was falling apart. In fact, by the mid–8th century B.C.E. it was.

CHAPTER VI

Towns, Villages, and Everyday Life

PART I: THE ARCHAEOLOGICAL DATA

We have already noted that the seventy-five or so archaeologically attested and mapped sites in figure IV.1 are only the tip of the iceberg when it comes to demography, "facts on the ground." For instance, we can actually document only a dozen or so agricultural villages, not the hundreds of others that must have housed the overwhelming majority of the population of Israel and Judah in the 8th century B.C.E. From intensive archaeological surveys done recently by Israelis, we know that there were hundreds and hundreds of additional settlements, mostly rural, nearly all unexcavated.[1]

We also know that the rural sector of the population was continually expanding from the 10th century and the early days of the monarchy onward. This happened despite some trends toward urbanization, centralization, and the concentration of the powers of the states of Israel and Judah as they evolved in the course of reaching their zenith by the late 8th century.

I shall examine the socioeconomic, cultural, and political implications of this fact in Chapter VII. Meanwhile, let us look at villages, where most ancient Israelites and Judeans lived, analyzing their character and distribution, their society, economy, and resources, attempting particularly to discern what it was really like in the 8th century B.C.E.

---

1. See references in Chapter IV, n. 20: some 450 sites in the north, 70 sites in the south. For Iron II Israel and Judah as a "rural society," see Hopkins 1985; Stager 1985; Perdue, Blenkinsopp, and Collins 1997; McNutt 1999; King and Stager 2001, 21-35; Ofer 2001; Borowski 2002; 2003; Bunimovitz and Faust 2003a; and especially Faust 2011.

Villages of the 8th Century B.C.E.

We have designated a dozen or so Tier 4 villages that are archaeologically attested in the 8th century (fig. IV.1). Some of these sites are insufficiently excavated or too poorly published to yield much pertinent information, but there are a few illustrative examples.

Tell Qiri

Tell Qiri is a 2.5-acre low mound near the large tell of Yokneam, at a major pass through the Carmel Mountains out into the Jezreel Valley. It was excavated in 1975-77 as part of a regional project carried out by Amnon Ben-Tor. Str. VI belongs to the 8th century, but Str. IX-V, spanning the entire Iron I-II period (ca. 900-600 B.C.E.), show so much continuity that "building phases" can scarcely be separated. Tell Qiri was an unfortified village, not destroyed or even substantially changed, for hundreds of years. The population appears to have been stable and reasonably prosperous, the economy based on agriculture. The houses are small, tightly compacted, sharing some common walls. Interestingly they are not the usual "four-room" houses we so often see in villages and towns, perhaps because they needed no pillars. In the courtyards there were many stone-lined silos. There were also a few olive presses. The large number of basalt grinders and pounders in all the houses attests to the processing of agricultural products, as do the abundant flint sickles. Seeds of wheat, pomegranates, chickpeas, and vetch were found. The animal bones were mostly sheep and goat (80 percent) with some cattle (15 percent).[2]

Kh. Jemein

This is a small late Iron Age hilltop site, about two to three acres in extent, in western Samaria. There are some twenty four-room houses, tightly clustered and surrounded by a boundary wall. In the vicinity were found terraces, cisterns, a lime kiln, an oil press, and a wine cellar. The impression is that of a prosperous agricultural village with a population of about 100.[3]

2. Ben-Tor and Portugali 1987.
3. See Faust 2011, 132-34.

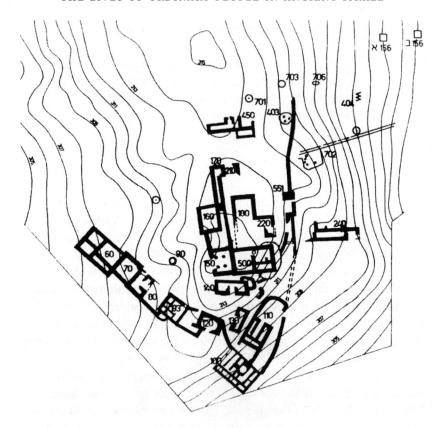

Fig. VI.1. Plan of village at Kh. Jemein.
Faust 2011, fig. 22

Beit Aryeh

This is a well-planned late Iron Age village from one to two acres in size, with ten four-room houses enclosed by a boundary wall. Not only are the houses standardized, but they share many common walls. There is a large courtyard in the center. In and around the site were found thirty-three oil-processing installations, large water cisterns, and a quarry.

While the buildings were not excavated to floor level, it is clear that there is a striking homogeneity. The excavator regarded the site as a "fortified royal village," perhaps supplying oil for trade.[4]

4. See Faust 2011, 135. Faust discusses several other rural sites, especially Kh. Banat

The Naḥal Refaim

One of the few archaeological projects that has investigated a larger area characterized by rural settlements is the Naḥal Refaim project. This project investigated an area of twelve acres on the southwestern outskirts of modern Jerusalem. Most of the remains on the agricultural terraces above the Sorek Valley leading up to Jerusalem from the Shephelah are earlier than our period. But some of the farmhouses scattered along the terraces above the spring are relevant. Here the earlier Bronze Age terraces (Str. II-III) were rebuilt and augmented when new farmhouses were erected sometime in the 8th-7th centuries. This no doubt occurred because the population of Jerusalem was now reaching its peak, after an influx of refugees from the north (Chapter X).

The scant Iron II remains are said to be similar to other finds on the terraces at nearby Manahat, as well as at Giv'at Masura and the farm at er-Ras. With nothing available beyond preliminary reports, we can only say that more rural settlements and suburban villages are surely to be discovered when archaeologists build the search for them into their strategy, which has heretofore been focused mainly on urban sites.[5]

Tell el-Oreime

Finally, we have the small site of Tel Chinnereth (Kinrot) on the northwest shore of the Sea of Galilee. Str. II, belonging to the 8th century, succeeds a much larger Middle-Late Bronze Age city in ruins, substantially reduced now (2.5 acres). This level was only partially excavated, but there is a row of pillar-courtyard houses near the village wall and gate. A larger such building stands on the other side of the mound, with a cistern. There are a few other scattered, simpler houses.[6] (See fig. VI.3, p. 147.)

Although these data are scant, we may infer (1) that some small villages did have enclosure walls, even gates; (2) that the stereotypical earlier four-room houses could be adapted in various simpler ways; and (3) that many of these poor villages barely survived. The latter means, of course,

---

Barr, Horvat Eli, Kh. er-Ras, Pisgat Zeev A, Kh. Jarish, and many other 7th-century farms and villages. These are too poorly published, however, to utilize here.

5. See Edelstein in Stern 1993, 1277-82.

6. See Fritz 1990; 1995, 83-87 (summary). The site is known as "Kinneret" or "Kinrot."

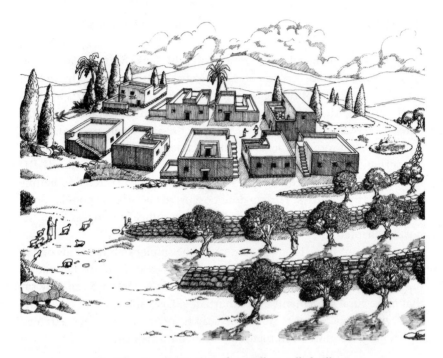

Fig. VI.2. Reconstruction of a small unwalled village.
Drawing by Giselle Hasel

that their remains are fragile and thus not likely to have come to light in conventional excavations. That surely skews our picture of rural life in the 8th century.

Vernacular Houses: Furnishings, Functions, and Families

We have characterized the stereotypical Israelite-Judean four-room (or "pillar-courtyard") house in some detail in Chapter V. Those houses dominate nearly all the smaller towns and villages that we have, so we shall discuss them here. They are almost the exclusive type of house in villages and towns, even in urban centers, since palatial buildings of any kind are rare. Thus it is in these houses and their furnishings that we will see reflected the reality of life for the overwhelming masses.[7] What can we say then of

7. On typical houses see Hardin 2010, 7-34, 44-55; Chapter V, nn. 39-49 above, and ref-

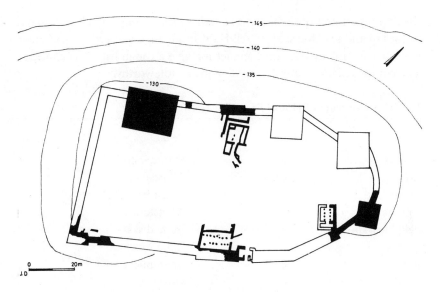

Fig. VI.3. Plan of Tell el-Oreime (Kinrot), Str. II.
Fritz 1995, fig. 29

the life of the bourgeoisie? Can we only speculate, or do we have some actual facts? In the following discussion I will illustrate the lifestyle of ordinary folk with a nearly complete catalogue of typical items that we now have from archaeological excavations, nearly all of them from clear 8th-century contexts, especially in houses like House F7 of Tell Ḥalif. Very few archaeologists, and almost no biblicists, have tried to imagine "what it was really like." But before we indulge in too much speculation, let us examine the basic data.

To begin with the larger rural landscape, a typical village of a few dozen people would have been made up of several family compounds of two or more so-called four-room houses each. A small town might have had a dozen or so such family compounds. This arrangement reflects the familial socioeconomic structure (the "house of the father") that we shall come to in treating the biblical evidence below (and again in Chapter VII).

In the houses themselves that we now know, especially the few with an almost complete repertoire of material culture remains, a number of items reflect daily life. As we noted above, the two excavated houses with

---

erences there. On "women's space" in particular, see Meyers 2003a; Ebeling 2010, 29-33, and references there. See also n. 30 below.

the best repertoires of items are (1) a 12th-century house at Tall al-ʿUmayri in Jordan and (2) House F7 at Tell Ḥalif in Judah, destroyed in 701.[8] Since the latter is directly relevant here, let me give a rough list of its contents. The complete lack of any "luxury" items is noteworthy.

Fig. VI.4. Contents of House F7 at Tell Ḥalif

Item	No.	Item	No.
Storage jars	19	Hammerstones	6
Jugs	6	Ballistae	1
Decanters	3	Crucibles	1
Amphora	2	Whetstones	1
Amphoriskoi	1	Stone disks	3
Flasks	2	Stone weights	4
Juglets	9	Jar stoppers	2
Kraters	9	Knives	1
Bowls	13	Arrowheads	3
Mortaria	1	Nails/rods	1
Plates	1	Spindle whorls	1
Cooking pots	3	Spatulas	1
Cooking jugs	2	Beads	2
Lamps	6	Seals	1
Scoops	1	Bullae	1
Strainers	1	Shells	1
Funnels	1	Horn core	1
Stands	2	Figurines	6
Pestles	2	Grinders	6
Misc. stone	3	Clay loomweights	7

8. Cf. Clark and Herr 2009; Hardin 2010, 124-60. The ʿUmayri house belongs to early Iron I (12th century), but the Ḥalif house is late 8th century, destroyed in the campaign of Sennacherib in 701. These are the only two excavated Iron Age houses thus far from which we have complete inventories. An Iron I house with a rather full inventory has now been published from Megiddo (House 00/K/10; Str. VIA, 11th century). But the excavators regard it as a "domestic industrial" installation, rather than a typical U-dwelling. See Finkelstein, Ussishkin, and Halpern 2006, 232-34, 583-97. There are two 12th-11th-century courtyard houses at Gezer; but they are not necessarily ethnic "Israelite," and they produced almost no *in situ* objects. See Dever et al. 1986, 88-117.

Terminology and Summary of Tell Ḥalif

House F7 may be taken as an example of a dwelling in a rural area, even though it may not be as typical as some might think. That presupposes that the site was about three acres in extent, with a population of some 300, that is, on the borderline of my "village"/"town" demarcation (Faust's "rural" by any criterion).[9]

Many recent discussions emphasize the widespread distribution of these stereotypical "four-room" houses throughout the Iron II period (ca. 1000-600). They also take the homogeneous plan as evidence of ethnicity and of certain distinctively "Israelite" cultural values.[10] Too often these dwellings are called simply "four-room" houses, whereas in fact the standardized courtyard plan can yield many variations. One finds four rooms off a courtyard; three rooms off a courtyard; or in some cases more rooms. It appears that the typically smaller urban courtyard houses are more standardized, often with the common divisions, whereas the larger rural houses show more variation, sometimes with only three divisions.[11]

In very small villages and at farmsteads, often neither the four-room plan nor the three-room house is found, only a sort of agglutinative plan.[12] Finally, the very notion of three- or four-"room" houses is misleading for several reasons. (1) The courtyard in the U-shaped ground floor is not really a room, especially if unroofed; it is a sort of entry area. (2) The areas surrounding the courtyard, making the house add up to two or three "rooms," are usually subdivided into more rooms than three or four. There are actually four or three *banks* of rooms.

Because of the many types of house plans, even though most do

9. Faust's examination of social structure based on archaeological data is the most thorough yet attempted. Yet he does not develop anything like the multitiered hierarchy adapted here. He distinguishes only two levels of society: rural and urban. His "rural" society evidently comprises my farmsteads, villages, and towns (at least the smaller towns). Cf. nn. 11, 12 below.

10. See below and references in n. 45.

11. On the apparent pattern of size difference, see Faust 2011. Urban houses average 485-865 square feet of floor space (presumably for only one story), while rural houses average about 900-1,300 square feet of floor space. On the designation "room," see below. On the problem of a second story and calculations of living space, see below and n. 15.

12. That is clear at sites like Banat Barr, Beit Aryeh, Kh. Jarish, Kh. Jemein, Tel Qiri, and other village and rural sites. Pillar-courtyard houses of such sites are the exception. The larger vernacular houses and agglutinative clustering probably reflect the special needs of extended farm families. See Chapter IV above; and cf. Faust 2011.

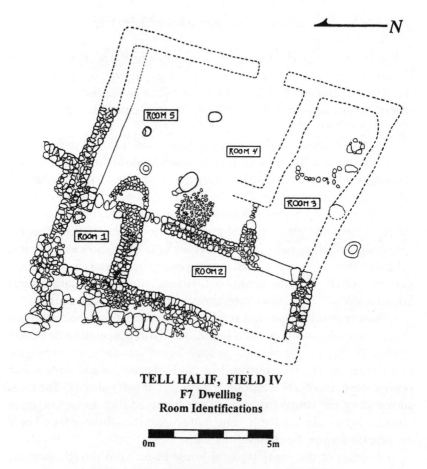

TELL HALIF, FIELD IV
F7 Dwelling
Room Identifications

0m   5m

Fig. VI.5. Schematic plan of House F7 at Tell Ḥalif.
Hardin 2010, fig. 5.3

seem to be variations on a theme, I shall avoid the usual designation and focus on the features that virtually all types have in common, the courtyard (whether roofed or not) and the pillars supporting the upper story, sometimes partly solid walls. Therefore, I suggest calling these simply "pillar-courtyard" houses.[13]

13. King and Stager now prefer "pillared house"; 2001, 28-35. Hardin uses the term "pillared building"; 2010, 44-56 (with full references to the origin and construction of these houses). I acknowledge the presence of pillars (and also masonry) as roof supports, but the central courtyard is even more universal.

Drawing on the extensive presentation and analysis of the nearly complete inventory of this house in Hardin's 2010 study, we may summarize the data from House F7 as follows (converting the usual meters to feet):

Room 4: open courtyard; ca. 200 sq. ft; probably stable
Room 5: probably roofed; ca. 230 sq. ft.; food preparation
Room 3: roofed; ca. 200 sq. ft.; multipurpose
Room 2: roofed; ca. 140 sq. ft.; multipurpose and cult
Room 1: roofed; ca. 65 sq. ft; storage[14]

If House F7 consisted of only a ground floor, the total living space would be about 865 square feet, including the open courtyard, or about 665 without it, that is, *roofed* living space if the courtyard were open (below). The Naroll coefficient of one person per 10 square meters of living space (or ca. 105 square feet per person) would yield a family unit of nine or ten persons for the larger floor space, or six persons for the smaller floor space.[15] The latter is close to the size of the "nuclear family" agreed upon by nearly all scholars today, based largely on ethnographic data. Adding the presumed upper roofed story, however, would give us anywhere from 1,300 to 1,700 square feet, providing for an "extended" family of between thirteen and seventeen (below). The latter fits the biblical description of the *bêt-'āv*, the "house of the father," consisting of a man, a woman, perhaps two or three surviving children; a married son, a wife, and a child or two; perhaps even a servant — ten or more people (below).

The question of whether the central courtyard was roofed is not easily resolved, since most descriptions do not present evidence that was sufficiently well excavated or recorded to settle the matter. The absence of evidence is not, of course, evidence of absence. A solution based only on common sense would argue that since the abundant objects, especially pottery, are almost always found in the side rooms, the courtyard may have been the only open work space. In the Ḥalif house, all four rooms off the central courtyard (Room 5) were cluttered with pottery and other objects, leaving

14. This is my summary of Hardin 2010, 124-60. I convert his meters to feet for convenience.

15. See Naroll 1962 for the model. Virtually all Palestinian archaeologists have adopted this model. For its application to our data, see for instance Shiloh 1979; Stager 1985; Holladay 1992; Broshi and Finkelstein 1992; Zorn 1994; Netzer 1992; Faust 2011, 109, 110. The result has been a lowering of estimated nuclear family size to about five, admittedly a minimal figure.

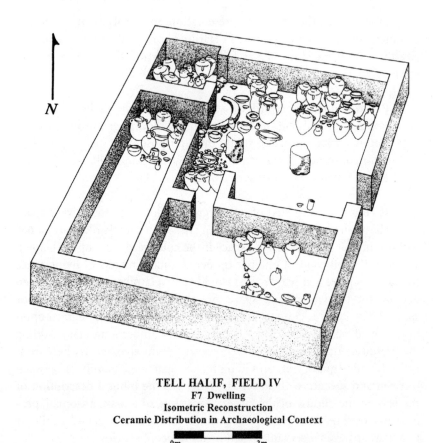

TELL HALIF, FIELD IV
F7 Dwelling
Isometric Reconstruction
Ceramic Distribution in Archaeological Context

0m   3m

Fig. VI.6. Contents of House F7.
Hardin 2010, fig. 4:9

the courtyard much more accessible. According to the excavators, it appears to have been unroofed (although one reconstruction shows it roofed).[16]

16. Whether the central courtyard was roofed continues to be debated. Arguing for a complete roof are Stager 1985, 15; Holladay 1992, 14-17; Netzer 1992, 196; Clark and Herr 2009, 85. Fritz is virtually alone in proposing an open courtyard, largely on the argument that the width of the courtyard was too wide to be bridged with the timbers available there; Fritz 1995, 131. Hardin is somewhat ambivalent, but he thinks that most, if not all, of the Ḥalif house was roofed; 2010, 51-58. This is also an excellent review of the literature. Some earlier scholars had opted for an open courtyard, including Shiloh 1970; Herzog 1984; and in particular the distinguished architect G. R. H. Wright 1985. I still believe that part of the courtyard

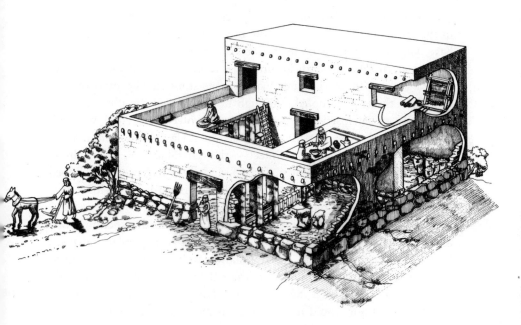

Fig. VI.7. Reconstruction of a village house.
Drawing by Giselle Hasel

At Megiddo, a 12th-century courtyard house was excavated that had been suddenly destroyed, probably by a fire set off by an earthquake (Building 00/K/10). The well-preserved roof fall extended over most of the side rooms but was conspicuously absent in the large central courtyard. The courtyard also contained far fewer objects, almost all of them storejars in one corner. The two *tabûns,* however, were not in this presumably open courtyard, but rather in one of the side rooms. The excavators conclude that the courtyard was used mainly for food preparation and consumption.[17]

---

area might have been open to the sky. From living in Arab villages, I know personally how suffocating dung smoke in an enclosed area can be. These *tannûrs* (Ar. *tabûn*) are never found in the house proper. In any case, *tannûrs* in small roofed areas would have been used primarily in inclement weather. See further n. 17 below.

17. See now the excellent study of the distribution and functions of *tannûrs* in Baadsgaard 2008, with special reference to women's cooperative labor. She shows that the distribution of *tannûrs* is random. She follows McQuitty in distinguishing the *tannûr* (Heb.) from the Arabic *tabûn,* on the assumption that the latter was fired from the outside. From my experience in Hebron hills villages, that is not usually the case. Cf. n. 16 above. The Ḥalif house has a *tannûr* in Room 5.

House 1727 at Shechem, violently destroyed in the Assyrian conquest in the late 8th century, is one of the most carefully excavated houses we have. The interior space of the ground floor plan was circa 675 square feet. The large central courtyard (Room 1) was taken by the excavators to have been a sort of "industrial" area, with a large stone-lined central fire pit. Campbell thought it roofed, although he recognized the difficulty that smoke in an enclosed area would have involved. He cited Watson's ethnographic data on hearths in closed spaces at Hasanabad in Iran. As for the presumed roof, the dig's architect — the venerable G. R. H. Wright — observed that the burnt roof material found there had probably slipped from the side rooms as the building collapsed inward. Thus House 1727 may have had an unroofed central courtyard.[18]

The Shechem excavators point out that it was the destruction debris of House 1727 that clinched the notion that these typical pillar-courtyard houses had a second story. The foundation walls were thick enough to have supported such a second story, where the room-dividing walls would necessarily have followed the same floor plan. It is now generally agreed that the first floor would have been used primarily for stables, storage, and food preparation, while the second story was the family's principal living domain.[19]

Here is introduced a problem not usually confronted when "living space" is calculated, then used to estimate family size, social structure, and other variables. As far as I can see, almost all authorities count only the living space for the ground floor. But should we double that figure if we have a second story? If we do, then the estimated family size of a typical pillar-courtyard house would double, throwing all our estimates off.

In particular, we should reexamine the proposed dichotomy between larger village/rural and smaller urban houses. Estimates put the average size of the former at circa 925 to 1,300 square feet, translating into a family size of from nine to thirteen, or a multiple-generation extended family.[20]

18. For a comparison of urban and rural house size, see Faust 2011, 32-38, 109-14. Cf. also nn. 11-15 above.

19. I cannot find any other writers who define precisely what they mean in presenting an estimate of "living space." For evidence for stables, storage, food preparation, and various domestic industries in the central courtyards, see Hardin 2010, 48-53, 151-57, with full references.

20. All recent discussions assume a second story where the family would have conducted most of its activities. This is partly on the assumption that otherwise the total living space would have been too small, partly on the observations that the activities on the ground

Such larger families would have been better suited to an agricultural life-style. The smaller houses average about 485-865 square feet, giving us a typical "nuclear family" of from five to nine, typical or slightly larger than estimates based on ethnographic data (above). These smaller houses may reflect less cohesive families, where people had probably migrated to the urban centers; we may also be dealing with restricted space for construction within the town walls. At Tell el-Far'ah north, de Vaux took the disparity in the size of Iron Age houses for evidence of socioeconomic inequalities (presupposed by prophetic protests). That interpretation, however, is open to question. We may be dealing simply with functional differences.[21]

A Case Study: Kh. er-Râs

One way out of the dilemma I see in house size and family size is to regard the ground floor of these pillar-courtyard houses not as true "living space," but rather as areas used mostly for stables and storage (the side rooms), as well as for food preparation, weaving, and other outdoor activities (the open courtyard). The upper rooms would then be seen as the *true* "living space": sleeping chambers, with some degree of privacy, as well as larger family gathering places for eating, relaxing, and other communal activities. In the following discussion, I shall try both scenarios simply as a trial. The hypothetical house on which this discussion is based (Kh. er-Râs) is therefore what I presume to be a typical larger dwelling in a village or small town, conforming to the above norm in size up to 1,100 or 2,200 square feet for both roofed stories, capable of housing an extended family of up to twenty-one people.[22] (See pp. 159, 160.)

The plan of the second story of this pillar-courtyard house can be reconstructed hypothetically on the basis of several considerations. (1) The major partition walls would have to be built directly on top of the load-bearing walls of the first story (dividing Rooms 7, 11, 12, and 13). A short,

---

floor best attested archaeologically are related to stabling, storage, domestic production, and the like. Yet the Ḥalif house remains suggest some domestic activities like cult practices and food consumption on the ground floor; Hardin 2010, 133-43. For the evidence of ladders and steps to give access to the second floor, see Hardin 2010, 51, and references there. For my theoretical reconstruction of a second story, see below.

21. For the site of Kh. er-Râs, see Faust 2011, 180-83.

22. See n. 15 above.

lightweight crosswall might rest on a beam stretching from one of the pillars below to the sidewall of the house (i.e., dividing walls between Rooms 8, 9, and 10).

(2) Access would most likely be by a ladder going up from one of the small side rooms off the courtyard if it was roofed (Room 13?). It could go from one of the stables between the pillars (Rooms 1, 2), but that would make for foul-smelling air in the living quarter above.

(3) The floor space of the second story can be calculated rather accurately on the basis of the rooms on the first story. For instance, in our Kh. er-Râs example (fig. VI.8, p. 160), Room 12 (above Room 4) would be about 8 feet by 8 feet, a very comfortable space for an adult sleeping chamber. Next door, Room 11 (above Room 3) would be about 5 feet by 8 feet, ideal for children's sleeping quarters. Room 7 (above Room 6, not able to be partitioned) would be about 8 feet by 20 feet, or 160 square feet. That would be well suited for various family activities, including common meals.

If we were dealing with a nuclear family of five or six people, the total living space of these three rooms would be only about 265 square feet, not enough to meet Naroll's 105 square feet per person. If we suppose, however, that the other side of the upper story was also utilized (Rooms 8-10), that could add another 150 square feet or so. In that case, a total second story living space of about 400 square feet would still house only four people. If we added to this the space above a roofed courtyard, about 200 more square feet (entered perhaps from Room 7), we could reach a total of nearly 600 square feet. That would translate into a family of about five or six people, well within the description of a nuclear family.

For an extended family, however, usually thought to be from ten to fifteen people, we would need to factor in the 600 or so square feet of the ground floor as living space, for a total of circa 1,200 square feet. Obviously we cannot reach firm conclusions on family size and structure until we decide what we mean by "living space." At present, the question may have to remain open, although the ethnographic data suggest counting the area of the entire house as living space.

House Plan and Social Structure

The implication of these calculations, based on a well-attested house plan, would seem to be the following. If we use the Naroll coefficient of 105 square feet of space per person, the estimated family size, with *both* floors counted as living space, would be from ten to twelve people (above). That would be well within the expected size of an extended family.

These calculations suggest that most authorities must be *assuming* a living space using both stories, even though they do not specify this. If so, we have the following scenario for a large rural dwelling housing an extended family of from ten to twelve.

> *Ground floor:* Rooms 1-5: stables, storage, food preparation, domestic production, perhaps sleeping area as well.
> *Upper floor:* Rooms 11 and 12: one family. Rooms 8-10: second family. Room 7: Common area. Ten people. Courtyard: perhaps for drying food.

By contrast with rural houses like House F7 at Ḥalif or the Kh. er-Râs house, which average 975-1,300 square feet on the first floor, typical urban houses average only 485-865 square feet on the ground floor (above). That would work out to from five to eight people, a bit large for the estimated size of a nuclear family. Doubling the living space by adding a second floor would yield a higher figure of from ten to thirteen people, more like an extended family. To maintain the prevalent notion that the urban dwellings house smaller *nuclear* families, we would have to consider only one story — presumably the upper story — as true living space. That would leave the small first floor for the differing needs of urban families: few if any animals to stable; limited storage space; and perhaps a shop, which many modern Middle Eastern townhouses include.

Combining the results of several recent studies of ancient Israelite social structure — based on biblical, ethnographic, and archaeological data — we may arrive at something like a three-tier structure, although necessarily simplified here.[23]

1. The basic level of society is the *nuclear* family, consisting of a father, mother, and two or three surviving children. This would be the equivalent of the biblical *bayit*, or house of the individual *(gĕvĕr)*. This fundamental unit of society is presumably reflected in the smaller pillar-courtyard houses of the urban centers, averaging some

---

23. The fundamental study is Stager 1985, followed now by virtually every authority. See discussion and references in Hardin 2010, 177-85. The following is a summary of this model and may be somewhat oversimplified.

486-865 square feet of living space, adequate for from five to eight people.

2. The middle level of society is the still patrilineal, the *extended, multiple-generation family*. It would consist of the nuclear father, mother, and children, plus one or two married sons, their wives and children; perhaps an unwed aunt or uncle; and even a servant or two (the biblical *gērîm,* "sojourners"). This larger group of from ten to fifteen individuals would be the biblical *bêt-'āv,* or "house of the father." It is the equivalent of the *za'ila,* or "joint family" of the ethnographic literature, still prevalent in the Middle East. This larger unit is reflected in the larger pillar-courtyard houses we have in smaller towns, villages, and the rural countryside. There the average living space of 900-1,300 square feet (or double if we include the presumed roofed second story) could accommodate as many as fifteen people.

3. The largest social unit would be the *hamula,* or *"stem family"* of the ethnographic data, comprising several extended families to form a village or even a small town (perhaps totaling 100-200 people). It corresponds to the biblical *mishpāḥā,* the larger family or "clan" of ancient Israel, and to the several dozen villages and small towns now attested in the archaeological record. Above that level there would be the "tribe" *(shevet; māṭṭeh)* and the whole people of Israel *(bēnê-yiśrā'ēl).*

These theoretical considerations fit Hardin's reconstruction of House F7 of Tell Ḥalif. Although he does not deal very specifically with the presumed second story, or the double-size floor space that would entail, he concludes: "The F7 Dwelling was perhaps occupied by a small extended family that included the father, mother, and unwed children as well as the wedded sons and their wives and children, and possibly even unwed paternal aunts and sometimes even unwed paternal uncles. It also is possible that slaves were brought into the dwelling."[24] This House F7 can be taken as typical overall of the nonurban houses in which the majority of Israelites and Judeans lived in the 8th century B.C.E.

---

24. Hardin 2010, 172. But if that large a family is envisioned, both a lower and an upper living space must be presupposed, totaling some 2,000 square feet rather than only 1,000 square feet. The latter would yield an estimate of only about seven or eight people (i.e., assuming one person per 130 square feet of living space, equal to Naroll's one person per square meter). That *could* be taken as a very small extended family; but most scholars use the figure of ten to twenty.

A Theoretical Rural House

While House F7 at Tell Ḥalif is our most complete example of an 8th-century house and its contents, the plan is not altogether typical. Let us therefore use it, together with many more contemporary Israelite and Judean houses, to generalize in the following discussion of village or small-town houses. Despite many variations, these generalizations may still be useful.

For a typical plan, I have chosen an 8th-century "pillar-courtyard" house at Kh. er-Râs, a small agricultural settlement on terraced hillsides on the outskirts of Jerusalem. It has a one-story floor space of circa 1,100 square feet, which on our model would have accommodated some ten people — a typical small rural extended family. Here I have produced a plan of what I believe the upper story might have looked like. The interior walls shown, while theoretical, must have rested on the lower load-bearing walls, not on the flimsy roof. The entrance into Room 7 (?) is presumed to have been by a ladder. Room numbers in the following discussion will refer to this plan.[25]

Let us look first at a typical courtyard (Room 1), with its beaten earth surface. Hearths and cooking pots found in the central courtyard show that simple meals were prepared here, no doubt by women. The hearths may be simply a circle of small stones to contain the fire. A cooking pot could rest on several other stones, directly above the coals. The fact that handles occur on many that we have suggests that they could be suspended over the coals (below).

The more common oven, or *tannûr* (Heb. = Ar. *tabûn*), was made of thick terra-cotta walls founded on a ring of small stones. The sidewalls may have extended as high as two feet, sloping inward to a smaller opening at the top. Stone lids could have closed the opening. To judge from the ashes found inside, the fuel was twigs and sun-dried dung patties, the ashes cleaned out from time to time. To help insulate the oven, potsherds were sometimes plastered around the outer wall. *Tannûrs* are found sometimes near the entrance to the courtyard, in one of the side rooms (Room 3), or nearby outdoors.[26]

These *tannûrs* are still in use today (as I know from living in Arab villages in the West Bank). A cooking pot can be placed on the coals inside or on the open top. More often, a thin layer of dough is placed directly on a layer of heated stones in the bottom, or even plastered on the inner side-

25. See n. 17 above.
26. The schematized plan here is adopted from Clark 2003, 36.

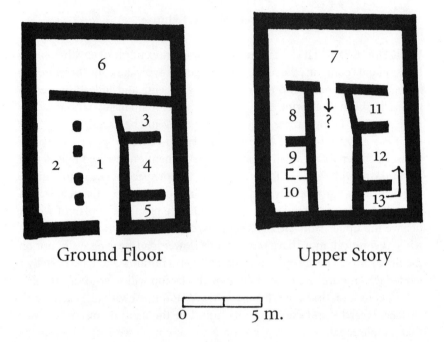

Ground Floor   Upper Story

Fig. VI.8. Reconstruction of a typical "pillar-courtyard" house of the 8th century
B.C.E. (Kh. er-Râs).
Adapted from Clark 2003, 36

walls. The bread bakes in a few minutes. A woman could easily bake a full day's supply for the family in an hour or less after the flour was prepared, although grinding grain for the flour would have been tiresome.

The dough was made of water mixed with wheat or barley. Coarse upper and lower grinding stones ("saddle querns"), sometimes of porous basalt, are found in the house courtyards and elsewhere (several kinds in the Tell Ḥalif house). Grinding grain for bread (or possibly cracked-wheat gruel, a sort of couscous) would have been onerous, consuming hours of time each day. It was undoubtedly done by the women and girls of the household as part of their daily chores. The grain supplies were close at hand, in the large storejars in the back room (Room 6), just off the courtyard (nineteen overall in the Tell Ḥalif house). Sometimes groups of women collaborated in this process (below).[27]

27. The literature on women's roles in domestic life has been scant but is now burgeoning. See especially Ackerman 1989 on bread making; Meyers 1999; 2002; 2003a; 2003b;

Fig. VI.9. A *tannûr* at Gezer, set in plaster floor

The cooking pots (five in the Tell Ḥalif house) pose no problems of interpretation. These unique vessels, always recognizable, were made of heavy clay, tempered with numerous large limestone grits to resist breakage when fired. The 8th-century examples are squat and round, with a grooved ring that could accommodate a ceramic lid if necessary. The earlier examples usually have no handles, but smaller Judean cooking pots of the late 8th-7th centuries do have handles (fig. VI.12, nos. 19, 20).

2007; 2009; Baadsgaard 2008; Ebeling and Homan 2008; Ebeling 2010, 48-53. The more recent publications on women's studies, such as Nakhai 2008; Ebeling 2010, include thorough references to broader literature on women in antiquity.

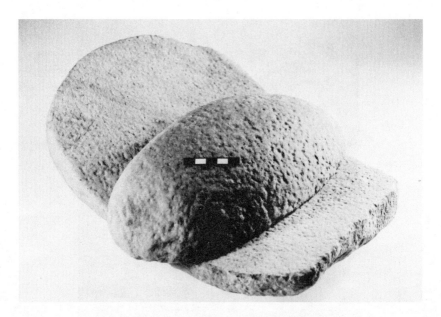

Fig. VI.10. Upper and lower basalt grinding stones.
Photo: W. G. Dever

Fig. VI.11. Palestinian woman taking bread from the *tannûr*

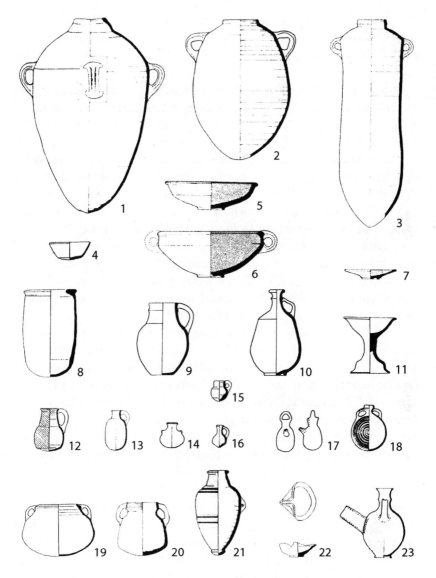

Fig. VI.12. Repertoire of typical pottery of the 8th century, mostly southern.
Scale = 1:10.

Their capacity runs from one-half quart to two quarts. They fired well, but the coarse ware was difficult to keep clean. They would have been used to cook meat in a broth, vegetables of all kinds, and other foods (below).

Several recent studies by women biblicists and archaeologists have shown that bread making in biblical times was not merely a chore. It had religious (though not "theological") connotations, because women who had little independent status could excel in this role. They could provide the basic foodstuff for a family. They could be valued and respected for their virtuous labor. And that is what religion is all about — doing the right thing. Several scholars who have looked at the textual, artifactual, and ethnographic evidence conclude that bread baking was probably accompanied by various rituals to make the baking a "blessing."[28]

Other foodstuffs could also be processed in the courtyard. Small stone mortars and pestles (several in the Tell Ḥalif house) were used to crush vegetables, and perhaps spices. We have a few iron knives, and whetstones that indicate the sharpening and use of cutting tools, such as those used for butchering and carving meat.

Water for cooking and what little personal sanitation existed was readily available in large storejars in the nearby back room. We also have pitchers, decanters, flasks, jugs, and small juglets (fig. VI.12) for pouring liquids (twenty-nine in the Tell Ḥalif house). Sometimes the water came from a well or a cistern, either inside or outside the house. In many cases, however, young girls would have gone back and forth part of the day, carrying spring or well water to the house where it could be stored. But water would always have been in short supply, especially in drought years.

The several side rooms off the central courtyard (Room 2) were usually cobbled to enable them to be mucked out regularly. These are clearly animal stalls, large enough to house a cow or two, a donkey, and perhaps a few sheep and goats. The space between the pillars could have a trough for feeding and watering the animals. The dung was saved, mixed with straw or chaff, plastered on a stone wall to dry, then used for fuel. The heat from the animals sheltered in the stables at night would rise to warm the living spaces on the second story. There were no doubt larger animal pens outside, but we have little evidence.

Ethnographic data suggest that a typical rural village family in preindustrial times would have had a cow or an ox, a donkey (perhaps a

28. See n. 27 above for references.

horse), as many as thirty sheep and goats, and perhaps pigeons kept in dovecotes for consumption. Families a bit better off might have had a camel, but these large animals were costly and difficult to manage.[29]

A wooden upright loom could be placed in the courtyard in good weather. We have good evidence for weaving, even though the wooden uprights do not survive. Baked clay or stone loomweights (eleven or so in the Tell Ḥalif house) are easily recognized by the hole pierced through them to attach them to the bottom of the warp threads. Occasionally they are found in large quantities in a room that was destroyed, fire-hardened and all lined up in a row just where they fell. A burnt room may contain a hundred or more of them.[30]

We also have a few bone or ivory shuttles that were used to push the woof threads back and forth. These may have been made of bone or stone, probably also of wood that would not survive (below). We also have a few iron trimming knives (found in the Tell Ḥalif house). In inclement weather, the loom could be stood against the walls of the house inside.[31]

We have many stone, ceramic, and bone spindle whorls (only one in the Tell Ḥalif house). These were used as weights, attached by their pierced hole to the shaft of a bone or wooden spindle to add to its momentum as it spun. A bundle of wool would be grasped in one hand, while the other hand teased out strands and spun them into yarn. When the yarn accumulated on the shaft of the spindle, it would be taken off and wound into balls. Spinning in this fashion is well known from antiquity in many Levantine societies, and it is still practiced in villages today. But it is very tedious and time-consuming.[32]

Women and girls were probably always spinning yarn, even while minding other chores. The yarn would have been dyed using natural colors: white and cream from sheep's wool; black from goat's hair; tan from

---

29. Classic works on Iranian villages are Kramer 1979; Watson 1979. On Palestinian villages, see Canaan 1933; Dalman 1935, 1942; Lutifiyya 1966; Seger 1981. See Hardin 2010, 161-73, for an excellent summary; and cf. the earlier discussion of Holladay 1992.

30. See Shamir 2007; Cassuto 2008 and references there for loomweights. At Gezer, the 1984 season produced more than 100 loomweights from a single casemate just west of the gate; cf. Dever 1986. Oddly enough, the Tell Ḥalif house has only a few examples; Hardin 2010. See also nn. 29, 32.

31. For women as weavers, see Meyers 2003a; 2003b; Shamir 2007; Cassuto 2008; Ebeling 2010, 6-95. For looms and weaving in the Hebrew Bible, see Deist 2000, 216-20. The best evidence from antiquity comes from Egypt. Cf. n. 29 above.

32. See Cassuto 2008 for illustrations and references. See also nn. 26, 27 above.

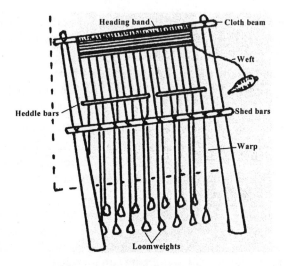

Fig. VI.13. An upright loom.
King and Stager 2001, fig. III.76

camel's hair; red from the root of the madder plant; yellow or green from saffron; and blue (rare) from cobalt or indigo.

Just as bread making was elevated to a virtue, so was weaving. Here, too, women and girls could prove their dexterity, their diligence, their own valuable role in the all-important task of sustaining the family. Ritual acts may well have accompanied weaving, like bread making, even though we have no artifactual evidence. We do know, however, that in 8th-7th-century domestic oil-pressing installations at Tel Miqneh a small horned altar for incense is found in nearly every room, suggesting that cultic activities accompanied many domestic chores.[33]

We must keep in mind that our modern distinction between "sacred" and "secular" was foreign to the ancient mind. Religion permeated every aspect of life, and it was inseparable from even the most mundane chores. And in their practice of what they knew instinctively to be the right thing, women found themselves in harmony with their world (see further Chapter VIII).

Food prepared or cooked in the open courtyard or a side room (Rooms 3, 4, 5) would be consumed either there or, in bad weather, in one of the upper rooms (below). Excavations of 8th-century sites have pro-

33. Gitin 1993.

Fig. VI.14. Palestinian woman spinning wool

duced one of the most complete and practical repertoires of domestic pottery that we have from any period. In addition to cooking pots, pitchers and jugs, and large storejars, all for storing and pouring, we also have abundant examples of smaller jars, large kraters (two-handled bowls), small bowls of various sizes, several kinds of very small juglets, shallow plates and platters rarely found in any period, and simple spouted saucer lamps. In figure VI.12 I present an almost complete repertoire of pottery forms of the 8th century, including those already discussed.[34]

Several vessels invite further comment. Any kind of drinking vessel is rare, but one could easily drink out of some of the bowls or jugs. We also have vessels called "water decanters," almost exclusively confined to Judean sites in the 8th-7th centuries. These are very distinctive one-spouted jugs, with a globular lower body and a slight carination (shoulder) on the upper body. They are usually well burnished or polished, especially in the earlier 8th century, which makes the clay impervious to liquids. They may well have been used as canteens, especially for carrying water to the workers in the field. We also have two-handled vessels called pilgrim flasks, which would have been even more practical, with their provision for carrying straps.

We have beer jugs, one-handled jugs with a pouring spout that features a perforated strainer. These could have been used to strain the husks from barley beer while drinking it. Another specialized vessel for liquids is a large ovoid jar with four handles at the rim, one of which is pierced and conducts liquids into the jar. This was undoubtedly used to store olive oil, the dipper juglet placed back to rest on the pierced spout to allow excess oil to drain back and thus be preserved. Olive oil was a precious commodity, used for cooking, for fueling saucer-lamps, and for cleansing and anointing oneself (below).

A small one-handled juglet with a long, very spindly spout is sometimes interpreted as a lamp-filler. But it might have been more readily used as a nursing bottle for weaning babies. Finally we sometimes find very small or even miniature juglets. Some of these, highly burnished, were probably used as unguentaria, and we do find them in tombs (above). The miniatures are presumed to have been used in cultic practices (see Chapter VIII).

The number of ceramic vessels found in some houses is revealing. The ʿUmayri house produced nearly 150 vessels, presumably the entire repertoire in use at the time of its destruction (12th century), and there were

---

34. Cf. Dever 2001a, 230-34, and references there. In that book I suggested a biblical term for almost every 7th-century ceramic form illustrated (eighteen in all), something otherwise attempted (independently) by King and Stager 2001, 144-45; cf. also the general discussion, pp. 133-46. No reviewer seems to have noticed. Most of those terms, however, would apply here to 8th-century forms. Thus for storejars in fig. VI:12, nos. 1-3, 8, *kad, nēbel, 'āsîd*; for cooking pots in nos. 19, 20, *dûd, sîr*; for bowls in nos. 4-6, *'arǎn, sēpel, sallahat*; etc. For the sources of fig. VI.12, see Amiran 1967, nos. 7, 9, 10, 11, 14, 16-18, 20, 21, 23; Gitin 1990, nos. 1-3, 5, 6, 13 (Gezer Str. IA); Hardin 2010, nos. 4, 8, 12, 15, 19, 22 (Tell Ḥalif Str. VIB).

some 83 vessels in the Tell Halif house.[35] Eleven were ordinary domestic forms, with storejars of various kinds accounting for one-fourth to one-half of the total. Another 40-50 percent consisted of serving vessels. The relatively small number of serving vessels, for a presumably large family, indicates that meals were an ad hoc affair.

People probably ate standing or sitting on the floor between chores (snacking), or perhaps sitting down together for an evening meal in one of the upper rooms (fig. VI.8, Rooms 7-13). The men would have had a small midday meal in the field. We have no indication whatsoever of tables and chairs, or for that matter of any eating utensils. Food was probably parceled out from a large krater, or more likely spooned out directly from the still-warm cooking pot. People would have scooped their food out into the small bowls or saucer-plates we know, eating with their hands. We have a few stone bowls, but these were too heavy to be convenient, and they would have been hard to clean. Wooden furniture and utensils may have been used, but they would not be preserved in the typical archaeological assemblage.[36]

Food Production and Consumption

Several studies of the diet of ancient Israel have been done, but the most recent and best is Nathan MacDonald's *What Did the Ancient Israelites Eat? Diet in Biblical Times* (2008).[37] He shows that the famous biblical phrase

35. The older village houses I knew, some deliberately preserved by the locale as museums, had almost no furniture such as tables and chairs, beds, or cupboards. Bedclothes were stacked during the daytime, sometimes on a stone bench or in a wall niche. People ate, slept, worked, and socialized on mats on the floor. Clothes hung from pegs on the wall. A few water jars and a wooden bowl, some woven baskets or mats, were seen, perhaps a woven baby sling, but little else in the way of furnishings or decorations. The only real "furniture" were large benches for stacking clothes and bins for storing grain, made not of wood but of thatch and mud plaster (Ar. *khābiyeh*). As much family activity as possible was carried on in the large outdoor courtyards interspersed with the houses, often the scene of communal activities like churning, cooking, weaving, and the like. These vivid recollections of forty years ago, about a world that has now disappeared, are detailed precisely in *The Palestinian Village World,* by Soad Amiry and Vera Tamari, the latter of the British Museum (1989). See also n. 27 above, on village life in both Palestine and Iran.

36. Clark and Herr 2009, 86-88; Hardin 2010, 124-60.

37. The following summary on diet is derived largely from N. MacDonald 2008. See also King and Stager 2001, 93-106.

"land of milk and honey" is an ideal description, that is, a metaphor. The reality was very different. In fact, the diet of the average person in the Iron Age was monotonous, highly varied and selective, depending on the season, and barely adequate. Many of the more exotic foods mentioned in the Hebrew Bible probably did exist, but they were rarely if ever consumed by most people.

The basic diet was based on the well-known Mediterranean triad: grain (bread), wine, and olive oil. Bread may have made up to one-half of the per capita caloric intake, made of either wheat *(Triticum durum)* or barley *(Hordeum vulgare)*. Wheat needs twenty to twenty-five inches of annual rainfall, continuing into April, and it flourishes best in the smaller valleys. It was sown in November, harvested in May or June. It could be eaten raw (after being soaked in water or milk), roasted, or, more commonly, ground into flour for bread (sometimes used to make beer). For a family of six, it has been estimated that up to four hours of milling a day would be required, plus another hour or so for baking. (Bread was so basic that the word itself becomes a synonym for "food" in many biblical passages.)

Grapes for regular or dried consumption, and primarily for winemaking, require sixteen to thirty inches of annual rainfall. They do well in a range of temperatures, and they flourish in the hilly areas in the loamy and stony soils where other crops may fail. The vines are pruned in the winter, then the grapes are ready for picking in July-August. The wine was "bottled" in large jars for fermentation and storage (fig. VI.8, Rooms 3, 4, 5). Adults may have consumed up to a liter of wine a day per person. The many biblical passages referring to wine and winemaking testify to its importance. Wine "makes the heart glad"; when "the wine dries up, the vine languishes, all the merry-hearted sigh" (Isa. 24:7). Beer was also consumed in large quantities.[38]

Olives prospered on the terraced hillsides throughout the country, but well-drained soils were preferred. Olives need a minimum of fifteen inches of annual rainfall. Olives were probably not eaten as a fruit, since they are bitter unless processed. They were utilized mostly for processing olive oil, used for cooking, anointing oneself, and fueling lamps. Olives were in fact sort of a luxury item, providing no more than about 10 percent of the diet. Some of the oil was probably traded. Olive presses are ubiqui-

38. On wine and winemaking in ancient Israel and on beer, see MacDonald 2008, 22-23 and the Tell Ḥalif house.

Fig. VI.15. Harvesting olives in November by beating a tree with a stick.
Photo: W. G. Dever

tous in the Iron Age, and many studies of olive processing have been done. In the Hebrew Bible olive oil is mentioned frequently, but little is said of its processing.[39]

Other foodstuffs were less common. Vegetables and fruits were poorly regarded. They were often wild and harvested only by the poor. Pulses (leguminous crops) like lentils, broad beans, chickpeas, and vetch are all known. They were winter crops, most requiring a mild climate and fifteen inches of rainfall or more. They could have been a valuable source of protein, since meat (mostly sheep and goat) was a luxury and rarely consumed. Vetch could also have been used as fodder, or plowed under since it is a source of nitrogen. We know of a few spices and condiments, and also of honey used for sweetening.

Milk and dairy products were very important, even though available only part of the year. Goat milk has twice the yield of cow milk, and it was drunk fresh, or more often made into yoghurt *(leběn)* or cheese for drying. Cow milk, while less common, could be churned for buttermilk, butter, or cheese.

39. On ancient processing and use of olive oil, see MacDonald 2008, 23-24.

Fig. VI.16. Terraced hillsides near Bethlehem.
Photo: W. G. Dever

Fig. VI.17. Early plowing in March, Hebron hills.
Photo: W. G. Dever

Despite the wide variety of foods available in theory, variable rainfall and frequent droughts (perhaps once every five or six years) meant that famine, and even starvation, was a constant threat (cf. below and Gen. 4; 12; 26; the book of Ruth; etc.).

Garbage and other rubbish were disposed of in pits outside the house, what New World archaeologists call "kitchen middens." At 'Umayri these pits, about seven feet from the house, produced 70 discarded artifacts; some 7,000 potsherds (pottery breaks easily); and 25,000 fragments of animal bones. These artifacts and many others illustrate the daily lives of most folk.[40]

In addition to the time-consuming tasks of food preparation, spinning and weaving, and tending to the animals, what other domestic activities may have gone on in the courtyard and first-story rooms? The above tasks were almost certainly performed by women and girls. But the men and older boys, who would have been out in the fields with the crops and the flocks much of the day, had some leisure time off, especially in the off-seasons of the year. They would likely have made and repaired their tools in the courtyard and stored them nearby (Rooms 1-5). Since these tools — plows, hoes, rakes, threshing sleds, and the like — were made mostly of wood, they have not survived the ravages of time. We do have, however, iron plow-points, as well as goads, sickles, chisels, and other tools. We also have flint sickle blades, since flint was more readily available than iron.

We have a few small stone olive presses, as well as some evidence for grape processing (fig. V.10 above). Most of the larger-scale pressing operations would more likely have taken place outdoors, especially in large multifamily "industrial" installations (below). Here, there would also have been the communal threshing floors, but the wooden threshing forks (or horse-drawn sleds, as still used) would not have survived.

It is now commonly thought that the upper story (and even the flat roof) was the family's primary living quarters (Rooms 7-13). Here anywhere from three to five separate rooms might be discerned, totaling up to

---

40. Clark and Herr 2009, 89. See also King and Stager 2001, passim; Ebeling 2010, 120-22. Cf. Deist 2000, 185-87. Much of the discussion here is based on my experience living for months in the West Bank villages of Deir Samit and Simiyeh in the Hebron hills in the summers of 1967 and 1968 and the spring of 1971. The diet of the villagers with whom I lived and worked was almost the same. Only coffee and tea were additions. Now, of course, "modernization" has changed all that. The old village houses, already going out of use in the late 1960s, featured little in the main part of the house except bedclothes stacked against the wall, and perhaps a table or chair or two. Cf. n. 35 above.

Fig. VI.18. Olive press in the bedrock.
Photo: W. G. Dever

600 square feet in the larger houses. (That would be the equivalent of about five typical ten feet by twelve feet bedrooms today; see further Chapter VII.)

Here there was ample room for a family of ten or more to share common meals, pass the time of day, do small chores, play the games for which we have some evidence, and bed down at night with some privacy. One shared activity was probably storytelling. Parents would regale their children with stories they had learned from their parents — stories about "who we are" and "where we came from." These myths were part of the practice of vernacular religion, that is, oral tradition, that may have been written down only centuries later (see below, on Scripture). Traditional poems were often sung, but we have scant archaeological evidence for music.[41]

Just as we have no preserved evidence of chairs and furniture, such as tables, we lack any evidence for wooden couches or beds of any sort (although we have ceramic miniatures in tombs). Family groups no doubt

41. On ancient Israelite music, see Braun 2002; King and Stager 2001, 285-98; and especially the work of my student, Burgh 2006. For the 8th century we have evidence for some bone flutes, or frame-drums.

Fig. VI.19. A threshing sledge, showing the embedded stones that crush the grain.
Photo: W. G. Dever

Fig. VI.20. Winnowing grain with a wooden rake.
Photo: W. G. Dever

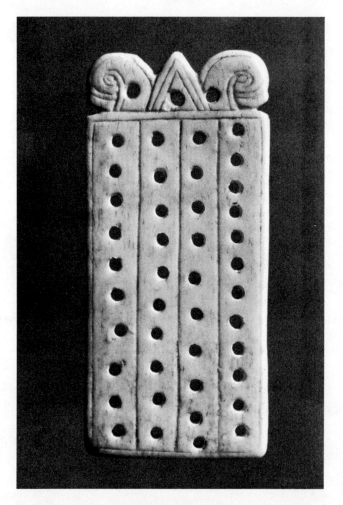

Fig. VI.21. A bone calendar (or game board) from ʿArôʿer.
Courtesy of Hebrew Union College

huddled together on the floor, the children and adolescents perhaps in a separate room or two, sleeping on mats and straw. Coverings of wool and probably of sheep and goat hides would have been piled on according to the season. During the day all these "bedclothes" would be stacked in a corner, sometimes aired out on the roof.[42]

What about clothing and storage? Since textiles are rarely preserved,

42. See n. 35 above.

Fig. VI.22. Judean captives being led away from the destroyed city of Lachish.
Ussishkin 1982, plate 86

we have little or no evidence. There are fragments of linen and wool at Kuntillet ʿAjrûd in the Sinai Desert, where organic materials may be better preserved. But these are likely to be textiles used for cultic purposes.[43] We also have the Lachish reliefs, commemorating the Neo-Assyrian conquest of Sennacherib at Lachish in 701 and found in Nineveh. Presumably eye-witness portraits, they depict both men and women in long shapeless shifts with short sleeves, no belt. The men are heavily bearded, the women with covered heads (see Chapter X below).

The flat roof of the houses was probably accessed by wooden ladders. As we know from excavations, the roof was made up of branches, twigs, and mud plaster, laid over evenly spaced wooden beams supported by several stone and wood pillars. The mud plaster had to be renewed each year after the rains, new layers of mud and straw being tamped down with a large stone roof-roller (sometimes preserved). The flat, spacious roof readily served for drying, processing, and storing food in good weather. The roof could also be used for airing clothes and bed coverings. In the really hot weather of summer, some people no doubt retreated to the cool airy rooftop to sleep (as they still did in the villages until recently).

Items from Daily Life

We have relatively little archaeological evidence for the smaller objects that would have been used in daily life in villages and small towns, since the lifestyle was simple. And the objects we do have are often found in rubbish from the courtyards, streets, or pits, that is, not *in situ* in a context that might illuminate their use.[44]

Domestic tools are what we might expect from villages and small towns. Stone tools were still in use: basalt querns (top and bottom grinding stones), digging-stick weights, chert ballistae (pounders), mortars and pestles, celts (small axes), bowls and basins, flint blades (for hafting into a

43. Sheffer and Tidhar 1991, 14. Most of the 100 textile fragments adhere to the regulations in Lev. 19:19 and Deut. 22:11. Cf. also King and Stager 2001, 140-62; Ebeling 2010, 58-60.

44. Exceptions are the near-complete inventories in Clark and Herr 2009; Hardin 2010, 123-60. On material culture and evidence for everyday life, see generally nn. 17, 27-30, 40 above. Add Ebeling and Homan 2008 and Homan 2010 on beer making; on wine making, Dayagi-Mendels and Weigl 1999; Walsh 2000; McGovern 2003; on olive processing, Frankel, Avitsor, and Ayalon 1994; on ground stone objects, Eitam 2007; Wolff 2007; Ebeling and Rowan 2008. For related biblical terminology, see Deist 2000, passim.

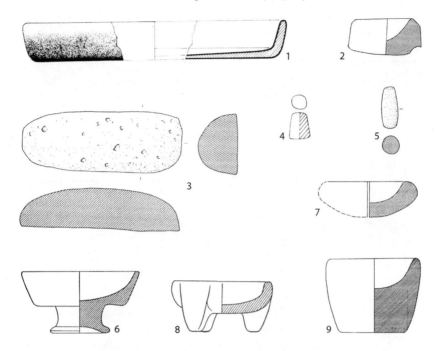

Fig. VI.23. Stone bowls, mortar and pestles. (1) Limestone platter, Tell el-Far'ah
VIId; (2) Basalt grinding stone, Megiddo VA; (3) Limestone mortar, Lachish III;
(4) Limestone pestle, Tel Qiri VI; (5) Limestone pestle, Lachish III; (6) Limestone
mortar, Lachish III; (7) Basalt pedestal bowl, Hazor VA; (8) Basalt tripod
bowl, Hazor VA; (9) Limestone mortar, Megiddo VA.
Scale = 1:4 (nos. 1, 2, 5-7); 1:10 (nos. 3, 4, 8, 9)
Chambon 1984, pl. 77:26 (1); Finkelstein, Ussishkin, and Halpern 2000, fig. 12.5:3 (2); Ussishkin 2004,
fig. 28.3:8 (3); Ben-Tor and Portugali 1987, fig. 58:17 (4); Ussishkin 2004, fig. 28.5:1 (5); Ussishkin
2004, fig. 28.3:7 (6); Yadin et al. 1989, pl. CCCXXXIII:5 (7); Yadin et al. 1989, pl. CCCXXXI:8 (8);
Lamon and Shipton 1939, pl. 112:8 (9)

wooden sickle handle), and stoppers. Loomweights could be made of stone
or ceramics but were usually baked clay.

A few iron tools are also now in evidence, such as scratch plow
points, ox goads, knives, axes, chisels, drills, scrapers, spears, and arrowheads. Bronze was used for awls, needles, and pins, as well as for most arrowheads. Animal horns could be used to make punches or pounders, as
well as various ad hoc tools. Bone, and more rarely ivory, was used for
making spindle shafts and whorls; spatulae for weaving; awls and punches.

Even poorer people cared about personal adornment. Jewelry is attested here and there, rarely of silver or gold, as one might expect. We

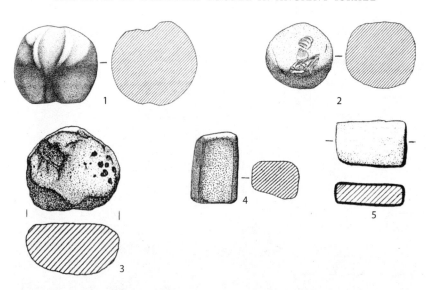

Fig. VI.24. Stone objects — large. (1) Chert ballista (maul?), House F7, Tell Ḥalif;
(2) Chert ballista (pounder), House F7, Tell Ḥalif; (3) Basalt grinding stone,
House F7, Tell Ḥalif; (4) Diorite whetstone, House F7, Tell Ḥalif;
(5) Limestone grinding stone, Tell el-Farʿah VIIe. Scale = 1:4
Hardin 2010, pl. 9:1 (1); pl. 11:4 (2); pl. 11:5 (3); pl. 8:4 (4)

have bronze bracelets and rings, and fibulae (safety pins). Beads and amulets, bone or ivory pendants, and hair pins are known, often from tomb
deposits. (From a slightly later tomb in Jerusalem we have a large collection of jewelry.) We have a few shallow limestone saucers, apparently for
mixing cosmetics such as rouge or eye shadow (kohl). Ivory or bone ap-
plicators are often decorated. Small juglets could contain olive oil, used
for cleansing and anointing oneself. Marine pumice, floating ashore
from distant volcanoes, was shaped into rubbers for exfoliating skin (a
"scoria").

There are very few luxury items: an occasional cylinder seal or engraved signet ring, carved bone or ivory inlays for wooden objects, an
"Eye-of-Horus" or Bes good-luck charm, an inscribed shekel weight, perhaps even a ceramic inkwell if anyone could write.

A woman's most valuable possession might have been a richly em-
broidered dress, her own handiwork, to be handed down to a daughter.
And then there was her dowry — the little bag of silver that went with her
to her marriage bed, perhaps some gold jewelry, which would be her salva-

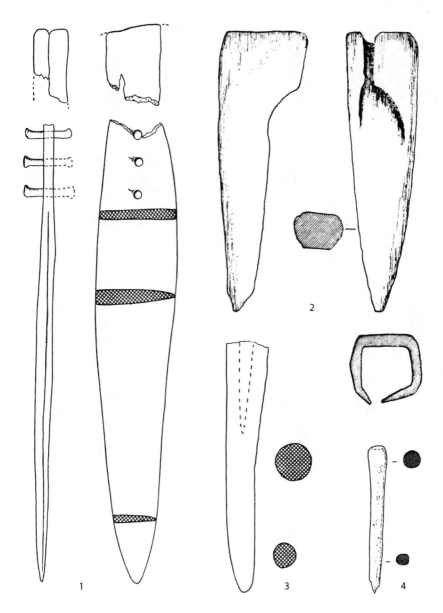

Fig. VI.25. Metal objects. (1) Iron knife, Hazor VA; (2) Iron plow point, Beersheba
III; (3) Iron goad, Hazor VA; (4) Iron point, Lachish III. Scale = 1:2
Yadin et al. 1989, pl. XXXIV:3 (1); Aharoni 1973, chapter 9, fig. 1 (2); Yadin et al. 1989, pl. CCXXI:15 (3);
Ussishkin 2004, fig. 28:16:9 (4)

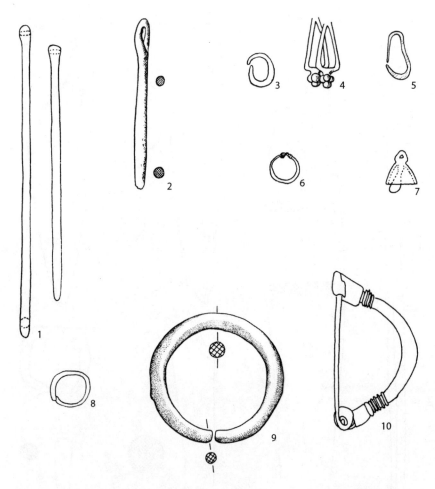

Fig. VI.26. Bronze objects. (1) Kohl-sticks, Lachish, L. 1007, 1009; (2) Needle, Hazor VA; (3) Earrings, Lachish, L. 4005, 4021; (4)-(7) Earrings, Lachish, L. 4005, 4021; (8) Ring, Lachish, L. 223; (9) Bracelet, Beth-shan S-1a (= V); (10) Fibula (safety pin), Beth-shan IV. Scale = 1:2

Tufnell 1953, pl. 57:35, 37 (1); Yadin et al. 1989, pl. CCXXI:12 (2); Tufnell 1953, pl. 57:40-42, 47, 48 (3); Tufnell 1953, pl. 57:40-42, 47, 48 (4-7); Tufnell 1953, pl. 56:8 (8); A. Mazar 2006, fig. 13.11:3 (9); James 1966, fig. 118:2 (10)

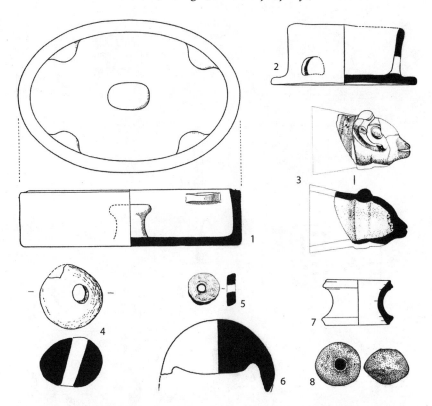

Fig. VI.27. Ceramics/clay. (1) Footbath, Samaria, southern tombs; **(2)** Brazier, Hazor IA; **(3)** Terra-cotta rhyton, Tell el-Farʿah VIIe; **(4)** Clay loomweight, Megiddo VA; **(5)** Ceramic spindle whorl, Tell el-Farʿah VIIe; **(6)** Ceramic jar stopper, Lachish III; **(7)** Jar stand, Hazor VA; **(8)** Ceramic inkwell, Gezer VI. Various scales

Crowfoot, Crowfoot, and Kenyon 1957, fig. 21:16 (1); Yadin et al. 1989, pl. XXXII:23 (2); Chambon 1984, fig. 64:4 (3); Finkelstein, Ussishkin, and Halpern 2000, fig. 12:16:10 (4); Chambon 1984, pl. 77:4 (5); Ussishkin 2004, fig. 12:28.4 (6); Yadin et al. 1989, pl. XXXII:14 (7); Dever 1986, fig. 5 (8)

tion if she was not a satisfactory wife and was renounced. There were few luxury items, only necessities, if those.

We have a few dice, gaming pieces, and gaming boards, although children would have made toys out of almost anything available.

We will discuss household shrines further below (Chapter VIII). But many houses would have had such shrines (as the Tell Ḥalif house; above), because religious practices were mostly family centered. The items we usually find are sometimes near a niche in a wall, on a bench, or in a small separate room. These items might include a ceramic offering stand; a small lime-

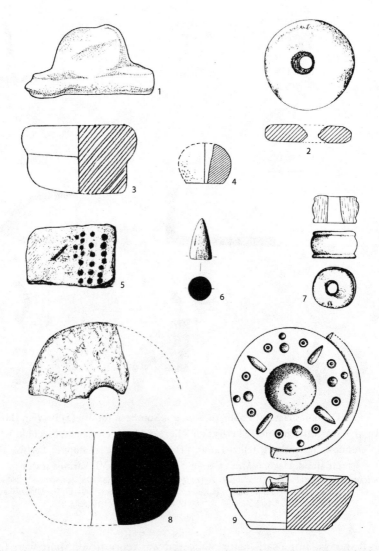

Fig. VI.28. Smaller stone objects. (1) Marine pumice rubber ("scoria"), Beth-shan P-7 (= V); (2) Limestone spindle whorl, Tel Qiri VI; (3) Limestone jar stopper, Tel Qiri VI; (4) Limestone dagger pommel, Lachish III; (5) Limestone game board, Tel Qiri VI; (6) Limestone game piece, Tell el-Far'ah VIId; (7) Limestone spindle whorl, Tel Qiri VI; (8) Limestone loomweight, Tel Qiri VI; (9) Limestone cosmetic dish, Hazor VA. Scale = 1:2

A. Mazar 2006, fig. 13:8:5 (1); Ben-Tor and Portugali 1987, fig. 56:3 (2); Ben-Tor and Portugali 1987, fig. 56:9 (3); Ussishkin 2004, fig. 28.9:21 (4); Ben-Tor and Portugali 1987, fig. 58:10 (5); Chambon 1984, fig. 69:3 (6); Ben-Tor and Portugali 1987, fig. 57:19 (7); Ben-Tor and Portugali 1987, fig. 56:1 (8); Yadin et al. 1989, pl. CCXXXIII:2 (9)

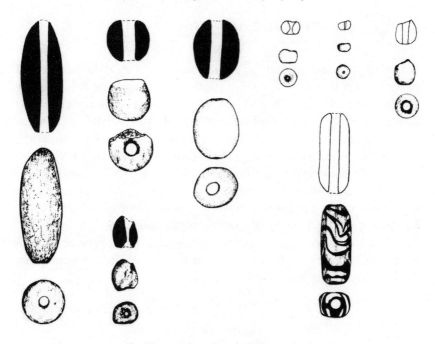

Fig. VI.29. Faience/semiprecious stone.
A selection of beads and amulets, Tel Qiri VI.
Ben-Tor and Portugali 1987, fig. 57

stone altar; a few exotic vessels, some for offerings, others for pouring liquids (libations); a terra-cotta zoomorphic or anthropomorphic (fertility) figurine; some astragali (polished sheep or goat knuckles) for divination; and perhaps some luxury items as gifts for the gods (see further Chapter VIII).

In the immediate space around the house we have some evidence of cisterns or wells, stone-lined silos, and perhaps sheepfolds and goatfolds. Here and there we have rubbish pits, and these can yield a great hoard of evidence, even if much of the rubbish has decayed (above). We might expect some sanitary facilities, such as latrines or toilets. But we do not recognize any. In elite houses in Jerusalem we have real toilets in a few rooms. But in rural areas, people simply relieved themselves outside. One can only imagine what these towns and villages smelled like.[45]

45. R. A. S. Macalister, who excavated Gezer in 1902-9, says the Arab village at Abu-Shusheh, near the mound, was "practically girdled by a ring of excreta, which taints the air hideously from whatever side the village is approached"; Macalister 1912, 1:5.

PART II: THE BIBLICAL DATA

Wherever we have adequate exposure, we have seen that stereotypical pillar-courtyard houses (or their slight adaptations) are often tightly grouped, sharing common sidewalls. Two or more may be arranged so as to share a common courtyard. Several such clusters, together with lanes, courtyards, and open spaces, constitute a typical village. Calculating the number of houses and averaging out the number of persons per house, we arrive at population estimates for these villages of 50-300 (above).

True to our principle throughout, we turn now to the biblical texts as a potential (secondary) source of information. What can we learn, and how may it affect the picture that we have drawn of the 8th century B.C.E.?

Much of the presentation of archaeological data above has to do with the typical Israelite or Judean house, its furnishing, and its functions. What do the biblical texts have to add to this picture?

The "House of the Father"

Following a brilliant 1985 article by Lawrence Stager, entitled "The Archaeology of the Family in Ancient Israel," most scholars correlate our ubiquitous pillar-courtyard houses and shared courtyards with the early biblical expression "the house of the father" *(bêt-'āv)*. This is a "nuclear family": father, mother, and unwed children — four to six people. An adjacent house or two, perhaps sharing a common courtyard, might house married sons and their families; a group that includes women brought into an "extended family" cluster is called in the ethnographic literature a "stem family" or an "extended family."[46] Most families in the Middle East have traditionally lived this way until recently, and many still do in small towns and villages. In the villages, several such extended families and household clusters, all sheltering blood relatives, would make up the entire population of a few hundred people. Within walking distance there would be other such villages, also kin-based and claiming descent from the same tribal ancestor, real or imagined. This pattern produces an extremely close-knit society, based on family ties, commonly shared traditional values, and loyalty to

46. See Stager 1985. Virtually every treatment of social structure and family life since then has cited this fundamental study. See most recently Hardin 2010, 169-70, 178-85; Faust 2011, 126-72.

the clan and to tribal sheiks rather than to any external authority such as the state.

Dozens of biblical stories about everyday life in ancient Israel reflect this family-based social structure. For instance, look at the story in Joshua 7. In assembling the people of Israel to punish Achan for his disloyalty at the battle of ʿAi, Joshua calls up the whole "tribe of Judah" *(shĕvĕt-yĕhūdāh)*. He then summons the "family of Judah," that is, the "clan" *(mishpaḥāh-yĕhūdāh)*. Finally, he brings out the "household" *(bêt)* of Achan, "man by man" *(lagvārîm),* that is, the whole family of Achan, "his sons and daughters." And as dramatic (and horrifying) evidence of family solidarity, when Achan is sentenced to death, his whole family is executed with him, and even his animals and property are destroyed. Collective punishment may be morally repugnant to us, but in ancient Israel it was deemed necessary to preserve the integrity of the larger family, the *bĕnê-Israel,* the people as a whole. Family — not the individual — was the core of society.

As Stager suggested, the typical Iron Age pillar-courtyard house is an almost ideal expression of the social, economic, and cultural values of the "house of the father." That is particularly true for the Iron I period when most settlements were small agricultural villages, and these dwellings were essentially farmhouses. But even in the later monarchy, when many people lived in larger towns, this "Israelite type house" and its values prevailed, as several scholars have recently shown.[47] In short, the "good life" was essentially rural, and society was still family- and clan-oriented.

Here, in the correlation of biblical ideals and the archaeological facts on the ground, we have one of the best examples to date of how texts and artifacts can be interrelated to illuminate real-life conditions.

Some of the above household tasks, presumably carried out by women, may be referred to in the biblical texts. Cooking indoors generated smoke, which could hurt the eyes (Job 20:26) or seem to drift out from a window (Hos. 13:3).

The celebrated description of the "virtuous wife" in Proverbs 31:1-31 includes, among many other tasks that she performs well, spinning and weaving.

47. See Chapter V, n. 40. On the notion that these distinctive houses give us a unique insight into the Israelite "mentality," see especially Bunimovitz and Faust 2002; 2003a; 2003b; Faust and Bunimovitz 2003; Faust 2006a, 71-84. Cf. Ebeling 2010.

She seeks wool and flax,
   and works with willing hands. . . .
She puts her hands to the distaff,
   and her hands hold a spindle. . . .
She makes herself coverings;
   her clothing is fine linen and purple. (Prov. 31:13, 19, 22)

Baking bread and spinning and weaving were commonplace domestic activities. The biblical texts acknowledge the central role of women in producing bread, a vital staple. Women use millstones to grind wheat or barley (Isa. 47:2; Job 31:10; Eccles. 12:3). The saddle quern that we have seen — a concave lower stone and a flat-bottomed upper stone — is referred to in several texts. Exodus 11:5 refers to a "handmill," using a dual Hebrew form *(rěhāyîm)*. Texts like Deuteronomy 24:6 and 2 Samuel 11:21 refer specifically to the upper grinding stone *(rekeb*, "to ride"). And Job 41:24 describes the lower millstone. So fundamental is grinding grain that the sound of this activity is equated with "the sound of gladness" (Jer. 25:10).

The smaller mortars and pestles that we have seen are referred to in Proverbs 27:22, used here for crushing grain, perhaps to make a sort of gruel. Cooking vessels like a "pan" *(lûlāh)* or "griddle" *(teʿsāh)* are mentioned in Leviticus 2:5, 7 (also 7:9). But we have no Iron Age vessels that would seem to match this description precisely.

Simple hearths are noted in texts like 1 Kings 19:6 ("hot stones") and Isaiah 44:19 (bread "baked on coals"). The terra-cotta ovens we have (or *tānnûrs*) are reflected in several texts. The fire inside has to be continually watched and stirred (Prov. 26:20; cf. Ps. 21:9; Hos. 7:4-7) before the bread is taken out.

Baking bread is usually assumed to be the task of each household, but in times of calamity as many as ten women may be forced to bake in a single oven (Lev. 26:26).

Spinning and weaving were also very common daily activities in the Iron Age, well attested archaeologically. The writers of the Hebrew Bible were obviously aware of this, so much so that they frequently used weaving as a metaphor in their discourse.

Some of the basic features of the weaving process are mentioned: the loom itself (Isa. 19:9); weavers and the weaving process (Judg. 16:13; 2 Kings 23:7; Isa. 19:9); the wooden beam (post) of the loom (1 Sam. 17:7; 1 Chron. 11:23; 20:5); yarn (Gen. 14:23); the warp threads (Isa. 19:10; Eccles. 4:12); the shuttle (Job 7:6); and the carding of the wool (Isa. 19:9).

Finally, several colors of yarn or fabric are noted: scarlet *(tōl'ā')* and purple *('argāmān)*, the latter much valued as a symbol of royalty and indeed probably rare because of the difficulties in its manufacture.

The only archaeological data we have for weaving, loomweights, show that our typical loom was a vertical standing loom *(dālāh)*. Such looms were presumably used by women in a domestic context. They are known elsewhere, in the Iron Age in Greece, for example. We also know of horizontal looms that were pegged to the ground, also used mostly by women. The biblical texts, however, are not decisive regarding these two loom types.

The passage in 2 Kings 23:7 suggests that women may have used the ground loom. The peg or pin that held it down is mentioned in the story of Delilah and Samson (Judg. 16:13-14; *yātēd*). The biblical texts seem to indicate, however, that both types of looms were in use in the Iron Age, even though we have no evidence of the horizontal ground loom (although wooden pegs would not have been preserved anyway).

As for male weavers, the ethnographic evidence suggests that the vertical loom was used by men. The archaeological data are not clearly gender-specific, of course. Some scholars suggest, however, that women wove at home on vertical or horizontal looms, either simply for family use or in a kind of small-scale cottage industry. Men used the heavier and more complex loom somewhere else on a quasi-industrial scale. But neither the archaeological data nor the textual data resolve the problem. Nor do the available ethnographic data.

"Convergences"

One striking convergence involves writing, an archaeological artifact that has an inscription, in this case an ostracon (although 7th century). Found at Yavneh-Yam, south of modern Tel Aviv, the ostracon is a complaint dictated to a scribe by a poor field laborer whose outer garment or cloak *(beged)* has been seized because of his alleged theft of goods or a poor performance.[48]

This reference to taking a person's garment as a pledge to repay a loan (in this case defrauding the person) provides a striking commentary on several references in Deuteronomy 24 that govern taking pledges. Just as

---

48. See Aḥituv 2006, 156-63.

taking a poor man's garment threatens his life, so is it unfair to enter a person's house and seize some necessary object as a pledge (vv. 10-11). One must not take one of a pair of millstones belonging to someone else, because this threatens his livelihood and thus his vital well-being (v. 6). Interestingly, two verses refer exactly to the situation described on the ostracon: taking a poor person's garment and keeping it overnight (vv. 12-13), or taking a widow's garment as a pledge (v. 17).

Is the Yavneh-Yam ostracon, an archaeological artifact, a commentary on the biblical text, something that might illuminate it? "Confirm" it? Discredit it? The answer seems to be that the two sources of information here are simply complementary. Neither needs the other, or in fact gains anything from it.

That raises the general issue of relating artifactual evidence to textual evidence, as we are attempting to do here, regarding each as a potential source for history writing. Let us take a few examples from the extensive data presented above. We have described domestic houses and their furnishings in some detail. We have cited most of the biblical references to these material things. There are interesting correspondences, but are they significant?

I would say that they are not — with one very significant exception. The stereotypical pillar-courtyard houses that we have described can easily be understood as a nuclear family's house, or in larger examples in a compound, evidence for multigenerational family houses. To be sure, we can extrapolate that from the archaeological data *alone,* as we have done. But without the biblical texts we would not be able to reconstruct the mentality of the *bêt-'āv,* the "house of the father." Here the biblical texts may go far in illuminating the style of life of the inhabitants. Is this information essential to understanding the houses and how they functioned? It is certainly very helpful. But recently archaeologists have begun to develop the "psychology" of ancient Israelite houses without texts (above).

To take some more specific archaeological data, what can we say from the texts of farming, herding, harvesting, cooking, weaving, or for that matter religious practices? Again the answer is very little, and perhaps nothing of any importance. Even if we could relate artifacts and texts directly, there would remain enormous difficulties.

Elsewhere I have addressed this problem with respect to pottery. The Hebrew Bible refers to specific ceramic vessels over thirty times. Few if any archaeologists have tried to correlate these terms with the actual pots we have. I tried it for the 8th century, with what seemed interesting results (above). But we simply cannot be sure that our correlations are one-to-one. And even if we could, would having a Hebrew name for a vessel make much difference? I think it would not. We already knew that lamps *(nērîm)* had a wick and could burn oil to give light. We already knew that a cooking pot *(dūd)* was used to heat food. Knowing the Hebrew name in such cases adds nothing of value.

Even with the rare specific correspondences, such as with the *pîm* weights (Chapter VII), we gain little from attaching a Hebrew name to the object. In this case, we happen to have the Hebrew name on the object. Furthermore, although the Bible gives no clue whatsoever as to its value (in silver), we know its value from independent sources.

The "Good Life": Myth or Reality?

We have described the rural life in some detail as the norm in 8th-century Israel and Judah, based on the archaeological data. We have treated the daily life of ordinary folk in particular in detail. Can any texts in the Hebrew Bible shed light on this lifestyle and its values?

There can be little doubt that the good life in the Hebrew Bible is the rural life, the lifestyle of villagers and townspeople who were mostly farmers. The writers usually assume an agricultural context and culture in their discourse, even when they seem to be addressing urbanites. And their own rhetoric is overwhelmingly antielitist, antistatist. That is transparently clear in the message of the presumed 8th-century prophets Amos and Micah.

For these writers, the good life consists of such elements as the following:

> Owning one's own house and fields (Mic. 2:2)
> Being independent, with no overlords to oppress a person (Mic. 4:4)
> No one seizes one's fields or property (Mic. 2:2)
> One is independent, can't be bought (Amos 2:6)
> Enjoying one's gardens (Mic. 7:14)
> Planting and sowing grain (Mic. 6:15)
> Threshing (Mic. 4:12; 6:15)
> Crushing grapes for wine (Mic. 6:14-15; 7:1)
> Herding one's flocks (Mic. 2:12; 7:14)
> Gathering summer fruits (Mic. 7:1)

Saving up for hard times (Mic. 6:14)
Eating and drinking (Mic. 6:14) but living frugally
Taking justice for granted (Amos 5:15, 24)
Being free of war (Mic. 4:3)

The supreme celebration of the good life is the well-known epiphany in Micah 4:3-4:

> They shall beat their swords into plowshares,
>   and their spears into pruning hooks;
> nation shall not lift up sword against nation,
>   neither shall they learn war any more;
> but they shall all sit under their own vines and under their
>   own fig trees,
>   and no one shall make them afraid.

There are also visions of the good life in other prophetic literature, as well as in other biblical texts that contain laws and customs related to rural life. Thus if we look at Isaiah and Deuteronomy, we obtain the following picture:

The land itself; flowing with rivers and streams, a land of wheat, barley, vines, fig trees, olives, lacking nothing (Deut. 8:7-10)
Living in villages and on the farm: houses and cisterns and wells, where one plows and plants, grinds wheat and bakes, following the rhythm of the sun, with lamps for the night (Deut. 6:10-14; 28; Isa. 42:3, 11; 43:17; 44:19; 49:7; 58:9)
Right relations with close neighbors (Deut. 5:20-22; 22–23)
Being charitable to the less privileged (Deut. 15; 16:18-20; 26:2-14, 17-19)
Fair and honest trade (Deut. 25:13-14; 24)
Maintaining the boundary walls (Deut. 19:14; 27:17)
The changing seasons and the rains (Deut. 11:14-16)
Planting, sowing, reaping (Isa. 5:1-10; 61:5; 62:8; 63:3; 65:10)
Tending the vineyards (Isa. 5:10; 62:8; 63:3)
Caring for the animals (Deut. 25:4)
Observing agricultural and other feasts (Deut. 18:3ff.; Isa. 56; 58)
Offering tithes and sacrifices (Deut. 12:17, 27; 14:22, 23; 26:1-4)
Satiety and simplicity (Deut. 7:25; 24:19)

A simple religion (Deut. 10:12)
The good life overall (Deut. 7:13-14; 28:3-6; Isa. 65:21-25)

A passage in Isaiah on the good life is very similar to the long list of elements above from Amos and Micah:

> They shall build houses and inhabit them;
>   they shall plant vineyards and eat their fruit.
> They shall not build and another inhabit;
>   they shall not plant and another eat;
> for like the days of a tree shall the days of my people be,
>   and my chosen shall long enjoy the work of their hands.
> They shall not labor in vain,
>   or bear children for calamity;
> for they shall be the offspring of the blessed of the LORD —
>   and their children with them. (Isa. 65:21-23)

It should be obvious from these and other passages (Leviticus; Jeremiah) that the fundamental ideal of the good life — the right way to live, in harmony with nature and the gods — was the rural life. Cities, kingship, central government — all these were familiar to large elements of the population throughout the monarchy. But they are linked with wretched excess, corruption, and the perversion of religion.

The society, the economy, and the basic cultural values were those of the agricultural sphere. This is what we will describe below as a society based on the "domestic mode of production": free men and women, living unhindered on their own land, self-sufficient, rearing their children, passing on their heritage. This is a *rural* lifestyle. But did it ever really exist?

What Does the Bible Do to Help?

We must confront the fact that nearly all the biblical texts that we have cited were probably based on oral traditions that were reduced to writing much later, perhaps in the exile to Babylon in 586-535 B.C.E., or even later. Simply put, the question is: Does this portrait of ordinary life during the monarchy (ca. 900-600) contain any reliable *historical* information? Is the portrait, despite its seemingly authentic setting and wealth of realistic detail, simply an idea or is it a reality? Perhaps it is a sort of "nostalgia for a past that never was."

What the prophets rail against is the abrogation of these very inalienable rights that we have outlined above. They protest against such abuses as the rich who

> pervert justice (Amos 5:10, 15),
> expropriate the fields of farmers (Mic. 2:2),
> seize even their garments (Amos 2:8),
> sell human beings for a "pair of sandals" (Amos 2:6; 8:6),
> "reap what they do not sow" (Mic. 6:15),
> loll about on "beds of ivory" (Amos 6:4),
> gorge themselves on expensive lamb (Amos 6:4), and
> drink until they are drunk (Amos 2:8).

One argument for the historicity of the biblical portrait is that the prophets condemn *precisely* the abrogation of the inalienable rights that we have outlined above. Why such a heated protest — unless a real-life situation provoked the rebuke of the prophets and reformers? They are not simply setting up a straw man. It is their very denunciation of abuse by the elites who wrote these texts that proves that they wrote the truth when they could. And it is a truth that is confirmed by the archaeological evidence that illuminates the life of the rural folk that we have been describing, precisely in the 8th century B.C.E.

PART III: WHAT WAS IT REALLY LIKE?

Drawing upon the artifactual evidence we have presented that gives some information on daily life in the 8th century, I have attempted to reconstruct a typical household and to describe the routines of family members. We have even given some evidence for gender-specific roles (only now becoming a focus of attention for archaeologists). Here and there we have indulged in some speculation, based, however, on both artifactual evidence and relevant ethnographic information. But is this narrative and descriptive account really "history"?

"How It Really Was"

In the nineteenth century, as the modern academic and professional discipline of history writing was taking shape, some cautious scholars chal-

Fig. VI.30. A house and courtyard in the village of Deir Samit, west of Hebron.
Photo: W. G. Dever

lenged the prevailing optimism. They insisted that we can never really know "what it was like in the past" (in German, *wie es eigentlich gewesen war*). Yet here, on the basis of the best information we have, I shall attempt just that, to draw a picture that captures at least something of what life was like in towns and villages — perhaps even some of what it *felt* like. I acknowledge that I would not presume to do such a thing had I not lived in primitive Arab villages in the Samaria and Hebron hills for many months, in all seasons of the year (above).

The Perception of Nature

First, everyone in 8th-century Israel and Judah lived in a marginal physical environment, and they were constantly made aware of that fact. In Chapter III we described the natural conditions of life in this small corner of the Levant, which determined nearly every facet of daily life. In the small agricultural villages where most people lived, farmers confronted rocky hillsides that had to be cleared and terraced, the terraces constantly rebuilt by arduous labor. The soils in the small intermontane valleys, although deep, were often chalky, hard packed, and difficult to plow. Summers were long and hot, with no rainfall between early May and late October. The scarcity of water generally was exacerbated by seasonal rainfall that was unpredictable — too little or too much. At best springs ran dry, and cisterns became polluted. The human family was at the mercy of nature, and nature often seemed inhospitable.

The Rhythm of the Seasons

The fundamental rhythms of life in ancient Israel and Judah were governed by the cycle of the changing seasons.[49] The year began in the fall, with the late harvest and the beginning of the annual rains, usually in mid to late October. This was a time of celebration as nature came to life once again after the long deadly summer months, when fields and animals and people had literally dried up. This — not our modern Western calendar — would have marked the New Year, the beginning of the agricultural year (later "historicized" as Rosh Hashanah). Even without texts, we know intuitively that fall festivals of one sort or another would have been celebrated. During Succoth (or "Booths," later connected with the wandering in the Sinai), the last of the summer produce would have been brought in — figs, grapes, and melons — and the winemaking and the plowing and planting for the winter season would have been completed. Judges 21:13-24 contains a delightful description of the fall festival, when whole families camped in the vineyards. The young people, escaping the watchful eyes of the elders (undoubtedly emboldened by the fresh wine), celebrated, danced, and made alliances. Stone towers in the fields where whole families lived and worked in the harvest season are still seen in the terraces area north of Jerusalem, used until recently. One may recall Isaiah 5:1-7, describing just such a "tower" in the vineyard.

The ensuing winter, while a welcome change, was a difficult time. Stored food had to be watched carefully and often rationed. There were no fresh fruits and vegetables. Caring for the animals, often stabled now, became more difficult. Even though fresh grass was now available in the fields, herding the animals outdoors in the harsh weather was difficult.

---

49. See Dever 2005a, 133-35; Ebeling 2010, 37-41. For agriculture generally, and its importance in particular, see Hopkins 1985; King and Stager 2001, 85-124; Borowski 2002. The origin in the Canaanite calendar and its consequent rituals is clear. See further King and Stager 2001, 85-89, 353-62; Borowski 2003, 27-28, 80-84.

Fig. VI.31. Early rainclouds over the Sea of Galilee.
Photo: W. G. Dever

It was difficult to cook anything, except on occasional clear days. Shut up in houses with no heat (and no privacy), everyone would have had constant respiratory diseases (not to mention diarrhea), with nothing but folk remedies to ease the discomfort. Young children, and old people as well, were now especially susceptible to disease and death. The fall plowing and planting had finished, and boredom took its toll as winter dragged on.

As spring came in April and the rains gradually tapered off, spirits rose and there were high hopes for a good harvest of grain by May or early June. The plowed fields in the valley were deep green; the pasture lands on the hillsides were grassy; and bright red poppies (anemones) dotted the landscape like glowing jewels. The almond trees were laden with white blossoms. Other fruit trees were in full bloom during the fleeting spring. Clear water flowed in the springs and freshets, some of it fed by melting snows higher up in the mountains. The long dry riverbeds (or *wâdīs*) were now filled with flowing water and seemed as though they would never run dry again. By April young lambs and goats, born in November, were ready for slaughter (also commemorated at Pesach, or Passover). The cows, better fed, calved. And children, conceived in the long off-

Fig. VI.32. A "watchtower" in the Samaria hills, formerly used at harvest time.
Photo: W. G. Dever

Fig. VI.33. Tending flocks in the Hebron hills in March.
Photo: W. G. Dever

Fig. VI.34. Men going to the fields and terraced hillsides, Hebron hills.
Photo: W. G. Dever

season, were born. Life was good, and it would go on for another season if the gods willed.

If the late spring and early summer harvest was bountiful, there would be an abundance of food. In late May or early June the wheat and barley harvest was ripe. Whole families worked together in the nearby threshing floors (the feast of Shavuot, or "Weeks"). Men, and women too, cut the wheat in the field with wooden-handled iron sickles and bundled it up (backbreaking stoop labor). The bundles were taken to the threshing floor on donkey back, then trodden out by wooden sleds to crush the stalks and free the grain. Wooden threshing forks were used to toss everything up into the air again and again until the wind blew away the chaff and the heavier grain fell back to the ground. It was scooped up, sieved, and put into large storejars or bags for transport back to the village. This was also a time when early summer fruits were in season: figs, early grapes, and other fruits and vegetables. Plowing again prepared for the summer harvest.

Even though the spring and summer harvest was often good, there were problems in storing it for the long months until the next harvest. Storejars invited mold and pests of all kinds. In the unprotected silos out-

Fig. VI.35. A village threshing floor.
Photo: W. G. Dever

side, not much more than large holes in the ground, rot and rodents could destroy half the harvest. Spring fruits could be dried, like fall fruits such as grapes (to make raisins). But preservation of any foodstuffs was inefficient and wasteful. Even in the village there were thieves. Food was precious but never taken for granted.

Food was precious also because most families needed to produce a surplus in order to barter with other families. Ordinarily a farm or village family unit was self-sufficient; self-sufficiency not only was a necessity but was also thought to be a virtue. The 8th-century shekel weights and balance pans that we have are found in bigger towns and cities and give evidence of regulated trade. In the countryside, however, certain families probably specialized in some modes of production (weaving, pot making), in addition to being self-sufficient. Thus one had to barter various goods to obtain what could not be produced at home.

It is obvious that in ancient Israel and Judah the old Canaanite calendar, based on the agricultural seasons, was adopted (above). Now, however, at some time in the monarchy at the latest, the old harvest festivals were "historicized" and given new theological meanings, as we have seen (further Chapter VIII).

Survival

Even if the family could manage to avoid malnutrition (or fend off starvation), there were many other health risks. Food was easily contaminated in storage or in preparation. What little evidence we have (from latrines) suggests that most people had constant intestinal diseases. There was little personal hygiene, and no sanitation facilities whatsoever, so intestinal and skin diseases spread. Ivory and bone combs indicate that head lice was a common problem. Living in close quarters meant that infectious diseases spread quickly.

Men and boys working in the fields were prone to accidents of various kinds, struggling as they did with large animals and crude implements. Working at household chores, they, like the women, could easily cut themselves. Children at play hurt themselves, as always. There was little treatment for any accident. A broken limb could not easily be splinted and healed. A badly injured limb meant amputation and likely death. A deep cut could not be stitched. A minor wound, even a splinter, would likely become infected. Few adults still had all their teeth.

Childbirth could present almost insurmountable difficulties. Women were married early, as young as thirteen. By the time they were thirty they had probably borne as many as a dozen children, plus having had several miscarriages. At birth there were only family members and perhaps a village midwife to help. A prolonged and difficult labor, a breech birth, septic infection, hemorrhaging — these often resulted in the death of the child and the mother. After delivery a woman had to nurse the infant, even if she was ill and undernourished herself. Ubiquitous childhood diseases took the lives of the majority of children in infancy.

What information we have indicates that only three or four children (out of a dozen) would have survived to young adulthood. Life expectancy was probably no more than thirty or forty. Beyond that most people were truly old, afflicted by pulmonary diseases, heart ailments, arthritis, and other maladies. Many women had already died in childbirth. Those who lived into their fifties were revered elders, wise and honored; in their sixties, they were miraculous, almost saints.[50]

---

50. On health and hygiene, see King and Stager 2001, 68-82; Borowski 2003, 74-79.

Life Cycle Events

The experience (or perception) of reality stemmed largely from what are called life cycle events, especially so-called rites of passage. These unfolding and changing events are what anthropologists sometimes call "punctuated equilibria." These are recurring singular events that temporarily disturb the equilibrium of life, but that pass, leaving an interval of stability.

The major events in the lives of individuals that would have most affected villagers and townspeople would have been the following:

Birth
Circumcision or other birth rites
Weaning
"Coming of age" rites in early adolescence
Betrothal and marriage rites
Conception and childbirth
Attaining one's majority
Decline and old age
Death and burial rites

These are not isolated events, nor are they simply individual events. The whole community participates and commemorates such events. They become part of the "corporate mentality," the collective consciousness of the community. Taken together, they constitute the experience of reality, the common historical memory (real or imagined) of the group, the oral traditions, the heritage that defines the individual within the community ("ethnicity") and must be preserved and passed on. *This* is the belief system, the "religion." But since these anonymous folk were almost illiterate, they have left us no scripture — only the artifacts they made, used, discarded, and perhaps reused. From these bits and pieces, we must try to write their history.

The "Domestic Mode of Production"

One of the most provocative attempts to define ancient social and economic groups is that of Marshall Sahlins, a distinguished American anthropologist. In his book *Stone Age Economics* (1972) he describes family-based communities like the one at hand as a "tribal community in miniature . . . politically underwriti[ng] the conditions of society — society without a sovereign." Elsewhere Sahlins describes the typical economy as the "domestic mode of production." That, of course, distinguishes it from the more typical description of ancient "Asiatic" or "despotic modes" of production (as well as the Marxist, capitalist, or other modern modes of production).[51]

I cannot think of a more apt description of early Israel, or of the later Israel that we are trying to characterize here. Even as late as the 8th century, Israel and Judah were still essentially tribal communities. Their political entity was the family and the local community. There was no "sovereign," not even a distant would-be king. This astute observation of Sahlins leads us to the biblical worldview: "In these days there was no king, and every man did what was right in his own eyes" (Judg. 21:25).

Viewing the World

Rural villages universally exhibit a distinctive lifestyle, as well as a peculiar outlook on the larger outside world. We must not underestimate village psychology in ancient Israel, despite our lack of direct testimony. First there was the small-town insularity, where there was no privacy and everyone knew everyone else's business. Close family relationships and ties, and frequent intermarriage (first cousins preferred), meant that the inevitable petty quarrels escalated into village uproars. Land and inheritance disputes divided many families, especially upon the death of an elder or a patron. Dealing with all these petty daily affairs required maintaining good relations with a hundred or more close neighbors.

Unhappy women, married off in adolescence to older men (and possibly competing with a second wife), enjoying few rights, might have made for frustrated mothers. Younger women were sequestered, and even a casual encounter with a young man outside the family could result in a blood feud in which her family could kill the man, and even the girl herself. "Honor" was everything, and however mythical, something to be preserved at all costs.

The *family* was the essential element of the society, economy, and polity. "Family" included the multigenerational nuclear family, plus the extended family both by birth and marriage, plus related families in the

51. See Sahlins 1972, 95.

village and the next village. "Family" even extended to the larger clan, where there were also blood relations. Beyond that world there was no other into which one needed to venture.

Most people in the villages had never traveled to a big market town twenty miles distant. They had never encountered a government official, unless one came around to levy taxes, or conscript the young men for military service. Few had ever met an official priest, or visited the temple in Jerusalem. Traveling on donkey back meant making about five miles a day, sleeping overnight in a cave or shelter, trying to carry enough food to tide one over. A long journey was simply not worth the effort.

There was little sense of the individual or of individual rights or opinions. (That is a modern construct.) There was probably also no sense of the state, or indeed of any authority beyond the village or the district. The egalitarian nature of the village meant no local elites who might adjudicate disputes — only a few old wise men, or a diviner, whose advice might be sought. Few people were educated, except in the school of hard knocks. In practice, people simply did the best they could under the circumstances. As the British say, they "muddled through."

There must have been an almost overwhelming sense of isolation, of being alone and helpless in the world, at the mercy of the unknown, poorly informed about the dangers rumored to be on the horizon (especially in the mid to late 8th century). One could depend only upon the closest resource at hand: one's own family, the only security there was. Thus the family, and the family heritage, was the fundamental social value. If religion had anything to offer in coping with reality, it had to deal with the ultimate reality: survival (Chapter VIII).

Another aspect of village mentality has to do with the inherent insularity and conservatism of rural folk everywhere. There was little tolerance for new or "foreign" ideas; no allowances were made for aberrant behavior, for nonconformists of any kind. Some of the "others" would have been regarded with suspicion or even as outcasts: "accursed ones": the ubiquitous village idiot, the physically handicapped, the leper, the homosexual, even the girl or the boy who never married. The egalitarian nature and the cohesiveness of the society meant that enormous social pressure would have been exerted on nonconformists. Life in 8th-century villages and towns in Judah went on as it had for at least two centuries, since the early days of the monarchy. One hoped not for change, but for stability.

Archaeology demonstrates such continuity throughout our Iron II A-C phases (even earlier, in the Iron I settlement period), so much so that inner phasing of the sites is quite difficult. Between the Egyptian Shishak raid circa 918 and the Assyrian destructions in the late 8th century, we have no major interruptions.[52] And most people in the long interlude were oblivious to anything other than the relentless cycle of the seasons and the local perturbances that we have documented. Life went on, even if it was inscrutable, "nasty, brutish, and short."[53]

52. A. Mazar 2007b, 160-66; cf. Finkelstein 2007, 147. There are, for instance, no definitive destructions between the Shishak raid, circa 915, and the late-8th-century Assyrian destructions. Cf. Chapter X.

53. For ancient Israelite life in general, the standard works are King and Stager 2001 and Borowski 2003, although in my judgment they give a somewhat too positive picture, as well as neglecting *women's* lives. For the latter, see n. 17 above; and add Willett 2008, on the difficulties of women's lives; and Ebeling 2010, for a partly fictional account of the life of one woman ("Orah"), though based on expert use of the archaeological data.

CHAPTER VII

Socioeconomic Structures

PART I: THE ARCHAEOLOGICAL DATA

In presenting our database in Chapters IV-VI, we necessarily touched upon questions of social and economic structure, especially in discussing the rural lifestyle. We spoke occasionally about an "egalitarian" society, arguing that the bulk of the population of Israel and Judah in the 8th century B.C.E. lived in rural villages and towns where there was an essentially homogeneous or nonstratified society. Indeed, the archaeological record bears out the notion of a simple, poorly developed society and economy, based on agriculture and a self-sufficient lifestyle.

The fact, however, is that no entirely egalitarian society has ever been well documented, nor does it seem possible. As we say, some are always "equaler than others." It is unlikely that a truly unstratified society could sustain itself. All such utopian dreams have failed, because elites will inevitably emerge in time. Some sort of leadership, even if imposed, is required.

Social Structure

Elite Structures and Social Structure

If we confine ourselves strictly to the archaeological evidence, as we are doing initially, social stratification will be difficult to ascertain, much less to describe in any detail. Our best option is to examine several sites where a few large distinctive structures stand out, presumably palaces or administrative centers, or possibly a combination of the two. These would have housed elite classes and should reveal something of the roles and functions that set them apart from ordinary folk. Unfortunately, the plans of these buildings are not always clear, and they are usually found with little of their original contents. Thus scholars will disagree on the interpretation. So we must engage in a bit of imaginative reconstruction, but sticking to facts where they seem reliable.

The Palace at Samaria

I have already described the site in general, suggesting that it was a royal stronghold on the basis of the location, the monumental architecture, and the luxurious furnishings (Chapter IV). The major complex on the acropolis is a large rectangular courtyard surrounded by solid and casemate (double) walls. These walls, originally some five feet thick, enclose about 17,000 square feet, or four and a half acres — an area larger than many of the small towns we know in this period (figs. IV.1, IV.2).

By the 8th century the walls had been augmented to enclose some five and a half acres, now surrounding a rectangular courtyard or plaza, the whole area measuring 345 by 625 feet, or 23,300 square feet. The rectangular palatial building in the southwest corner, measuring about 55 by 32 feet (totaling ca. 1,800 square feet), has a large courtyard at one end and an adjoining complex of fourteen rooms surrounding a small inner courtyard, probably open. A side room may contain stairs to a second story. If there had been a second story, the living space might have been as much as 3,000 square feet. This is at least double the larger village and town houses, and the floor plan differs altogether.

The palace is constructed of the finest chisel-dressed (ashlar) masonry found anywhere in the country, confined to only a few sites at palaces and elite structures elsewhere. The large rectangular blocks are laid with no mortar, yet one cannot insert even a knife blade into the joint. This masonry is well known in Syria and is of Phoenician style and manufacture. Either the masons were imported, or they were local workers trained by foreign artisans. This is royal masonry by any criterion. No wonder that these magnificent blocks were largely quarried out by later builders, all the way down to the Roman period, posing severe stratigraphic problems for the American and British excavators in 1908-10 and 1931-35.

The supposition that this was a palace is further supported by its lo-

Fig. VII.1. Ashlar masonry in the palace compound at Samaria.
Photo: W. G. Dever

cation with a separate, large, walled compound. Also, an adjacent building with many smaller rooms was found partitioned off by a light wall, no doubt a palace archive. There are fifteen small rooms of some 100 square feet each, their entrances leading off two corridors. A pair of long, narrow corridors gave access to this building.

Any doubts that the latter building was a chancellery are removed by the discovery of a hoard of ostraca (inscribed potsherds) on the floors of this building, as well as bullae for sealing documents. They are all receipts or dockets for taxes paid in kind to the palace with a regnal year (of a king?); the names of the payers, recorded apparently by an official; and the types of the commodities given (such as "old wine," "bathing oil"). A number is given like "the 15th year," but since the names of the pertinent kings are absent, these ostraca have been dated anywhere from the reign of Ahab in the 9th century (873-852) to the days of Menahem (748-738). All the ostraca were found in the 721 destruction debris and should be from a period not much earlier than that, even if they are archives. In any case, they probably belong broadly to the 8th century.

The Samaria ostraca have several implications for social structure. (1) These taxes surely were not paid voluntarily, but were extracted from

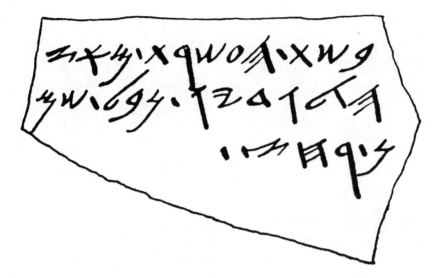

Fig. VII.2. Ostracon no. 17 from Samaria.
McCarter 1996, 103

landowners by a king with enough power to do so, whether we know his name or not. (2) This king had a bureaucracy working for him, as well as administrators whose names we do know, and who were housed in offices and archival buildings in the capital compound close to the palace. (3) Studies reveal the names on the ostraca to be tax collectors and wealthy landowners in the Samaria district. (4) Beyond that level of social organization, we seem to have clans and clan names. (5) A class of commoners can be presumed to have been somewhat like peasant farmers on the large estates that paid the taxes.[1]

If this analysis has any merit, we have at least a three-tier society: a small ruling elite class, a larger entrepreneurial and proprietary class, and a much larger working class. If we had a few more of these precious written materials, we could no doubt reconstruct social and economic structure for other parts of Israel and Judah.

The only other building known inside the palace compound is a large, partially preserved structure in the central courtyard, also destroyed in 721. Here excavators found hundreds of burned fragments of Phoenician-style carved ivory inlay panels. They are clearly expensive imports and testify fur-

1. For the ostraca, see Reisner, Fisher, and Lyon 1924, 1:227ff. For discussion, see Aharoni 1967; Kaufmann 1982; Rainey 2006, 221-22.

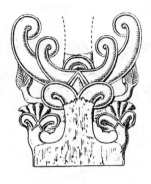

Fig. VII.3. Ivories from Samaria.
Crowfoot and Crowfoot 1938, pl. 5, 6, 17

ther to the luxurious lifestyle of the rulers of Samaria, and perhaps the noble families attached to the court. This structure — as large as the palace —
may have been a well-furnished subsidiary residence, or perhaps a storeroom for booty taken in various military campaigns.

We know from archaeological evidence elsewhere, such as Phoenician remains on Cyprus, that these carved and inlaid ivory inlays of the
10th-8th centuries were used to decorate elaborate wooden furniture such
as beds and chairs. The best examples of ivory carving come from north
Syrian workshops of the 9th-8th centuries. They are found only rarely elsewhere in Israel and Judah, and never in a hoard, only as a fragment or two.
The ivories clearly suggest great wealth and prestige.[2]

In the northwest corner of the palace compound was a deep pool,
seventeen by forty-three feet, which would have held many thousand gallons of water. The remainder of the vast plaza seems to have been devoid of
major buildings and could have served as a parade ground for ceremonial
events or for military exercises.

Since we are attempting to do history — to chart change over time
— it is noteworthy that this monumental palace, built in the mid–9th century, continued in use for a century or more, until the Assyrian destructions in 721. Sometime in the early 8th century another large multiroom
structure was added (Building 4; fig. IV.3). It was about half the size of the
original palace, but it was outside the walled compound. It would seem to
be an additional residence or administrative building, as the growth of the
northern kingdom came to a peak. But while new, it honors tradition.

We are not simply speculating about Samaria having been a capital
city. The Neo-Assyrian annals specify that their western campaigns in 732-
721 (Chapter X) were directed against a site named *sāmārina,* and for 150
years afterward the whole subjugated area was designated the "Province of
Samarina."[3]

The Palace at Lachish

Str. III at Lachish in the hills of southern Judah has revealed the largest and
best-preserved palace we have to date.[4] It is situated near the center of a

2. Crowfoot and Crowfoot 1938. Cf. Winter 1976, 1981; Barnett 1982; Tappy 2006.
3. Cf. *Sāmārīna* on Sargon's *Great Display Inscription;* see Rainey 2006, 234. The name
may refer to the capital city or the larger district (as often in the Hebrew Bible).
4. Ussishkin 1982, figs. 2, 3; and add now Ussishkin et al. 2004.

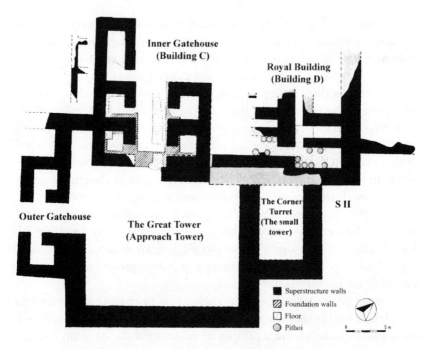

Fig. VII.4. Major elements of the upper "City of David," on the Ophel.
E. Mazar 2006b, fig. 2

large thirty-one-acre Bronze Age mound that was already high and steep. It was defended in the 8th century by a double-wall system and a three-entryway gate (fig. IV.14).

A huge podium, 105 by 100 feet, was erected at the heart of the city in the 9th–early 8th century (Podium A-B), so high that it commanded a view in all directions, even far beyond the site. On the podium there would have been a palace, the largest Iron Age structure ever found in the country. Today the foundation still stands, so prominent that it can be seen from miles away. Its walls were from 6 to 12 feet thick, of cyclopean masonry filled inside with a deep tamped fill of stones and earth — an impregnable fortress. In the Phase C stage (mid–8th century) the podium was expanded to the east to form a foundation some 118 by 248 feet, an area of about half an acre. There was now a major transformation, with a rectangular courtyard or plaza constructed to the east. To the northwest, attached to the palace itself and complementing its plan, were six long narrow rooms, perhaps for storage.

Extending the plaza to the south, where a four-entryway gate was incorporated into the plaza, two very large buildings flanked the gate to the right. On the left were three of the long three-room buildings that we have interpreted elsewhere as government storehouses.[5] The new compound was 228 by 345 feet, or about 78,000 square feet. The total area of the palace and the plaza with its building was 345 by 423 feet, or some 145,000 square feet, about three and one-third acres. That would be the equivalent of a typical American suburban block, which with two-thirds-acre lots could accommodate five large houses.

There can be no doubt that the monumental 9th-8th-century structures of Str. V-III at Lachish do reveal a major palace — on a scale as large as, or larger than, Samaria. But these structures were badly destroyed, then looted, and finally robbed out. So we have no contents on the basis of which to specify their nature or functions. Yet the palace complex was so large that it took up about one-fourth of the occupied area inside the walls. And it was made even more conspicuous by being set off from the domestic quarter by its own thick perimeter wall and sloping ramp.

A Palace at Jerusalem?

Jerusalem may have been just as important a capital as Samaria, but very limited access to the Old City has prevented archaeologists from saying very much. The Solomonic Temple, however early, certainly existed in the 10th century B.C.E. and continued into the 8th century. On the Hill of Ophel, several monumental structures have been revealed. First is a large complex just outside the south wall of the Temple Mount, consisting of a three-entryway gate flanked by storerooms. This gate complex appears to have been the entryway into structures on the acropolis above. It may date to the 8th century. To the south, as part of the City of David area, Eilat Mazar has recently found the remains of a massive citadel. It dates perhaps to the 10th century, but it would have been in use into the 8th century.[6]

5. On these storehouses, some examples as at Megiddo thought to be "stables," see Chapter V; and cf. Herzog 1992, 223-39. Cf. Chapter IV, n. 16; Chapter V, nn. 24, 29, 30, and references there.

6. B. Mazar and E. Mazar 1989; E. Mazar 1987. Cf. Cahill 2003, 70, for the possibility that these structures originated in the 10th century. See also B. Mazar and E. Mazar 1989; E. Mazar 1987, 2002, 2006b. The 10th-century date is disputed, some scholars preferring the 9th century; cf. Finkelstein 2003. But see Cahill 2003, 72-79; A. Mazar 2007b, 152-53, for more

Fig. VII.5. Slopes of the "City of David," with Iron Age wall.
Photo: W. G. Dever

Elsewhere, scattered monumental and domestic remains do attest to a capital city in the 8th century, even if largely still unexplored. The principal remains are found on the slopes of the Ophel south of the Temple Mount (Shiloh's "City of David"). First, there is a monumental city wall midslope to the south. Below that, nearer the valley floor and the Spring of Gihon, a lower wall has been found. These walls enclose a group of well-constructed houses situated on a series of terraces, the front terrace of each extending over the roof of the one below. These houses were originally built when the "stepped stone" structure south of the Temple Mount was abandoned, perhaps in the 9th-8th centuries, continuing in use until the Babylonian destruction in 586. One house yielded the name of the owner, one "Ahiel," whose name was found on the lintel of the doorway.[7] These elaborate, closely related houses, occupied in the 8th century, all within sight of the Temple Mount, were in all likelihood the residences of elite families connected to the court and the Temple.

---

balanced treatments. In any case, the 8th century would be the latest possible date. For a lower 8th-century city wall; see Reich, Shukron, and Lernau 2008. Cf. also n. 9 below.

7. See Shiloh, in Stern 1993, 698-712. See also Cahill 2003, 56-66.

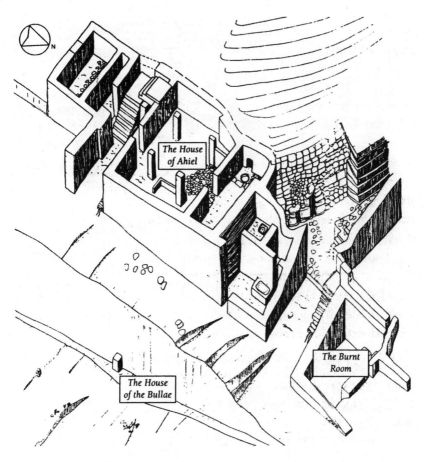

Fig. VII.6. The "House of Ahiel" on the lower terraces of the City of David.
Barkay 1992, fig. 9:44

Further, direct evidence of socioeconomic structure comes from a rock-cut tomb across the Kidron Valley, below the modern Arab village of Silwan (ancient "Siloam"). The sheer cliff here, with many tombs (all robbed), was probably the area of an Iron Age cemetery where upper-class families had tombs. In one of these tombs was found an 8th-century inscription reading as follows:

This is [the sepulcher of . . .] yahu
    Who is over the house.
There is no silver or gold here

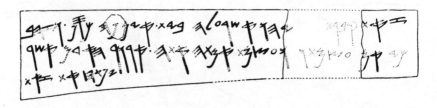

Fig. VII.7. The "Royal Steward" tomb and inscription
found in the cliffs of Silwan village.
Barkay 1992, fig. 9:49

> But [his bones] and the bones of
> His slave wife with him.
> Cursed be the man who will open this.

In 1953 Nahman Avigad first deciphered this inscription, found in 1870, and he suggested to restore the name as "Shebnayahu," interpreting the phrase "over the house" as meaning "Royal Chamberlane." Thus we probably have a direct witness to Shebna, Hezekiah's royal chamberlain in the late 8th century (Isa. 22:15-18; cf. 36:3; 37:2). Incidentally, there is a reference here to an offensive, conspicuous tomb, in full view of the Temple — a "tomb on the height, a habitation for yourself in the rock" (Isa. 22:16). This is an apt description of the Silwan tomb.[8]

More written evidence would of course be helpful, and it may be at

8. See Avigad 1953; cf. Dever 2001a, 219-20.

216

hand. In excavating around the Gihon Spring area, Israeli excavators have recently found a hoard of 130 9th-century bullae, or clay stamped seals for papyrus scrolls. They are not yet published, but they are reported to contain iconographic motifs relating to elites, probably officials who dealt with archives.[9] This would suggest socioeconomic stratification even before the 8th century.

Midlevel Elite Residences

We have looked at several capital cities and district administrative centers that feature a palace compound with attached administrative structures (Chapter IV). We have taken these as evidence for an elite ruling class, however small. But we also have a few elite structures of the 8th century that are impressive but are not palaces. These we know are usually adjacent to the city gate and probably housed middle-echelon city officials and administrators, or possibly well-to-do merchants.

Hazor

On the acropolis at Hazor, a large rectangular structure was added to the buildings within the walled citadel in Area B, probably during the early 8th century (Str. VI). This multiroomed structure was located just inside a

---

9. Reich, Shukron, and Lernau 2008. Cf. also E. Mazar 2007, 165, who sees the bullae as evidence of "central administration and organized commerce." For the latest and most authoritative survey of Jerusalem in the 10th-8th centuries, see the essays in Vaughn and Killebrew 2003, especially the chapter by Cahill (13-80), the only contributor to have been one of the excavators. For the city wall, see Cahill 2003, 67-68; for the private houses in Area G and elsewhere, 56-68; for the infamous "stepped-stone" structure (the biblical *millo*), 33-57. On the Solomonic Temple, see Dever 2001a, 144-57, and references there; cf. also Miller and Knauf in Miller 1997; for Hebrew studies, see Cahill 2003, 54 n. 111. On the famous "Hezekiah's tunnel," the city's water system in the late 8th century, see Chapter X below. Other structures related to the Spring of Gihon, which we now know originated in the Middle Bronze Age, may have continued in use into the 10th-8th centuries. See Reich, Shukron, and Lernau 2008; and cf. Cahill 2003, 71-72. See also Reich and Shukron in Stern 2008, 1801-37, for updated information.

Finkelstein's much-debated "low chronology" is not relevant here, since even he admits that by the 8th century there was a Judean "state" with its capital in Jerusalem; see Finkelstein 2001, 105-15; 2007, 110-16. On the origins of the state, see Chapter IV, nn. 14, 23.

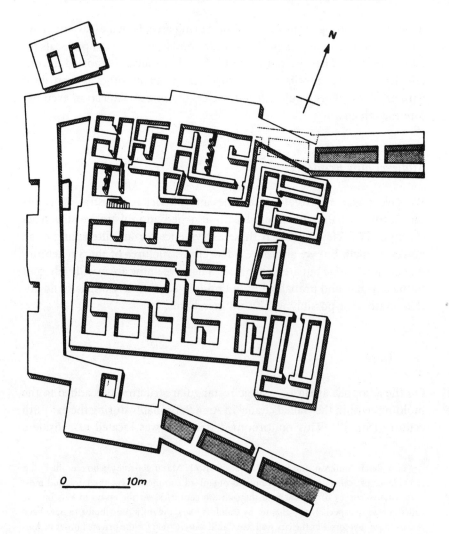

Fig. VII.8. Citadel and elite houses near the citadel at Hazor.
de Geus 2003, fig. 17

stretch of the casemate city wall in the huge citadel on the summit. Measuring about twenty-one by twenty-five feet (some 5,500 square feet), this building featured two long narrow corridors running its length. The remainder was a U-shaped structure like the usual four-room house, with a dozen smaller adjacent rooms.

An exterior stairway led to the second floor. If the second floor had a

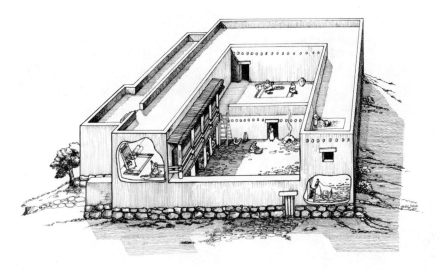

Fig. VII.9. A larger elite house.
Drawing by Giselle Hasel

similar arrangement, the building could have had up to 10,000 square feet of living space. (The average American house is about 2,500 square feet.) The contents of this structure are not very helpful, but the size alone, together with its strategic location, would qualify this as an administrative structure. Near the citadel, but with a bit of privacy, were two very large "pillar-courtyard" houses, possibly the residences of high-ranking officials.[10]

Tell el-Farʿah

At Tell el-Farʿah in the north, once the capital, we have a rare opportunity to document changes from the 9th into the 8th century. In the northwest quarter, immediately inside the two-entryway city gate and adjoining the gate plaza, there is a large block of four-room houses, dating from the 10th century (Str. VIIb) to the 8th century (Str. VIId). In particular, the earlier small four-room houses give way to several very large houses that now dominate the gate and plaza.

10. Yadin et al. 1958, pl. CCV. Cf. Herzog 1992, 207-8. This structure was built in Str. VIII of the 9th century, but it seems to have continued in use into Str. VI of the 8th century. On the site in general, see Yadin in Stern 1993, 601-3.

Fig. VII.10. Elaborate 8th-century houses near the gate at Tell el-Far'ah N.
Reconstruction by Giselle Hasel. Cf. fig. V.2

The clearest example is House 148, right inside the gate and opening directly onto the plaza. The house itself measures about sixty-five by thirty-two feet, with a living space of some 2,000 square feet — double that if it had two stories, as is likely. There are about ten rooms surrounding a rectangular inner court. While this is reminiscent of the older four-room plan, this house, with its size and large outer courtyard (more than 1,000 square feet), represents a radical change. House 148, with its size and prime location, is surely the residence of an upper-class patron or official.[11]

Tell en-Naṣbeh

At Tell en-Naṣbeh, a few miles north of Jerusalem, a small (seven to eight acres) administrative or residential complex can be discerned near the 8th-

11. Chambon 1984, plans II-IV. Cf. Fritz 1995, 96-99. On the site in general see Chambon in Stern 1993, 439-40.

century city gate. Here the American excavators in the 1930s cleared almost the entire top of the mound — an ill-advised strategy, but one that at least gives us an unprecedented exposure. The stratigraphy was faulty, but it is generally clear that a small town of the 9th century was transformed into a moderate-sized administrative center by the 8th century.

The expanded fortifications included a massive solid wall with numerous towers, bastions, and a two-entrance offset city gate. Immediately inside the gate on the left was a large square building that resembled the typical four-room Israelite house (Chapter V) in plan, with several rooms around the courtyard, set off by two rows of pillars (A). A storeroom is adjacent. It is significant that this structure was about forty-five by forty-five feet, or about 2,000 square feet. That is somewhat larger than the typical four-room house. It was probably not a private house, to judge from both its prime location and its size.

Another complex lies some distance to the south of the gate (B), but still built anew right up against the city wall. The plan, unfortunately, is not clear. But the total area occupied by these buildings, all unusual in type, is at least three times that of the building near the gate. One building in this area fortunately is clear (A). It again has the typical four-room plan, but it is somewhat larger than many of these houses, some 1,600 square feet. Perhaps this is the residence of a lower-ranking official housed near the gate.[12]

Tell Beit Mirsim

At Tell Beit Mirsim, a larger provincial town in southern Judah (ten acres), much of the town plan of the 8th century can be discerned. In the northwest quadrant the city wall is clear, with a group of densely grouped domestic houses just inside the wall, even incorporating sections of it into their back room (as at Beersheba III-II). But one large, multiroomed building built into the wall extends well beyond the wall, like a projecting tower.[13]

Few scholars have analyzed this structure in detail,[14] but in my opinion it must be either an administrative building or an elite residence. Its

12. McCown 1947. Cf. McClellan 1984; Herzog 1992, 201-63; Fritz 1995, 100-102; add now Zorn in Stern 1993, 1108-12.

13. On the site in general see Albright in Stern 1993, 179-80; cf. Fritz 1995, 108-9.

14. See, however, Shiloh 1970, 150-90; Holladay 1992, 316-17; and cf. Herzog 1992, 201.

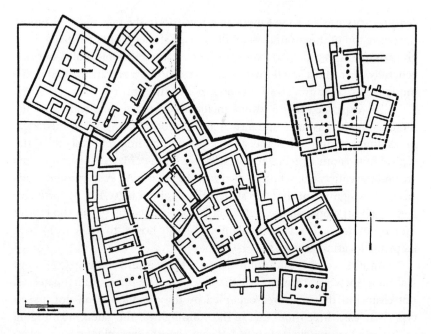

Fig. VII.11. The West Tower of Str. A$_2$ at Tell Beit Mirsim.
Fritz 1995, fig. 39

plan, rather like the Assyrian-style *bit hilāni* discussed above, would suggest the former, but its location in the midst of domestic houses seems to rule that out. It is more likely an elite residence, commanding a magnificent view, but still near ordinary houses. Its size is impressive: seventy-two by seventy-two feet, or some 5,000 square feet, two or three times the size of the ordinary houses nearby. It features a large entrance court (actually part of the city wall) and seven rooms grouped around a central court. Whatever this structure may be, it is no ordinary house. Only a very high-ranking official, perhaps the governor of the town or a wealthy businessman, could have afforded such real estate.

Beersheba

We have already described Beersheba as a planned barracks town and local administrative center, farther south in the country (Chapter IV). We would expect to find a governor or military commander there. That draws

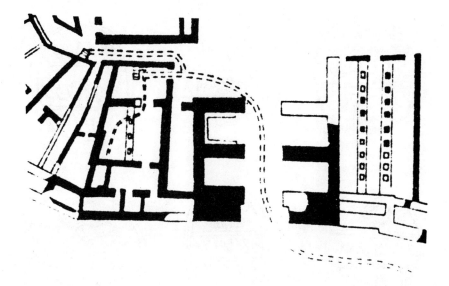

Fig. VII.12. Palatial building adjoining the Str. II gate at Beersheba.
Herzog 1997, fig. 5.31

our attention to a large building that differs from all the other very stereo-
typed four-room houses. It is about thirty-three by sixty feet, or 2,300
square feet, more than four times as large as the other houses, and it is
partly built of finer ashlar masonry.

This structure is located immediately off the plaza right inside the
gate, overlooking the three large government storehouses on the opposite
side of the plaza. The plan differs from all the other Str. III buildings at
Beersheba. It features two long corridors off one side of a small central
court, and five or six other small rooms. This building, dubbed the "Governor's House," would have been an ideal combination of residence and
business office for a midlevel official.[15]

Seals and Status

I come now to a very particular class of objects that often turn up in excavations, stamp seals. These are small gemstones, usually carnelian or some

15. Cf. Reich 1992, 210-11; Fritz 1995, 109-10. For other elite residences, see Singer-Avitz
2002, 171-72 (nos. 812, 855).

Fig. VII.13. A selection of 8th-7th-century seal impressions. (1) Seal of "Jaazaniah,
Servant of the King," Tell en-Naṣbeh (7th century); (2) bulla of "Hanan, son of
Hilkiah the Priest" (8th century); (3) bulla of "Baruch, son of Neriah the Scribe"
(7th century); (4) seal from Samaria, Pottery Period IV; (5) seal from Megiddo, Str.
IVA; (6) seal from Tell Ḥalif, Str. VIA
McCarter 1996, 147 (1); McCarter 1996, 146 (2); McCarter 1996, 149 (3); Crowfoot, Crowfoot, and Kenyon
1957, pl. XV:23 (4); Finkelstein, Ussishkin, and Halpern 2000, fig. 12:42.4 (5); Hardin 2010, pl. 13:10 (6)

other semiprecious stone. They were engraved with images and/or personal names, and when mounted in a gold ring setting they could be used
as signet rings. You could seal a legal or other document by rolling up the
papyrus, tying it with a string, then fixing the knot with a patty of wax (or
mud) into which the ring could be pressed. Thus you could "seal" the document to keep it from being opened, and more importantly to document
its authenticity. We almost never find the papyrus roll, because it would
have rotted away, but we can often recover the patty of baked clay, or bulla.

These seals have a long history in the Levantine world. We have
thousands of them, of which perhaps several hundred can be dated to the
Iron II period, several dozen to the 8th century.[16] They are even more com-

16. For a general introduction to seals and seal impressions, see Avigad 1987, 195-208.
For definitive catalogues of Hebrew and other Iron Age seals, see Sass and Uehlinger 1993;

mon in the 7th century in Israel and Judah, when they often carry only the name of the owner and a patronymic (the father's name). If we isolate a corpus of such seals specifically from the 8th century, what can we learn?

First, the iconography — the artistic motifs — of the engraved seals usually draws upon Phoenician art. This is an eclectic art form, borrowing familiar motifs from both Egyptian themes on the one hand and Mesopotamian themes on the other hand.[17] Sometimes these foreign themes are faithfully translated, in which case they are easily recognized, and their meaning can be explained. Often, however, the motifs are some-what bungled, in which case we must grapple with a vernacular art form that may not be familiar.

Since most of the ones we find in Israel and Judah are Phoenician in style, and presumably imports, we are dealing with objects that are twice removed from their homeland, and even more distant from their concep-tual world. But in any case, they are luxury items and denote the high sta-tus of the owners. The seals and bullae found in ordinary houses feature very simple iconographic motifs, or only names.

Literacy and Social Status

In attempting to use material culture objects to identify social status, I have already looked at engraved gemstones, some of which have inscrip-tions on them, that is, personal names and possibly titles. Owners of these seals could stamp their name on anything soft, such as wax or clay, but could they themselves read or write? Did they need to do so? And if they could read and write, what might that tell us about their social status?

Most authorities estimate that no more than about 1 percent of the population of Israel and Judah in the Iron Age was literate.[18] Even those few could not have read much of the complex poetry and prose that we

---

Keel 1997; Avigad and Sass 1997 (ninety provenanced seals); Reich, Shukron, and Lernau 2008 (bullae recently found in the Gihon Spring excavations). See also Avigad 1986; Reich and Shukron 2000; Hestrin and Dayagi-Mendels 1979.

17. On Phoenician art see Winter 1976, 1981.

18. On the problem of Israelite literacy, see Ben Zvi and Floyd 2000; Schniedewind 2000; Sanders 2008, and references there. On ancient literacy in general, see Harris 1989. Cf. further in n. 19 below. On literacy and state formation, see D. Carr 2008, with reference to Knoppers 1997; Millard, Hoffmeier, and Baker 1997; Miller 1997; King and Stager 2001, 300-317. See also n. 19.

have in the Hebrew Bible. A few people were what we might call "function-ally literate," but fewer still were really fluent in reading and writing. We have good evidence that even kings were illiterate. They had to employ the few professional scribes trained here and there in scribal schools.[19] As late as the Roman period, it is estimated that no more than 5 percent of the population was truly literate.

The personal names, presumably of the owners of the seals, and sometimes a title, can be engraved at the bottom, or even up the side. Many are Hebrew names familiar to us from the Hebrew Bible. But we also have dozens of new names. If we consider the much larger corpus of 7th-century seals and bullae (seal impressions), we have even more names, both biblical and nonbiblical.[20] That seals were so commonly used suggests that literacy was uncommon, and therefore the seal itself was a mark of high status. You sealed because you could not write. One could be wealthy enough to employ scribes and thus be able to conduct one's personal business, as well as political affairs, with other elites who similarly used written records. One might even correspond with someone of a neighboring culture, such as a Phoenician merchant or an Aramean entrepreneur. A scribe might attain status professionally, since scribes were highly valued and no doubt well rewarded. (See further below.)

A Bureaucracy

By the 8th century the royal court at Samaria was documenting taxes paid in kind to the crown and was keeping archival records on ostraca. Written records like the Samaria ostraca are rare, but the fact that we have one archive suggests that there were many more. Here we have a treasure trove of information. After all, the ostraca are well preserved, and many are complete. And they are written in good biblical Hebrew, which scholars know quite well. Therefore, we ought to be able to pick up an ostracon, scan it, and say, "Aha! So that's how it was." But it is not that easy.

Most of the Samaria ostraca have names of individuals with the Hebrew prefix *lāmed*. Unfortunately *lāmed* can mean "to," "for," or "with re-

19. On scribal "schools" see Heaton 1994. For more skeptical views and late dates, see Jamieson-Drake 1991. Add now D. Carr 2008; Sanders 2008. See also n. 18.

20. See references in n. 16 above.

spect to . . ." Most authorities, however, read it to mean "for," that is, "taxes to" or "for the crown."[21] Those names would then be the names of the individuals who collected the taxes, middle-class government officials. Other names specify "from," so these are the taxpayers.

I have already noted the importance of the Samaria ostraca for filling the lacuna on our map of the Samaria district in the 8th century. Some sixteen sites are named, of which we can identify as many as ten with sites excavated or known through archaeological surveys, working from Arabic place-names. But only a few of these sites are named in the Hebrew Bible, and of those, to date only Shechem has been excavated.[22]

The names of the individuals are equally informative on several topics. Many scholars have pointed out that about one-third of these personal names are compounded with the old Canaanite divine name "Ba'al," rather than "Yahweh," presumably the Israelite-Judean national god. Thus we have for instance the contrast in

"Meribbaal" *(měrib-baʿal)*
"Gaddiyau" *(gāddî-yau,* like *yāhû)*[23]

Such percentages in presumably typical documents suggest a degree of religious syncretism, in which some were more devout Yahwists than others. In view of what we shall say about "folk religion" in Chapter VIII, this should not be surprising.

Most if not all the individuals paying these taxes were wealthy landowners, noblemen who lived in large towns but nevertheless owned and managed extensive agricultural estates in the hinterland, on the produce of which they paid substantial taxes. Several are also styled as "leaders of clans." This datum alone would confirm that we have not only a three-tier (above) but often a four-tier social structure:

21. On the Samaria ostraca generally, see n. 1 above. On the interpretation of the *lāmĕd* prefix, see Aharoni 1967, 322 ("l" = tax collectors); Yadin 1959, 184-87 ("l" = owners); Rainey 1996, 221 ("l" = recipients, but from their own estates).

22. Aharoni 1967, 324-27. On the more recent Israeli surveys in Samaria, see Dar in Stern 1993, 1314-16; Finkelstein in Stern 1993, 1313-14; Zertal in Stern 1993, 1311-12; Finkelstein, Lederman, and Bunimovitz 1997; Faust 2000.

23. In Judah theophoric personal names end in *-yāhū,* for example, "Shebna-yahu." In Israel, however, the theophoric element (name of the deity) is shortened to *-yaw,* for example, "Obdyaw" ("Obadiah"). For a corpus of Israelite-Judean names, see Tigay 1986. On the much larger corpus of names on seal impressions, see references in n. 16 above.

Tier 1: Ruling class: kings and noble families at court
Tier 2: Upper class: clan leaders and wealthy landowners in cities
Tier 3: Middle class: a professional middle class, including government officials and scribes in towns and cities
Tier 4: Lower class: a peasant class, subsistence farmers tilling the land in villages and on farms

The Samaria ostraca allow us a glimpse into the relationship of literacy to social structure. In the above four tiers, perhaps only some in Tier 3 could really read and write well, that is, a few middle-class individuals. But everyone in Tiers 1 and 2 benefited from literacy, indeed could not have maintained their high status without it. And perhaps some upper-class persons — the occasional businessman — could read and write. But in any case, the lower classes were almost entirely illiterate and would remain so for centuries.

The Further Development of Literacy by the 8th Century B.C.E.

To appreciate the substantial growth of literacy by the 8th century, which might seem like an overnight phenomenon, we need to look at the previous several centuries in which the momentum was gained. The earliest "Hebrew" inscriptions we have are in fact in the Old Canaanite script as it was in the process of being adopted at the time that Hebrew was emerging, soon to become the national language of Israel and Judah. From the 11th century we have our earliest such inscription, significantly an "abecedary," or a list of the twenty-six letters used in the Canaanite alphabet, in their accepted order. It is an ostracon from a silo in Str. II at 'Izbet Ṣarṭah, a small site of the settlement horizon near the Philistine plain. It is probably a schoolboy's exercise tablet because it reverses the standard order of two letters. And while the bottom line is not bad, although quite crude, the three lines above that are gibberish. Furthermore, the letters are written from left to right (although the order of the letters may still have been in flux).[24]

A second abecedary has recently been found at Tell Zayit in the southern Judean hills. From a 10th-century level there comes an abecedary carved on a large stone incorporated into the wall of a courtyard.[25] This

24. Demsky and Kochavi 1978. See also references in nn. 18, 19 above.
25. Tappy and McCarter 2008.

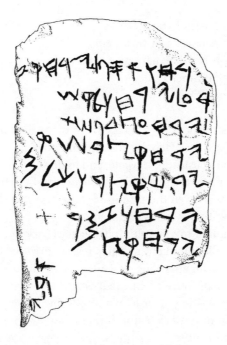

Fig. VII.14. The Gezer Calendar.
McCarter 1996, no. 80

may either be in reuse, or it may have been what we call a "display inscription," that is, designed for the edification of the public. In any case, this and the 'Izbet Ṣarṭah abecedary show that by the 11th-10th centuries at the latest, some people even in small villages were learning to write. Nevertheless, it would be a long time before many mastered the art.

The well-known Gezer Calendar was not found in our excavations, but by Macalister in 1902-9 in an unstratified context. It is a soft limestone hand-sized palette, dated paleographically (by comparative analysis of the evolving letter shapes) to the 10th century. This, too, may be a Hebrew (or Phoenician?) practice text. It is a short mnemonic poem, that is, like "thirty days hath September," an easily memorized ditty that gives the seasons of the agricultural year. It reads as follows:

1. His two months: Ingathering
   His two months: Sowing
2. His two months: Late Sowing
3. His month: Chopping flax (or grass)

229

4. His month: Barley harvest
5. His month: Harvest and measuring
6. His two months: Vine harvest
7. His month: Summer Fruit
    Bottom: "Abiya"[26]

Despite what we call "the accidents of discovery," it may be significant that all the earliest Hebrew inscriptions that we have are practice texts. People are now learning to write, and to do so with the vastly simplified Canaanite alphabet. It has only about twenty-five characters, instead of many hundreds or even thousands of characters that the Egyptian and Mesopotamian writing systems required.

The invention of this simple alphabet goes back to Canaanite groups in the early 2nd millennium B.C.E. When it was borrowed by the early Israelite settlers in Canaan after 1200, it would eventually make literacy widespread, potentially universal.[27] But that would take time. Meanwhile, the ability to read any writing — or to exploit the few who could — helped to create and sustain in power an elite ruling class.

The few 10th-century inscriptions that we have notwithstanding, literacy does not make much more immediate progress. We have almost no 9th-century inscriptions, even though among Israel's neighbors we have Phoenician, Aramaic, Moabite, and other inscriptions — some of them monumental royal inscriptions. One Aramaic royal inscription was even found in Israel, the famous Dan stele, commemorating a victory over the Omride dynasty, dated to circa 840.[28] It mentions a known Israelite king (Jehoram/Joram, 851-842/41) and refers to "the House (dynasty) of David." Yet we have no Hebrew royal inscriptions from ancient Israel (except possibly for the Hezekiah tunnel inscription).

26. Rollston 2008, 80-81, and references there. See also McCarter 1996, 100-101; Aḥituv 2006, 252-57.

27. See especially Naveh 1982. On the implications of the spread of literacy, see Havelock 1982. Add D. Carr 2008; Sanders 2008. On the significance for state-formation processes, see n. 18 above.

28. For the original publications, see Biran and Naveh 1993, 1995. Early revisionist attempts by Lemche, Thompson, Davies, and others to dismiss the Dan inscription as a "forgery" are transparent propaganda for their nihilistic notion that there cannot have been a "united monarchy." See Lemche and Thompson 1994; Davies 1992; and cf. the devastating rebuttal in Rainey 1994. On the genuineness of the inscription and its significance, see Lemaire 1998; Schniedewind 1996b. See also Chapter IV, n. 9.

In any case, it is significant that in the 8th century, which represents the zenith of the society and culture of northern Israel, we have a relatively sudden upsurge of inscriptional evidence. In addition to the Samaria ostraca we have a large corpus of slightly later ostraca from the 7th-century fortress at Arad, near Beersheba.[29]

One reason we have so few inscriptions is that if they had been written on papyrus, as in Egypt, they would not have survived, due to the damp climate in Palestine. However, in the desert — one of the few places where papyrus could be preserved — we do have a papyrus. This papyrus, a letter, was found in one of the Dead Sea caves, in the Wadi Murabba'at, and dates to the 8th century.[30]

Among the other 8th-century written remains we have, I note here graffiti in a cave on the shores of the Dead Sea, graffiti in a cave near Jerusalem, and a few of the Arad ostraca.[31]

I will discuss in Chapter VIII two very important 8th-century religious texts: the tomb inscriptions from Kh. El Qôm in the Hebron hills and the large corpus of graffiti from the fort/shrine at Kuntillet 'Ajrûd in the eastern Sinai Desert. Here we simply note that both of these sites are somewhat remote, especially the latter. Thus it appears that by the 8th century some people could read and write, in villages, even in forts in the desert.

Before leaving this topic, we note the only possible Hebrew royal inscription we have, precisely dated to the years immediately before the Assyrian invasion of 701. This inscription, often called the "Siloam tunnel inscription," commemorates the completion of a long underground tunnel that carried the waters of the Gihon spring below the city of David under the city wall and into a secure reservoir (Chapter X). This Hebrew inscription, inscribed in an exquisite hand, even with word dividers, describes the cutting of the tunnel. It was found in 1880 and is now in the Istanbul Archaeological Museum, but the top half is missing. What is left reads as follows:

> [The matter of] the tunnel. And this is the matter of the tunneling (tunnel?). While [the hewers were swinging the] axe, each towards his companion, and while there were still three cubits to hew, there was hea]rd

29. See Aharoni 1981. All in all, few inscriptions can now be attributed to the 8th century; see further Aḥituv 2006, 92-123.

30. Stern in Stern 1993, 833-35.

31. See Bar-Adon 1975; Naveh 1963; and for Arad, n. 29 above. See further Aḥituv 2006, 233-39.

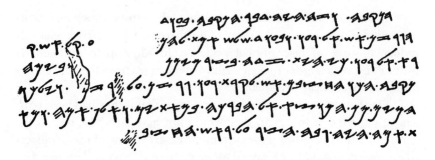

Fig. VII.15. The Siloam tunnel inscription from Jerusalem.
McCarter 1996, no. 90

the voice of a man calling to his companion because there was a fissure (?) in the rock, on the left and on the right. On the day of the tunneling through, the hewer struck each man towards his companion, axe towards axe, and the waters flowed from the outlet to the pool, one thousand and two hundred cubits, and a [hu]ndred cubits was the height of the rock above the heads of the hewers.

Some scholars have argued that the Siloam tunnel inscription is not really a royal inscription. They seem to ignore the fact that such a monumental feat of engineering could only have been undertaken by the central authorities and the king himself. And it is difficult to believe that the contractors arbitrarily attached their names to the project, with a sort of plaque placed at the very entrance to the tunnel. Finally, the elegant script must have been carved by a very professional artisan whom only the court could have employed.[32]

If we even have an 8th-century royal inscription (at last), we can surely assume that by the 8th century literacy was becoming somewhat more widespread, adopted not only for public but also for many private affairs. Nothing could associate literacy with status more than a royal inscription.

The rapid growth in literacy at all levels of society in the 8th century (if only relative) will have far-reaching implications for the origin and nature of the biblical texts, as we shall see in Part II below.

---

32. For this translation, see Rainey 2006, 253. Rainey points out that the upper smoothed portion of the rock was left blank, so the inscription was never finished. Thus the absence of a king's name is irrelevant. Those who assert that this is not a "royal" inscription overlook this fact. Cf. Chapter IV, n. 7 for references.

A Middle Class?

Thus far the archaeological evidence alone, when carefully considered, has allowed us to reconstruct first a three-tier, then a four-tier, society in the 8th century in Israel and Judah. We have no statistics for the small ruling and elite class, but this upper class must have constituted only about 1 percent of the population, or no more than 2,000 or so individuals. Such a small number of people could easily have been housed in the several large cities and administrative centers that we discussed above, with a total estimated population of 18,000 (fig. IV.1).

If 2,000 or so high-ranking officials and elites lived in these places, they would have been a minority, but a sizable and distinct upper class. At Beersheba, for example, out of a population of 300 or so, perhaps 15-20 people had a higher status than the ordinary soldiers stationed there. They would have included the governor, administrative officials, and a few military officers.

The existence of a very large, rural lower class — probably at least 80 percent of the total — can easily be documented, as we have done in Chapter VI. That leaves a middle class to be described, probably in the larger towns and cities discussed in Chapter V. But what archaeological evidence do we actually have for such a middle class?

To begin with, we must assume the existence of such a middle class, fairly sizable, if larger towns and cities were to support their society and economy. No known urbanized society, such as Israel and Judah certainly were by the 8th century, consisted only of a huge lower class and a very small ruling class. At minimum we must presuppose people who were purveyors of commodities, suppliers of services, middlemen, traders, importers, lenders, financiers, realtors, and entrepreneurs of all kinds. In addition, some people made it into the middle class as artisans, craftsmen, masons, metalsmiths, jewelers, ivory and seal cutters, leather workers, weavers, and others.[33]

Our best hope for actually illustrating such a middle class is to look at the plans of the larger towns and cities discussed in Chapters V and VI above. All we can really discern beyond the few public areas, however, is a group of tightly compacted buildings, most of them not the typical four-room houses of the period.

Take, for instance, our most complete plan, that of Tell en-Naṣbeh 3A,

---

33. Cf. Dever 1995; Holladay 1995, 381-82.

Fig. VII.16. Central section of the plan of Tell en-Naṣbeh 3A.
Fritz 1995, fig. 35

a small city of about 800. The several distinctive structures near the gate are no doubt those of a few officials. Many of the other buildings — several dozen — are unclear, but those whose plans we can make out are mostly four-room houses. Nevertheless, at least half of the others could easily have been small shops of artisans and craftsmen and even some small-scale industrial installations. Indeed, we must presume so, even though the state of excavation and publication has left us ambiguous evidence.[34]

One area is promising, however. Right in the middle of the city, surrounded by a relatively large open area, are two or three clusters of closely grouped buildings. None of the dozen or more structures in this area bears any resemblance to the many clear four-room houses elsewhere in the city. Might it not be reasonable to interpret these as the shops and businesses of a mercantile class, that is, our missing middle class?

Here in a separately designated commercial area there could have been shops where potters, woodworkers, smithies, weavers, and other

34. See n. 12 above.

craftsmen worked. And here were probably also the storerooms and shops for food and provisions that an urban population would have required, but which had to be brought in from the countryside. Another such group of buildings is situated to the north, separate from nearby domestic structures.

We can see similar possible commercial and industrial areas at the few other sites whose plans we can discern. Tell Beit Mirsim A_2 reveals two clusters of houses, one near the southwest gate, the other near the "tower" (or elite residence; above) to the northwest. But again, each area contains a cluster of buildings that does not look like the typical four-room houses at the site, and each is set off somewhat from these houses (see fig. V.3).

A row of five buildings near the "tower" and running right alongside the city, several of them nearly identical, is very likely to have been just the sort of commercial area about which we have been speculating. Finally, many of the private houses must have belonged to middle-class shop owners, businessmen, entrepreneurs, providers of various services, and petty officials of all kinds, as well as some landowners and agriculturalists who commuted to nearby fields.[35]

This is not all speculation, however. Numerous ethnographic data support our reconstruction. In the less developed areas of the West Bank, until twenty years ago one could visit just such small towns, and even a few cities, where the lifestyle we have imagined could actually be seen.[36] In the center of the town or city is an area of small shops and businesses of all kinds, with some larger adjoining industrial areas. Everything the population needs is available here. And in many cases the owners and their families live on the second story of these buildings.

The Old City of Jerusalem today, with its crowded population of some 80,000 within the walls, and its innumerable shops and houses all intertangled, provides a parade example of a traditional town or city in the Middle East. It is likely that little has changed over the centuries until recently, except for a larger population agglomerate and a thin veneer of modern sophistication. This reflects the *longue durée* of the *"annales school"* (above).

---

35. See n. 13 above.
36. This observation is based on my twelve years of residence in Jerusalem, with regular visits to the Old City, as well as to many other towns and villages in the West Bank. For broader ethnographic data, see Kramer 1979; Watson 1979.

Fig. VII.17. Crowded shops and dwellings in the Old City of Jerusalem.
Photo: W. G. Dever

The Economy

Economic structure cannot be separated from social structure, which it supports and legitimizes, except as we do here for practical purposes of analysis. But the rather limited archaeological data that might be relevant are difficult to interpret.

The "Domestic Mode of Production"

In looking at small villages and the typical rural lifestyle, based almost entirely on agriculture, I have characterized a "domestic mode of production" (Chapter VI). In terms of the four-tier social structure delineated above, this would represent the economy of the lower classes, mostly farmers. These individuals would have produced virtually every commodity that the village required. But in addition, the rural sector necessarily produced everything that towns and especially cities needed as well. The only question remaining is how these goods were marketed. In short, was there any "economic system"?

At the local village level there can be little doubt that nearly all economic transactions were carried out by barter. Each household could simply trade its surplus of any one product for the balance that it needed from a neighboring household. No shops were needed. But if foodstuffs, for instance, were sent to nearby market towns, as must have been the case, how were the villagers compensated? The towns and cities apparently produced a few things that the villagers wanted or needed, since they were not completely self-sufficient.

A "Redistributive" Economic System?

Scholars have offered several solutions to the above questions. One popular model is called the "redistributive" economic system.[37] According to this theory, the economy works something like this (much simplified here):

1. Some individuals accumulate a surplus that creates wealth, that is, capital.
2. These entrepreneurs prosper largely by coercion, by manipulating

---

37. On "redistribution" models and "down-the-line trade," see Holladay 1995, 368-91.

the masses so as to "disembed" goods and services, further multiplying their wealth and emphasizing their class distinction.

3. But a central government imposes taxes on the wealth of the middle and upper classes, thereby creating a royal treasury.

4. The government then either "redistributes" its accumulated wealth by dispensing it to the masses in exchange for labor or the like, or uses it to trade abroad for luxury items and enhance its status.

Obviously such a redistributive economic system cannot work unless some central authority has the power to assess and collect taxes, either in kind or in some hard form of currency like silver or gold. The income would have been used to hire a large palace workforce, the construction workers for building the administrative centers that we have seen, and some district administrators. These individuals would all constitute a small upper-middle class, as well as a much larger contingent of lower-class laborers in many professions (above).

We have already shown beyond doubt that a centralized government did exist in Israel and Judah in the 8th century, along with an upper class of wealthy taxpayers and a middle class of administrative officials to process taxes. That is abundantly clear from the Samaria ostraca (above). To document a putative middle class, in this case petty bureaucrats, let us look at these written documents more closely. We may also be able to flesh out the rather meager archaeological evidence for a middle class.

Ostracon no. 13 identifies a certain "Abiezer," apparently from a clan named "Tetel," an unknown site. Abiezer's taxes were paid to "Shamaryau" and "As[a]," presumably the tax officials at Samaria, but no commodities are mentioned. From other ostraca we learn that a typical payment was one or two "jars of old wine," or a "jar of oil."

For some of the clans mentioned we have the names of several senders. Thus from "Shemida" we have five senders (plus a number of illegible names), for a total of fifteen transactions. That seems to suggest that a number of clan leaders might have jointly owned lands in a particular region. The fact that the names of certain individuals occur frequently may indicate that some landowners accumulated considerable wealth.

These ostraca, however valuable, cannot of course be taken as anything more than a small, random sample. But they do reflect what seems to be a dense network of small towns and rural settlements, where a relatively few entrepreneurial landlords organized agricultural production, paying taxes on their profits with superior quality wine and oil.

The individual payments are small, but these ostraca are only a few of what would have been regular payments. And a "jar" — a large Iron II storejar of the type we have — would have held fifteen gallons or more, no pittance for aged wine or something like "virgin olive oil." Incidentally, two place-names in the ostraca suggest large vineyards:

"Kerem-Hattel" ("Vineyards of Hattel," the latter apparently a place-
name), and
"Kerem-Yehoeli" ("Vineyards of Yehoeli").

These vineyards might be compared to famous wine-growing districts in France or other places. They made fine "varietal" wines.

The evidence thus suggests a middle class of entrepreneurs and purveyors of agricultural products, managing farms in the countryside where peasant labor was employed. Whether these middlemen lived on rural estates (which would remain unexcavated) or in the towns and cities mentioned in the ostraca, or even in some of the cities we know in the area, is impossible to say.

Further Archaeological Evidence for Trade

I have mentioned silver as a medium for transactions that go beyond barter. In the 8th-7th centuries we find a new system of weights that were used in trade and commerce.[38] These small dome-shaped limestone weights are inscribed, and they come in designations of 1, 2, 4, 8, 12, 16, 24, and 40. The numerical signs are Egyptian for some reason.

There is also a smaller series of fractional weights, or gerahs, in units of 1-20. By averaging all the weights we have we can calculate that the sheqel should have weighed circa 11.33 grams. The *pîm* is thus circa two-thirds of a sheqel; the *neṣef* circa five-eighths; the *beqaʿ* circa one-half.

Each weight also carries a bag-shaped sign, undoubtedly depicting the leather or cloth pouch in which silver was carried. The sign must mean "sheqel," from the Hebrew verb *šql*, "to weigh" (below). One paid by weighing out silver fragments to balance the stone sheqel weights on the other side of a balance pan where the appropriate stone weight was.

Not only do we have several dozen sheqel weights, we even have a number of metal balance pans and chains. Furthermore, the balances are

38. See Kletter 1991, 1999.

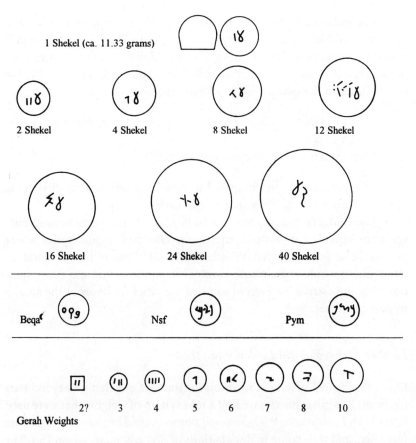

Fig. VII.18. The Judean sheqel-weight system.
Kletter 1999, fig. 6

often found in the area of the city gate, along with grain scoops, where we know that trade was carried out.[39]

Finally, we know that these stone weights were made slightly oversize, then chiseled down to the correct size. What is interesting are the chisel marks on the flat bottom of some weights that were left about 10 percent overweight — "the butcher's thumb on the scale." (Even today we speak of cheating as "chiseling.") We have several hoards of sheqel weights — money in the bank.[40]

39. For the balance beam see Barkay 1996. For grain scoops, see Gitin 1993.
40. See Yeivin 1987, 426 (Eshtemoa, 10th-9th centuries; five jugs totaling 26 kilograms

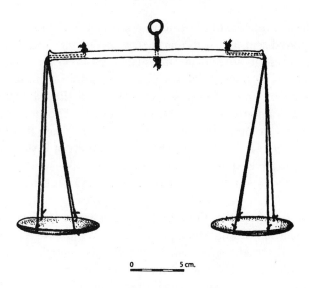

0   5 cm.

Fig. VII.19. Balance beam and scales.
Barkay 1996

Foreign Trade

One way of discerning trade in the wider sphere is to look for imports. Both Israel and Judah, for instance, had been in close contact with neighboring Phoenician peoples along the coast from at least the 10th century on, and even earlier. Do we find any of the Phoenician items that we might expect in the 8th century? Despite the geographical proximity and well-excavated Phoenician sites like Dor, Shiqmona, Achzib, and others (Chapter IX), we find only a few ordinary Phoenician ceramic vessels here and there in most sites listed in figure IV.2. We would not expect, of course, to find luxury items, among them imported Phoenician pottery, in villages or small towns. But in the cities? In fact, we do have Phoenician imports just where we would expect to find them, in the northern capital of Samaria.[41]

I have already described the large collection of carved ivory panels found there as either direct Phoenician imports from Syria, where the art of ivory carving flourished in the 9th-8th centuries, or manufactured lo-

---

of silver); Gitin 2004b, 1956 (Tel Miqne/Ekron, 7th century, three hoards); Stern 2008, 1699 (Dor 9th-8th centuries, seventeen sealed bags in a jar, totaling 8.15 kilograms of silver).

41. Holladay 1995, 379-81.

cally under the tutelage of Phoenician craftsmen.[42] The same can be said of the engraved gemstone seals that we have noted, on which nearly all the iconographic motifs are Phoenician. Finally, we can now say that the finest ceramic vessels — the well-known "Samaria wares" — are so closely related to contemporary Phoenician sites at Syrian sites like Sarepta that they are either imports, or manufactured locally in Phoenician style.[43]

At Hazor, comparative studies have shown similarly that there were frequent Phoenician ceramic imports or imitations of luxury wares, declining by the 8th century, but still in evidence (ca. 4-6 percent).

At Dan, right on the Syrian border, the excavators discovered several small adjoining buildings outside the gate, on the edge of the outer plaza. It has been suggested that this may have been a sort of "duty-free zone," where Phoenician or other foreign merchants could have set up bazaars, having struck a trade agreement that gave them certain concessions.[44] Given the number of Phoenician imports that we have, this suggestion is not fanciful. In fact, we can document the penetration of Phoenician culture well into Israel by looking at the excavation at what appears to be essentially a Phoenician site, at Rosh Zayit in lower Galilee (on the border with southern Phoenicia; cf. below, and Chapter IX).

When we move down the Levantine coast, we come to an area of late Philistine culture, now partly assimilated. In Chapter IX we will say more of these "Neo-Philistine" sites, like Ashkelon and Ashdod (also Ekron and Gath). What we can say here is that we do not see much archaeological evidence of trade between the Philistine plain and Judah. In fact, if we look at a distribution map of such typical Judean artifacts as the Judean Pillar Base figurines to be discussed in Chapter VIII, we see that the border with Philistia was rather nonporous.

Moving north and northeast to Israel, always more open to foreign influence, we see that a few Aramean sites that represent the spread of the contemporary Aramean culture of Syria actually penetrate into nominal Israelite territory. These include particularly Bethsaida, Tel Hadar, and 'En-Gev around the north and east shores of the Sea of Galilee. At these sites the material culture is mostly Aramean. Yet here, too, the archaeological record shows little trade or cross-fertilization, even with sites not too far distant that are clearly Israelite. The one exception might be Tel Reḥov,

42. See nn. 3, 17 above.
43. See n. 41 above.
44. Biran 1999.

ten miles to the south on the west bank of the Jordan. By all accounts this ought to be an Israelite site. But the material culture known from excavations thus far has some enigmatic features, perhaps due to Aramean influence (Chapter IX).

The closest neighbors of Israel and Judah were the peoples of Gilead, Bashan, Ammon, Moab, and Edom in Transjordan. A generation ago these peoples were poorly known apart from the biblical and extrabiblical texts. Today, however, thanks to extensive archaeological surveys and an increasing number of excavations, we begin to know these cultures in some detail (Chapter IX). Yet we have little evidence of trade with Israel and Judah.

The area north of Ammon is still largely *terra incognita* archaeologically. Ammon and Moab, however, and Edom to some degree, give us some basis for comparison. These essentially tribal states were reaching a level of complexity only by the 8th century (see Chapter IX). Yet here, too, we see little evidence of trade — perhaps because these states were not yet mature.

PART II: THE BIBLICAL DATA

As we do in each chapter, we shall now look separately at any texts in the Hebrew Bible that may reflect a knowledge of the "facts on the ground" that archaeology has provided. Social and economic factors are basic, but because they are usually assumed rather than made specific in our texts, they are somewhat difficult to draw out and relate to the archaeological evidence. Nevertheless, there are some correspondences.

The Fact of Social Stratification

We have reconstructed a four-tier society above on the basis of the archaeological data alone. Do the biblical authors and editors supply any additional information on what we call "complex society"? The short answer is: Yes. And they don't like it. In describing the biblical ideal of "the good life" in Chapter VI, we have shown that while the writers are not necessarily aware of social stratification in our sense, they do use language that shows that they were familiar with the abuses that we now know archaeologically.

This explains the Bible's condemnation of the idle rich in the Samaria district who live in "houses of ivory" and loll about on "beds of ivory" (Amos 6:4). These are metaphors that we now actually understand on the basis of archaeologically attested ivories. And their condemnation of wealthy landowners who "add field to field" (Mic. 2:2) and "sell the poor for a pair of sandals" (Amos 8:6) makes perfect sense in the light of the Samaria ostraca that we have analyzed in some detail above.

The biblical writers excoriate the wealthy and generally dismiss the kings, saying only of the latter that they "did evil in the sight of Yahweh." They do seem to accept the fact of a middle class and its values. But without exception it is the ordinary folk that they celebrate — the "people of the land" (ʿām hā-ʾārets) — the lower classes that archaeology now illustrates so well (Chapter VI).

The Economy

Above we presented archaeological evidence for a series of sheqel weights in discussing local trade in the 8th century. The Hebrew Bible gives us evidence that fits. The basic unit of currency in the Hebrew Bible is the sheqel, the Hebrew term deriving from a root meaning "to weigh," that is, to pay by weighing out silver. Sheqel units are mentioned in many biblical passages. The booty from the Israelite conquest of ʿAi was reckoned in sheqels (Josh. 7:21). Similarly, Goliath's armor is evaluated in sheqels (1 Sam. 17:5; cf. 2 Sam. 21:16), as is Absalom's hair (14:26). The prices of various commodities are also given in sheqels: fields (1 Chron. 21:25; Jer. 32:9), oxen (2 Sam. 24:24), measures of barley (2 Kings 7:18), and daily rations of food (Ezek. 4:10; 45:12). When an ox gores a slave, recompense is figured in sheqels (Exod. 21:32). In addition, tribute is given in units of sheqels (2 Kings 15:20; Assyrian tribute). Sheqel weights could be altered; Amos 8:5 protests the "enlarging" of weights in the merchants' favor. Special sheqel weights "of the sanctuary" are mentioned (Exod. 30:13, 24; Lev. 5:15; Num. 3:47, 50; 7:13).

Sheqel fraction weights, that is, specific weights smaller than one sheqel, are also mentioned in the Hebrew Bible. Thus we have references to weights of a half-sheqel (Exod. 30:13-15; 38:26); of one-third sheqel (Neh. 10:32); and of one-quarter sheqel (1 Sam. 9:8). Also mentioned are smaller fractions, gerahs, of which there were twenty to the sheqel (Exod. 30:13; Lev. 27:25; Ezek. 45:12). Several specific fraction-weights are mentioned by name in biblical texts: the beqaʿ, or half-sheqel (Heb. beqaʿ, "to split"), and the pîm (only in 1 Sam. 13:21, etymology unknown). We have all these and other sheqel weights in well-stratified archaeological contexts of the late 8th and early 7th centuries. Thus we are now in a position to understand several hitherto enigmatic biblical passages. Deuteronomy 25:13-16 describes a "bag" *(kîs)* for weights *('eben)*, and speaks further of the cheaters who have "two kinds of weights, large and small." Amos 8:5 complains of "false balances." Finally, Micah 6:11 condemns those with "wicked scales" and a "bag of dishonest weights."

In addition to references mentioning the sheqel, we have, as expected, texts referring to the balances with which the sheqel weights were used. The Hebrew term for balance is *mō'znāyim*, a dual noun that really means "ears" — apparently from the fact that the flanking balance-pans could be seen as resembling two ears. A number of biblical passages refer to balances in general, such as Ezekiel 5:1, describing how the prophet's severed hair was weighed. Leviticus 19:36 mentions balances in connection with sheqel weights, and Proverbs 16:11 mentions "balances" in parallel with "scales." These passages show familiarity with the archaeological data for balances and trade that we adduced above.

The prophets are obviously calling for the reform of an economic system that actually existed, and for which we have the pertinent physical evidence, thanks to archaeology. We even have a unique convergence of data in the fact that the *pîm* weight is actually mentioned in the Hebrew Bible in 1 Samuel 13:21. The word *pîm* occurs only here in the Hebrew Bible, and its precise meaning was not understood until the first discovery of the *pîm* weights in the early 20th century.

These biblical passages, even if written or edited later, have the ring of truth about them — especially since we have the doctored weights, as well as some inscribed with the correct Hebrew term. And they were in fashion in the late 8th and early 7th centuries, especially in Judah. This is a remarkable convergence, not a coincidence.

Luxury Items

In discussing luxury items above, we noted the widespread use of engraved gemstones as signet rings. Here, too, we have some direct convergences between artifact and text. The Hebrew word for seal *(ḥôtām)* occurs a number of times in the Bible. In Genesis 38:18, 25, Tamar demands from Judah his "seal and cord" as a pledge that he will keep his promise of a gift. Signet rings themselves are described as gifts or offerings to God in Exodus 35:22

and Numbers 31:50. According to Exodus 28:11, 21, 36; 39:6, 14, 30, priests serving in the temple possessed "engraved seals," some with "the names of the sons of Israel." The king and other high state officials in ancient Israel had seals as symbols of their authority, worn on the right hand (Jer. 22:24).

Seals often were not only symbols of wealth or authority, but were also used in a practical way to designate ownership. In 1 Kings 21:8 Jezebel seals Ahab's documents, that is, she affixes a signet ring to a wax or clay patty that binds the strings and knots surrounding a rolled-up papyrus or parchment document. Jeremiah 32:10-44 refers several times to "sealing" deeds of purchase. In Nehemiah 9:38, 10:1 the priests "seal" a covenant document. Certainly seals were intended for making seal impressions, as proven by the fact that all the hundreds of examples we possess are engraved in the negative, even though that was technically difficult. Both the Song of Songs 8:6 and Isaiah 8:16 use the term "seal" as a metaphor (the latter in reference to a *mĕgillāh*, or scroll), referring to God's promise to "bind up my testimony, seal my teachings." While these and a few other passages in the Bible attest to the rather widespread ownership of seals, many of the texts themselves cannot be dated precisely. Nor can it be assumed that everyone who possessed and used a seal could read or write — indeed, the inability to do so might have been one reason for having a seal, although someone must be presumed to have been literate or the whole business of sealing something would have been pointless.

Literacy

I have regarded literacy as one criterion in discerning an upper class of society. Do the biblical texts add any essential information? Many scholars have suggested that biblical texts such as Deuteronomy 6:6-9 — God instructing the Israelites to "write" the commandments on their doorposts — indicate early and widespread literacy. But this passage, although set by the Deuteronomistic editors in the Mosaic era, is almost certainly quite late, probably postexilic, and it offers no real evidence for the early Iron Age. In fact, the text actually implies that the oral tradition was still the primary means for transmitting knowledge. Many of the other allusions to writing in the biblical patriarchal and Mosaic eras reflect the same preliterate stage of cultural evolution, such as Exodus 17:14. This passage relates how, after the battle of Amalek, God said to Moses: "Write this as a memorial in a book and *recite* it in the ears of Joshua." Thus the mention of writing in these and related texts is really an anachronism, not historical evidence.

In any case, the important point is that the biblical writers, whose oral and written traditions go back at least to the 7th if not the 8th century, assume that literacy was relatively widespread in the days of the monarchy. The archaeological data corroborate that, but they do so independently.

A Very Specific Convergence

Rarely does one specific archaeological discovery find direct mention in the biblical texts, for reasons that we have noted frequently. The biblical writers' cosmic overview often makes them oblivious to the details of ordinary life. However, the excavations at Dan, on the northern border, recently brought to light a large plaza outside the city gate. Here there was a series of several unique structures that suggest extramural "bazaars," or marketplaces. One is inevitably reminded of the *ḥuṣṣôt* (outer installations) that Ahab was given permission to construct in Aramean Damascus, and that the Arameans were granted reciprocally in Samaria (1 Kings 20:34). These were like "duty-free" shops (above).

Primary Data

In all the above cases (and in other chapters) where we can make a correlation between archaeological data and the biblical text, we have raised the question of what these texts contribute to our history of the 8th century B.C.E. And the answer again is: not much, and nothing essential, or even helpful. For instance, we actually have the ivories, the seals, the weights that the biblical writers mention occasionally. We even have the correct names and values of all the weights, whereas the biblical writers mention only a few, like *pîm*, and they don't know or don't give either its name ("sheqel") or its value. Again, our ivories are mentioned a few times, but these references remained enigmatic for centuries until the modern discovery of the actual ivory panels that we now know were used to decorate expensive Phoenician-style furniture.

So which are the "primary data," the essential sources of reliable information for history writing? A fair-minded observer, free of biblical or antibiblical bias, can only conclude that the archaeological evidence must now take precedence. In other words, it is the artifact that illustrates and "corroborates" the texts, not the texts that corroborate the archeological data. These artifacts do not need corroboration. That fact will have significant implications below.

PART III: THE MEANING OF THINGS

The vast majority of people in ancient Israel and Judah lived in smaller towns, villages, and farmsteads in the countryside. So I have offered a detailed discussion of "how it really was" for them in Chapter VI. Here I will instead try to imagine how the elite ruling classes and the upper middle class in the large urban centers might have seen their world.

For one thing, kings and their retinue would probably have felt how heavy the crown weighed on their heads. Kings everywhere in the ancient Near East ruled by a presumed "divine right." But the gods were capricious, the oppressed masses restless (coups were frequent and violent). Kings grabbed what they could and enjoyed it while it lasted. Archaeologically we now know something about the conspicuous consumption — the wretched excess — of the kings of Israel (if not Judah). But if kings were routinely deposed, those who connived with them went with them. Collective guilt was assumed.

The relatively few who rose to the ranks of the middle class in the larger towns and cities did so by ingenuity and sheer determination. No one had any real education, or for that matter much experience of the wider world. How would an aspiring trader in a village amass any capital to move up the economic and social ladder? Yet some did.

We have seen what amounts to villas in a few cities. These would have been the residences of a few businessmen or landowners who had made it. If one demonstrated managerial skills, and especially if one had learned to write a bit, an administrative post might have become available. A degree of wealth and status accrued to that. But being near the top of a rickety ladder would have brought little lasting satisfaction or confidence. Life may have been brutal for the masses, but it was hard even for the few elites. And when the long-expected Assyrian threat materialized (Chapter X), the elites knew that they would be the first target.

CHAPTER VIII

Religion and Cult

Widespread religious beliefs and practices characterize every ancient society of which we know anything. Ancient Israel and Judah were no exception. From the beginning of both critical biblical study and archaeological investigations in Palestine (the Holy Land) in the 19th century C.E., religion has been a major topic as well as the motivation of many scholars. Indeed, until recently the archaeology of the region has been widely understood as biblical archaeology. Today, however, the discipline is often called Palestinian, Syro-Palestinian, or Levantine archaeology. Alternately, some speak simply of the archaeology of Israel, Jordan, Syria, etc. However, the story of the demise of classic biblical archaeology and the growth of an independent, secular, professional discipline that has come of age is one that has been told many times before and need not detain us here.[1]

PART I: THE ARCHAEOLOGICAL DATA

After some years of neglect (or revulsion), the study of Israelite religion has recently burgeoned. Yet most treatments have typically focused on the analysis of the biblical texts, even though many recognize that this is largely the study of texts *about* the religion, not the phenomenon itself. Even at best, this inquiry focuses on the theological ideals of the Hebrew Bible — on "Book religion" — rather than on the real religions (if numbers count) of most in ancient Israel and Judah, that is, folk religion. And

---

1. See, most recently, Dever 2000 and references there, especially 1985a, 1992. Portions of this chapter are adapted from Dever 2005a. See also Chapter II above.

virtually no recent scholar, not even the archaeologists who now control the fundamental data, has done an adequate study of the latter.

In writing my 2005 book on folk religion, *Did God Have a Wife? Archaeology and Folk Religion in Ancient Israel,* I attempted a synthesis of all the known archaeological data. I also surveyed nearly all the more conventional, text-based works on Israelite religion, pointing out why none is satisfactory. By far the best was by a biblical scholar unusually familiar with archaeology, Ziony Zevit. His *Religions of Ancient Israel: A Synthesis of Parallactic Approaches* (2001) is a magisterial work, more valuable than most precisely because it takes archaeological data seriously.[2]

Here I shall draw on the archaeological data once more, but this time with several differences. (1) The period covered will be restricted to the 8th century B.C.E. (2) The treatment will be less topical, more diachronic, focusing on change and the explanation of change. (3) The influence on the environment, both natural and cultural, will play a more important role.

In Chapter VII, I discussed the several annual feasts and festivals that followed the rhythm of nature's cycle, all based originally on the old Canaanite agricultural calendar. These were not at any time specifically "sacred" celebrations, rather than secular. There simply was no such distinction in the ancient world, and certainly not in ancient Israel and Judah. The *whole* of life was permeated by the presence of the gods. These annual observances were instinctive, intuitive. They were given systematic theological meaning only toward the very end of the monarchy (or even later in the exile and return) when the centuries-old oral traditions were reduced to written form as Scripture — the Hebrew Bible substantially as we have it, the foundation of still later rabbinic Judaism.

That means that in assessing earlier Israelite religion in the Iron Age, we must always remember that ordinary folk had no written Bible, nor, being mostly illiterate, could they have read a Bible had they had one. For most people there was no Sinai covenant, only vague stories of a Moses; no written code like our Ten Commandments, only folk wisdom that was often sufficient to govern rural life in preindustrial, tribal societies. Perhaps natural customs like observing a weekly day of rest, or celebrating the monthly New Moon, had been in place from earliest times. Circumcision

---

2. Dever 2005a, 32-62. In addition to Zevit 2001, see also Hess 2007, from a more conservative approach. For my critique of Zevit see Dever 2005a, 45-46. For an excellent brief survey of archaeology and cult, see Vriezen 2001. See also King and Stager 2001, 319-63 (although not specifically on folk religion).

and avoiding pork may well date back to Israelite origins as well. But these were probably more "ethnic markers" than written law. The prevailing law was that of the village elders.

Certainly no one in villages and towns in ancient Israel could have known in detail the more than 600 laws in the book of Deuteronomy (even if it had been written already). And many of the rigid rules, like the one requiring all males to attend festivals in Jerusalem three times a year, or letting the land lie fallow every seventh year, would have been impossible to observe in the life of an agricultural society and economy.

The fact is, most ancient Israelites had never been to Jerusalem in their whole lives; had never seen the Temple or met an official Levitical priest; had little familiarity with the developing "Book religion" of the elite establishment; and remained largely polytheistic (and naturalistic) until the end of the monarchy. We are dealing here with "folk religion," the religion of the masses, which ironically is illuminated sometimes by its *condemnation* in the Hebrew Bible. But it is better illuminated by the mounting archaeological data we have. It is this new understanding that prompted my 2005 book.

Having described the general religious ethos, let me now turn to specific cultic places and religious rites, those best illuminated by archaeology, and only incidentally by the biblical texts.

Before turning to more specific archaeological sites and data, let us offer some criteria for defining "cult," that is, the *practice* of religion.

1. A cultic site is one that is deliberately "consecrated" for religious rituals, often marked off from other public and especially private sectors, perhaps even isolated.
2. Cultic sites are often located on elevated sites, such as promontories or hilltops, in order to be "nearer" to the deities.
3. Cultic installations exhibit unusual architectural features, such as a series of small rooms, standing stones, altars, basins, and other unusual features.
4. The artifacts are "exotic," such as offering stands, chalices, figurines, etc.
5. There is material evidence (optimally) for sacrifices, such as food or drink offerings.

For heuristic purposes, we can divide our survey into several categories, the first being cult installations. By "cult" I refer simply to the practice of religion, rather than beliefs, since archaeology is better suited to document the former. (I gladly leave the latter to theologians and clerics.) In doing so, we shall move generally from the north to the south.

Cult Places of the 8th Century B.C.E.

Temples, Sanctuaries, and Shrines

I have already dealt with the site of Dan on the northern border, an administrative and cultural capital.[3] A major feature in addition to the monumental fortifications is a large cultic installation on the highest summit of the mound, but still near some of the springs. This impressive installation began in the 10th century according to the excavators, when a "high place" (the biblical *bāmāh*) was built. This was a massive stone platform, approached by a steep flight of steps and topped by a series of small adjoining rooms. The foundation was built of well-fitted masonry, the upper courses dressed in fine Phoenician style (ashlar).

In front of the high place was a public courtyard or plaza, the sole architectural feature being a large stone "four-horned" altar with its own temenos (or enclosure) wall. The only parallel for such an outsize altar has been found at Beersheba; Dan and Beersheba were reputed to be the borders of ancient Israel.[4] A small horned altar, of the usual type, was found nearby. Off to the side of the plaza was a tripartite building on a longitudinal axis, in the first room of which was a low stone altar built into the floor, with three iron shovels lying nearby. This, however, was a later addition to the high place.

Faulty excavation and sketchy publication make the phasing of the Dan cultic installation difficult. But by the 8th century, it appears that the high place (Bamah A and B) and the large horned altar were still in use. Several Phoenician-style figurines, both male and female, probably belong to this horizon (below). A large olive press and a bronze-working installation may also date to the 8th century. A spring pool with a large tub nearby appears to have been connected with lustrations. House 9235 is also associated with the plaza. Finally, in the courtyard between the two city gates there was found a low stone altar with five small standing stones behind it (below).

3. Chapter IV; cf. Dever 2005a, 139-51. See also Biran 1994; Zevit 2001, 180-96.
4. See Dever 2005a, 139-41, 158-59; Zevit 2001, 180-96. For a reworking of Beersheba, see Herzog, Rainey, and Muskovitz 1977.

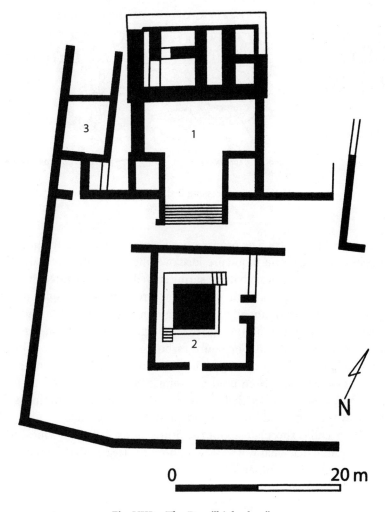

Fig. VIII.1. The Dan "high place":
(1) the bāmāh; (2) the large altar; (3) the liškah, or tripartite building.
Sharon and Zarzecki-Peleg 2006, fig. 10

On the basis of these archaeological data alone, what can we say of the religious practices (if not beliefs) of those who frequented the shrine at Dan? First, we must consider the probable overall function of the shrine. Because of Dan's strategic location, as well as the public plaza and the monumental character of the architecture, it is reasonable to conclude that Dan was a well-known sanctuary that served a large area of the northern king-

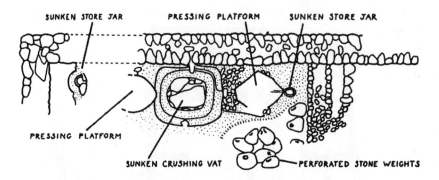

Fig. VIII.2. Olive-pressing installation at Tel Dan.
Stager and Wolff 1981, fig. 1

dom in the 8th century. The bronze priestly scepter, made on the premises, suggests that a local priesthood presided over the shrine. But the scale of the installation makes it clear that the shrine served a larger clientele.

The olive oil press in the temenos (sacred precinct), under priestly supervision, was undoubtedly used for anointing both priests and worshipers. The spring pool and nearby tub suggest lustrations, also well known in the ancient cult. The figurines, both male and female, will be discussed below. Finally, the stone altar and iron shovels (if contemporary) would obviously have been used for animal sacrifices, and indeed burnt bones and ashes (unspecified) were found nearby. The offering stand could have served in addition for food and drink offerings.

If we could speculate about the liturgical uses of the shrine and its cult paraphernalia, what would we say about the larger environmental setting and its possible influence? Dan is unusual among the sites in Israel in its situation among the perennial underground springs that form the headwaters of the upper Jordan River. Its cool, luxurious surroundings are enhanced by groves of trees, making it look more like Switzerland than the arid Middle East. It is a truly miraculous site. It is hard to believe that the ever-flowing springs and evergreen trees would not have had a mesmerizing effect on worshipers visiting the site. Dan was unique in the entire region, and its fame must have spread far and wide. Pilgrims who came to Dan would undoubtedly have left feeling cleansed and renewed, and blessing whatever deities they had venerated there. Shrines connected with groves of trees on elevated heights, as well as chthonic deities associated with fresh-flowing springs, are known everywhere in the ancient Near East, and for obvious reasons. Water is a potent symbol of life everywhere

Fig. VIII.3. Oak trees at Horshat Tal.
Photo: W. G. Dever

in the arid lands of the Levant: the reassurance of ongoing life in the midst of the omnipresent threat of death and oblivion. Even today, the national park at Horshat Tal, in lower Galilee, is frequented by admirers, as it has been from time immemorial, who revel in the huge native Palestinian live oak trees (the last ones remaining) and the hot springs that bubble up everywhere from the ground.

The sacrifices, lustrations, and libations carried on at Dan were also typical of ancient Near Eastern religions and folk practices generally, and they too would have been deemed efficacious in placating the deities and securing their favors. If folk religion is "what works," Dan was probably a justly famed sanctuary in the 8th century b.c.e., as it already had been for two centuries, if not longer.

Samaria, the capital some thirty-five miles to the south of Dan, was principally a royal stronghold in the 8th century. The acropolis has only been excavated in select areas. But there is evidence for a cult installation, however small.[5] Locus E 207, a rubble-filled trench, produced a substantial quantity of cultic objects and pottery similar to those from Cave I in Jerusalem (below). Perhaps this is evidence of "feasts for the dead," well known from earlier Canaanite rituals (the marzēaḥ banquet; cf. below). But we do not know whether such feasts at the site, if any, were private or for public officials. Once again, however, religious practices were traditional, yet capable of adapting to changing conditions, such as the impending Assyrian threat. The name Samaria in Hebrew means "watchtower." What would be more appropriate than watching and waiting with the deities venerated there?

Jerusalem, the other state capital, in the south, would be expected to exhibit monumental cultic structures. Yet the presumed Temple — the national shrine — is not attested archaeologically at all save for a possible artifact or two. A small ivory pomegranate scepter, inscribed "Sacred for the priests of the Temple of . . . ah," may be a relic.[6] But it was purchased on the open market and could be — the inscription at least — a forgery. An Iron Age temple probably did once stand beneath the present 7th century c.e. Dome of the Rock, a Muslim shrine. But the barring of archaeologists from conducting excavations or surveys anywhere in the area of the Temple Mount precludes our knowing anything more than the probable loca-

---

5. See Dever 2005a, 117; Zevit 2001, 234. See also Chapter IV above.
6. There is a formidable literature pro and con. But see conveniently Hess 2007, 276-78, and references there.

Fig. VIII.4. Ivory scepter head from Jerusalem

tion. All present reconstructions are based on supposed parallels with Canaanite or Phoenician temples excavated elsewhere, when compared with the somewhat obscure biblical references in 1 Kings 5–9.[7]

However, at least two other cultic installations in the Jerusalem area have been excavated and have better credentials, possibly also "high places" (although this identification depends upon the biblical term). Dame Kathleen Kenyon excavated a large natural cave, somewhat artificially enlarged, a few hundred yards south of the Temple Mount.[8] Cave I was filled with several hundred objects, including nearly 100 anthropomorphic and

7. On the Solomonic Temple see Dever 2001a, 144-47; add Bloch-Smith 2002b; cf. also Monson 2000.

8. Kenyon 1974, 143; Holland 1977, 154; Holladay 1987, 265, 74; Zevit 2001, 706-13; Dever 2005a, 155-57. Cf. n. 9 below.

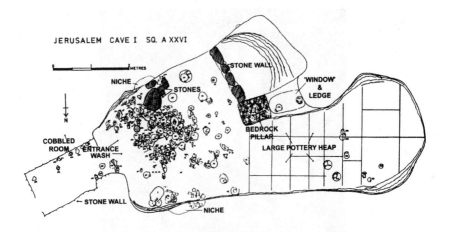

Fig. VIII.5. Plan of Cave 1, Jerusalem (7th century B.C.E.).
Zevit 2001, fig. 3.44

zoomorphic figurines. Other cultic objects included offering stands, a model shrine, miniature couches, and a terra-cotta "rattle" (below).

There is also a substantial amount of domestic pottery (ca. 1,200 vessels, or about 90 percent of the finds). Thus scholars are divided over whether Cave I was simply a dump for ordinary debris, a *favissa* (cult repository) for a nearby sanctuary, or a full-fledged cult installation. The pottery suggests final use of Cave I in the 7th century B.C.E., but it may have been first used in the 8th century, with a long life span typical of most cult sites (below). Jerusalem itself was probably a cult place for centuries prior to Israelite times. It is significant that despite all vicissitudes it remains a renowned holy place today.

The other possible cultic site in the Jerusalem area consists of twenty large tumuli (stone heaps) on hilltops on the western outskirts of Jerusalem. They were partially excavated in 1923, then reinvestigated in 1953. Associated with this complex are a perimeter wall, a large platform, a paved area, some pits, and an enclosure full of burned animal bones. The few tumuli excavated produced quantities of 8th-7th-century pottery, especially cooking pots and bowls. These tumuli may have had a cultic function, probably associated with feasting of some sort, and possibly connected with funerary rites, especially those connected with nonroyal observances or folk religion.[9]

9. See Amiran 1958; Holladay 1987; Dever 2005a, 157-58; Zevit 2001, 206-10.

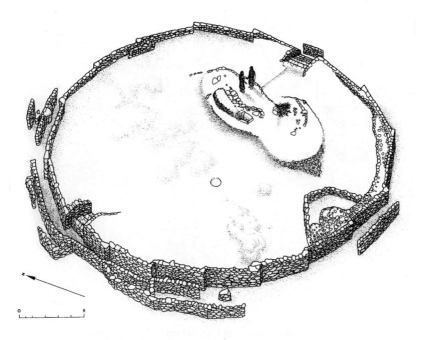

Fig. VIII.6. Plan of a large 8th-century tumulus near Jerusalem.
Zevit 2001, fig. 4.4

A small temple has been thought to exist at Beersheba, clearly a regional administrative center in the 8th century. However, this "temple" was reconstructed largely on the basis of negative evidence — what was not found. Yohanan Aharoni recovered several large stone blocks that once had made up the four-horned altar we have noted (like Dan), not *in situ*, but dismantled and incorporated into later walls. He associated the altar that had once stood somewhere else with a "basement building" that he thought had been originally a temple, destroyed when the altar was dismantled. That hypothesis has been contested; in any case, Aharoni's 8th century has been lowered to the 7th century by general consensus.[10]

At nearby Arad there can be no doubt about a full-fledged temple, with priestly personnel and cultic objects clearly attested. It was excavated by Yohanan Aharoni in the 1960s. This building was controversial from the moment of its discovery. Some scholars argued that it could not have been a "temple" (there weren't supposed to *be* any). Others thought it simply a

---

10. Aharoni 1973; Zevit 2001, 171-74; cf. Dever 2005a, 158-59. Cf. also n. 4 above.

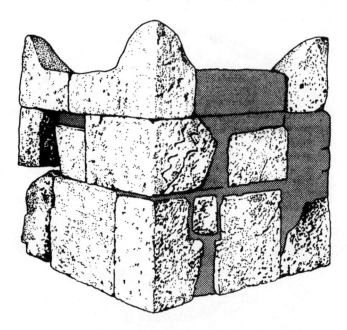

Fig. VIII.7. The Beersheba four-horned altar, reassembled.
Adopted from a photo. Israel Antiquities Authority

desert "tabernacle." Still others assumed that it might have been a temple of sorts, but surely not "Israelite." And estimates of the date ranged all the way from the 10th century to the 7th century. No final publication ever appeared, but several recent reexaminations of the excavated material have clarified matters considerably, especially the question of date. All now agree that the temple must be 8th century, that is, post-Solomonic by some two centuries. The temple was thus in use not through four or five strata, but only in Str. 10-9.[11]

Iron Age Arad was a small fort east of Beersheba, on the Judean border with the Negev Desert. The complex is roughly square, with thick walls with offsets-insets. The temple occupies almost one-quarter of the interior space, located in the northwest corner. It is the only well-preserved element within the fort. The use of the other spaces is uncertain, but they were probably the living and storage areas for the troops of the garrison, which must have been quite small. Some light is thrown on the size and

11. Herzog 2001; Herzog et al. 1984; Herzog, Aharoni, and Rainey 1987. Cf. Dever 2005a, 170-75; Zevit 2001, 156-57. For the plan, see fig. IV.31.

Fig. VIII.8. The Arad temple complex.
Photo: W. G. Dever

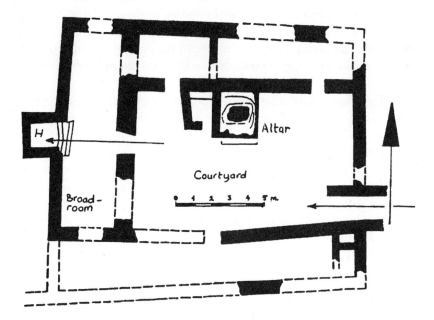

Fig. VIII.9. Plan of the Arad temple.
Keel 1997, fig. 170

function of the fort by the more than 100 ostraca found, documents written in ink on pieces of broken pottery (above). Most have to do with provisions, but some mention names that are known from priestly families in the Bible. One (no. 18) refers to the "temple of Yahweh," which I interpret not as the Jerusalem Temple but as the local temple at Arad.

The rectangular temple, like the one in Jerusalem, is basically tripartite in plan, with three rooms arranged along a central axis. The first room, with an off-center entrance, is an open courtyard with a large stone altar on one sidewall and a corridor or storage area *(favissa?)* behind that. Near the altar in a walled-off compartment to one side were found an offering stand with a removable bowl and a large oil lamp. Nearby was a small bronze weight in the form of a crouching lion.

The next chamber was shallow but wide. There were probably low stone and mud-brick benches around the walls, but these were poorly preserved. Beyond that, the third room was only a small niche (five by three and a half feet), approached by a single step. The entrance was at one time flanked by two square, finely dressed stylized horned altars, which had some traces of burned organic material on the tops (unfortunately not analyzed). A curtain may have closed off this inner sanctum. At the back wall apparently stood two large undressed standing stones, one larger than the other, one with faint traces of red paint. But these *māṣṣēbôth* (above) were not found there *in situ*. They were recovered (along with a third) from under a later plaster floor, along with the two altars mentioned above (there is some confusion in preliminary reports).[12]

If physical setting influences the location and function of sanctuaries and temples, as I argue here, then the Arad temple has a clear rationale. Here on the edge of the hostile Negev Desert and along the border of neighboring Edom was a fort where a military garrison was stationed, clearly in harm's way. If religion has to do with "ultimate concern," the soldiers at Arad would have been moved to appeal to any gods they knew (not just Yahweh).

The most spectacular Israelite or Judean sanctuary ever found is part of a 9th-8th-century fortress in the eastern Sinai Desert at Kuntillet ʿAjrûd (fig. IV.34 above).[13] It was excavated by Israeli archaeologists in

12. For the notion of some biblical scholars that dismantling of the *māṣṣēbôth* was due to the reforms of Hezekiah, see Herzog et al. 1984 and references there. For the biblical terminology, see LaRocca-Pitts 2001. See also Dever 2005a, 118, 136-54.

13. Publications on ʿAjrûd are numerous, but see Meshel 1978; Beck 1982; and cf.

1975-76, but it remains largely unpublished, possibly because of the sensa-
tional and troubling graffiti and drawings found there (below). It looks
like a typical Middle Eastern caravansary, or stopover station on one of
the desert routes crisscrossing the eastern Sinai between the Mediterranean and the Red Sea. It is on an isolated hilltop near small wells, still frequented by Bedouin.

Kuntillet ʿAjrûd is essentially a one-period site, occupied continually
in the mid–9th to mid–8th century. The pottery not only confirms that
date but makes it clear that, although remote, this is an "Israelite" site, with
both northern and southern (or Judean) contacts. The main structure atop
the mesa is a rather typical Iron Age Judean desert fort, rectangular in plan
with casemate (double) walls and square towers at the corner, and a partially open courtyard in the center. There are food storage and cooking facilities on the lower level, and steps indicate an upper level, no doubt with
sleeping quarters. This complex was probably staffed and guarded by a
small permanent force, but it would also have provided shelter and provisions for many desert travelers and traders. Scholars have debated the
function of Kuntillet ʿAjrûd, especially whether it was a sanctuary site.[14]
But there is clearly a shrine incorporated into the gate, and this shrine was
a center for cultic activities.

The site is thus a fort, but it also served quite sensibly as a sort of
"inn"; and it had, as other sites did (above), an indisputable "gate shrine."
The shrine consists of two rooms flanking the offset gateway as one
comes into the courtyard from the plastered outer plaza. There are low
benches around the walls of these rooms, and each is partially partitioned
off across the back wall to form a *favissa*, or place to discard cultic items
that must not be profaned by ordinary use. The walls and benches of the
two siderooms are plastered, as are other portions of the larger complex.
The rationale of the plan is clear; anyone coming or going must pass
through the sacred area. There were two fragmentary outlying buildings
at the far side of the plaza, but the gate shrine was the focal point of the
entire complex.

In the two bench rooms, the *favissae*, and in the courtyard nearby

Holladay 1987; Keel and Uehlinger 1998, 210-39, 259-63; Day 2000, 104-25; Hadley 2000, 104-
25; Dijkstra 2001, 17-31; Zevit 2001, 370-405 (the best discussion); Aḥituv 2006, 313-30. The
following discussion is based on Dever 2005a, 170-95, 219-24.

14. See references in n. 13 above. The view of some that the site was not a religious
center appears to rest on a very simplistic view of religious practices.

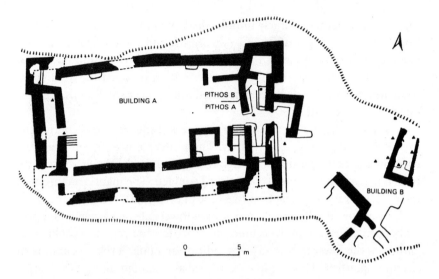

Fig. VIII.10. Plan of the Kuntillet ʿAjrûd complex.
Barkay 1992, fig. 9:30

were found several inscriptions painted in the plaster walls, two large storejars with painted scenes and inscriptions, and quantities of pottery. Elsewhere in the complex were other painted plaster inscriptions and drawings, as well as a large, heavy stone bowl inscribed around the rim "Belonging to Obadiah, the son of Adnah; Blessed be he by Yahweh," no doubt a votive.

Many fragmentary Hebrew inscriptions were found at Kuntillet ʿAjrûd, but neither a catalogue nor adequate photographs have yet been published. Zevit's translations, based on firsthand examination in the Israel Museum, are among the best.[15] Of particular interest here is that the corpus of Hebrew inscriptions contains clear references to at least four deities: Yahweh, El, Baʿal, and Asherah. Where the names of these well-known deities are paired, their occurrence is even more significant. Thus we find the names of male deities in parallel, indicating that they are held in equal esteem, in texts like this one:

> To bless Baʿal on the day of w[ar,
> To the name of El on the day of w[ar.

15. Zevit 2001, 370-405. See also Aḥituv 2006, 313-30, and references there.

More revealing, however, are the names of "Yahweh" and "Asherah" paired on several inscriptions. A wall inscription in one of the bench rooms of the shrine reads

To [Y]ahweh (of) Teiman (Yemen) and to his Ashera[h.

ʿAjrûd is thus an atypical archaeological site in many ways, in particular because of the wealth of written material it has produced. I cite these texts because they are nonbiblical and indeed are archaeological artifacts that fit our category of primary evidence. Again, we know even the names of the deities venerated there (at least four of them).

Several large storejars were found in the shrine, also with Hebrew inscriptions. One (Pithos A) has a long inscription that ends "I [b]lessed you by (or 'to') Yahweh of Samaria and by his Asherah." The second storejar (Pithos B) is similar but reads "Yahweh of Teiman and his Asherah." Both storejars also have elaborate, rather exotic painted scenes. Pithos A depicts the well-known Phoenician motif of a cow suckling her calf (identical to the motif on 9th-8th-century carved ivory panels); a stylized palm tree (looking rather phallic) flanked by two rampant wild goats, a common motif in earlier Canaanite iconography; a large lion; what may be a bull; and, most importantly, a scene showing two standing males (?). The Phoenician and Canaanite motifs are familiar, and they are not really unexpected if we are dealing with syncretistic folk religion, as is certainly the case here.

On Pithos A there is an intriguing painted scene below the inscription discussed above. It shows two figures that are best understood as the Egyptian god Bes, very popular in the Levant in the Iron Age as a deity of good luck and also of celebrations in the cult like music and dancing. To one side is a seated half-nude female figure, playing a lyre. Scholars have been puzzled by this figure, but I have long argued that the lion throne, reserved for royalty and deities in the ancient Near East, identifies her as a goddess. In this case, she must be the very goddess named in the inscription above: Asherah, the old Canaanite Mother Goddess and consort of the chief male deity El.[16]

16. This view of Asherah as Yahweh's consort, which I first advanced in Dever 1984, was initially controversial but has since become the view of many scholars. Cf. Olyan 1998; Day 2000; Ackerman 1992, 2003a; Keel and Uehlinger 1998; Toorn 2003; Hadley 2000; Smith 2001; Wiggins 2001; Becking et al. 2001; Dijkstra 2001; Vriezen 2001; and Cornelius 2004. Cf. my full-scale treatment in Dever 2005a, 176-251.

Fig. VIII.11. Pithos A, Kuntillet ʿAjrûd.
Meshel 1978, p. 12

What explains such an elaborate cult installation far out in the Sinai wilderness, dozens of miles from the nearest civilization (and it is our best-known example)? For one thing, the ʿAjrûd fort served only a small garrison, members of which were well aware of their exposed position. Moreover, what would have been more natural for travelers and traders on the well-worn routes nearby than to stop off and pray for a safe journey? It appears that ʿAjrûd may have also served as a pilgrimage site (like the nearby fort at Kadesh-barnea?). Finally, as many of us know, the Sinai Desert is awesome in itself and has inspired mystics and saints over long centuries. Why not a temple there?[17]

Household Shrines

We have looked at a few monumental temples and smaller village sanctuaries. Presumably, however, most cult practices were carried out in house-

17. Ancient Judaism, like early Christianity (and Islam), exhibits a marked "wilderness motif."

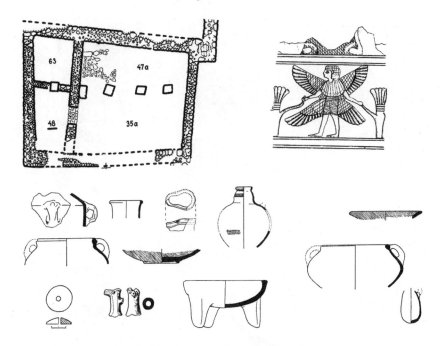

Fig. VIII.12. Household cultic items from L. 47a, 48 (= Str. VI) at Hazor.
Yadin et al. 1958, pl. LCV: 6:20; CLXXIII

hold shrines, especially since Israel and Judah were primarily rural societies. It has been suggested that wives and mothers were often the real "ritual experts," not priests of any sort. They would have officiated in various religious rites, perhaps daily, surrounded by their families. If there was any other religious functionary in most small towns or villages, it would have been a soothsayer, or shaman. Yet we have seen to date very little evidence of family shrines, in part because until recently archaeologists were preoccupied with public rather than domestic architecture. Now there are a few clues in published field reports.[18]

At Hazor in upper Galilee, finds in Str. VI of the early to mid 8th century illustrate what household shrines of the period would have looked like. In Area A, L. 47a and 48, belonging to a typical 8th-century four-room house,

18. The following discussion treats individual sites, but the only extensive synthetic treatment is ironically by a biblicist, Rüdiger Schmidt, of the Westphalian Wilhems University in Münster, Germany. I have not cited his work in the bibliography, listing only works in English.

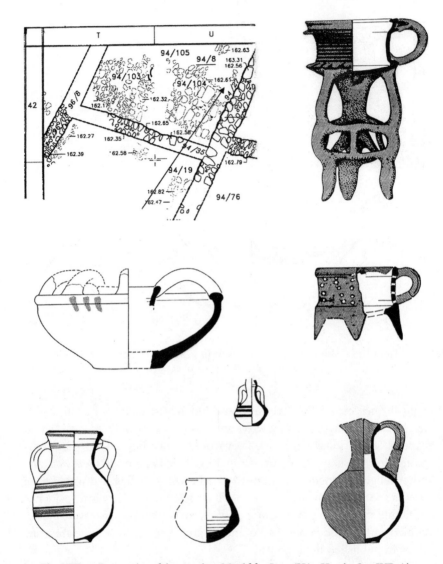

Fig. VIII.13. Domestic cultic remains, Megiddo, L. 94/H/8, H-3 (= Str. IVB-A).
Finkelstein, Ussishkin, and Halpern 2000, figs. 11.43:13, 15, 19; 11.44:5; 11.45; 11.46.2, 6, 8; 11.47; 11.48

were found, among other things, a tripod basalt offering bowl, a zoomorphic figurine head, and a carved ivory panel depicting a griffin. Str. V, of the late 8th century, yielded information from other four-room houses in Area A (L. 13-16; 44). One item was a fragment of a terra-cotta "cultic mask."[19]

Megiddo, another district administrative center, provides additional evidence for household shrines. A cultic niche was found in a room of House 2081 of Str. IVB. Among the contents were three other offering stands; two small stone altars; several unusual Cypro-Phoenician vessels; a censer, several amulets and stamp seals; and several metal objects.[20] One room of a complex dated to Str. IVA (L. 99H8) yielded a large group of ceramic vessels, including several fine Phoenician-style pitchers, along with an elaborate offering stand, a rare censer cup, and a fragment of a zoomorphic vessel.

Tell Ḥalif (Lahav), L. G8005, is interpreted as a household shrine with objects similar to those described above at Megiddo, and it is clearly late 8th century in date.[21]

Rooms of several houses of Beersheba Str. III produced assemblages of cultic items, including a chalice fragment, a Judean Pillar Base figurine, a miniature lamp, and a miniature couch (L. 25). Another figurine came from L. 48 of Str. III. From L. 442 and 443 in a courtyard house there came a figurine head, two miniature limestone altars, and a miniature couch. House 808 yielded two zoomorphic figurine fragments. All in all, Beersheba has produced our largest assemblage of 8th-7th-century cultic artifacts, including forty-three Judean Pillar Base figurines and eleven horse-and-rider figurines.[22]

What do these (and several other) Iron Age "cult corners" imply for the practice of folk religion, especially in the predominant rural areas? The Tell Ḥalif house may be illuminating. The contents include (1) items typically used in food production and consumption (storejars; jugs and juglets, cooking pots; plates and bowls; and grinding stones; plus some cow and sheep bones); (2) a few utilitarian items, perhaps consecrated for daily use by both sexes (spindle whorls, bone discs, arrows); (3) and a few more specifically cultic objects (an offering stand, two *māṣṣēbôth* [standing stones], two female figurines).

These objects suggest that among the religious rites that went on at

19. See Yadin et al. 1958, 14-20; pl. LVI:9; LVII:22; LXV:13-20; CLI; Yadin et al. 1960, pl. LX:10; CCII.

20. Finkelstein, Ussishkin, and Halpern 2000, 145-47, 301-13; fig. 11:43-51; fig. 12:38.

21. Hardin 2010, 133-34. See also above, Chapter VI.

22. Aharoni 1973, pl. 6, 22-28, 45, 52, 70, 71, 75, 84, 94; cf. Zevit 2001, 175-76.

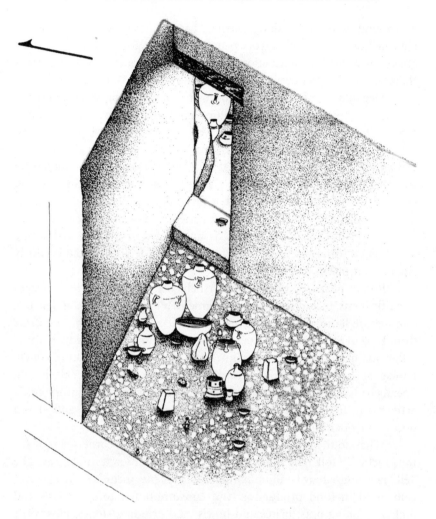

Fig. VIII.14. Household shrine at Tell Ḥalif.
Hardin 2010, fig. 5:12

Tell Ḥalif were the presentation of food and drink offerings to the gods, hoping for continued fertility; communal feasting; the blessing of beasts and fields; consecration of everyday utensils; and no doubt prayers (and perhaps songs) to the goddess for the conception and safe rearing of children. The wives and mothers were probably the real ritual experts at the household shrines. In any case, we may be fairly sure that no one read the book of Deuteronomy, quoted our prophetic works by heart, or sang the

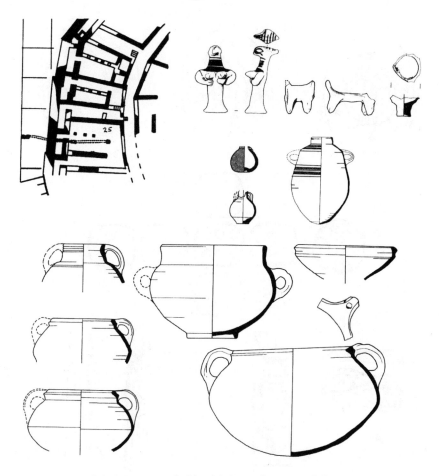

Fig. VIII.15. Household cultic items from Beersheba III.
Aharoni 1973, pl. 70:16-21; 71:1-6; 94

Psalms we now have. The overriding concern (which finally became enshrined in Book religion) was not verbal formulations of any kind, but a ritual practice that would placate the gods and secure their favor.

One class of smaller cultic objects is difficult to illustrate for the 8th century specifically. It would include items used for divination or "magic."[23] Earlier tombs have yielded dice and polished astragali (sheep/

23. On "magic," see Dever 2005a, 125-35; cf. further Jeffers 1986; Dolansky 2008. For miscellaneous cult objects, see Bloch-Smith 1992, 86-90, 94; Dever 2005a, 133-35.

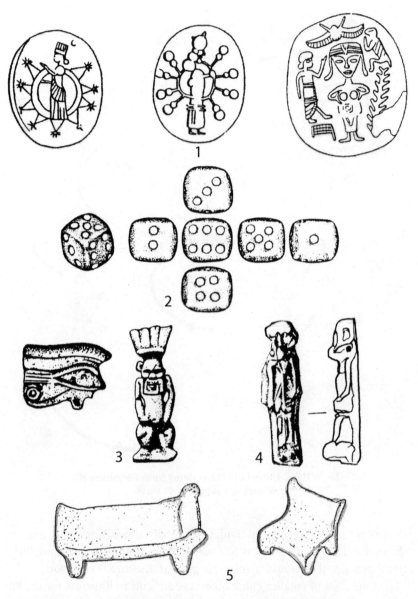

Fig. VIII.16. Items used for divination or magic. (1) Seals depicting Ishtar; Lachish,
Ornan 2001, fig. 9.17; (2) a faience die and its six sides; (3) Bes figurine and Eye-of-
Horus amulet, Lachish; (4) faience Sekhmet amulet, Tel el Far'ah; (5) miniature
couch and bed, Lachish tomb

Keel and Uehlinger 1998, fig. 288a, b (288b, Beth-shan) (1); Biran 1994, fig. 157 (2); Tufnell 1953, pl. 34:8, 14
(3); Chambon 1984, fig. 63:7 (4); adapted from Tufnell 1953, pl. 29:21, 22 (5)

goat knuckle bones) for casting lots. In the Iron II period we find hundreds of images, which when found occasionally in cultic context were no doubt used as good-luck charms. The miniature furniture discussed above would also likely have had magic connotations, since they model other, less visible phenomena. Among the most conspicuous apotropaic devices in late Judean tombs are Egyptian-style faience Bes figurines and Eye-of-Horus amulets, whose function as popular good-luck charms throughout the Levant is well known.

Other Cult Paraphernalia

I have suggested above that cult places are usually fairly obvious, both from the unusual architectural features and from the "exotic" small finds. These criteria may more readily characterize large public temples and sanctuaries. They also apply, however, to smaller village or household shrines, although these by nature are less visible in the archaeological record. And until recently many archaeologists neglected to look for them, or missed the clues. Only recently in our discipline has the "archaeology of cult" resurfaced, this time with some intellectual rigor and better-excavated materials.

In spite of the importance of architecture, cult places are also recognized by the artifacts associated with them. Long ago the Megiddo excavators published a volume entitled *Material Remains of the Megiddo Cult.*[24] It is these remains — the small finds — that most directly reflect the behavior of devotees, which is after all what we want to get at. And if these objects are found in an otherwise "cultic" context, we have two lines of evidence that converge. Let us see, therefore, what we can sort out from the archaeological data alone, without any input from biblical texts.

Mās̄s̄ēbôth

Several sites thought to be cult places have produced unusual artifacts. First we have large standing stones.[25] These stone slabs, some six feet high or more, are found in the earlier (10th century) gateway at Tell el Far'ah

---

24. May and Engberg, 1935.
25. See Dever 2005a, passim. On the biblical terminology see Zevit 2001, 256-63; LaRocca-Pitts 2001; Bloch-Smith 2004.

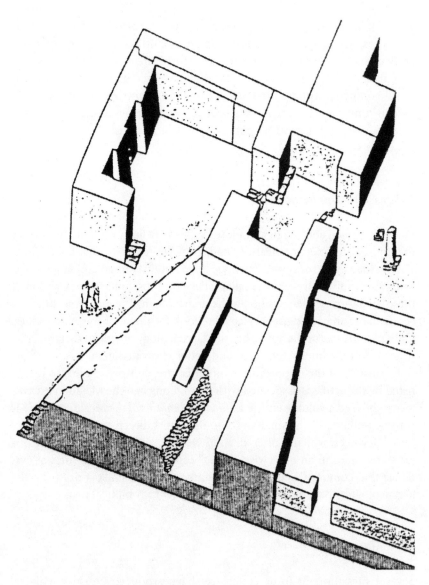

Fig. VIII.17. *Māṣṣēbāh* in the Tell el-Farʿah N. gate area.
Chambon 1984, pl. 66

(Tirzāh), and notably in the inner sanctum of the Arad temple, where they are paired (above). A group of five smaller standing stones forms the backdrop of a low stone altar in the outer gate plaza at Dan. While those standing stones are not self-explanatory, they are unusual, and their deliberate placement and use surely reflect some sense of the numinous, the "other." The association with altars and gate-shrines strengthens this assumption.

Altars

Similarly conspicuous stone structures are the single or grouped stones that form what appear to be altars or "offering tables." The ones we happen to have from ancient Israel and Judah are relatively obvious.[26] The low stone platform in the Dan gate complex, referred to above, is an excellent example. Small bowls found placed on the altar confirm its use for food and drink offerings.

The platters for offerings were found at the foot of an obvious stone altar in the forecourt of the temple at Arad (above), one of them happily supplying a text. It is inscribed with the Hebrew letters *qōf kāf*, no doubt an abbreviation for *qôdesh kōhānîm,* "set aside/sacred for the priests." Several other nonbiblical texts on the Arad ostraca (potsherds with inked inscriptions) actually mention priestly families connected with "a temple of Yahweh." Here we even have the name of the deity worshiped at Arad — Yahweh — a rare bit of written evidence from excavations.[27]

Another class of altar is the "four-horned" altar.[28] We have already discussed the two large ones known from the 8th century, found at Dan and Beersheba. At Arad, two very stylized medium-sized horned altars (?) flanked the entrance to the inner sanctum.[29] The more common variety, however, is a small portable altar, only a foot or so high, undoubtedly used for burning incense. We have dozens of examples, most dated to the Iron II era, a few to the 8th century, most of them in domestic, not temple, contexts.

26. See Zevit 2001, 288-314; Dever 2005a, passim.
27. On Arad generally, see n. 11 above. On the Arad inscriptions, see Aharoni 1981; Aḥituv 2006, 92-154.
28. See Gitin 2002.
29. See nn. 10, 11 above.

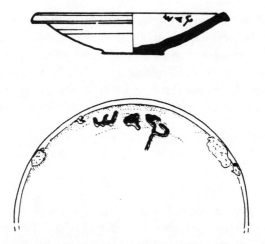

Fig. VIII.18. Offering bowl from the altar at the
Arad temple, reading "Holy."
Aharoni 1981, 35

Facilities in Preparation for Liturgical Rites

Serving in the ancient Near East temple, and probably in smaller sanctuaries as well, required anointing oneself with oil or aromatic substances,
preferably produced on-site under priestly supervision. Just such an installation is the large olive press and basin found in the temple precinct at Dan
(above). Very similar presses and basins have been found elsewhere, notably 10th-century examples at Tell el-Farʿah (N.) and Taʿanach.[30]

Lustrations with purified water were also apparently common in antiquity, as they remained so into much later times. Possible examples
would include the spring pool in the Dan temple compound discussed
above. The symbolism — cleansing oneself of pollution — is transparent.

Terra-Cotta Implements of the Cult

Small cultic artifacts made of baked clay would have been ubiquitous in
any ancient sanctuary — indeed, they are one way of defining a cult instal-

30. For Tell el-Farʿah, see Lapp 1964; for Dan see Stager and Wolff 1981; Chambon
1984, pl. 63:1. For Taʿanach, see Stager and Wolff 1981; cf. Zevit 2001, 181-96, 235-41; Dever
2005a, 115-16, 142, 151-55.

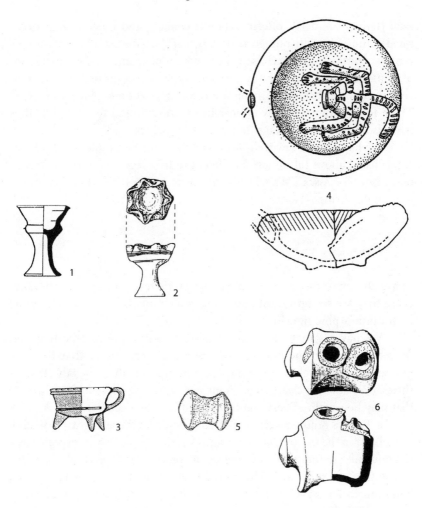

Fig. VIII.19. Small cultic artifacts. (1) Chalice, Hazor VA; (2) seven-spouted lamp, Dan; (3) censer, Ammon tomb; (4) *kernoi*; (5) terra-cotta rattle, Lachish tomb; (6) ceramic zoomorphic vessel (for libations?), Gezer. Scale = 1:10.

Amiran 1967, pl. 68:18 (1); Biran 1994, fig. 128 (2); Amiran 1967, pl. 101:11 (3); Bloch-Smith 1992, fig. 130 (4, 5); Dever, Lance, and Wright 1970, pl. 37.9 (6)

lation. None of these were common domestic items. They were "exotic" by nature, often one of a kind, and therefore set aside or consecrated for sacred use (although the distinction between "sacred" and "secular" was not common in the ancient world generally).

Such easily recognized cultic artifacts would include the following:

naoi (temple models); offering stands; chalices and bowls (often decorated); unusual multispouted lamps; *kernoi* ("trick vessels" for libations); censers; "rattles" (and perhaps other musical instruments); various kinds of miniatures, usually furniture; various types of vessels probably used as votives; and especially anthropomorphic and zoomorphic figurines.[31] These terra-cottas typically appear in sanctuaries and temples, but they may also be found in village and domestic shrines.

We have only a few well-attested 8th-century examples of the terra-cottas listed above (although for the entire Iron Age we could cite examples from all classes). We will discuss those we do have when looking at household shrines (below).

Figurines

I have chosen to discuss these obviously cultic terra-cottas separately, because they are so significant and yet so enigmatic. Let us first look at the anthropomorphic figurines.

We have as many as 3,000 terra-cotta anthropomorphic figurines from ancient Israel and Judah. They range in date from the 12th to the early 6th century, although they are most common in Judah in the 8th-7th centuries. (We have no clearly male figurines, from any context, for whatever that may be worth.) These can be divided into two general types.[32]

a. Figures holding a circular disclike object to the left breast (usually). The object in the figure's hand or hands has been variously interpreted as a tambourine, another type of frame-drum, or a molded bread cake or a representation of a sun disc.[33] The frame-drum theory is supported by several ethnomusicologists (you can't play a tambourine clutched to your breast). I have suggested along with a few other scholars that the object is best seen as a mold-made bread cake. We have archaeological evidence elsewhere for bread molds, as well as for the tradition of baking special cakes for religious festivals and feasts. These figurines are found both in the north and the south, from the 10th to the early 6th century.[34]

31. See n. 23 above on *naoi,* see Dever 2001a.
32. On the figurines see Holland 1977; Kletter 1996 (a corpus); Vriezen 2001, 58-60; Zevit 2001, 267-76; Moorey 2003; Meyers 2007; Dever 2005a, 176-95, 219-24; Dever 2010; Dever forthcoming. On the biblical texts, see Toorn 2002.
33. Paz 2007.
34. See references in nn. 30, 31 above.

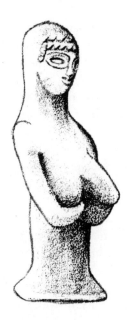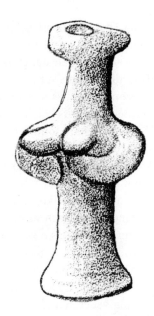

Fig. VIII.20. Judean Pillar Base and Pinched Nose figurines, 8th-7th centuries.
Vriezen 2001, fig. 13

b. Figures with outstretched arms, usually supporting the breasts. This type can be further divided into those with separately mold-made elaborately coiffured heads, and a vernacular type with a face formed simply by pinching the clay to shape a nose and two eyes. Both subtypes are called Judean Pillar Base figurines, because of their columnar lower body and also because they occur only in Judah after the Assyrian destructions in the north (late 8th to early 6th century).

The main issue concerns the use of these figurines. That may be relatively easy, since these nude figurines obviously emphasize the female breasts — especially when compared with their much more flagrant Canaanite predecessors, which have long been called "fertility figurines." Thus all the figurines of this type, early or late, have also been called fertility figurines, often thought to represent the great goddess Astarte. Today the term "fertility" is in some disrepute because of the tendency of earlier scholars to regard the Canaanite cult as lascivious. And in the Iron Age, the principal female deity was not Astarte, but Asherah. Nevertheless, these figurines are not Barbie-like dolls. They clearly have to do with reproduction: the desire of their users to be able to safely conceive, bear children, and lactate. These are in effect "prayers in clay": talismans to aid women in having children, nursing them, and rearing them through childhood. These were all extremely dangerous times for women in antiquity, yet they desired children intensively.

A second issue has to do with the identification of female figurines. Context often helps to explain exotic or enigmatic artifacts, but not in this case. The figurines are found in houses, streets, dumps, fills, tombs, sanctuaries, and elsewhere. Relatively few come, however, from clear cultic contexts. An exception would be Jerusalem Cave I, which produced a group of sixteen, but it may or may not have been a cult site (above). More significant is the mold for making the disc-type figurines, from a 10th-century village shrine at Ta'anach in northern Israel.[35] This was found in a clear cultic context, but it was obviously intended for mass producing the figurines for use *elsewhere* — probably in domestic contexts. This may be our best clue to their use.

But who *is* the figure represented? Do the figurines depict a goddess who is being venerated? Or do they depict humans, in which case they would be simply "votives," in effect stand-ins for the worshiper, like votive candles in a church. That question, too, is much debated.[36] To simplify the discussion, the evidence suggesting a goddess is chiefly that the figure is nude, which seems unlikely if she represents ordinary women. Furthermore, these figurines seem to be the Iron Age successors of the Canaanite ones that undoubtedly depict a goddess (usually Astarte, but sometimes Asherah). On the other hand, many of the similar images found elsewhere in the Levant, as for instance in Cyprus in this period, are votives.[37]

I do not find the latter argument persuasive, based as it is on comparisons that may not be relevant. Therefore, I identify the figurines with the popular Iron Age goddess Asherah. However, since the figurines do not come labeled, we have no direct textual evidence telling us whom they represent. (Obviously the biblical texts must be left out of consideration at the moment.) If they do represent Asherah, however, they need not be understood as "idols." Rather they are symbols, physical manifestations of deities whose presence and power are invisible. Would knowing the name of the goddess make much difference?

---

35. Lapp 1964; cf. Dever 2007, 151-54.

36. The literature is vast, but see the references in n. 16 above; cf. Dever 2005a, 176-251. See also Dever forthcoming, contra Meyers 2007.

37. See Connelley 1989; cf. Dever 2010.

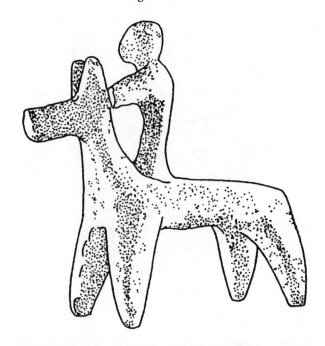

Fig. VIII.21. Horse-and-rider figurine, Lachish tomb (7th century).
Keel and Uehlinger 1998, fig. 33b

Another category of figurines is the horse-and-rider figurine, although some have no rider.[38] These, too, are enigmatic. They are similar to the Judean Pillar Base figurines in date and distribution. Some scholars have regarded the obviously male rider as a male deity, perhaps Baʿal, who in Canaanite lore is called "Cloud Rider" (as is Yahweh in some biblical passages).[39] All we can say is that they are not toys; they surely have some cultic connotations. Yet context is unhelpful here as well. Most come from late Judean tombs. Again, no labels. (On tombs, see further below.)

Cultic Objects in Use

If we look only at the above artifacts, what could we conclude about the cult and cult practices in 8th-century Israel and Judah? Many of the objects

38. There is little discussion, but see Taylor 1993.
39. See Day 2000, 91-95; cf. Deut. 33:26-27.

Fig. VIII.22. Small four-horned limestone incense altar, Megiddo.
Vriezen 2001, fig. 10

are clearly intended for animal sacrifices, such as the larger stone altars. Smaller stone altars could also be so used; but the horned varieties are known to be used mostly for burning incense.

The small cup-censers, although rare in western Palestine, were obviously used for burning and probably waving incense. The large cylindrical offering stands, when fenestrated, were also designed for burning incense. Whether or not they were fenestrated, a removable bowl at the top would have been ideal for food and drink offerings. Footed chalices would have served a similar purpose.

Kernoi, or "trick vessels," while rare, are well designed for ceremonially pouring liquids, that is, for libation offerings.[40]

The clay "rattles" (as well as a few terra-cotta flutes, etc.) would have been part of the musical performances that characterize nearly all religions.[41]

40. See Dever 2001b.
41. Cf. Meyers 1991 on music in the cult; Braun 2002 and Burgh 2006 on ancient Israelite music; and King and Stager 2001, 285-98, generally.

The few *naoi* we have from Iron II are model temples, whose function is clear, especially from iconographic motifs associated with a deity or pair of deities.[42]

The various miniatures — lamps, chairs, and couches — were probably symbolic offerings of familiar household items to the god.

Various "luxury" items, usually ceramic vessels, would obviously be gifts for the gods for answered prayers, or "payment" for vows made.

The identity and function of the ubiquitous female figurines have been explored above. The almost universal absence of male figurines might indicate either that female deities dominated in the cult, or that it was permissible to model female deities but not male ones.

Tombs and Burial Practices

Archaeologists have long regarded tombs and burial practices as particularly illuminating, especially with regard to religious beliefs. Fortunately we have a great deal of relevant evidence. The Iron II tomb plans themselves are instructive.[43] The typical 8th-century tomb is a rock-cut, multiroom chamber with benches that seems to represent a "house for the dead." These tombs were used for generations, sometimes producing dozens of burials and hundreds of objects. The bones of previously buried individuals were periodically removed to repositories under the benches when other individuals were interred. All this implies that in ancient Israel and Judah, rural societies and economics, the family, and the continuity of the family were the fundamental values in life and in death. Again, we do not require texts to tell us this.

Nevertheless, we do happen to have some Iron II tomb inscriptions. An 8th-century rock-cut tomb within view of the Temple Mount in Jerusalem (fig. VII.7 above) has a Hebrew inscription that reads:

This is the tomb of (Shebna)-Yahu,
who is "over the house." There is
no silver or gold, only his
bones and the bones of his slave-wife

---

42. Dever 2001b; and most recently Dever 2008.

43. See Dever 2003b, 131-35. The standard reference is Bloch-Smith 1992; add Lewis 1989; Schmidt 1996.

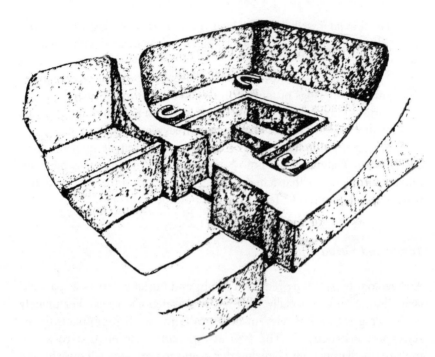

Fig. VIII.23. Schematic plan of a typical 8th-century Judean bench tomb.
de Geus 2003, fig. 41

with him. Cursed be the person
who opens this tomb.[44]

Here we actually have a family tomb. And the inscription helps to preserve the legacy of the individual and his family.

Another Judean tomb of the 8th century is the one I excavated in 1968 at Kh. el-Qôm in the Hebron hills (probably biblical Makkedah).[45] Here there are two inscriptions in one typical bench tomb. One inscription, beside the doorway in one chamber, reads "Belonging to Ophai, son of Netanyahu. This is his tomb-chamber." The other, above the door to another "room," reads "Belonging to 'Uza, daughter of Netanyahu." This, too,

44. See Avigad 1953; cf. Dever 2001a, 219-20; see also Aḥituv 2006, 44-48. See also fig. VII.7 above.
45. See Dever 2005a, 131-33, 196-98. There is now an extensive literature, but cf. references in Dever 1999b; and add Day 2000, 49-52; Zevit 2001, 359-70; Aḥituv 2006, 220-26; and especially Lemaire 2006.

Fig. VIII.24. Repository under benches in Kh. el-Qôm tomb

is obviously a family tomb of one named "Netanyahu," a good Hebrew name meaning "Yahweh has given/provided."

Another inscription from Tomb II is even more revealing. Here we have a Hebrew inscription contemporary with the Kuntillet 'Ajrûd inscription (above). This inscription reads

> Belonging to 'Uriyahu, the governor. This is his inscription.
> Blessed be 'Uriyahu by Yahweh:
> He has been saved from his enemies by his Asherah.
> (Written) by 'Oniyahu.[46]

Here we have another inscription with a blessing formula naming a pair of deities. Nothing could better illustrate the intersection of religious beliefs and burial practices.

If we did not have these tomb inscriptions, what would the remaining archaeological evidence tell us of religious beliefs in the 8th century? First, the typical rock-cut multichambered tomb resembled a house, even to its central courtlike *arcosolium*. That concept — a "house for the dead"

46. See the résumé in Dever 1999b. See also Zevit 2001, 359-70; Aḥituv 2006, 180-200.

Fig. VIII.25. Inscription no. 3 from Tomb II at Kh. el-Qôm.
McCarter 1996, no. 87

— is another reminder of the centrality of the family in the Israelite-Judean worldview.

The practice of multiple burials over very long periods of time and the conservation of the bones of previous burials carries with it the notion of continuity with deceased family members, as though to preserve their memory and heritage. Some of the ceramic offerings, usually ordinary bowls and the like, might indicate that feasts were held either at the time of death or when visiting the family tomb on special occasions. Other grave goods are obviously cultic: Bes, Eye-of-Horus, and other good luck amulets; miniatures of one kind or another (above). These were surely deposited in the belief that the dead somehow continued to exist after death and could even be blessed by the actions of the living. These are indeed speculations; but they are reasonable, and they accord well with what we know of almost all ancient societies.

One final tomb inscription underlines this point, an inscribed silver

286

amulet from Ketef Hinnom, from a tomb in the cliffs overlooking the Hinnom Valley south of the Temple Mount in Jerusalem. Although it is later (late 7th century) and beyond our purview here, it does attest to the confluence of religion and burial practices. The inscription reads in part:

> May Yahweh bless you,
> keep you.
> May Yahweh make his
> face shine upon you
> and grant you peace.[47]

PART II: THE BIBLICAL DATA

As I argued in some detail in Chapter II, virtually all histories of Israelite religion have been little more than histories of the literature *about* that religion. The Hebrew Bible, written by elitists (and propagandists), is an ideal portrait, not of what most people actually believed and practiced, but of what they should have believed and practiced — and would have, had these theologians, these nationalist orthodox parties, been in charge. The Hebrew Bible is thus best considered as a "minority report." The real report — the more accurate portrait — is the one that we can and must now derive from information supplied by modern archaeology.

Sometimes the two sources converge, but more often they do not. The disconnect between artifact and text means that, ironically, it is the biblical texts that condemn folk religion that best illustrate it. Thus the religion of the masses consists of almost everything that the biblical writers forbade. So the texts do have at least a negative value. Beginning with temples and sanctuaries, let us look at some specific instances where there may be a possible correlation between text and artifact.

We have noted 8th-century temples and sanctuaries at Dan, Arad, and Kuntillet ʿAjrûd (there may have been others). The Hebrew Bible does mention cultic installations in general, but only to declare that they must be dismantled, or to deny that they even existed. References are too numer-

---

47. See Barkay et al. 2004. In ancient Israel, when one died he/she was "gathered to the fathers." See further Bloch-Smith 1992. Add now Faust 2008b on the similarity of the four-room house and the Judean rock-cut tombs, emphasizing the centrality of the family in a time of social change in the 8th-7th centuries. Cf. Yezerski 1999.

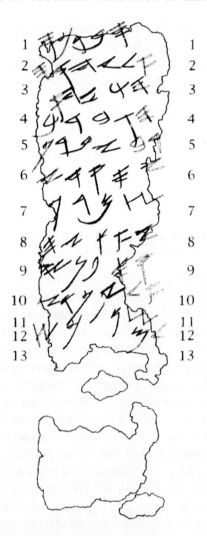

Fig. VIII.26. The first Ketef Hinnom silver amulet.
Barkay et al. 2004, fig. 30

ous to mention, mostly in Kings and the prophetic works. The only legitimate temple is Solomon's Temple in Jerusalem, the political and religious
capital of the united monarchy, remaining so throughout the divided
monarchy. But we know virtually nothing archaeologically of that temple,
except for Iron Age parallels elsewhere (above). We have never been able to
excavate the Temple Mount. Thus we must move on.

I have cited virtually all the evidence, both archaeological and textual, in my *Did God Have a Wife?* (2005). Let us look first at the only full-fledged temple we have, at Arad (above), which we can safely date to the 8th century. There is no reference to that structure in the Hebrew Bible, or even to Arad itself, that yields any information. Some scholars have suggested that the deliberate burial of the three *māṣṣēbôth* (standing stones) in the inner sanctum of the temple may be evidence of the reforms of King Josiah of Judah. 2 Kings 18:4 specifically states that Josiah "removed the high places *(bāmôt)* and broke down the pillars *(māṣṣēbôth)* and cut down the Asherah *('ăšērāh)*" of such sanctuaries. Skeptics argue that this and other such passages about a "cultic reform" under the leadership of Deuteronomistic reformers and prophets are simply propaganda.

I would suggest that at least the biblical writers describe the general religious situation accurately, because they knew it well. I have argued that we now have archaeological data to illustrate and document almost every single item that Josiah is said to have thrown out of the Temple in 2 Kings 23.[48] Thus archaeology can supply a "real-life" context for such reforms, whether they were actually carried out or not. But the archaeological data, in themselves, are not decisive.

At Dan in the north, we have somewhat better prospects. The extensive cult installation at Dan, particularly the large open-air platform-altar, is clearly what the Bible calls a *bāmāh*, or "high place." I have discussed this installation and its history at length elsewhere. We may note here that the Dan "high place" may actually be mentioned in the Hebrew Bible (1 Kings 12:30-31).

The remote 8th-century sanctuary at Kuntillet ʿAjrûd, in the eastern Sinai Desert, offers several intriguing possibilities for correlations.[49] First, there are Hebrew inscriptions mentioning "Asherah" alongside Yahweh in a context of blessing. These inevitably recall the prohibition of this very goddess in the Hebrew Bible. The word *'ăšērāh* occurs some forty times in the Hebrew Bible and often refers only to a treelike symbol of the goddess, which one ought to cut down and burn, since it was a cult symbol of the old Canaanite religion.

In half a dozen or so instances, however, the word *'ăšērāh* can refer only to the goddess herself. In 1 Kings 15:13, King Asa's mother Maacah "made an abominable image for Asherah." The reference here is clearly to

48. See Dever 1994.
49. See the discussion in Dever 2005a, 32-62. Cf. also references in n. 13 above.

the goddess herself: one does not make an image for an image. Compare this with 2 Kings 21:7, which states that Manasseh "set up an image of [the] Asherah." 2 Kings 23 couples Baʿal with Asherah, for both of whom "vessels" were made but condemned. So if Baʿal is a deity, so is Asherah. Thus the Kuntillet ʿAjrûd inscription referring to "Asherah" (and, I would argue, the seated half-nude figure on a large storejar) must be taken as a direct three-way connection between artifact and two texts, one nonbiblical, the other biblical.

Above I have distinguished several smaller cult installations, that is, household shrines. Obviously these are too inconspicuous to have been noted in the biblical texts. Furthermore, they are not supposed to have existed, so why mention them? In any case, we have no direct textual correlations of the archaeological examples we have.

We can say something, however, about certain items of cult paraphernalia. First, we have references to standing stones, or *māṣṣēbôth* (from a verb meaning "to stand").[50] These large standing stones, some reaching heights of ten feet, are generally proscribed, because they are associated with the old Canaanite cult. To judge from the numerous references in the Hebrew Bible, they were erected to commemorate an epiphany, the appearance of a deity (Gen. 28:18; Exod. 24:4; Josh. 24:26-27). They are often said to be associated with a *bāmāh*, or "high place" (1 Kings 14:23; 2 Kings 18:4; 23:13-14), or a temple (2 Kings 3:2); or located near an "idol" (Lev. 26:1; Deut. 7:5; 12:3; Mic. 5:13).

Do these biblical references throw any light on the large standing stones we actually have, such as those in the inner sanctum at Arad? They only confirm what we already surmised, namely, that these very impressive standing stones were meant to command one's attention, to inspire one with awe. Such obvious symbols of the "numinous" are to be found in many ancient (and modern) religions.

We have cited both large horned altars and smaller limestone altars. A few biblical texts refer to large altars. Exodus 21:14 describes how an innocent person can cling for dear life to what is obviously a larger-than-life altar. It is interesting, and perhaps significant, that the two archaeological examples we have of such monumental horned altars come from Dan and Beersheba — precisely the biblical borders of Israel (2 Chron. 30:5).

The smaller horned altars, about a foot or so high, are well attested; some forty-five are known to date. They were almost certainly used for

50. See n. 12 above.

burning incense. Sometimes they are found near domestic installations such as oil presses.[51] The Hebrew Bible refers to them numerous times; they are used specifically for burning incense (Lev. 26:30; Isa. 17:8; 27:9). Yet all references to such altars condemn their use for burning incense. So here again it is the biblical prohibition of the small altars that illustrates just how common they were. None of these references, however, mention the "horns" we have. One reference is especially intriguing, the mention of King Ahaz's "altar on the roof of the upper chamber." Precisely such an altar has been found in the debris of a fallen roof at Ashkelon.

The most intriguing cult objects we have are the terra-cotta female Judean Pillar Base figurines, so dubbed because almost all of them are found in Judah, and precisely in the late 8th and early 7th centuries, the period that concerns us here. We have 3,000 or more of them; they are found mainly in domestic contexts (above). So the biblical writers must have known about them. Yet never once are they mentioned anywhere in the Hebrew Bible.

A close examination of all the possible terms for "household gods" *(tĕrāphîm),* "idols" *(gillūlîm),* "graven image" *(pesel),* "molten image" *(māssēkāh),* and "image" *(sēmel)* yields nothing. None of these terms, judging from etymology or usage, can possibly refer to our Pillar Base (or other) figurines. Here the silence of the biblical texts is deafening. Did the biblical writers deliberately suppress any mention of these "pagan" artifacts? And does the widespread popularity — precisely in the era of the so-called religious reforms — say anything about their real significance?

A number of other cultic artifacts well known to us through archaeological discoveries are similarly overlooked for one reason or another by the biblical writers. Among these are *naoi,* or temple models; *kernoi,* or libation vessels; and perforated tripod cup-censers. The *naoi* that we have are earlier than the 8th century, but examples of *kernoi* and censers are known in our period.[52] The surprising thing is that both libations and the burning of incense are acceptable to the orthodox writers of the Hebrew Bible (incense only for the priests, however). Yet they never mention the actual ritual implements used in such rites, like ones that we actually have found.

In summary, it is sometimes the "silence" of the biblical texts, sometimes the condemnation, that conforms to the cult paraphernalia brought

51. See Zevit 2001, 156-70; Dever 2005a, 173-75. See also nn. 27, 28 above.
52. See Dever 1994.

to light by archaeology. But in no case do the biblical texts actually do much to illuminate the artifacts that we actually have. They speak by and large for themselves.

PART III: THE MEANING OF THINGS

In keeping with our intent to focus on the lives of ordinary people, as illuminated primarily by material culture remains, we must now move to a more speculative level of interpretation, risky though it may be. What do all the above artifacts and the texts mean? What was the nature of the cult and of the deities it venerated? What did people feel when they engaged in cultic activities, at home, in a village sanctuary, at a shrine dedicated to a saint, in one of the few temples we have?

Of course, it is impossible to know in detail (even with textual evidence; below). But the material culture remains we have discussed are far from "mute," as some biblicists maintain. Nor do texts necessarily illuminate them. Taken together, these remains make it abundantly clear that in ancient Israel and Judah, as in the Levantine world generally, we are dealing with "fertility religions." For the masses it was practice that mattered, not the correct theological formulations of a few literati (including those idealists who wrote the Hebrew Bible). Thus we cannot look to the textual traditions to illuminate practical or folk religion. Only archaeology can do that.

"Religion" is almost impossible to define in any case. But what is clear is that it attempts to deal with ultimate concern. And it is beyond doubt that in ancient Israel and Judah that concern was fundamentally for survival. In a harsh environment, at the mercy of the elements, surrounded by hostile foes, most people sought to placate the gods and seek their favor as best they could. And in a predominantly rural and agricultural society, that meant giving back, as a token to the gods, what they had provided: the surplus of the flocks, the produce of the fields, and perhaps even progeny. Only these offerings could secure "plenty," without which the human family and its heritage could not survive.

Perhaps 99 percent of the population in ancient Israel and Judah were illiterate. They couldn't have read Bibles even if they had them. They had never met a priest of the royal establishment, nor even visited the Temple in the capital (perhaps not even a regional administrative center). Their entire life revolved around the family, the village, the clan, the world of nature, and the rhythms of the changing seasons (see further Chapter VI).

Some of the upper classes in the few larger towns and cities might have been more theologically sophisticated. But for most, the household shrine was the only temple they knew: the religion of hearth and home. And women of the household — wives, mothers, daughters — were just as likely to serve in the role of ritual expert as any priest. Unless religion worked in that small sphere, it was of no use and would not have survived. It is the artifacts that people made, used, discarded, reused — not the texts of the Great Tradition — that reveal the most about the reality of their daily lives. If histories of Israelite religion are to be written in the future, they will have to incorporate the vast array of information that we now have, thanks to the archaeological revolution that Albright confidently predicted. It has come, even if with some unintended consequences.

CHAPTER IX

Israel's Neighbors

It is obvious that ancient Israel did not exist in a vacuum, even though that may have seemed the case until recently. The birth of modern scholarship — especially the 20th-century archaeological revolution — has brought to light these long-lost neighboring peoples and their cultures.

Here I shall consider in turn Neo-Philistines and Phoenicians along the coast; Arameans to the north; and Ammonites, Moabites, and Edomites in Transjordan. The biblical data, since it is scant and rarely helpful, will be brought in section by section rather than appended as usual. And because we have so little information, I will not attempt the usual "how it really was."

There are useful summaries elsewhere of the cultures of all these peoples,[1] so the treatment here will concentrate on (1) the political and cultural relations with Israel and Judah and (2) those changes over time that we can chart.

Neo-Philistines

The original Philistines were one group of "Sea Peoples" who came from the breakup of the Mycenean world around 1200 B.C.E. and settled the

---

1. See LaBianca and Younker 1995 for orientation and especially the handbook edited by Adams (Adams 2008). See also references in nn. 2, 39 below. The encyclopedia that covers most sites (Stern 1993; 2008) now extends its coverage into Jordan and all the major sites there. For a detailed summary of Jordanian sites, see Stern 2008, 1840-91. See also works cited in nn. 19, 25, 32, 34, and 35 below.

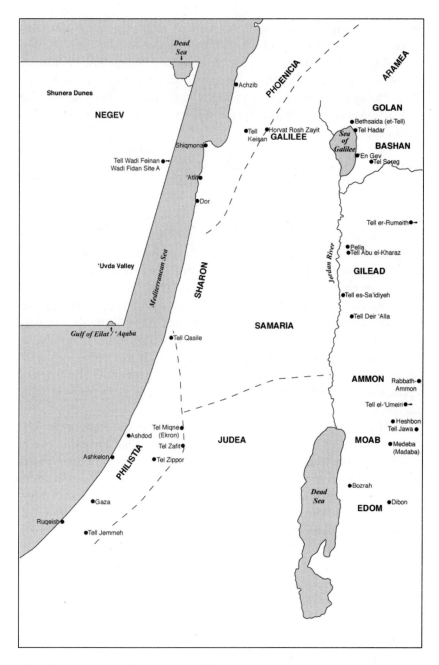

Fig. IX.1. Map of Israel's principal neighbors in the Iron Age, showing a few of the
better-known excavated sites

southern Levantine coast shortly thereafter.[2] After expanding somewhat inland in the 11-10th centuries B.C.E., they appear to have been checked thereafter by the rising kingdoms of Israel and Judah. The continuing Philistine presence along the coast, partly acculturated, may be termed "Neo-Philistine."[3] This culture persisted until disrupted by the Assyrian destructions in the late 8th century and was finally destroyed in the Babylonian conquest in 604.

Here we shall survey only the 8th century, basing our résumé mainly on the few well-excavated and published sites.[4]

Ekron

Philistine Ekron is to be located at Kh. el-Muqanna' (= Tel Miqne), one of the largest mounds in the country, with a forty-acre lower city and a ten-acre upper city. Located at the western border of Judah's inner Coastal Plain, Ekron lay along the major east-west roads. Judean Timna (Tel Batash) was some five miles to the east, and Beth-Shemesh was only about seven miles distant. Ekron thus fronted Judah from its foundation by Philistines in the 12th century (Josh. 15:45-47). It was known in the Bible as the northernmost city of the Philistine pentapolis (Josh. 13:2-3; 1 Sam. 5:10; 7:14). The writers gloat at the prospect of its desolation (Zeph. 2:4; Zech. 9:5-7).

The site was excavated by a joint Israeli-American team under Seymour Gitin and Trude Dothan in 1981-96. The original Philistine city of Ekron had been characterized by distinctive Aegean-style pottery, figurines, temples, and architecture with hearths, as well as heavy fortifications (Str. VII-IV). By the beginning of Iron II (Str. III, 10th/9th century), however, the city had shrunk to no more than ten acres. Str. II B-A of the 8th century produced mostly domestic houses built along several streets, with

2. For orientation to Philistine history and culture, see Dothan and Dothan 1992; Gitin 1998; Killebrew 2008, 197-245; and especially the chapters in Oren 2000. A short summary is found in Stern 2001, 102-29, with bibliography (594-96). See also Katzenstein 1992 on history.

3. This term, while seemingly appropriate, is not yet common. "Neo-Philistine" sites recently or currently being excavated would include Ashdod, Ashkelon, Ekron (Tel Miqne), and Gath (Tel Zafit). The term would best suit the 10/9th-to-late-7th-century period.

4. These résumés depend principally on the anonymous entries on Israel and Jordan in Stern 1993; 2008.

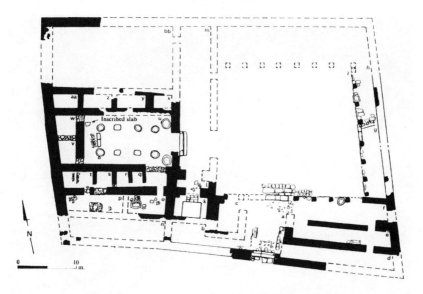

Fig. IX.2. Plan of Str. I temple complex at Tel Miqne (Ekron).
de Geus 2003, fig. 34

pottery that combined coastal Philistine and Judean forms. There were traces of a mud-brick city wall.

Under pressure from the Neo-Assyrian king Sargon II in his campaign down the Levantine coast in 712, Ekron, Ashkelon, and other Philistine towns had paid tribute. But in the pivotal invasion of Judah by Sennacherib in 701 these towns rebelled. The Neo-Assyrian annals record, however, that while the people of Ekron supported the revolt, their king Padi did not, and he was imprisoned and turned over to the Judean king Hezekiah in Jerusalem. (The biblical accounts do not mention this incident.) Thereupon Sennacherib took Ekron, slew the officials and impaled them on stakes, and reinstated his vassal Padi, finally imposing tribute upon him. The archaeological evidence reflects major changes thereafter but no destruction.

Despite being overrun by the Assyrian advance in 701, Ekron quickly recovered, and throughout the 7th century (Str. I) the city flourished under Assyrian tutelage as a major olive-oil-producing and textile center. It thus remained a prosperous outpost along Judah's borders during her final century of existence.

Several ostraca written in the Phoenician script mention a sanctuary dedicated to the old Canaanite goddess Asherah. Nude female figurines

Fig. IX.3. Silver hoard from Tel Miqne (7th century).
Courtesy of Ilan Sultzman/Tel Miqne-Ekron Publications Project

seem to represent the goddess, similar to the contemporary Judean Pillar Base figurines yet distinctive. Here language and cult reflect a degree of assimilation by the 8th century. In Str. IB of the late 7th century a monumental dedicatory inscription found in Temple 650 mentions "Achish, son of Padi," who ruled until the destruction of the site by the Babylonians under Nebuchadnezzar in 604.[5]

Gath

Tell es-Sâfi (Tel Zafit), five miles south of Ekron, opposite Azekah on the Judean border, is certainly ancient Gath, another of the biblical pentapolis cities, although earlier identifications placed it at other sites. It has been excavated since 1996 by Aren Maeir and others. It is even larger than nearby Ekron, consisting of some 100-125 acres. The extent of the original Philistine city of the 12th century has not yet been determined. Provisional Str. 3 belongs to the 9th/8th centuries. It gives evidence of substantial domestic occupation, brought to an end by a fiery destruction that produced hundreds of ceramic vessels. The repertoire includes Cypro-Phoenician types as well as distinctive black-on-red "Ashdod" ware. There were also many types of cultic vessels and even a few Philistine inscriptions, so far not well deciphered.

The destruction has been attributed to the Aramean king Hazael (ca. 840; cf. 2 Kings 12:17), whose siege works may be reflected in the huge ditch found encircling the entire lower city of Gath. In any case, Sargon II later seized the town, along with Ashdod, in 712 (cf. Isa. 20:1).[6]

Ashdod

The large mound of Ashdod (Ar. Isdud; lower city about 70 acres; acropolis about 20 acres) was excavated by the Israeli archaeologist Moshe Dothan and others in 1962-72. Now in decline, the city of Str. VIII, belonging to the 8th century, produced several domestic structures as well as a small temple. Near the altar and in surrounding rooms were found quantities of cult objects: anthropomorphic and zoomorphic figurines, *kernoi*

---

5. Dothan and Gitin in Stern 1993, 1051-59; 2008, 1952-58.

6. Maeir in Stern 1993, 1522-24; 2008, 2079-81.

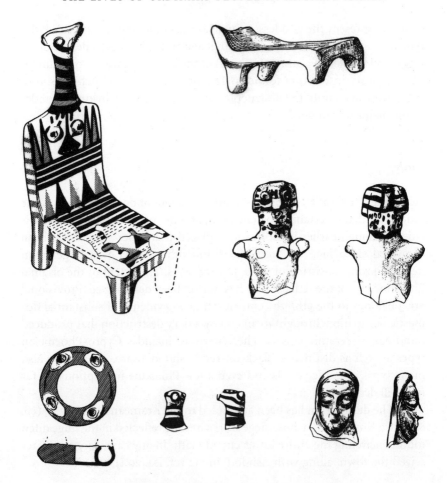

Fig. IX.4. Philistine cultic items from Str. VIII at Ashdod.
Dothan 1971, figs. 62:3, 63:6, 64:8, 66:7, 71:3, 91:1

(libation vessels), miniature couches with the heads of Aegean-style mourner-goddesses ("Ashdodas"), and offering stands.

To judge from Neo-Assyrian texts, Ashdod was destroyed in the campaigns that had earlier obliterated the northern kingdom of Israel. Ashkelon (below) and Gaza are both specifically mentioned in texts of Tiglath-Pileser III (ca. 734). Gaza and Ashdod were finally taken by Sargon II in 712, then Ekron (and possibly Gath) fell to Sennacherib in 701 (cf. Isa. 20:1; Amos 1:8; Zeph. 2:4).

At Ashdod dozens, perhaps hundreds, of burials and secondary burials in refuse pits of Str. VII yielded many human skeletons, some with funerary offerings. These are almost certainly the victims of the Assyrian destruction.

Even more compelling evidence comes from three fragments of a large basalt victory stele with an Assyrian cuneiform inscription. Although these fragments do not mention Ashdod itself, the stele is very similar to one found in the Neo-Assyrian capital of Khorsabad. Nearby Ashdod-Yam ("Ashdod of the Sea") was fortified but also destroyed at this time.

Renewed salvage excavations at Ashdod in 2003-4 revealed an Assyrian-style palace, extending over at least 25 acres (Str. 7). It marks the postdestruction horizon of the 7th century.[7]

Ashkelon

Ashkelon is a huge mound (ca. 150 acres) on the Mediterranean some twelve miles south of Ashdod. It was excavated in the 1920s by British archaeologists, and after 1985 by an American expedition led by Lawrence Stager for Harvard University. Like nearby Ashdod, Ashkelon has yielded extensive evidence for an original Philistine settlement of the 12th-11th centuries. But by Phase 15 of the 9th century, Ashkelon was also in decline. Little has been brought to light except one house with a subterranean grain silo in the courtyard. Refuse from the silo contained imported Phoenician pottery, as well as some fine Samaria-style bowls. No evidence of the 734 destruction known from texts (above) is reported.[8] Judah's hostility is reflected in passages like Judges 1:18 and 2 Samuel 1:20.

Other Neo-Philistine Towns

Other Neo-Philistine towns are known, such as one of the pentapolis cities, Gaza, as well as Raphia and "towns of Ashdod" like Beth-dagan, Joppa, Benei-beraq, and Azor (all up the coast toward Tel Aviv). Gaza presumably lies under the modern city of Gaza and thus remains unexcavated. The location of Raphia is known, but we have only a few chance finds.

7. Dothan in Stern 1993, 93-102; Kogan-Zechavi in Stern 2008, 1573-74; Nachlieli in Stern 2008, 1575-76.
8. Stager in Stern 1993, 103-12; 2008, 1577-85.

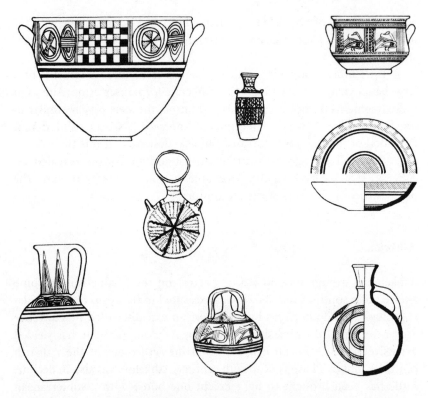

Fig. IX.5. Early Philistine pottery (12th-11th centuries).
Amiran 1967, pl. 90:1, 2, 6, 9, 13; 91:4, 5, 10

Tell Jemmeh, farther south, possibly ancient "Arza near the Brook of Egypt," is mentioned in texts of the Neo-Assyrian king Esarhaddon (ca. 681), but it may have been destroyed earlier. In any case, a unique mud-brick vaulted building in Assyrian style with Assyrian "palace ware" reflects Assyrian domination in the 7th century.[9]

In summary, the Philistine Plain in the 8th century continued several distinctive "foreign" cultural elements that distinguished it from Judah inland, even though the border was not fixed. Distribution maps based on Judean sheqel weights and Pillar Base figurines have shown that such cultural type-fossils did not extend into Philistia. Conversely, many Philistine pottery types did not penetrate inland, even though there was a certain degree of cross-fertilization. While a form of Mycenean Greek was

9. See generally Stern 2008, 1840-91, and bibliography there.

no doubt spoken by the early Philistine invaders, it is clear that their descendants came to speak a Semitic language related to Hebrew. They also adopted the Phoenician script that was closely related to Hebrew. Inscriptions from Ekron in the 7th century reveal that the cult of the goddess Asherah was common to both peoples (above). And both shared the same fate at the hands of the Assyrians in the late 8th century, although Philistia was far less affected, and even flourished in the 7th century.

Despite a degree of accommodation in the 8th century, the biblical writers (from a later perspective) speak of conflicts. In the north, King Uzziah (788/7–736/5) is said to have "made war against the Philistines" (2 Chron. 26:5-8). And King Ahaz of Judah (742/1–726) suffered Philistine raids into the Shephelah and the Negev (2 Chron. 28:18). There is, however, no archaeological evidence of such conflicts. And while the Chronicler makes the above claims, writing perhaps 300-400 years later, the authors of Kings make no reference to such events. Finally, we note what is surely more rhetoric, the implication in such passages as Amos 1:4-8 and Micah 1:10 that the cities of Gaza, Ashdod, Ekron, and Gath will rejoice in Israel's and Judah's defeat (i.e., by Sennacherib).

Phoenicians

The southern Levantine coastal plain was occupied in the 8th century by Neo-Philistines. But farther north, toward Tyre and Sidon, the Phoenicians — descendants of the Late Bronze Age Canaanites — prevailed.[10] Here the border was with western Galilee. A number of Phoenician sites have been excavated, several of which have 8th-century levels (fig. IX.1 above).

Dor

Dor was founded as an early Phoenician site in the 12th-11th centuries, possibly by one group of the Sea Peoples known as the "Sikil." It was excavated from 1980 onward by Ephraim Stern and others. Dor possessed one of the best deepwater harbors along the southern Levantine coast. Close

10. See conveniently Stern 2001, 58-101, and full references there; Lehmann 2001. On Phoenician history and culture generally, see Peckham 1992; Aubet 1993; Lipinski 1991.

relations with Cyprus are witnessed by large quantities of early Cypro-Phoenician pottery. By the 8th century, however, Dor had become a minor Phoenician site, its population probably somewhat acculturated. Scant material from Ph. 9-10 of Area D3 belongs to the 8th century and consists of mostly pottery and objects said to be typically Phoenician. A seal is inscribed "the priest of Dor."

The most important find at Dor was a hoard of nearly nineteen pounds of silver fragments, packed into seventeen cloth bags of about one pound each, each sealed with a clay patty and a signet ring. The bags were packed into a large jug, covered by a bowl, and buried beneath a floor. Such a hoard attests to the wealth of the city, even if little of its architecture has been brought to light.[11]

'Atlit

Some eight miles up the coast, the Phoenician site of 'Atlit is best known for its vast cemeteries, with burials from the 8th century to the Hellenistic era. Some of the early burials were cremated, accompanied by typical Cypriot and Phoenician pottery. There are also shaft graves with similar grave goods.

The Phoenician harbor is the only one sufficiently well preserved along the coast of Israel to yield evidence for early Phoenician maritime engineering methods. Most of the finds of shipwrecks and cargoes, however, date to the Persian and Hellenistic periods.[12]

Shiqmona

Shiqmona is a small low mound (about two acres) situated on a natural promontory that marks the southern limits of the Bay of Haifa. It was excavated in 1963-79 by J. Elgavish of the Haifa Municipal Museum of Ancient Art. Continuous occupation is reported from the 12th to the late 7th century. Town B appears to have been destroyed in the late 9th century, probably by the Arameans. Town C was then destroyed in the mid–8th century, Town D in the late 8th century. These may have been Neo-Assyrian destructions, part of their campaigns down the Levantine coast.[13]

11. Stern in Stern 1993, 357-72; 2008, 1695-1703.
12. Johns in Stern 1993, 112-17.
13. Elgavish in Stern 1993, 1373-78.

Tell Keisan

Tell Keisan, originally near the Bay of Haifa but now inland, is a large steep mound (fifteen acres), possibly ancient Achshaph. From 1971 to 1980 it was excavated by the École Biblique et Archéologique Française in Jerusalem, under Pères J. Prignaud, J. Briend, and J.-B. Humbert.

The 12th-11th-century levels (Str. 10-9) show Cypro-Phoenician as well as Philistine ceramic influences. Str. 8-5 belongs to the 10th-8th centuries, ending perhaps in the Assyrian destructions. The best indication of Phoenician culture is the popularity of Phoenician storage jars, used for far-reaching trade until the late 7th century. Similar jars, mostly for shipping wine, have been found in Cyprus, Turkey, North Africa, and Spain.[14]

Acco

Much of ancient Acco lies inaccessible under the modern town. Nevertheless, recent excavations by Moshe Dothan have shown that there was a fortified Phoenician city in the 8th century. A silver hoard was found in what appears to be the Assyrian destruction in 701.[15]

Achzib

Achzib is on the Levantine coast only five miles south of the modern Lebanon border. The site has been sporadically excavated from the 1940s onward by several archaeologists, among them Immanuel Ben-Dor, Moshe Prausnitz, and Eilat Mazar. The early Phoenician levels exhibit Cypro-Phoenician wares and their imitations. Most of the evidence, however, consists of burials in several cemeteries. Some of the 8th-century burials are cremations, like those in the Phoenician "Tophet" at Carthage. Others are shaft tombs with Phoenician-style pottery. Particularly important are distinctive red-polished jugs, horse-and-rider figurines, and female figurines playing a drum (cult musicians?). The site was destroyed in the campaigns of Sennacherib in 701.[16]

14. Humbert in Stern 1993, 862-67.
15. Dothan in Stern 1993, 17-24.
16. Prausnitz in Stern 1993, 32-35; Mazar in Stern 1993, 35-36.

Fig. IX.6. Phoenician "fertility figurine,"
a cult musician (Achzib).
Vriezen 2001, fig. 15

Rosh Zayit

Rosh Zayit is a small mound (six acres) situated in the foothills of lower Galilee, some ten miles inland from Tell Keisan. It was excavated in the 1980s by Zvi Gal. The principal discovery was a large fortress resembling Assyrian courtyard buildings (the *bit hilāni* model) that had been destroyed in the 9th century. From the ruins came many Phoenician-style storejars, as well as Cypro-Phoenician juglets. Building A, belonging to the 8th century, had an associated oil press. Although somewhat inland for a Phoenician site, Rosh Zayit is probably best identified with biblical Cabul (Josh. 19:27). There is some evidence for trade relations between sites like Cabul and Israelite sites in the north (cf. 1 Kings 20:34, "bazaars").[17]

In summary, the Phoenicians were the northern coastal neighbors of Israel from earliest times in the Iron Age until both peoples fell victim to the Neo-Assyrian campaigns in the late 8th century. Both were heirs of the

17. Maeir in Stern 1993, 1522-24; 2008, 2079-81.

old Late Bronze Age Canaanite civilization. It is significant that Samaria, the northern Israelite capital, was admittedly Phoenician in its culture: ashlar masonry and architecture, carved ivory inlays, red-slipped pottery, even a Phoenician princess (Jezebel). And even in Solomon's Jerusalem, the Temple was constructed by Phoenician artisans and craftsmen. Despite the harsh polemics of the biblical writers (mostly southerners), Israelites and Phoenicians managed to live together in relatively peaceful conditions. That was partly due to their borders being porous (fig. IX.1).

Recent studies have suggested that following the Assyrian destruction of Neo-Philistine sites to the south, Phoenicians penetrated into the area as far as Gaza and even Ruqeish. These movements of peoples were typical of the post-Assyrian conquest period, and they were probably encouraged by the new overlords.[18]

The Arameans

The Arameans of the Iron Age had a similar origin to that of the early Israelites. Both peoples emerged from partly nomadic tribes of the Levant, becoming sedentarized in the 12th century as the Egyptian empire in the Levant collapsed. Coming originally from northern Mesopotamia, the Aramean tribes moved westward and settled in Syria, eventually coalescing into several city-states by the 10th-9th centuries. Thereafter, they pressed to the south and are known from sites such as Yamhad (Aleppo), Qatna, Hamath, and Damascus, especially the Arameans of Damascus (fig. III.1).[19]

We have already noted in general Aramean incursions into northern Israel in the 9th and 8th centuries (above). Let us now look more closely at the excavated sites we have in Israel or on her northern and northeastern borders.

Bethsaida

Bethsaida (Ar. et-Tell) is a twenty-acre mound on the east bank of the Jordan River, where it empties into the Sea of Galilee. Since 1987 it has been

---

18. Rainey 2006, 255.

19. See Daviau, Wevers, and Weigl 2001; Sader 1992. On ancient Ammon generally, see Millard 1992 and the chapters in MacDonald and Younker 1999 and bibliography there.

Fig. IX.7. Gate stele depicting the Aramean deity Ba'al-Haddad.
Bethsaida, 8th century

excavated by an American team under Rami Arav. Iron Age Bethsaida began in the 10th-9th centuries with the Str. 6a-b city walls, gate, palace, and granaries, all destroyed in a great conflagration sometime in the 9th century. Str. 5a-b sees an 8th-century refounding of the fortifications, with a massive triple-entryway gate and several gate shrines. Flanking the entrance to the gate, one shrine had a large basalt stele depicting the Aramean god Ba'al-Haddad. The whole area was violently destroyed, leaving badly burned brick debris a meter or more thick everywhere, undoubtedly the work of the Assyrian campaigns of Tiglath-Pileser III in 732 B.C.E.[20]

Tel Hadar

Tel Hadar is a small mound (2.5 acres) on the eastern shore of the Sea of Galilee, about two miles south of Bethsaida. It was founded in the 11th century (Str. II) as a heavily defended "royal stronghold" according to the Israeli excavator Moshe Kochavi. By the time of Str. I, however, in the 8th century, the site was reduced to little more than a farming village, perhaps

20. Arav in Stern 2008, 1611-15.

Fig. IX.8. The site of Tel Hadar.
Photo: W. G. Dever

a satellite of the newly fortified site of 'En Gev just six miles farther south. It was destroyed in the campaigns of Tiglath-Pileser III in 733-732 and never rebuilt.

During its heyday Tel Hadar was an outpost of the Aramean kingdom of Gesher extending up onto the Golan Heights, whose ruler was one "Talmai, the son of Ammihud." According to the Bible, he was related to King David by marriage.[21]

'En Gev

'En Gev is a low mound on the eastern shore of the Sea of Galilee, excavated in the 1960s by Israeli archaeologists and in the early 1990s by an Israeli-Japanese team. It was founded in the 10th century (Str. 5-4) as a fortified citadel. In the 9th century (Str. 3-2) it was refortified, probably in the course of the Aramean campaigns to the south. Str. 1 represents an unfortified site that was destroyed in the Assyrian campaigns of 733 and 732.

21. Kochavi in Stern 1993, 551-52; Yadin and Kochavi in Stern 2008, 1756-57.

The identification of the site as Aramean rests partly upon Str. 3-2 material, especially an Aramaic inscription on a storejar reading "Belonging to Shaqia (the cupbearer)." In addition, some of the pottery types come from southern Syria. The strong fortifications and public buildings suggest an identification with Aphek (1 Kings 20:30; 2 Kings 13:14-17), an advance Aramean outpost of the 9th century. Tel Soreg is thus eliminated as a candidate for Aphek.[22]

Tel Soreg

Tel Soreg, five miles inland from 'En Gev on the lower Golan Heights, was a small wayside fort in the 9th century, excavated in the 1980s. The fort continued in use into the 8th century, after which it fell into decline. It was presumably an Aramean outpost.[23]

In summary, the Arameans, especially those of Damascus, penetrated deep into Israel periodically throughout the 9th century. The Aramaic royal inscriptions, together with the Neo-Assyrian annals, testify to the extent of these raids. The biblical texts agree broadly, although they are silent or in error here and there.

The Arameans eventually overran all of Israel, Judah, and Philistia under Hazael (ca. 840-810), according to most scholars. These Aramean campaigns ended, however, toward the very end of the 9th century, after the death of Hazael and the succession of his son Ben-hadad (III). According to 2 Kings 13:1-6, 22-25, Jehoahaz king of Israel (819-804/3) repelled Hazael and Ben-hadad. In Judah, Jehoash (Joash; 842/1–802/1) is also said to have withstood Hazael, although he was forced to pay tribute (2 Kings 12:17-18). Thus for the next fifty years or so, there seems to have been an armed truce between Israel and the Arameans.

By the 8th century, both peoples had to put aside past grievances to confront the more urgent Assyrian threat, sometimes perhaps collaborating. The biblical writers have the names of the Aramean kings right. But they were mistaken in continuing to suppose that the Arameans, and not the Assyrians, were their main enemy.[24]

---

22. Kochavi in Stern 1993, 409-12; Kochavi and Tsukimoto in Stern 2008, 1724-26.
23. Kochavi in Stern 1993, 1410.
24. Grabbe 2007, 164-65.

The Peoples of Transjordan

The Ammonites, Moabites, and Edomites in Transjordan were in effect first cousins of the Israelites and Judeans on the other side of the Jordan River, which was never a fixed border (fig. IX.1). They were all northwest Semitic tribespeople who, like Israel, had emerged in the early Iron Age after the collapse of the Late Bronze Age Canaanite culture and Egyptian hegemony. Their languages were very similar to Hebrew, as were the scripts they adopted. Nevertheless, the marginal environment of Transjordan, on the edge of the desert, meant that the trajectory toward statehood of peoples there was much slower. In the light of the burgeoning archaeological evidence, most authorities today agree that true statehood was never achieved, that the more appropriate model is the "tribal state." And even this level of centralization is not evident before the 8th century, if then.[25]

Although these Transjordanian peoples were less integrated, they were seen as posing a threat to the states of Israel and Judah. The famous Mesha Stele, a monumental Moabite royal inscription found in 1868, depicts 9th-century campaigns of the Israelite king Omri against King Mesha. Mesha, however, rallies to retake his cities, where the Israelites had even erected "Davidic altars." Some of the sites mentioned on the stele have now been identified or excavated (especially Madeba and Dibon; below). However, there is no archaeological evidence of the conflicts described on the stele.[26]

By the 8th century it would appear that several Israelite and Judean kings carried out raids into Transjordan. Amaziah of Judah (805/4–776/5) is said to have killed 10,000 Edomites in the "Valley of Salt" (2 Kings 14:7; cf. 2 Chron. 25:14).

In the days of Uzziah (788/7–736/5), the prophet Amos rails against Gilead, Moab, Kirioth, Bozrah, and Teman, well-known towns of Transjordan. Again, however, this may be simply rhetoric; no archaeological evidence supports any actual aggression against these peoples.

Jotham (758/7–742/1) is said to have fought against the king of the Ammonites and prevailed (2 Chron. 27:5), as well as taking tribute.

With this general summary in mind, let us turn now to a brief sum-

---

25. See Sawyer and Clines 1993; Dornemann 1983; Bartlett 1989; Bienkowski 1992; Edelman 1995; MacDonald and Younker 1999; B. MacDonald 2000; Levy et al. 2007; Adams 2008.

26. Rainey 2006, 203-5, 211-12. For more detail, see Dearman 1989.

mary of what we know archaeologically of some of the major regions and
sites of Transjordan.

Bashan

The area designated Bashan is generally opposite the Huleh Basin and the
Sea of Galilee, south of the Golan Heights, down to the Yarmuk gorge (fig.
IX.1). The major sites we know include Rumeith, on the modern Jordanian
border with Syria; Karnaim; and Ashtaroth. Only Rumeith has been excavated, by Paul Lapp in the 1960s (below). The Hebrew Bible regards
Rumeith ("Ramoth Gilead") as a city in Gilead of the tribe of Dan (Deut.
4:43; Josh. 20:8; 21:38). But the size of the site seems too small to permit
that identification (cf. 1 Kings 22; 2 Kings 8:28–9:10). Rumeith is characterized mainly by a large fort constructed in the 10th century (Str. VIII), destroyed and rebuilt in the 9th century (Str. VII-VI), and largely reduced by
domestic occupation by the 8th century (Str. V). Str. V appears to have
been destroyed in the campaigns of Tiglath-Pileser III in 733 and 732.[27]

Pella belongs generally with Gilead, but it is very far to the west, near
the Jordan River.[28]

Gilead

Gilead, south of Bashan, extends from the Yarmuk gorge southward to the
Jabbok River and to the area north of Ammon (fig. IX.1). The only known
Iron Age sites are Ramoth-Gilead (not "Rumeith"; above) and Jabesh-
Gilead, but neither has been excavated. Elsewhere there are a few excavated
sites, but little clear 8th-century material.[29]

Jabesh-Gilead may be located at Tel Abu el-Kharaz, near Pella in the
Jordan Valley. It is a large mound, twenty-five acres at its base, and about
four acres on its flat summit. It was excavated from 1989 to 2005 by a Swed-
ish project directed by Paul M. Fischer. Substantial Iron II remains are reported, including a large building of ashlar masonry and a defensive system with towers.[30]

27. Lapp in Stern 1993, 1291-93.
28. Smith in Stern 1993, 1174-80.
29. See generally B. MacDonald 2000, 195-208, and references there.
30. Fischer in Stern 2008, 1840.

A few other Iron Age sites in Gilead are known but scarcely excavated, like Irbid, but we can say little about 8th-century remains. Sites down in the Jordan Valley, like Deir 'Allā and Tell es-Saiʿdiyeh, are probably not typical.[31]

Ammon

The boundaries of ancient Ammon are not easily determined, since its peoples were often seminomadic (fig. IX.1). The writers of the Hebrew Bible, working perhaps with older sources but writing in the 7th-6th centuries, view Ammon as extending from the Jabbok River (Wadi az-Zarqa), north of modern-day Amman, southward all the way to the Arnon gorge (Wadi el-Mujib), halfway down the eastern shore of the Dead Sea. More realistically, the southern border of Ammon can be said to extend southward only to the plains of northern Moab and including the sites of ancient Heshbon and Madeba (below).

The Hebrew Bible, supplemented by Neo-Assyrian texts and now a few Ammonite inscriptions, yields a few ancient Ammonite placenames. Among them are ʿAi, ʿArôʿer, Abel Keramim, Heshbon, Jazer, Madeba, Minnith, and Rabbath-Ammon. Only a few of these sites can be identified, however, and of these few only Heshbon (Tall Hisban) has been systematically excavated (below). Madeba is known mainly from surface surveys.[32]

Rabbath-Ammon, modern Amman, has produced only chance finds and some tombs. This meager information can be supplemented by several Ammonite inscriptions, including an 8th-century inscription that names several Ammonite kings. A number of towers have been found around Amman, which suggests a fortified kingdom. To this information we can add several surveys and excavations of a number of sites whose ancient names we do not know or can only guess.[33]

31. On Deir 'Allā, see van der Kooij in Stern 1993, 338-42; on Tell es-Saaidiyeh, see Tubb in Stern 1993, 1295-1300.

32. See generally the chapters in MacDonald and Younker 1999; B. MacDonald 2000, 157-70; Stern 2001, 237-58, 605-85, and references there.

33. See n. 32 above, especially MacDonald and Younker 1999.

Fig. IX.9. The Jabbok River.
Photo: W. G. Dever

Moab

Extensive excavations have been carried out by American archaeologists such as Siegfried Horn, Roger Boraas, Lawrence Geraty, Larry Herr, and others in the Madeba Plains Project from 1968 to the present. Initial work at Tall Hisban (clearly biblical Heshbon) concluded that while there was some evidence of occupation in the 10th-8th centuries, the best-preserved data came from the 7th-6th centuries (fig. IX.1).[34]

A similar picture emerges from the project's excavations at Tall el-'Umeiri, a few miles south of modern Amman. Here there are fairly extensive Late Bronze and Iron I remains (13th-11th centuries). But the excavators can only say of Str. 8, which belongs to the 8th century, that there are a few houses, none suggesting a significant settlement.[35]

Nearby Tall Jawa was excavated in 1989-95 by Randall Younker and P. M. Michèlle Daviau. Some 8th-century remains (Iron IIB) are reported,

34. On ancient Moab generally, see Miller 1992; B. MacDonald 2000, 171-83, 609; Stern 2001, 259-67, 609; Routledge 2004. For Hisban, see Geraty in Stern 1993, 626-30.
35. Herr in Stern 2008, 1848-51.

Fig. IX.10. The Arnon gorge; the King's Highway, on the Moab border.
Photo: W. G. Dever

Fig. IX.11. Ammonite round tower at Rujm Malfuf, on the outskirts of Amman.
Photo: W. G. Dever

including well-preserved houses and domestic installations, as well as a casemate city wall.[36]

Another excavation of the Madeba Plains Project is Tall Jalul, three miles east of Madeba. It has been dug since 1992 by Randy Younker and David Merling. Most of the remains are from the Iron II period, but they date mainly to the 7th-6th centuries.[37]

In summary, the tribal states of Ammon and Moab were beginning to form by the 8th century. But they seem to have flourished mainly in the 7th century — in part because they escaped the worst of the Assyrian depredations — and survived until the Babylonian destructions in the early 6th century.

The biblical writers are ambivalent about the Ammonites. They regard them as ancient rivals from the patriarchal and settlement eras. Yet by the Iron II period, there seems to have been a sort of accommodation. The biblical accounts of the reigns of Israelite and Judean kings of the 8th century (2 Kings 13–21; cf. 2 Chron. 24–32) rarely mention Ammonites. The

36. Herr in Stern 2008, 1845.
37. Herr in Stern 2008, 1844-45.

book of Kings does not contain any references. Chronicles, later and less reliable, refers to raids of Amaziah (805/4–776/5) and Jotham (758/7–742/1) against the Ammonites (2 Chron. 25:14; 27:5). Thus far it has not been shown that the periodic destruction of some sites in Jordan can be correlated with the events claimed in Chronicles. Both peoples may have been forced to put aside their differences in order to focus on the growing Assyrian threat.

Edom

Edom stretches south of the Zered Brook (Wadi al-Hasa), at the southern end of the Dead Sea, all the way to the Red Sea. Since most of this region is semiarid and borders on the desert, there was never any large sedentarized population (nor is there today; fig. IX.1).[38] The biblical writers regard the Edomites, like the peoples farther north, as rivals and enemies. According to 2 Kings 14:7, Amaziah invaded southern Edom (near Petra), slaughtered 10,000 Edomites, and renamed the territory (cf. above, on the Ammonites). 1 Chronicles 1 begins a genealogy with Adam (!) and moves on to the kings who "reigned in the land of Edom before any king reigned in Israel" (1 Chron. 1:43). A number of Edomite rites are named, as well as the "clans of Edom" (1:51-54). This passage is strikingly similar to Genesis 36, which is probably somewhat older in its present form (6th-5th centuries). The list of names is almost the same, but of these sites only Bozrah can be identified.

Buseira (biblical Bozrah) is some fifteen miles south of Tafila on the fabled King's Highway skirting the edge of the desert. It was excavated by the British archaeologist Crystal Bennett in 1971-80. She dated a massive building (palace?) in Area A built in "Assyrian style" to the 8th-7th centuries, but she claimed that a destruction within its phasing should be attributed to the Assyrians.[39]

When Bennett dug the site, the pottery of Jordan — particularly the southern region — was not well known. Extensive reworking after her death by Piotr Bienkowski, who has published the material, provides some

---

38. On ancient Edom generally, see Bartlett 1992; B. MacDonald 2000, 185-94; the chapters in MacDonald and Younker 1999; Stern 2001, 268-94, 609-12; and especially Bienkowski 1992.

39. Reich in Stern 1993, 264-66.

clarification. He regards the building in Area A as possibly a temple, but he concludes that Bennett's work was so poor that no precise dates can be assigned to any of her material. The local pottery, however, does seem to show many continuities from the late 8th century (like that at other Edomite sites) all the way to the Hellenistic era. All things considered, we can only conclude that the monumental architecture suggests that Bozrah may indeed have been the capital of Edom at the time the biblical writers compiled their narrative (above; 6th-5th centuries).[40]

Only two other Edomite sites have been sufficiently excavated, nearby Tawilan and Kh. el-Kheleifeh, on the Red Sea. Tawilan was excavated by Bennett in 1968-70 and in 1982, and again inadequate stratigraphy (and publication) leaves us little to say. It appears that "Str. 1-5" all postdate the 8th century (7th-6th centuries) and that the site was not, as previously thought, a major site but only an unfortified town.[41]

Tell el-Kheleifeh, just north of the port of Aqabah, was excavated in the 1930s by the American rabbi/archaeologist Nelson Glueck. He dated a large fortress compound to the 10th century (fig. IV.32 above) and claimed that the site was Solomon's seaport of Ezion-geber (1 Kings 9:26). The material was much debated but not published until it was extensively reworked by Gary Pratico in 1992. Period III belongs generally to the 8th century, perhaps destroyed in the Aramean wars between Judah and Edom (cf. 2 Kings 16:5-7). A rebuild in Str. IV extends into the 7th century.[42]

The most recent work by American archaeologists and others under the direction of Thomas E. Levy has capped many years of investigations in the Wadi Feinan area (ancient Punon) and has clarified a vast copper-smelting installation that goes back to the third millennium B.C.E. Of particular interest are 10th-9th-century pottery and a fortified site with a city gate. This may suggest that these smelting operations began early and had some contact with Judah across the border.[43]

Although they postdate the period under review here, two unique 7th-century cult sites have been found west of the Jordan in Judah: Horvat Qitmit, east of Beersheba, and 'En-Ḥazevah, in the Jordan Valley south of the Dead Sea.[44]

40. Bienkowski 1992.

41. Bienkowski 1992.

42. Pratico in Stern 1993, 869-70.

43. Levy et al. 2007 and references there.

44. On Qitmit, see Beit-Arieh in Stern 1993, 1230-33; Beit-Arieh 1995; Zevit 2001, 142-49. On 'En-Ḥazevah, see Cohen and Yisrael 1996.

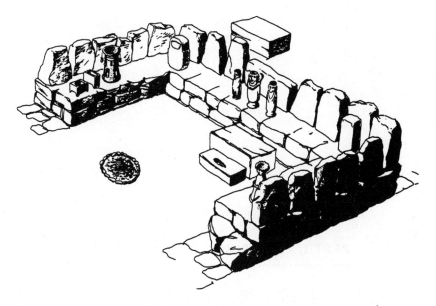

Fig. IX.12. The Edomite shrine at ʿEn-Ḥazevah.
Stern 2001, fig. I:113

From the foregoing it is clear that Edom was very peripheral and largely *terra incognita* to Israel in the 8th century. According to Assyrian sources, Sennacherib's campaign of 701 extended not only into Judah but even to Moab and Edom. Current archaeological evidence, however, does not confirm this. Most of Transjordan apparently continued into the 7th century and even flourished, probably in the same sort of *pax Assyriaca* that allowed Judah to prosper (above). However, the Babylonian destructions in the early 6th century ended much of that. But again Transjordan, on the periphery, fared better than Judah, which suffered a final catastrophe.

CHAPTER X

Warfare and the End

PART I: THE ARCHAEOLOGICAL DATA

The period we are surveying here — the mid to late 8th century B.C.E. in Israel and Judah — was a time of war. The Neo-Assyrian empire began pushing westward in the early 9th century (under Asshur-Nasirpal; 883-859), intent upon reaching the Mediterranean before marching down the coast to invade Egypt.

Setting the Stage

In 853 B.C.E. Shalmaneser III came up against a coalition of petty princes in the west who had hastily convened in order to head him off at Qarqar, in the Orontes Valley in Syria. From the monolith inscription of this king we learn that in league with the Arameans of Syria (Chapter IX) was one "Ahab," the king of Israel, who had more forces than any other leader — 10,000 foot soldiers and 2,000 chariots.[1]

The Assyrians were temporarily checked, but in 841 they came knocking at the door again under Shalmaneser III. This time the Assyrians were satisfied to take tribute and withdraw. One register on the famous Black Obelisk now in the British Museum depicts an Israelite general named Jehu who had staged a palace coup and killed Jehoram/Joram, Ahab's grandson, who had been ruling in Samaria. The middle register of this victory stele shows poor Jehu on his hands and knees, kissing the feet

1. Rainey 2006, 199-203.

Fig. X.1. The Black Obelisk, depicting the Israelite king Jehu (or his emissary?)
doing obeisance to Shalmaneser III.
King and Stager 2001, fig. III:134a

of the Assyrian emperor. Ironically, this is the only eyewitness portrait we
have of an Israelite king, in what we can truly call a compromising position.[2] Thus begins a campaign of humiliation (and ultimate defeat) that
would consume Israel's energies and resources for more than a century.

While Israel could negotiate a treaty of allegiance with the kings of
the Aramean city-states in Syria, now approaching their own zenith, these
Arameans (Chapter IX) soon constituted another threat to the northern
kingdom. And they were much closer, right on the northern border (Chapter IV; fig. IX.1). Israel had encountered Ben-Hadad II ("Hadadezer") at the
conflict with the Assyrians, when he was already threatening to bolt the coalition and seize power himself. From that point on, Israel had to face both
the Assyrians and the Aramean kings, especially those of Damascus, barely
twenty miles from their northern border with Syria, and of Tyre on the
coast, actually south of their northernmost border.[3]

City Walls and Gates

In Chapter V I described city walls and gates while characterizing the major
cities of 8th-century Israel and Judah, all of which were now heavily fortified.

2. Rainey 2006, 209-10. Some scholars argue that the kneeling figure is not Jehu himself but only an emissary.

3. On the Arameans generally, see Pitard 1987. Cf. Rainey 2006, 190-95, 199-202, 207-
11, 214-21. See now the more recent work of Sader 1992.

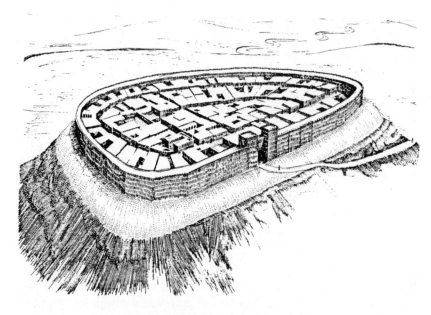

Fig. X.2. A reconstruction of Beersheba.
Herzog 1997, frontispiece

The ramparts of a typical town or city sometimes featured a massive solid stone wall with a high, thick mud-brick superstructure, and often an outer wall studded with a series of towers. An outer *glacis*, or steep reinforced slope, could augment these walls, as at Beersheba. Alternatively a lighter double wall (casemate), constructed with inner chambers, could prove equally effective, yet cheaper to construct and more practical in peacetime.

No studies of these city walls have been carried out by military engineers or economists.[4] But a typical city wall would have taken hundreds of men many years to build. Some sites as small as two acres are fortified, and there the relative investment of men and material was truly enormous. And in every case, very sophisticated engineering techniques were involved. In describing skilled technicians and laborers in Chapter VII, we argued that just such a middle class must be presumed. Here is the proof.

All the known city walls have but a single gate, obviously to reduce

---

4. A useful but brief summary is Herzog 1992. On earlier fortifications (Middle Bronze Age) see the detailed work of Burke 2009.

Fig. X.3. The Field III city gate at Gezer, 10th-8th centuries.
Photo: W. G. Dever

the number of weak sections of the wall to as few as possible. While four-entryway gates prevailed in the 10th century, simpler three-entryway and two-entryway gates were now more typical. But these were also multi-entryway gates, sometimes with external flanking towers, and they could also be quite effective.

The opposing inner chambers of these gates, often called guard-rooms, cannot actually have had any such function. In peaceful times these small rooms, which often had benches around the walls, could serve as a meeting place for such people as the village elders, sitting in judgment (as we know from biblical texts; Chapter V). We have grain scoops, balance pans, and shekel weights from some gate areas, so these rooms could also serve for business transactions (Chapter VII).

The inner chambers were clearly not intended to be defensive. Guards in these very small areas (ca. ten by fifteen feet, the size of a large closet) would be trapped if the gate was breached. The only real defense of the gate had to be mounted from the upper story or atop the roof of the outer towers. These projected out beyond the gate and allowed the defenders to fire down upon the attackers, or throw heavy stones or boiling water on their heads. Like the city walls, these gates were two or three stories

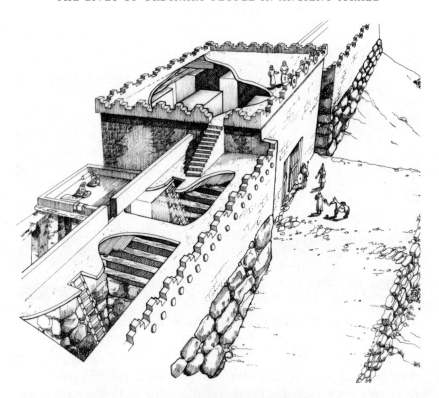

Fig. X.4. A three-entrance gate and casemate wall.
Reconstruction by Giselle Hasel

high, in effect citadels, as we know from Neo-Assyrian reliefs depicting the Gezer gate.[5]

The Lachish reliefs (below) give us an eyewitness portrait of what these 8th-century city walls and gates actually looked like — and moreover how they functioned in the event of a sustained siege and attack (they didn't).

Other Instruments of War

Given the archaeological evidence we have seen, one would expect Israel and Judah to have anticipated the Assyrian threat (which we know well

5. See conveniently Lance 1971. The word for "Gezer" is partially broken at that point, but the restoration is almost certain. Unfortunately, the inscription is said to be lost. Cf. n. 43 below.

from extrabiblical data; below) and taken measures to raise a standing army. In fact, we know that Israel did just that. The Neo-Assyrian annals specify that one "Ahab of Israel" brought to the coalition of western princes at the battle of Qarqar in 853 B.C.E. 10,000 foot soldiers and 2,000 chariots. That is a larger contingent than any other of the ten or eleven kings.[6] Yet we have no actual archaeological evidence of Iron Age chariots (except Neo-Assyrian).

Earlier scholars interpreted the 9th-century storehouses of Megiddo VC-IVB as "Solomon's stables." But they turned out to be wrong on both counts: the so-called stables are probably royal storehouses, and they belong to the era of Ahab in the 9th century. Even in an obviously planned barracks town like Beersheba, there is no specific evidence that military personnel stationed there were anything more than peacekeepers, a sort of militia. And there is certainly no evidence of (and no provisions for) chariots.

Border Forts

Weapons were common and presumably made of iron, which was commonly available. But iron did not fare well in the damp climate of ancient Palestine, so little evidence of weapons has come to light even in our extensive excavations, except for a few spears and arrowheads (the latter usually bronze).[7]

We have distinguished several forts in working out our rank-size hierarchy above (Chapter IV; fig. IV.29). There are at least fifteen of these forts, all obviously defensive to judge from their strategic location and distinctive architecture, and all located on the natural borders with Israel's neighbors. Thus on the border with the northern Philistine plain we find Rishon le-Ziyyon. Farther north on that border we do not seem to have a fort, probably because of the economic and cultural interactions that we have noted. On the border with Aram (of Syria) to the northeast, we have a small fort at Tel Soreg (but it may be Aramean; Chapter IX). On the natural border with Transjordan, the Jordan Valley, we have several forts: Kh. Mahrûq; the small forts in the Buqeiah Valley of the Judean Wilderness,

6. See n. 1 above.

7. See Yadin and Ben-Tor 1993; Chapman 1997; King and Stager 2001, 223-58; Borowski 2003, 35-42.

east of Jerusalem; Kh. Abu Tuwein (somewhat up in the hills); Ḥorvat Radum in the eastern hills; and in the Negev Desert perhaps Tel Malḥata, farther west.

These forts, obviously government initiatives in both the north and the south, share several similar features. (1) The fort is relatively isolated and seems quite small. The only one for which we have an indication of size is Tel Malḥata, at some four acres, but the fort itself is only a small part of the site. The other sites have no real settlements, only the fort building itself. (2) The fort is square or rectangular, with unusually thick solid walls, and usually with corner (and other) towers. A single, double, or triple gate gives access. (3) Often a well and cistern provide water. (4) The fort contains only a few simple rooms for the needs of those stationed there. The sole exception is the fort at Arad, which has a substantial temple within the walls.[8] In any case, we need to see what the rationale of defensive forts was.

The Rise of the Aramean City-States

Recent studies have shown that the early Aramean peoples of Syria had a trajectory toward statehood similar to that of the Israelite peoples. Originally pastoral nomads along the fringes of the settled zone in north Syria and Mesopotamia, they slowly became sedentarized. They are first mentioned in texts from the time of an early Neo-Assyrian king, Tiglath-Pileser I (ca. 1116-1076), described as unsettled, hostile peoples.[9]

By the 9th century, these northwest Semitic peoples, first cousins of the Israelites, had founded a number of city-states (not a unified national state) in north and central Syria. We know the names of several of them from contemporary cuneiform texts: Alalakh, Yamhad (Aleppo), Hama, Qatna, Qadesh, and Damascus. All but one (Alalakh, in Turkey) are in modern Syria and have been positively identified. Of these 9th-8th-century Aramean city-states, four have been partially excavated and published to some extent: Alalakh, Hama, Qatna, and Qadesh.[10]

The kings of Israel first seem to have come into contact with their northern neighbor at the battle of Qarqar in the Orontes Valley in 853. The

8. The date of the impressive fortress at Arad is disputed. For the best reworking see Herzog et al. 1984; Herzog 2001. In any case, Str. 10-9 belongs to the 8th century and is thus relevant here.

9. See n. 3 above; in addition Rainey 2006, 207-21.

10. Pitard 1987, passim.

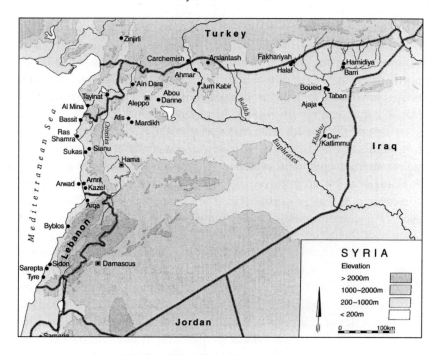

Fig. X.5. Map of Aramean sites in Syria.
Akkermans and Schwartz 2003, fig. 11.1

Israelite king Ahab joined a coalition of western petty states, which included an Aramean king.[11] According to the monolith inscription of Shalmaneser III, the Aramean king could field only 7,000 men, but the Israelite king outnumbered all his cohorts (above).

A few years later, another Israelite king whose name we know from contemporary Neo-Assyrian inscriptions to be Jehu (842/41–815) confronted Shalmaneser III somewhere near Tyre on the Levantine coast. Here, too, Damascene and Sidonian Aramean kings were involved in the coalition (Hadadezer of Damascus). The coalition was not decisively defeated, but the kings were forced to pay heavy tribute and swear allegiance (above).

From that point on, the Arameans turn against their former ally.[12] The Aramean king of the mid to late 9th century we know best from

11. Rainey 2006, 199-200, 212-13. Cf. nn. 1, 6 above. The Aramean king was Hadad-'idri of Damascus (biblical "Hadadezer").

12. Rainey 2006, 307-21.

extrabiblical inscriptions is Hazael of Damascus (ca. 844/42–800). He may have been the son of Ben-Hadad III ("Hadadezer"), or perhaps only a usurper. At first he continued his rebellion against the Assyrians to the north, where he lost considerable ground, even though Shalmaneser III retreated northward and did not campaign in this area again for years. Now Hazael could turn his attention to Israel, on his southern border.

During the late 9th century Hazael seems to have attempted to penetrate south of Damascus into northern Israel. We have, however, little or no extrabiblical epigraphic evidence. We have only an inscription of a king of Hamat, Zakkur, an archrival of Hazael and Bar-Hadad of Damascus (his son), found at Afis in north Syria. The context suggests a date of circa 796.[13] The description of defensive ramparts and moats is now seen to be significant (below, on Gath).

It is difficult to relate any archaeological disturbances or distractions at northern sites in Israel to Aramean incursions. Some years ago Israeli archaeologists Yohanan Aharoni and Ruth Amiran suggested a new Iron Age chronology, based largely on the supposition that there had occurred a series of Aramean campaigns between circa 840 and 810, which might be correlated with breaks in the stratigraphy of archaeological sites in Israel. That turns out, however, to be rather difficult except in a very few cases.[14]

The location of Philistine Gath has long been disputed, but it is now virtually certain to be equated with the huge mound of Tell es-Sāfî (Tel Zafit) on the border of the Philistine Plain and the Judean Shephelah.[15] Gath has been excavated since 1996. Among the finds that are relevant to our discussion here are (1) an enormous dry moat, a deep trench twelve feet wide and fifteen feet deep, running a mile or more, and enclosing the entire 100-125-acre mound. Dated to the mid to late 9th century, it is obviously defensive in nature. Nothing like this moat has ever been found in pre-Roman Palestine. (2) There is an enormous late-9th-century destruction level over much of the mound (temporary Str. 3).

The excavators relate these two phenomena to a presumed siege and destruction by the Arameans, in which case it is plausible to identify the Aramean king as Hazael. If so, that is one of the first archaeological cor-

13. Rainey 2006, 215, 220.

14. Aharoni and Amiran 1958. Particularly significant now is the indisputably 11th-10th-century fortress at Kh. Qeiyafa; see Garfinkel and Ganor 2009, 3-12.

15. Meir in Stern 2008, 2008-81; cf. Rainey 2006, 214-15.

roborations of possible 9th-century Aramean incursions into Israel —
surprisingly far south in Judah.[16] If Hazael's dates of circa 844/42–800 are
reliable, this destruction would probably mark the end of this particular
threat to Israel.

We now have an even better witness to the Aramean incursions into
Israel, brought to light by archaeology, even though it is somewhat earlier
than the period we are surveying here. In 1993-94 there were found at Dan,
right on the Syrian border, fragments of a large monumental Aramaic inscription. Probably a display inscription, the stele had been broken up and
the pieces incorporated into a stone wall in the outer gate plaza. There it
was found, in the debris of the 732 destruction. The stele, however, was no
doubt originally executed in the mid–9th century. This is clearly a victory
inscription. In it the Aramean king (Hazael?) claims that the Israelite king
(probably Jehoram/Joram, son of Ahab) had invaded his land, but he had
killed him and his son Ahaziyahu. Interestingly, the Dan inscription identifies a "king of Israel" and a king belonging to the "House (i.e., dynasty)
of David." So here we have (1) possibly the only extrabiblical reference to
the Davidic dynasty; (2) the name of two known Israelite kings of the 9th
century; and (3) clear evidence of the Aramean incursions.[17]

The End of the Northern Kingdom

By the middle of the 8th century a crisis mentality must have begun to prevail in Israel and Judah. As we know from cuneiform sources, the Neo-
Assyrian king Adad-nirāri III (811-783) had been preoccupied early in his
reign by the rise of the Urartian kingdom in what is today south-central
Turkey. In this interval Israel and Judah enjoyed a brief respite, as we can
gather from several Neo-Assyrian and Aramaic inscriptions.[18]

The Eponym Chronicle records a campaign of Adad-Nirāri in 796, in
which he received tribute from Damascus, as well as moved down the
Phoenician coast. In 775 his successor, Shalmaneser IV (782-773), also campaigned down into what today is the Lebanese coast. It was one of his

16. See n. 15 above.

17. On the now-famous Dan inscription, see Schniedewind 1996b; Na'aman 2000;
Rainey 2006, 212-13. Add now Hagelia 2004, with bibliography. The name of one of the Isra-
elite kings is partially broken, but the restoration of the name "Joram/Jehoram" is certain.
The name of the Aramean king is missing, but most scholars think it is "Hazael."

18. Rainey 2006, 219-20.

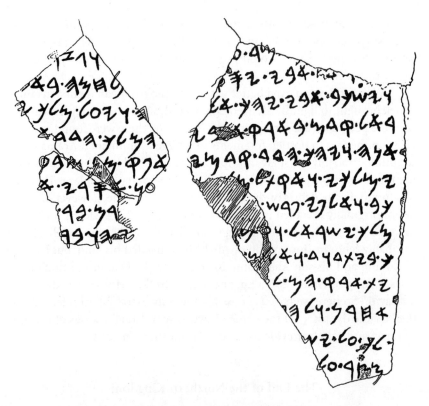

Fig. X.6. The Aramaic inscription from the Dan gate complex.
McCarter 1996, no. 70

namesakes, another Shalmaneser (V, 727-722), who would eventually be-
siege Samaria, Israel's capital. By now the handwriting was on the wall.

The notorious Assyrian king Tiglath-Pileser III came to the throne in
748 (reigning until 727). We happen to have fairly extensive cuneiform
sources for his eventful reign over the now rapidly expanding Assyrian Empire: the Neo-Assyrian Annals, the Nimrud Prism, the Asshur Chronicle, a
stele found in Iran, and particularly the Great Display Inscription (II).[19]

By his second year Tiglath-Pileser III claims to have taken tribute
from the king of Damascus (only forty miles from Israel's northern border
as the crow flies). Between 743 and 738 Tiglath-Pileser III campaigned in

19. On the pertinent Neo-Assyrian textual sources, see Rainey 2006, 213-45, with authoritative translations.

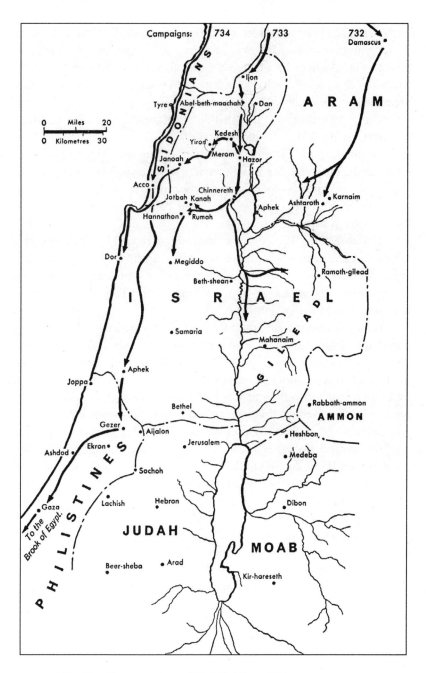

Fig. X.7. The campaigns of Tiglath-Pileser III in 734-732 B.C.E.
Aharoni 1967, map 30

north Syria, retaking some lost territories. The Eponym Chronicle seems to supply information that in 734 he even penetrated down the Philistine coast to Gaza, where he exacted tribute. It is claimed further that the "Arabs" in Transjordan were forced to pay tribute. If so, Israel was now threatened on two sides, soon to be three.[20]

The next year (732) Tiglath-Pileser III probably took Damascus. Moreover, in the Great Display Inscription (II) we have another Neo-Assyrian mention of "the House of Omri." In one text, Tiglath-Pileser III states that he despoiled the Israelite dynasty. But in another he names the king, "Hoshea," and says he deported large numbers of his (Israelite) subjects. If the document is reliable, there were campaigns, destructions, and deportations as early as 732.[21]

Tiglath-Pileser III died in 727 and was succeeded by Shalmaneser V (727-722). Unfortunately we have very few inscriptions from his brief reign. The Babylonian Chronicle gives him only four lines.[22] In 722 he was succeeded by Sargon II (722-705). Fortunately this emperor is relatively well known from the cuneiform records.

We know that it was Sargon II who took Samaria in 721, after a siege of perhaps eighteen months. The pertinent text is worth quoting in full. "The city of Samaria I besieged and I conquered. 27,290 people who resided in it I took as booty. I conscripted fifty chariots from them and the rest I had instructed in their proper behavior. My eunuch I appointed over them, and I imposed on them the tribute like the previous king."[23]

Since we know that "the previous king" was Shalmaneser V, who had died only shortly before (722), he was possibly the one who had laid the siege just as Sargon II was coming to the throne. And since Shalmaneser V mentions a king named Hoshea, we may assume that this king was the last ruler of Samaria (for the somewhat different biblical account, see Part II below).

A second inscription adds some details but differs slightly. It states that "the Samarians" had conspired with another king against Sargon II; that he took not only the same number of captives but also "deities"; that the number of chariots was not 50 but 200; that the deportees were settled in Assyria; and that he rebuilt Samaria "and made it greater than before." Sargon II even claimed to be "the subduer of the land of Judah, the loca-

20. Rainey 2006, 229.
21. Rainey 2006, 229-30, 232.
22. Rainey 2006, 234.
23. For the text, see Rainey 2006, 229-31.

tion of which is far away."[24] Finally, we know that Sargon II not only took refugees from Israel to Assyria but also brought in other conquered peoples to resettle parts of Israel — the well-known Neo-Assyrian policy of mixing various ethnic groups in conquered territories so as to shred the social and cultural fabric beyond repair. While Judah slipped from Sargon II's net temporarily, later Neo-Assyrians, in Sargon II's campaigns, extended down the coast to overrun Ashdod, Ekron, and Askhelon, as well as Beth-dagon, Joppa, Bene-baraq, Azor, and other cities in the Ashkelon district that were captured and looted.[25]

Meanwhile, Samaria and the northern kingdom of "Israel" disappeared forever. The archaeological evidence shows overwhelmingly the Assyrian presence and domination in the north, following the fall of Samaria (below).

Reviewing the Evidence: What Really Happened?

Most biblical scholars and archaeologists have assumed until recently that the Assyrian devastation of the north would be self-evident, especially in the archaeological evidence for the fall of Samaria in 721, so well attested by contemporary Neo-Assyrian texts. That, however, may not be the case, as I have recently shown in a critique of virtually all the data.[26]

The Neo-Assyrian texts mention, in addition to Samaria, only "Abilakka" (Abel-beth-Maʿacah); "the wide land of Naphtali"; "all Israel"; and possibly "Hannathon."[27] Anticipating a bit, we can add to this list a few names mentioned in the Hebrew Bible: Ijon, Janoah, Kedesh, Hazor, Gilead, and Galilee (the Assyrian names of "Abel-beth-Maʿacah" and "all Naphtali" are repeated in the Hebrew Bible; cf. 2 Kings 15:29).

Let us look first at Samaria. Samaria, mentioned specifically as an ally in the Neo-Assyrian texts, deserves special attention. This is because the relative wealth of information from all the potential sources — textual and archaeological — ought in principle to supply the convergences that might place us on firmer historical ground. Indeed, most scholars have assumed so. Unfortunately, it is not that simple, as more recent research has shown.

24. Rainey 2006, 234-38.
25. Rainey 2006, 234-36.
26. Much of the following discussion is dependent upon Dever 2007, with full references. On the later 701 destruction (below), see the excellent résumé in Hardin 2010, 80-83.
27. Rainey 2006, 229-45.

Despite the early intuition of authorities such as Albright and Wright that Dame Kathleen Kenyon's stratigraphy and ceramic analysis were flawed, her reputation as an innovator in field methods was so vaunted that few could offer a plausible alternative to her oft-repeated statement regarding the "Assyrian destruction" at Samaria (her Building Phase VI). Kenyon claimed that all the buildings below a sterile fill or "chocolate layer" were destroyed — "everywhere found covered by a layer of debris of destruction"; that "a 'sooty layer' covered the wall stubs." The floors of the "royal palace" rooms were littered with burnt ivory carvings and other debris. Subsequently, the walls were pulled down, then leveled over with redistributed destruction debris. "Alien pottery" (presumably Assyrian Palace Ware) was found in subsequent occupation levels (Phase VII).[28]

Fortunately, we now have Ronald Tappy's extensive reworking of Kenyon's 1932-35 excavation results at Samaria. Tappy has gone through all the original field records and has produced the first comprehensive, persuasive stratigraphic history of the site. He has not only wrung out of the complex data, published and unpublished, every conceivable scrap of information, but he has also fully integrated the pertinent data with both the biblical and the Neo-Assyrian texts in a remarkable *tour de force*. He shows that "'Building Phase' V" represents very scant remains, hardly "monumental architecture"; that scarcely any diagnostic pottery is published from the crucial loci; and that even Kenyon's famous section drawings are too schematic to be definitive. Accepting Albright's and Wright's attribution of the pottery of Pottery Period VI (rather than Kenyon's VII) to Building Phase V, Tappy finds the corpus astonishingly slight and Kenyon's confident dating precisely to 722/721 not credible. He regards the corpus as mixed and would redate it to "the last quarter of the eighth and the early seventh centuries BCE."

Tappy's overall conclusion after nearly 900 pages of discussion is worth quoting: "Ultimately, it is the lack of any stratigraphic bearings that hampers Kenyon's own reporting technique. . . . I have not encountered a blanket of destruction debris across the remains at the site; rather, diverse layers dating from many time periods and extending as late as the Late Roman period have emerged. . . . Kenyon's archaeological chronology seems tied too directly to generally accepted historical dates (Jehu's coup) and/or presumed historical events."[29]

To turn now to other sites, *Abilakka* of the Assyrian texts is to be identi-

---

28. For Assyrian Palace Ware see Amiran 1967, pl. 63:14.
29. Tappy 2001, 440, 444.

fied with the large tell of Abil al-Qamḥ (or Abel Beth-Maʿacah) at the southern end of the Ijon Valley. The prominent 35-acre site, on a high promontory overlooking the entire Huleh Basin, still preserves the ancient name in Arabic. The mound has never been excavated, but I conducted a thorough survey in 1973.[30] We located the surface remains of a large citadel, probably a fortress, on the upper part of the tell, as well as good quantities of 8th-century pottery, including some grooved storage jar rims identical to those published from Hazor VA, which was probably destroyed circa 734 (below). While there is no excavated evidence of a destruction at Abel Beth-Maʿacah, Assyrian forces moving from the Ijon Valley southward into Palestine could not have bypassed the site. The strategic topographical situation alone would have necessitated its conquest, as the Neo-Assyrian texts claim.

The "wide Land of Naphtali" in the Assyrian texts probably refers to upper Galilee generally (the relevant biblical text, 2 Kings 15:29, says only "Galilee"). This area does include Abel Beth-Maʿacah geographically, and thus would have been mentioned next in the list, just as it is. Next follow the names of "Samaria" (above) and "all Israel."

Now we need to look at the other sites in the supposed Assyrian itinerary, the names now being supplied by the Hebrew Bible (2 Kings 15:29) or possibly archaeological evidence (in geographical order).

Ijon may refer to the Valley of Ijon, on the border with Syria, near Abel Beth-Maʿacah. Alternatively it may refer to a town by that name, tentatively identified with Tell ed-Dibbîn to the north of Abel Beth-Maʿacah in the Ijon Valley (now in Lebanon). The latter has never been excavated, but like Abel Beth-Maʿacah, it was a gateway town that lay directly in the path of the Assyrian advance (see above). Whether the town was Aramean or Israelite, however, is uncertain.

Kedesh, obviously Tell Qades, a prominent 25-acre tell on the Israel-Lebanon border today, in the ancient territory of Naphtali (above), is the largest mound in upper Galilee. The lower tell is currently being excavated and has produced spectacular Hellenistic-Roman remains. The Iron II remains are known, however, only from a small salvage excavation in the place where the modern road divides the site. Yet this site was nearly as strategic as Abel Beth-Maʿacah for the Assyrian advance from the north, so its mention in the biblical list of sites destroyed by Tiglath-Pileser III makes good topographical sense.[31]

30. For my brief survey of Beth-Maʿacah, see Dever 1986.
31. Tadmor in Stern 1993, 855-57.

Fig. X.8. The imposing mound of Abel Beth-Maʿacah from the west, overlooking
the modern border with Lebanon and Syria.
Photo: W. G. Dever

Yiron in the Kings list is probably to be identified with Yārûn, just
southwest of Kedesh, but it has not been excavated. Merom, close by, is
possibly Tell el-Khirbeh ("mound of the ruin"), but it also remains
unexcavated.

Hazor

Hazor is certainly the 180-acre mound of Tell el-Qedah in lower Galilee,
another large fortress. Although not mentioned in the extant Neo-
Assyrian texts, it was the largest, most strategically located mound in the
region and lay directly in the path of any Assyrian advance into Galilee and
beyond, into the heartland of northern Israel. Hazor was extensively excavated by Yadin from 1955 to 1959, and the renewed ongoing excavations directed by Ben-Tor begun in 1990.[32]

The city of Str. VA is represented principally by a massive citadel, in-

32. Ben-Tor in Stern 2008, 1975.

corporating a watchtower, on a promontory at the western end of the upper mound (Area B). Apparently, the citadel had no surrounding city wall in the preceding Str. VB. But when the citadel was enlarged and additional buildings were added to the east, an offset-inset wall was constructed. Together with the enormous water tunnel dug in the 9th century (fig. IV.9 above), these constructions would have prepared Hazor quite well for the late-8th-century siege that surely had been anticipated (perhaps since the battle of Qarqar in 853).

Yadin describes the citadel as destroyed in a "final, complete" conflagration, "the entire area . . . covered with a layer of ashes and rubble about 1 m. thick." Area G was also destroyed — Yadin states that "the signs of the terrible destruction manifested in all the excavated areas were still 'fresh' when uncovered, and the next occupants did not trouble to clear the debris." Str. IV, which followed the destruction, is described as "a temporary unfortified settlement." Of particular significance to us is the Assyrian-style palace subsequently constructed in Str. III in Area B, occupying the whole of the western bluff, which was reused into Str. 1. But Yadin himself equivocated on its dating, allowing for either a 7th- or 6th-century (Babylonian) date. Its plan, however, is similar to the Assyrian citadel of Megiddo III (below).

Yanoah

Yanoah (Yānûh) is quite far to the west of the above sites, only ten miles or so inland from the Levantine coast. If the biblical account is reliable, the mention of Yanoah would indicate that the Assyrians intended to move down the coast toward Egypt, as we know in fact that they did (below).

There are at least ten excavated mid-to-late-8th-century sites in the north that are not mentioned in biblical or Neo-Assyrian texts where we might look for destruction levels between circa 734 and 722/721. We shall examine them briefly from north to south.

Dan

The long-running excavations at Tel Dan (1966 to date) might be expected to have yielded significant evidence. Dan was not only a principal cultural and religious site, but it was also strategically located on the border with

Aramea. Indeed, in the Neo-Assyrian military itineraries, Dan is mentioned along with nearby Ijon and Abel Beth-Ma'acah, the strategic importance of which has been noted above. Dan has been excavated since 1966 by the late Avraham Biran and his successors, but very little has been published to date. Biran's popular book *Biblical Dan* says that the pertinent Str. II, the city walls and gate (Areas A and B) and sacred precinct (Area T), was "destroyed." But there is no mention of the domestic areas, and indeed little evidence is presented to substantiate a deliberate destruction in a military campaign.

All one can say is that the scant Iron II pottery published from Str. II does appear to date to the mid to late 8th century. The gate area is the best candidate for a substantial destruction. This area was found in ruins, with up to one meter of fired bricks and ash overlying the piers and guardrooms. Biran attributes this destruction to Tiglath-Pileser III in 732 on the basis of the pottery. Among the objects retrieved from the last phase of the triple-entryway gate and its outer plaza was the well-known 9th-century "David Stela," which had been broken up and its stones reused in a retaining wall (above).[33]

Kinneret

This small but strategically located mound overlooking the northwestern shore of the Sea of Galilee stands guard over the main route around the sea to the west. It would have been on the natural invasion route south of Hazor. Excavated by Volkmar Fritz from 1982 to 1992, Kinneret Str. II is said to have been strongly fortified but destroyed by Tiglath-Pileser III in 733, after which it was settled only sparsely.[34]

Beth-Shean (Tell el-Ḥusn)

This is one of the most imposing mounds in lower Galilee, at the junction of the Jezreel Valley and the Jordan River. It was one of the major sites of the northern kingdom. Str. IV may date broadly to the 8th century, but it is said to be poorly preserved. The pottery as published may range from circa

33. Biran 1994, 203-6, 260-70. Cf. references in n. 17 above.
34. Fritz 1995, 83-87.

800 to 600 B.C.E. A gap in occupation follows until the Persian period. The recent excavations conducted by Amihai Mazar have yielded somewhat more information, deriving from a large, well-preserved building that was destroyed in a heavy fire, perhaps in the Assyrian campaigns. The debris yielded more than 100 restorable vessels, plus many more objects.[35]

Megiddo (Tell el-Mutesellim)

The name of Megiddo is virtually synonymous with famous battles, and here we might expect to have more persuasive evidence of the Assyrian campaigns (although the site is not named in the texts). Str. IVA is the pertinent horizon, with its offset-inset city wall, three-entryway gate, water system, three palace complexes, and storehouses (all probably continuing from Str. IVB of the 10th/9th century). Megiddo would have been an enviable prize for Tiglath-Pileser III, just as it was for Thutmosis III in the 15th century B.C.E.: "The capturing of Megiddo is the capturing of a thousand towns." Yet surprisingly, Yigal Shiloh's authoritative résumé does not mention any evidence whatsoever of an Assyrian destruction, stating only that it occurred. What is clear from the Neo-Assyrian texts, however, is that Megiddo became the capital of the new Assyrian province of *Magiddu* (below). The new Str. III two-entryway city gate provides some evidence of the takeover — it was buttressed by several large public and residential buildings that display clear Assyrian architectural features, such as central courtyards. Yet the current excavators, Israel Finkelstein and David Ussishkin, specifically note the absence of Assyrian objects.[36]

Ta'anach (Tell Ti'nnick)

Megiddo's nearby sister city of Ta'anach was excavated in the 1960s by Paul W. Lapp. The Iron II levels are published only in brief preliminary reports, and little can be said except that the scant remains of Period IV apparently belong to the mid to late 8th century. They are said to have been overlain in one small area by a single, black ashy layer, tentatively dated by the excavators to 733/732.[37]

35. A. Mazar 2001, 196-300.
36. Shiloh in Stern 1993, 1021.
37. Rast 1978, 41.

Yoqneʿam (Tell Qeiman)

Yoqneʿam (Jokneam), a steep, ten-acre mound guarding a major pass from the Ephraim hills into the Jezreel Valley, was excavated by Amnon Ben-Tor and others in the 1970s as part of a larger regional project. Str. XII of the 8th century had two heavy defense systems built on the slopes, replacing those of Str. XIV. The preliminary reports, however, do not mention destructions, only that the defenses went out of use and that the subsequent Str. XI had only fragmentary remains.[38]

Tel Qiri

Tel Qiri is a small, unwalled village, just southeast of Yoqneʿam on the lower slopes of the Carmel Ridge overlooking the central Jezreel Valley, excavated by Amnon Ben-Tor in 1975-77. No identification is suggested. Str. VIII belongs to the 8th century and represents a newly founded village. Nothing is reported regarding its end or destruction, but the subsequent Str. VIIB-A shows continuing architectural changes in the domestic architecture and the expanded development of the sort of agricultural industries that would befit a small village. The site would not likely have attracted the attention of invaders.[39]

Tirzah (Tell el-Farʿah [North])

Tirzah, briefly the first capital of the northern kingdom, is located prominently at the headwaters of the Wadi Farʿah in the hill country of Ephraim. It was excavated by Père Roland de Vaux in 1946-60 but has only been partially published. Str. VIId, belonging broadly to the 9th-8th centuries, is a fortified town with a solid city wall; an offset gateway; blocks of well-laid-out, multiroom houses; and a "palace" (fig. V.2 above). The pottery is reported to be characteristic of other 8th-century sites and includes Samaria Ware. The excavators attribute its destruction to Sargon II, but no details are given. Thereafter, in Str. VIIe, the town is said to have declined, but Assyrian Palace Ware may indicate an Assyrian presence.[40]

38. Ben-Tor in Stern 1993, 807.
39. Ben-Tor and Portugali 1987, 71-73.
40. Chambon in Stern 1993, 539-40.

Tell Keisan

The large mound of Tell Keisan, an important seaport near Acco, has been tentatively identified with several sites, none convincingly. It was excavated on a small scale by French scholars in the 1970s, and, to their credit, they produced a lavish final excavation report. Str. 6 apparently belongs to the 8th century, but it is described as a little village on the edge of the kingdom of Tyre, with typical Phoenician coastal pottery, and was thus probably not part of the northern kingdom of Israel. It is not likely that the site was in the path of the Assyrian advance down the coast, which concentrated rather on Philistia (see above). There is, however, some Assyrian Palace Ware, possibly trade items.[41]

Shechem (Tell Balâṭah)

Shechem, in the central hill country some eight miles south of Samaria, was one of the mid-sized towns in Iron II. It was excavated most recently by an American team under G. Ernest Wright and others from 1954 to 1973. Str. VII belongs to the 8th century, when a casemate wall in Field VI served as a defense. In Field VIII, House 1727 shows particularly clear and detailed evidence of violent destruction by fire. It provides perhaps our most carefully excavated evidence for destroyed domestic structures anywhere, although the pottery and objects are not yet published. The excavators proposed that the total destruction was the result of the Neo-Assyrian campaigns.[42]

Gezer (Tell el-Jezer)

Gezer, a thirty-three-acre mound at the juncture of the Judean foothills and the Shephelah near modern Lod, is one of the most strategically located Bronze–Iron Age sites in ancient Palestine. The city lay on the southern border of the northern kingdom, and after its late 8th-century destruction it was rejoined with Judah. It thus probably marked the southernmost point of the Assyrian advance toward Judah until the campaigns of Sennacherib in 701. The most recent excavations (1984-90) were carried

41. Humbert in Stern 1993, 866.
42. Toombs 1992, 1185.

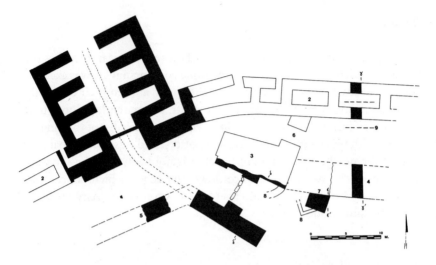

Fig. X.9. The city gate and casemate wall, Gezer.
Dever 1986, fig. 8

out by myself and other American staff. Str. VI of the 8th century is characterized by a multitowered city wall (the Outer Wall) with some casemate sections; a three-entryway gate with a lower gatehouse in Field III and an adjoining palace (Palace 8,000); and a large area of well-laid-out private houses in Field VII.

Our earlier seasons illuminated the wholesale destruction of some domestic areas (Fields II, VII), and the 1984 and 1990 seasons brought to light vivid evidence of the breach of the lower city wall near the gate and the fiery destruction of the upslope casemate wall. In the latter were found quantities of heavily burnt and calcified late-8th-century pottery; iron arrowheads; more than 100 burned clay loomweights; a carved ivory fan handle similar to one found in the 701 destruction at Lachish; a storage jar fragment reading *yayin* (wine); and rare examples of clay inkwells.

Gezer is unique in being able to boast an apparent eyewitness battlefield sketch, a Neo-Assyrian cuneiform tablet showing in detail the attack on the city gate and reading "the siege of Gezer" *(gaz[ru])*, found long ago in the ruins of the Assyrian palace at Nimrud.[43]

43. Dever 1985, 223-26; Dever 1993, 36-38. On the cuneiform relief depicting "Gezer" *(gazru)*, see Lance 1967, 42-44. Cf. n. 5 above. On the Assyrian period, see Reich and Brandl 1985.

Fig. X.10. A Neo-Assyrian tablet depicting the siege of the gate
at Gezer, our Field III gate and city wall.
Lance 1967, fig. 5

There remain two northern sites to be mentioned — Bethsaida and
Tel Hadar — on the northern and eastern shores of the Sea of Galilee, respectively. Both, however, are Aramean sites (Chapter IX).

The other regions named in 2 Kings 15:29 are Gilead and Galilee. The
second is obviously a region of northern Palestine, embracing the general
area of the tribal allotments of Naphtali (above) and Asher to the west. Including both upper and lower Galilee, the area would also likely have been
a target of the initial campaigns of Tiglath-Pileser III.

Gilead poses a problem, however, because it lies in north-central
Transjordan, where Assyrian destructions remain undocumented both
textually and archaeologically. Furthermore, how Israelite this area actually was in Iron II is debatable. Known Iron II archaeological sites both
north and south of this area of Transjordan — that is, Wadi Zarqa (the
Jabbok) — are rare, and few have been excavated. The recent exhaustive

survey of MacDonald lists some fifteen sites in Gilead proper (i.e., north of Ammon, on the border of ancient Ammon).[44]

The Post-Assyrian Horizon

The late 8th century in the north is a sort of postlude. The Neo-Assyrian forces under Sennacherib V and then Sargon II had overrun the northern kingdom, seized the capital of Samaria, killed thousands of people, and deported thousands of others to Nineveh as slaves. What follows is a century or so during which the north becomes the Assyrian province of "Samarina." And Assyrian rule extended far down to the coast of the Philistine Plain, and even into Transjordan as far south as Ammon. Tiny Judah was surrounded. Thus emerges the mystique of the "ten lost tribes of Israel." The archaeological evidence clearly reflects these drastic changes.[45]

Oddly enough, the city of Samaria itself does not become the new capital. In fact, Str. VII continues many of the older walls with little change. There were few finds from this stratum, none specifically Assyrian except for some imported Palace Ware, a fragment of an Assyrian stela attributed to Sargon II, and a cylinder seal from a letter to the local governor. Although Samaria was a district capital, the Assyrians deemed it expedient to keep their new province divided and impoverished, capable of producing only revenues sufficient to support the Assyrian occupation troops.

Megiddo was another Assyrian capital, one that illustrates better than any other the impact of Assyrian domination. An altogether new city replaces that of Str. IVA, laid out on an orthogonal plan, with blocks of houses flanking well-laid-out streets (Str. III). These were probably the residences of Assyrian officials and troops. The old offset-inset city wall was maintained, with a new two-entryway city gate. Near the gate were the residential quarters and administrative offices of the local governor, a combination of both Assyrian and Syro-Phoenician styles.[46]

Hazor also reveals major changes. Atop the ruined Str. V citadel in Area B, a large administrative stronghold was built similar to that of

44. B. MacDonald 2000, 195-205.

45. That the northern kingdom did virtually disappear is a matter of historical record. As a result, the surviving southern kingdom of Judah shaped the literature that has been handed down to us. What if we had a "*northern* Bible"?

46. Stern 2001, 42-51; cf. Herzog 1992, 253-58. For convenient overall summaries of the postdestruction horizon, see Stern 2001, 2-57; see also Blakely and Hardin 2002.

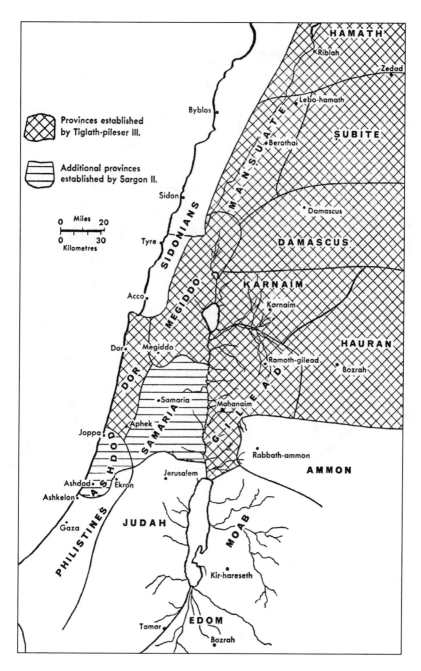

Fig. X.11. The Assyrian provinces in Palestine.
Aharoni 1967, map 31

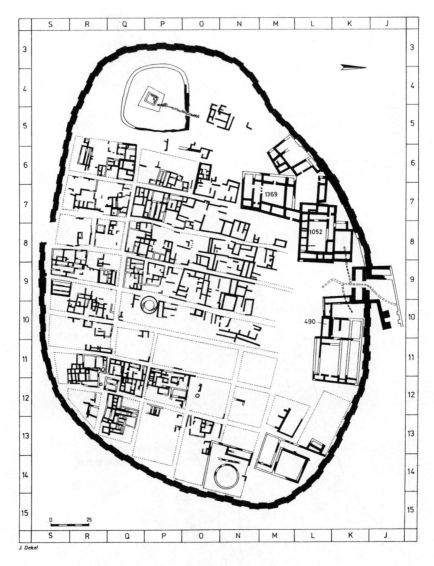

Fig. X.12. Plan of the Assyrian levels of Str. III at Megiddo.
Herzog 1997, fig. 5.35

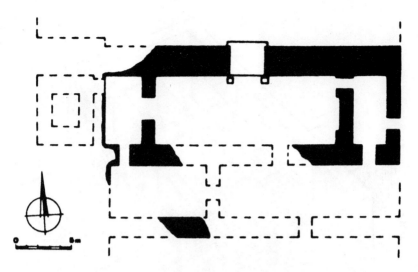

Fig. X.13. The Assyrian citadel at Hazor (Str. V).
Stern 2001, fig. I.14

Megiddo. At the eastern foot of the mound, now perhaps largely deserted, was a sort of palace with a reception hall.[47]

Tell el-Far'ah (N.) was immediately reoccupied in Str. VII, with few changes except for the blockage of the city gate and a few changes to the old palace and courtyard area. Assyrian Palace Ware, however, attests the presence of Assyrian officials.[48]

Gezer — as far south and central as the Assyrian campaigns penetrated at this time — shows clear evidence of the takeover. The older excavations produced two 7th-century Assyrian cuneiform administrative tablets, as well as a group of Assyrian objects and pottery.[49] More recent American excavators added to this picture, but it may be that Gezer, on the periphery of Assyrian power, remained less dramatically affected than other sites.[50]

Farther south, along the coast, Tel Sera' and Tell Jemmeh have produced evidence of Assyrian influence in building styles and objects. And many Neo-Philistine sites flourished under Assyrian rule (below).[51]

47. Yadin in Stern 1993, 601; Ben-Tor in Stern 2001, 1775.
48. Chambon in Stern 1993, 440.
49. Lance 1967; Dever in Stern 1993, 505; Reich and Brandl 1985.
50. Herzog 1992, 253-58.
51. On Tel Sera' see Oren in Stern 1993, 1332-33. On Tel Jemmeh, see van Beek in Stern

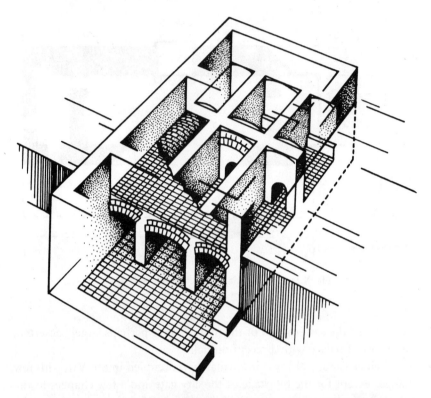

Fig. X.14. A Neo-Assyrian vaulted mud-brick structure at Tell Jemmeh,
late 8th–early 7th century.
Van Beek in Stern 1993, 671

Judah, encapsulated, somehow maintains quasi independence, but only briefly.

Preparing for a Siege: Judah Is Next

In 705 B.C.E. Sargon II died and was succeeded by Sennacherib, who initially was preoccupied by political instability and regional conflicts in Assyria. But by 701 he had campaigned westward to the Phoenician coast

---

1993, 670-72 (a unique mud-brick vaulted building in Assyrian style). On the fact that Judah actually flourished in the 7th century after the Assyrian destruction in the north, see Gitin 1997; and cf. Bunimovitz and Lederman 2009, 136-39.

north of Judah, and then had proceeded southward to menace the coastal Neo-Philistines who were Judah's closest neighbors. In the course of these expeditions Sennacherib penetrated into the heartland of Judah. The Neo-Assyrian sources document these campaigns in some detail, claiming the destruction of forty-six of King Hezekiah's "walled towns" (below). The writers of the Hebrew Bible, however, state simply that "in the fourteenth year of Hezekiah . . . Sennacherib attacked all the fortified cities of Judah and he took them" (2 Kings 18:13; cf. 2 Chron. 32:1; Isa. 36:1). Only Lachish (below) is named in addition to Jerusalem, and that only in one verse acknowledging that Sennacherib was present at Lachish (2 Kings 18:14). They then devote two chapters (2 Kings 18 and 19) to the miraculous lifting of the siege of Jerusalem — their only concern. Nothing illustrates more dramatically the fact that the biblical writers were largely oblivious to the fate of most of their countrymen, as I maintained at the outset of this work.

One of the most vulnerable points of any Israelite or Judean city, especially as it grew to maximum size in the 8th century, was the water supply. In looking at the major components that identify a city (Chapter V), we have noted several water systems. Some were built in the 9th century and were still in use in the 8th century, while others were constructed only then. We may assume that the date of these innovative and enormously expensive feats of engineering is not fortuitous. They were a direct response to the Assyrian threat that began in the 9th century and intensified in the 8th century as the danger obviously drew nearer.

The most impressive of all these water systems was an immediate response to the Assyrian presence hovering on the horizon, the famous water tunnel in Jerusalem (figs. V.12 and VII.15 above). This was surely built on the eve of the impending invasion in 701 precisely to augment and secure the city's resources by bringing the waters of the Spring of Gihon into a large reservoir inside the city walls. We have already discussed the late-8th-century monumental Hebrew inscription, found at the south end of the tunnel and describing the construction. Here it is worth assessing the enormous skill and effort this entailed.

Although perhaps hastily dug in desperation, this project was engineered with amazing expertise. The tunnel had to penetrate through some 400 yards of bedrock, as much as 100 feet below the surface.[52] We know from the inscription that the engineers and tunnelers for some inexplicable reason decided to start from both ends simultaneously. But how did

52. See references in Chapter IV, n. 7; VII, n. 32.

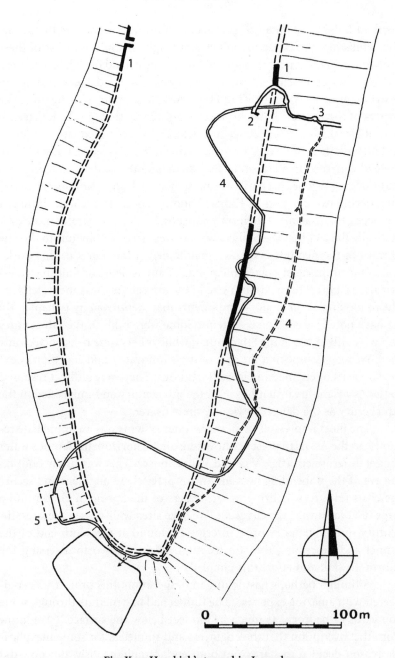

Fig. X.15. Hezekiah's tunnel in Jerusalem.
1. City wall; 2. "Warren Shaft"; 3. Gihon spring; 4. tunnel; 5. Siloam pool.
Fritz 1995, fig. 56

the diggers manage to meet almost precisely in the center, with nothing like modern surveying instruments to guide them? And why did they not suffocate, working in a narrow channel not even head-high in places? And why did the water, flowing all the time, not flood enough to drown them? We do not know the answers to these questions. But we can appreciate both the desperation and the ingenuity with which the authorities and their laborers had to work.

Probably related to the Jerusalem water tunnel is an enlargement of the city wall so as to incorporate and secure a much larger area. Termed the "Broad Wall," it was found by Nahman Avigad and dated to the mid to late 8th century by its archaeological context. Also found nearby in the current Old City were other contemporary fortifications, like towers. From this and the water tunnel, we can conclude that the kings of Judah in the 8th century anticipated, with good reason, the Assyrian invasions of 732-701.

Provisioning Store Cities

Among the epigraphic materials discussed in Chapter VII, we alluded to an intriguing class of objects, the so-called Royal Stamped Jarhandles.[53] These are the typical distinctive double-ridged handles of large ovoid storejars of the 8th century, but in this case they are stamped with an engraved signet ring.

Some impressions have a two-winged sun disc, others a four-winged scarab, and a few have a stylized four-wing symbol. The impressions all read on the upper register *le-melekh* ("Belonging to [or 'by'] the King"), thus the epithet "Royal."

On the lower register there is one of four place-names (giving here only the consonants): *mmšlt* (presumably for Heb. *memshālt*, "government," i.e., Jerusalem); *zp* (Ziph); *skh* (Socoh); and *ḥbrn* (Hebron). Three of these sites are located in the southern Judean hills, extending to the border with the Negev Desert, beginning at Hebron, some twenty miles south of Jerusalem, then to Ziph and Socoh.[54]

All these inscribed jarhandles are found in Judah, where they can be

---

53. Aharoni 1967, 340-46; Lance 1971; Ussishkin 1977; Na'aman 1979; Vaughn 1999; Kletter 1999; and see the summary in Rainey 2006, 251-53.

54. Virtually all the 1,200 or so known Royal Stamped Jarhandles (400 at Lachish alone) have been found in Judah. A few come from Bethel and Gezer, both sites right on the north-south border. See the summary in Rainey 2006, 251-53. Cf. n. 53 above; n. 55 below.

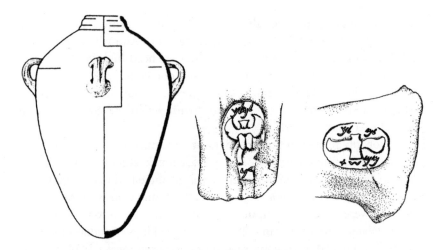

Fig. X.16. "Royal Stamped Jarhandles," reading *lmlk*, "Belonging to the King."
Gitin 2006, fig. 2:2, 3; McCarter 1996, no. 109

closely dated by their context to the mid to late 8th century. Studies of the hundreds of examples known suggest that a map of their distribution, like that of the Judean weights, coincides with the borders of Judah otherwise known.[55] Other studies have demonstrated that all the impressions were apparently made by only a few seals.

When these jarhandles began to come to light in early excavations, there was some problem in appreciating their meaning. But most scholars today agree that they indicate the attempt of the late-8th-century Judean kings to stock up provisions in certain district towns in anticipation of the impending Assyrian invasion of Judah. Grain, oil, and other supplies were stockpiled in depots, where the storejars were being mass-produced. When the drying clay was leather-hard, a government administrator with one of a few official signet-rings stamped the upper handles with the name of a destination. In fact, studies of many of the impressions show that they may all have been made with a relatively few rings (22 for some 500 handles).[56] These studies tend to support the notion of government supervision of the jars themselves, their contents, and their destinations.

55. See Kletter 1999 on weights and figurines.
56. Some have argued that no more than 22 signet rings were used for the total of known storejars. Others, however, count as many as 40 different rings, given more recent examples.

The most reasonable explanation of these hundreds of government-certified jars is that they were a defense mechanism. Anytime after the filled jars were stockpiled, they could be quickly shipped to the several regional depots from which they could then be disbursed to smaller cities and towns as needed. Just as the water supplies had to be protected against siege, the principal means of warfare, so did the food supply. And only a centralized government could have devised and implemented such measures. The store cities were in effect government-sponsored defense factories and warehouses. That the provisions were actually deployed can be seen from the fact that the destruction debris at Lachish, where we have a well-documented siege, produced hundreds of these stamped jarhandles.[57]

The Fall of Lachish

The best-documented battle of the ancient Near East is the siege and fall of Lachish in 701 in the campaigns of Sennacherib (705-681). We have four sources: (1) the Neo-Assyrian annals describing the events; (2) the famous reliefs from Nineveh depicting the battle itself, now in the British Museum; (3) two extensive, long-running archaeological excavations, fully published in many volumes; and (4) the laconic mention of Sennacherib and the siege of Lachish in the Hebrew Bible.[58]

Sennacherib succeeded Sargon II in 705 upon the latter's death, and he immediately began to campaign to the south against Babylon, soon to become his *bête noir*. The Phoenician/Philistine coast, however, was his objective on his third campaign in 701. Neo-Assyrian texts recount attacks on Sidon, Sareptah, Achziv, Joppa, Azor, Ekron, Ashdod, Ashkelon, and Beit-dagon (perhaps Azekah), as well as Moab and Edom in Transjordan. The routes to Jerusalem were now open from the east and the west.

In the follow-up to these successful southern campaigns, Sennacherib turned his face toward Jerusalem, which had eluded Assyrian ambitions for nearly forty years. He may not have succeeded there, but relevant levels of the city have been excavated only slightly, so the question remains open.[59] But he succeeded brilliantly at the great Judean for-

---

57. Ussishkin in Stern 1993, 9007-9. More than 400 Royal Stamped Jarhandles were recovered from the Str. III/701 B.C.E. debris.

58. No other battle of antiquity is so well documented.

59. Minimalist arguments on Jerusalem are based almost exclusively on the supposed lack of excavated evidence. For a much better, balanced view, citing considerably data, see

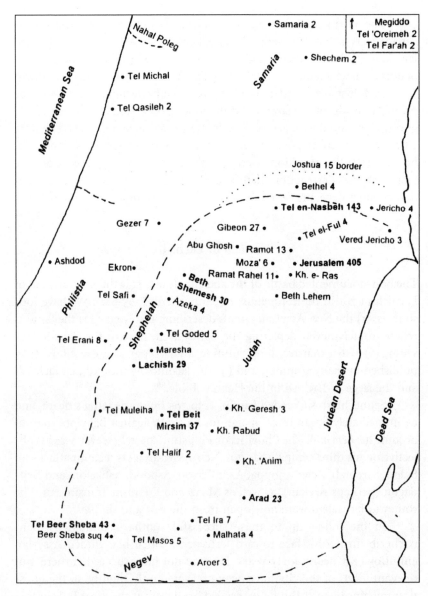

Fig. X.17. Distribution map of the Judean inscribed weights.
Kletter 1999, fig. 7

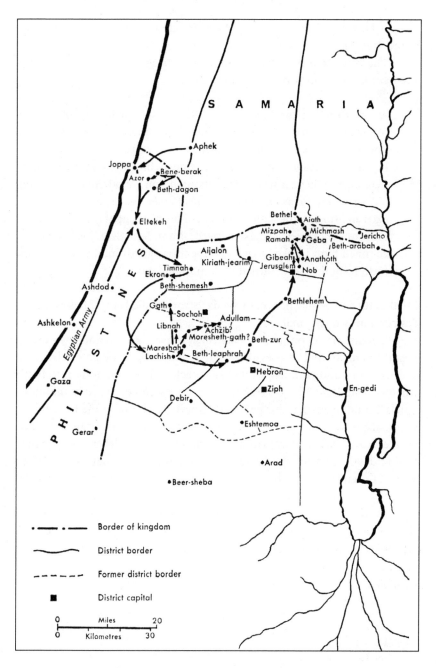

Fig. X.18. Sennacherib's campaigns in Judah in 701 B.C.E.
Aharoni 1967, map 32

tress of Lachish (Chapter V), and he celebrated it for all his world to see it and tremble.

The brief Neo-Assyrian account of the siege of Jerusalem is somewhat ambivalent, but worth quoting in full:

> As for Hezekiah the Judean, who did not submit to my yoke, I surrounded forty-six of his strong walled cities and the numberless small towns in their surroundings by laying down ramps and applying battering rams, onslaughts by foot troops, tunnels, breeches and siege ladders, I conquered them. Two hundred thousand one hundred and fifty people, small and great, male and female, horses, mules, donkeys, camels, oxen and small cattle without number I brought out of them and I . . . as for him (i.e., Hezekiah), like a caged bird in Jerusalem, his royal city, I confined him; I linked together siege forts against him, whoever came forth from the gate I turned back in humiliation.[60]

I shall return to Sennacherib's forty-six "strong walled cities" below, whose destruction is questionable.

Sennacherib's conquest of Lachish, however, is in no doubt — and he meant to ensure that. It is evident that Sennacherib anticipated the siege, and to record and commemorate his expected victory he took into battle what we would call "war correspondents." The series of monumental stone reliefs, found in a hall of his palace at Nineveh and now in the British Museum, are so detailed and lifelike (or deathlike) that they can only have been executed based on eyewitness sketches.[61] These reliefs portray in horrifying detail the iron-shod battering rams drawn up man-made ramps against the city walls; the ballistae, arrows, and shafts flying back and forth; the desperate attempts of the defenders atop the walls to rain down upon the attackers anything they could lay their hands on, trying to set on fire the wooden shafts of the rams; siege ladders thrown up against the walls and soldiers ascending them; rank upon rank of massed cohorts on the

---

Cahill 2003. The view of Finkelstein and a few others that Jerusalem was not the capital of any kingdom before the late 8th century is now effectively nullified, not only by the growing evidence from Jerusalem, but especially by the new excavations at Kh Qeiyafa, a well-planned Judean border fortress that all agree must date to the late 11th/early 10th century. Cf. Garfinkel and Ganor 2009.

60. Rainey 2006, 243.

61. For a superb visual treatment of the Lachish reliefs (lavishly illustrated), see now the definitive treatment of Ussishkin 1982.

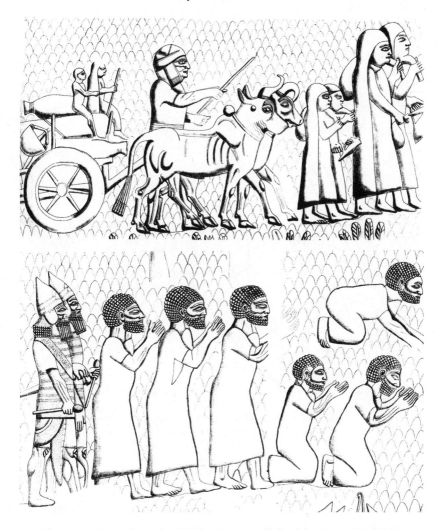

Figs. X.19. Scenes from the British Museum reliefs of the siege of Lachish.
Ussishkin 1982, pl. 86

ramp with their interlocking iron shields protecting them; a backup of row upon row of archers sending a cloud of arrows through the air.[62]

Simultaneously, as is typical of Neo-Assyrian art, the reliefs show the fall of the city: prisoners with knapsacks on their backs streaming out of

62. The Lachish reliefs are so detailed and lifelike that most authorities assume they were executed back home from sketches made on the spot at Lachish.

Fig. X.20. Prisoners leaving the city gate at Lachish.
Ussishkin 1982, pl. 86

the gate, while the battle is still raging and the city is blazing; begging captives dragged before a resplendent Sennacherib seated on his throne surrounded by his lackeys, his chariot and horses waiting behind the throne; a woman held by her hair with a soldier holding a sword over her bowed neck; men stretched on the ground and held flat while their skin is flayed off their backs; bodies impaled on long spikes and paraded around the toppling walls; severed heads piled up like watermelons on a rack.

Anyone who paused before these display reliefs in Sennacherib's audience chamber in his palace got the point: this is what happens to all who dare to defy the mighty king. To drive home the point, Sennacherib has himself portrayed over the eight-foot-high reliefs, seated on his throne and receiving booty and prisoners who are cowering before him. The inscription reads:

Sennacherib, King of the world,
King of the land of Assyria,
Set on a throne; the booty of
Lachish passed before him.[63]

This was not an idle boast, as the excavations prove. Lachish was excavated in 1932-38 by the British under the direction of the redoubtable
Starkey, and then in 1973-87 by Tel Aviv University under the able direction of David Ussishkin and a large team of Israeli specialists. Tufnell
published four large volumes; Ussishkin's elegant five-volume series is a
tour de force.[64]

The results of the excavations at Lachish present an almost uncanny
example of how artifacts and texts can corroborate each other — when
each is an unbiased, contemporary witness. The excavators found a steep
artificial stone and mud-brick ramp thrown up against the southeast corner of the city wall, with paved roadways to receive the heavy-wheeled Assyrian battering rams. A sounding into and around the ramp showed how
carefully it had been constructed. This is exactly what the siege looks like
on the palace reliefs. They even depict Sennacherib enthroned on a hill opposite the ramp — no doubt the perspective from which the Assyrian art-
ists had sketched the scene (above).

Immediately inside the wall at this point, the defenders had thrown
up a counterramp made of debris from everywhere. Here a second line of
defense had been hastily erected. Yet inevitably the Assyrian breach of the
wall occurred, and the evidence is horrifying.

Details of the siege were clear in Assyrian chariot horse ornaments; a
soldier's helmet; armor scales; long chains and perforated heavy stones,
used by the defenders against the battering rams; numerous ballistae (sling
stones); and more than 850 arrowheads.

When the wall was breached, the soldiers fired the city gate, the inner
chambers of which were found filled to the top with burned mud-brick
debris. The entire city was violently destroyed, the debris on the surface
and down the slopes below the city walls still visible today. Much of the
population would have been exiled, and the remainder slaughtered (as the
reliefs show). Some 1,300 skeletons were found in mass burials in several

63. Rainey 2006, 244.
64. For my rave review of Ussishkin's magisterial five-volume publication of his excavations at Lachish (2004), see Dever 2010.

caves — the bodies of men, women, and children. When analyzed, the skulls turned out to be typical of the local population at the time.

I visited the excavation nearly every season. Standing atop the Assyrian siege ramp with all the above in mind, staring down into the section through the counterramp, holding some arrows in my hand, I felt a chill. Archaeologists are notably blasé, in fact are very fond of destructions because of the useful information they provide. But here I could get at least an inkling of the sheer terror the hapless Judean defenders on the wall must have felt. They were doomed. It was only a matter of time (cf. Part III below).

The destruction of Str. III at Lachish is dramatic evidence of the campaigns of Sennacherib in 701. But the Assyrian king claims to have destroyed forty-six walled towns in Judah. In fact, there cannot have been forty-six walled towns in the whole of Judah. There are, however, several other sites that do have destruction levels that may be dated to this period.

Along the southern border with the Negev, the fort at Arad (Str. VIII) and the district administrative center at Beersheba (Str. II) were violently destroyed at this time. The debris yielded dozens of Royal Stamped Jarhandles (above) and hundreds of restorable vessels almost identical to those of Lachish III.[65]

In the heartland of Judah, the fortified town of Tell Ḥalif VIB has yielded a mass of information from recent American excavations, including a four-room house destroyed so suddenly that all its contents were recovered (figs. VI.5, VI.6).[66]

Beth-Shemesh, on the border with Philistia, was so severely destroyed (Str. IIB) that it never recovered.[67] Thus the raid of Sennacherib did have serious consequences for Judah, even if it was able to struggle on for another hundred years or so. Tiny Judah escaped the clutches of Assyrian forces, but it ultimately fell into the hands of no less a determined foe, the Babylonians.

Destructions at a number of other Judean towns are probably to be attributed to Sennacherib in 701: Ramat Raḥel VB, Tel Batash III, Rabûd B-II, and Tell Beit Mirsim A$_2$. Gezer is also destroyed on this horizon (Str. VII-VI), but it is on the northern border and may still be more Israelite than Judean. Even with these additions to our list, we do not come any-

65. For Arad, see Aharoni in Stern 1993, 82. On Beersheba, see Aharoni in Stern 1993, 171.

66. Hardin 2010, 80-83. For the discussion of other possible Sennacherib destructions in Judah, see Blakely and Hardin 2002; cf. Faust 2008a.

67. Bunimovitz and Lederman 2009, 136-39.

where near Sennacherib's forty-six towns. Some known from surveys, of course, might swell the total.[68]

Jerusalem was Judah's capital. What happened to it? Sennacherib claimed to have "shut up Hezekiah the Jew like a bird in a cage," that is, a siege (above), but he does not claim to have destroyed the city. Jerusalem Str. 12 belongs to this horizon, but the limited exposures we have described above mean that we have little stratified evidence. We know archaeologically that the city was well defended by Hezekiah in anticipation of a siege, the water tunnel and augmented Broad Wall being good evidence of that (above). But from what little we know, there was no major destruction at the time. In fact, Jerusalem continued to flourish for another hundred years.

PART II: THE BIBLICAL DATA

In keeping with our effort to consider our two sources for history writing separately, let us turn now to data derived from the Hebrew Bible.

City Walls and Gates

The writers and editors of the Hebrew Bible were well aware of the Aramean and Assyrian threats of the 8th century, as well as the defensive elements in play at the time (whenever the texts were written). There are references to massive walls like Jerusalem's Broad Wall (Jer. 51:58), but the ordinary city wall *(ḥōmāh)* is also well known. Unwalled towns and villages, however, "daughters" (above), are characterized as being insecure. The prophets specify that even walled cities will fall prey to Assyria (as indeed they did).

The city walls must be kept in constant repair (Neh. 3:14), but still the weak points may be breached (Job 30:14; Isa. 22:10-11, "two walls"; cf. 1 Kings 20:30; Isa. 30:13; 58:12; Amos 7:7; Ps. 106:23). So crucial are city walls that the term "wall" may serve as a metaphor for the city itself (Lam. 2:8).

---

68. Taking into account even the maximum number of possible Sennacherib destructions in Judah (cf. nn. 65-67 above), we are far from Sennacherib's boastful forty-six towns. Hardin's recent work is a good survey of the archaeological data on the 701 destructions, based on the detailed excavation of Tell Ḥalif VIB. Hardin adds some twenty destructions to the few I treat here; cf. Hardin 2010, 80-83.

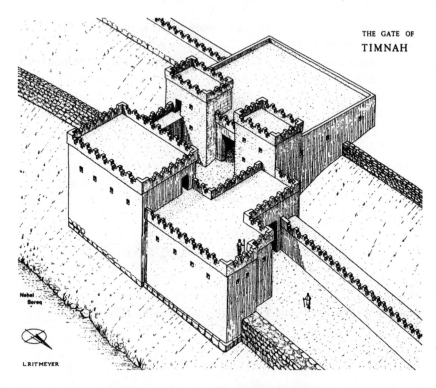

Fig. X.21. Reconstruction of the city gate at Tel Batash (Timnah).
Mazar 1990, fig. 12:1

These and a few other texts show that the writers of the Hebrew Bible were well aware of the ominous picture we have sketched above, that is, they knew intuitively what we now know in fact. But in all candor, their references, while realistic, add little to our understanding of the nature of defenses and warfare in the 8th century.

Similarly, the writers knew something of the typical city gates in use in their day. We noted that various important activities, trade being one of them (above), took place in the inner place and the benches surrounding the walls of the side chamber. About this the Hebrew Bible provides additional information. The gate *(sha'ar)* was a place where officials could hold audience, where public discourse was carried on, where the elders met and dispensed justice. We have cited all the relevant texts above, but here we should acknowledge that without some texts we would not be able to understand the full function of the city gates that archaeology has brought to light. Nevertheless, the information gleaned from the Hebrew Bible is off-hand, casual, not deliberately descriptive. It is incidental to the purpose of the biblical writers. It shows once again how oblivious they could be to history writing as we understand it.

The Aramean War and Other Wars

The Aramaic and Neo-Assyrian inscriptions that document Aramean incursions into Israel circa 840-810 have been summarized above, as well as the scant information we have from a few excavated sites (principally Gath). We even have the names of Aramean kings like Ben-Hadad III and Hazael who are mentioned in the Bible. But do the biblical texts provide any additional information?

What we might learn of the 8th century from our major source, 2 Kings 13–20, can be easily summarized as follows (adding dates known from extrabiblical sources):

1. Ben-Hadad (III; ca. 800-), the son of Hazael (842–ca. 800), oppressed Israel under Jehoahaz (819-804) but did not take any towns (2 Kings 13:1ff.).
2. Jehoahaz's son Jehoash (805-790) may have fought the Arameans at Aphek during campaigns by Ben-Hadad, but he recovered the towns lost by his father (2 Kings 12:7; 13:17, 24; 2 Chron. 24:17-25).
3. Jeroboam (II, 790-749) recovered the cities of Damascus and Hamath in Syria (2 Kings 14:25-28).

Here we have considerable difficulties in coordinating (1) the Aramaic and Neo-Assyrian inscriptions, (2) the biblical accounts, and (3) the scant archaeological data we happen to have. Several points may nonetheless be made.

First, the biblical accounts correlate the reigns of Jehoahaz and Ben-Hadad, who must be Ben-Hadad III, who was indeed the son of Hazael. But the range of dates when the two could have overlapped is narrow, if possible at all. Any campaigns of Ben-Hadad III would have to have taken place in his last few years and in Jehoahaz's last two years, that is, circa 805.[69]

---

69. The Hebrew Bible telescopes the dates of Hazael (844/42–ca. 800) and Jehoahaz (842/41–802/1), stating that "King Hazael of Aram oppressed Israel all the days of Jehoahaz" (= Jehoash) (2 Kings 13:22). "All the days" would then be only a year or two.

Second, an overlap of circa ten years between Jehoash (= Joash) and Ben-Hadad III is possible, circa 800-790, when the former died. "Aphek," however, cannot be Aphek on the Philistine border near Joppa. There is another Aphek on the Golan Heights, near 'En-gev, which is in the appropriate area. Recent excavations carried out at the small mound of Tel Soreq, near modern Afiq, have shown that this fortified Aramean town, like 'En-gev, may have been taken by Israel in the early 8th century (Chapter IX).[70] If so (the material has not been published), we have a corroboration of 2 Kings 12:7; 13:17, 24.

A few other towns said to have been retaken by Jehoash are mentioned in Amos 6:13: Karnaim and Lo-debar. But even if these sites can be identified, there have been no excavations.

Third, the claim that Jeroboam II took ("recovered") Aramean strongholds in southern Syria like Hamath and even Damascus seems fanciful, despite the efforts of some scholars to confirm this claim.[71]

In sum, what do we learn from the biblical texts regarding the Aramean advances? We already had the names of the Aramean kings, as well as the dates that the biblical texts do not supply (for Ben-Hadad and Hazael). We do learn the names of their Israelite opponents, for what that is worth. But it is only the context provided by Jehoash's resistance and the recapture of Aphek (and 'En-gev?) that adds anything of substance to the picture we already had.

Other biblical texts relative to the early to mid 8th century depict civil wars between Israel and Judah, as well as attempts by both Israel and Judah to expand their hegemony into neighboring territories. But since there is no direct archaeological confirmation of any of this political history, we will skip over it here. It must be conceded that all of this may be possible. But that depends entirely upon the biblical texts, whose political bias and a theocratic agenda limit their usefulness.

The Assyrian Invasions, 732-721 B.C.E.

We have discussed in some detail the archaeological and extrabiblical textual evidence for the Assyrian destructions in the north in 732-721. The relevant texts in the Hebrew Bible do not give us much additional detail, both

70. See Kochavi in Stern 1993, 1410.
71. For instance, Rainey 2006, 216.

because they are written from a southern, Judean, perspective and because they actually gloat about the defeat of their northern neighbor/enemy. In essence, they emphasize how all the Israelite kings "did what was evil in the sight of Yahweh," so they got what they deserved.

The entire account is contained in one verse in 2 Kings 15:29 and in portions in 2 Kings 17, concluding with the editorial comment that the Israelites "served their carved images to this day" (17:41). It claims even that the defeat "occurred because the people of Israel had sinned" (17:7).

To be sure, the biblical writers give us the names of the last Israelite king, Hoshea, and the Assyrian kings, Tiglath-Pileser (called also "Pul") and Shalmaneser. But we already had those names, and moreover, the biblical writers do not give the name of the actual conqueror of Samaria, Sargon II.

In their account of the fall of Samaria (two verses), the biblical writers attribute the victory to Shalmaneser (V). But the Neo-Assyrian texts attribute the victory to Sargon II. The apparent discrepancy is easily resolved, however. Shalmaneser V began the siege in 722, but he died shortly thereafter, and it was his successor, Sargon II, who actually conquered Samaria in 721. Thus the biblical writers are not wrong; they just don't give any details beyond those necessary to flesh out their own story. They discuss mainly Samaria. Most of the other northern towns and districts we have discussed above are not mentioned, even if the biblical writers did know something about them.

The account in 2 Kings notes the deportation of Israelites to "Halah, on the Habur (the Khabur river), the river of Gozan, and in the cities of the Medes" (2 Kings 17:6). The Neo-Assyrian accounts specify "27,900" deportees from Samaria, but that probably means from the entire province.[72]

Preparing for a Siege

We have described what appear to be late-8th-century preparations for an anticipated siege in Jerusalem, an ambitious water tunnel (Siloam), and the construction of the Broad Wall to extend and fortify the city (above).

It happens that we can illumine precisely these archaeological find-

---

72. The Neo-Assyrian texts specify "27,900" deportees, but that is likely to have been for the whole province of Samaria. The writers of the Hebrew Bible simply say "the king of Assyria captured Samaria; he carried the Israelites away to Assyria" (2 Kings 17:6).

ings with reference to the Judean king Hezekiah (whose name we already knew from Sennacherib's inscriptions, above). He is said in 2 Kings 20:20 to have "made the pool and the conduit and brought water into the city." 2 Chronicles 32:30 declares that this same Hezekiah "closed the upper outlet of the waters of Gihon and directed them down to the west side of the city of David." The first description is accurate enough in general, but that of 2 Chronicles is a spot-on description of the Siloam tunnel that we actually have. Here the biblical writers got it right — perhaps because the text exalts their favorite son Hezekiah.

Avigad's Broad Wall gets its name from a passage in Nehemiah 3:8, which describes the restoration of Jerusalem by returnees from Babylon in the late 6th century. The Broad Wall they restored was presumably in use first in Hezekiah's day, and the passage suggests that it was the wall to the far west that Avigad actually found.

The Campaign of Sennacherib, 701 B.C.E.

The fall of Lachish in 701 is the best-documented siege and destruction that we know from the ancient Near East. Thus it is astonishing that the biblical writers devote less than one sentence to it.

Isaiah gives three chapters to the deliverance of Jerusalem (chapters 35–37) but does not mention Lachish. 2 Kings does not mention Lachish either, but it devotes two chapters (chapters 18 and 19) to the miraculous deliverance of Jerusalem. Only the account in 2 Chronicles 32:9 takes note of Lachish in part of one sentence: "King Sennacherib of Assyria was at Lachish with all his forces." So he was.

The biblical sources are obviously preoccupied with Jerusalem and the fact that the Temple and their own royal court were spared, even though Jerusalem was besieged, as both our sources maintain (above). All along I have insisted that history writing requires not only accurate description but also an attempt at a rational explanation. The writers of Kings declare that the siege of Jerusalem was lifted because Yahweh intervened by sending a plague upon the Assyrian camp that killed 185,000 soldiers and forced Sennacherib to retreat (2 Kings 19:35-36). 2 Chronicles has essentially the same story, attributing the miracle to an angel but not specifying the number of those slain (2 Chron. 32:21). Isaiah has almost exactly the same account as 2 Kings.

Whatever one may say about exaggerated numbers, angels, and the miraculous deliverance of Jerusalem (unlike Samaria), these accounts hardly qualify as a believable explanation. The biblical writers must have known about the siege and fall of Lachish, only forty miles distant, not to mention other towns and cities destroyed by the Assyrians. But they are simply oblivious to the fate of hundreds, if not thousands, of their own countrymen. Not only is this horrifyingly callous, but it disqualifies these writers as anything like reliable historians.

PART III: THE MEANING OF THINGS

I have already described the chill I felt standing on the Assyrian ramparts at Lachish and imagining what was in the minds of those trapped inside, frantically trying to shore up the collapsing city wall. Soon they would join the hundreds of other corpses flung into the caves where we have found them. If they were spared, they would be marched off in chains to slavery in Assyria, 600 miles distant across the great Syro-Arabian desert. (We can even see the departing wretches on the Lachish reliefs.) How many other Judeans were uprooted from Sennacherib's "forty-six besieged towns" we shall never know, but there were probably several thousand deportees. Judah did survive the Assyrian campaigns of 701, and the biblical writers even hailed it as vindication for the Temple and the Crown. But that would have been poor consolation for those outside the capital, who knew in their gut that this was no victory and realized the mortal danger in which they and their children would now remain. A close call leaves one insecure forever. Perhaps Yahweh did save his Temple in Jerusalem and a handful of priests. But could he save his people in the countryside? The northern kingdom had been wiped off the pages of history within living memory. To many, it must have seemed that God was dead.

Conclusion

Having set out originally to separate and then compare our two sources for history writing — artifacts and texts — at least theoretically, it is time to sum up our inquiry.

Questions and Criteria

First, was the effort even possible? The answer is yes, with a few qualifications. The problem is that most archaeologists who work in Israel, whether American or Israeli, are influenced to some degree by biblical archaeology, however defined. For more than thirty-five years, however, I have been calling for a trial separation of archaeology and biblical studies. Not because the two inquiries are unrelated, but to the contrary, because until recently biblical archaeology was a monologue, rather than the dialogue that it should be.[1]

Most practitioners, especially Americans in the heyday of biblical archaeology in the 1950s-1960s, were biblical scholars (most clerics) who were amateur archaeologists at best. What I envisioned in my original critique was the experimental separation of archaeology from biblical studies so that it would be freed of theological biases to become an independent, mature, professional discipline. Then a dialogue between two honest and

---

1. See the classic description of the dilemma in Halpern 1997. I have called for a dialogue in numerous works for more than thirty years. Dever 2001a is almost entirely related to the possibilities and "rules" for the dialogue; see especially Chapter V. See further Dever 1992, 2003a and references there. See also the essays in Hoffmeier and Millard 2004.

critical disciplines might at last be possible. The effort, at first hotly contested, has met with mixed success. But in any case, today Syro-Palestinian archaeology (the term I prefer) or perhaps Levantine archaeology has made vast progress, and in principle it does strive to be an independent witness to the past.

How this all works out academically is a story to be told elsewhere.[2] Here I want to look only at the effects of the separation (not a divorce) on our attempt to write a sort of secular history of ancient Israel and Palestine. The fact is that while we can indeed separate our two sources (as all good historians do), we cannot make ourselves into schizophrenics, that is, separate two sides of our heads and our two realms of knowledge. It is impossible to forget the knowledge of the Bible that most of us have. Again and again I have had to rewrite portions of the text of this book so as to hold in suspension the biblical data I know all too well. And for some, it may be even more difficult to suspend their faith, that is, the hope, however subconscious, that the Bible may be "true" after all. But honest scholarship requires the effort (below).

It is the failure to be honest that lies behind my sharp critique of the biblical revisionists. Moreover, theirs is still the old-fashioned monologue, since they ignore or abuse the vast archaeological data that we now have — most of it readily accessible, even to nonspecialists.[3]

Second, we must ask how well the heuristic separation of sources worked. The test, of course, would be whether this tactic has produced a superior history — or any history at all in the real sense. Here a final answer is impossible, because we will never have an objective and therefore perfect account of the past against which to measure our own efforts at history writing.

Neither archaeologists nor biblical scholars have access to the whole truth, due not only to the limits of reliable information but also to their

2. Some tentative but promising steps forward are documented in nn. 4, 11, and 12 below.

3. The most instructive case study is Davies, who in his *In Search of "Ancient Israel"* (1992) cites only one archaeological source — Mazar's 1992 handbook — and that only to dismiss it in a single footnote as "irrelevant" for Davies' *Persian-period* "Israel." Whitelam is not necessarily oblivious, but his 1996 *Invention of Ancient Israel* is a caricature of archaeology and archaeologists throughout. His later works scarcely make the effort. So also Thompson 1999, even more outrageous. Lemche, at least, attempts to use archaeology fairly, although selectively (so his 1998a). There is no excuse for revisionists, if their European Seminar colleague Grabbe (2007) can show such critical mastery of the data. Cf. n. 4 below.

own inevitable subjectivity. History writing is about the present, as well as the past.

Despite these caveats, there are some practical criteria for evaluating the work of historians (and archaeologists *are* historians). (1) First, have the "facts" adduced been established as such? More information, so readily attainable today, is in itself little more than background noise — a distraction and an illusion that may obscure real knowledge. The raw information in both the biblical texts and the archaeological artifacts must be *interpreted* according to generally agreed principles (hermeneutics) before we can actually know anything, that is, before we have a database with which to proceed in any putative reconstruction of the past. And these facts become data (Lat. "things given") only when they can be related to appropriate questions. Thus at this initial level of inquiry, the answers we obtain will depend upon the questions we ask, and the way we go about the task.

Here a recent work of a biblical scholar is helpful, especially in the dialogue that we hope to foster: Lester Grabbe of Hull University in England, in his *Ancient Israel: What Do We Know and How Do We Know It?* I had already posed the question of Grabbe's subtitle and had urged other archaeologists to ask it of themselves.[4] That would be a beginning toward dialogue, one in which archaeological artifacts would play as strong a role as texts.

Artifacts such as those brought to light by archaeology are often called *realia* because they constitute tangible evidence. Texts, of course, are also artifacts, things made by human hands. But they are relevant only for the ideas they may encode, and these are often difficult to decode. New literary critics would assert that decoding texts is impossible, because the author's intentions can never really be known. The most radical critics argue that we cannot even speak of an "author." The text thus can mean anything the reader wants it to mean.

An archaeological artifact is more difficult to wish away. Its materiality, and the fact that some individual in a particular time and place made it for a purpose, is so clear that only a fool would deny this. To be sure, interpretation is as essential for an artifact to become a fact, in the above sense, as it is for a text. But here, I would argue, the interpretive task is somewhat

---

4. See my admiring review of Grabbe in Dever 2010. See also Grabbe's superb foreword and summary in the publication of a symposium he himself convened, Grabbe 2008. In my review I call again for a dialogue, emboldened by Grabbe's bold step forward.

easier than it is with biblical texts that have been worked and reworked for centuries and given widely different meanings, so much so that the original meaning is completely obscured. By contrast, an artifact is pristine until brought to light after centuries. And many archaeological discoveries, though they don't come labeled, speak for themselves in such a way that scholarly consensus about their meaning can be obtained relatively easily.

(2) Second, does our putative reconstruction adequately take into account all the data that we now have? Is it comprehensive, balanced, well documented? Is it the best explanation possible? And finally, is the result reasonable; does it appeal to common sense; is it ultimately satisfying?

These may seem to be subjective measures of evaluation, but that is inevitable, as we have already seen. Most historians acknowledge that history writing is not scientific, simply because human nature is not explainable or predictable in the same sense that, for instance, particles in physics are.[5] Thus a widespread test for all of us is what can be called "the balance of probability." That suffices in jurisprudence ("beyond reasonable doubt"), and it may be the best that we historians can do after querying our two witnesses, texts and artifacts.

(3) Finally, is our account of the past explanatory, at least as far as it is possible given the above limitations? Historians cannot simply put together past events like beads on a string. They do typically tell a story about the past ("narrative history"), but that story must be more than anecdotal, a mere description of what happened. To live up to its ideal, history writing must be *explanatory*. It must tell us not only what supposedly happened in the past, but why and what all this means. Otherwise the story is little more than a fairy tale — amusing, but finally dismissed as fanciful.

Has the coverage of the 8th century B.C.E. here been truly explanatory? I believe that it has been. Wherever possible I have shown a causal relationship. For instance, at the macro level I have not only described several 8th-century water systems, but I have also explained them as a response to the Assyrian threat at the time. At the micro level, I have described village lifestyles but have also explained those lifestyles as a response to the natural environment (Chapter VII). Cult is more difficult to explain, simply because religion is not rational and may defy any rational

5. Cf. Chapters I and II here. Ironically, some evangelicals, who would seem to require that the Bible be taken literally as "history," now concede this point. See, for example, the extensive discussion in Moberly 1999. Cf. also Martens 1994, even more candid (especially 330-40; one section is titled "History as Tangential to Theology").

explanation (Chapter VIII). Why people worshiped a particular deity, or enacted a particular ritual, may not be discernible. I would argue that even with texts, which some think indispensable, an explanation of religious phenomena may be impossible. If it were possible, scholars would have long since agreed upon an explanation of religion in ancient Israel. Clearly they have not.

Passing the Test?

In the light of the above criteria, let us see how well the present effort has fared. In the first case, have we actually been able to avoid a biblical bias? And even if we have avoided that obvious trap, have we succeeded in setting aside an agenda that was supplied by the biblical story (as we so often are accused of doing)?[6] I believe that in both cases we have been reasonably successful.

To be candid, having examined my conscience for many years, I am confident that I have neither a biblical nor an antibiblical bias. I am not trying to "prove" anything, only to summarize what we can actually know about one epoch in ancient Israel's past. As far as possible, I have eschewed any ideology, theological or political.[7]

As for an agenda, I would only observe that all scholars have an agenda. But mine has not been adopted from the Hebrew Bible, with its theocratic view of history. My agenda is drawn from the same questions that all good historians ask. And not once have I invoked "God's miraculous intervention" in history as an explanation (literally a *deus ex machina*).

Our fundamental appeal has been to the latest and best facts that archaeology provides, interpreted in the light of mainstream scholarship, as well as documented in footnotes and bibliography. Only in the last section

---

6. Examples of this charge of "biblical bias" from the revisionists are ubiquitous. Davies' most recent mindless comment is typical. Although he notes my 2001 book simply seeking "convergences" between classes of data — as all good historians do — he claims that "even those who pay lip-service to an independent archaeological history in fact fail to do so (on Dever's attempt [2001a], see Davies 2005)"; Davies 2007, 53. But Davies 2005, entitled "Crypto-Minimalism," actually contradicts the above statement, since he argues that there is not really much difference between his supposed "minimalism" and my (supposed) "maximalism." But one cannot have one's cake and eat it too. Davies cannot really co-opt me without undermining his own position.

7. On my own up-front ideology see Chapters I, II above. Of course, absolute objectivity is impossible; but I maintain that some objectivity is better than none.

of each chapter — "What was it really like?" — have I engaged in much speculation. And that has been deliberate and labeled as such but nevertheless based on relevant ethnographical parallels, as well as long personal experience in less developed areas of the Middle East where the biblical world survived until recently. In the second case, whether the phenomenological approach adapted here is thought to be a reasonable and satisfying account will depend largely on readers' response. I can only say that as far as I can tell, few thus far have done it at all. As I noted at the outset, few scholars in either of our fields have thought such a history possible, or even desirable.

This book does not purport to be the final history of the 8th century B.C.E., or even necessarily a history at all in the usual sense. It is an experiment in method, at a point where I consider that both biblical studies and archaeology have reached a historiographical impasse. As such, it is the culmination of concerns that have occupied me in publications over some thirty-five years, all of which can now be seen as a prolegomenon.

In one sense, this book has been begging to be written. I can only hope that, inspired by this effort, others will do it better. But whether a single individual will be up to the task in the future is open to debate. Will more conventional "histories of Israel" continue to be written? Of course they will. But they can no longer afford to depend on the biblical texts alone as their preferred "primary data." Even biblicists are beginning to see that (although not, of course, the biblical revisionists, who can only produce a "pseudo-history of non-events").[8]

Lastly, the issue of "explanation" may be the most pressing (above). This requires first of all a series of consecutive, datable events (or witnesses to events) that can be linked together in a causal relation. Some will argue that only the biblical texts can rise to that level of proof. They can be arranged along an extended time line, whereas real archaeological phases cannot be discerned within a century or so, as I have attempted here.

Here there are several objections to be raised. First of all, the various biblical texts (or "traditions") cannot in fact be dated very well at all. Even mainstream biblical scholars vary as much as 500 years in dating the materials that I have invoked here, such as the so-called Deuteronomistic History (essentially Joshua through Kings).[9] By contrast, we archaeologists

---

8. This apt phrase belongs to Knauf 1991, 41. Other memorable phrases of Knauf — his own kind of "revisionist" — will be found in Knauf 2008.

9. For references, see Chapter I, nn. 6, 7.

scarcely differ by more than 50 years for the most controversial eras, such as the evidence for a united monarchy in the 10th-9th centuries B.C.E.[10]

Furthermore, with vastly improved stratigraphical methods, buttressed by carbon 14 calculations and confirmed by historical records, archaeologists can often recognize and date subphases. As a single example, the diagnostic pottery that would characterize a Solomonic state in the 10th century is fixed by the well-dated raid of the Egyptian pharaoh Sheshonq in 918, which obviously dates pottery and other material found in the destruction layers related to that horizon or earlier.

Admittedly, in many of the instances discussed in this book we may not actually have such precisely dated archaeological phases. But even so, we have been able to project our coverage backward and forward a bit, so as to expand our database. And in any case, by restricting ourselves to roughly a century, we have already embraced a relatively brief interval in the *longue durée* approach that many archaeologists and historians now espouse.

What Have We Learned?

Since ours is an experimental exercise, not a definitive work, we ought to take away some lessons to guide future efforts. So what have we learned about each of our sources for history writing?

Archaeology and History Writing

First, the implication for archaeology is that we now have an abundance of data, even for our short century or so, more than we can profitably use. That should answer skeptics (almost always nonspecialists) who simply do not recognize the advances that modern archaeology has made. To be sure, twenty-five years ago a work like the present one would have been impossible. But today I can only wonder why someone else has not already attempted what I have tried here. (It was actually much simpler than I had thought.) Anyone who repeats the old canard that archaeology is "mute" is either ill-informed or simply defending textual turf.

---

10. The literature on the "conventional" versus "low" chronology is vast; but for orientation see now Levy et al. 2007; Sharon et al. 2007, and bibliography there; and update by references to Finkelstein 2007 and E. Mazar 2007 (although without footnotes); Garfinkel and Ganor 2009.

Of course, more archaeological data would always be welcome (there will be no more biblical data, an advantage we archaeologists possess). In particular, larger horizontal exposures of urban sites would yield better information on town planning. On the other hand, more attention to rural sites and the rural component of society would be even more important, since, as I have argued, this element was crucial in ancient Israel and Judah. In particular, we need to encourage recent emphases on "domestic archaeology," the archaeology of households, where we have a chance to document complete assemblages of objects from everyday life, including those that can illuminate gender-specific roles. Even so, I would insist that it is not the lack of data that is the problem but the lack of adequate syntheses.

Syntheses are risky in an age of rapidly expanding information, but it is time that some undertake them or we will make no further progress. Surprisingly, Israeli scholars, for all their supposed focus on "biblical" archaeology and the preponderance of the data they are producing, do very little of the kind of synthesis that I have attempted here. One can only cite some of Israel Finkelstein's popular works like *The Bible Unearthed: Archaeology's New Vision of Ancient Israel and the Origin of Its Sacred Texts* (with the journalist Neil Silberman).[11] More serious, but similarly with no documentation, is the recently published exchange between Finkelstein and another leading Israeli archaeologist, Amihai Mazar, entitled *The Quest for the Historical Israel: Debating Archaeology and the History of Early Israel.*[12]

The Hebrew Bible and History Writing

I began in Chapter I by noting the diminishing interest in history writing among mainstream biblical scholars worldwide. That may be because after 150 years of applying the methods of modern critical scholarship we have

11. This laudable effort, however, has been criticized for its lack of documentation, and in particularly for its (Finkelstein's) naïveté with regard to the biblical sources. See n. 12 below. See also Vaughn 2003, 427-29. In the same work Vaughn mischaracterizes me as an "essentialist" who runs the "risk of . . . creating a God who is a rational construct" (411; cf. also pp. 12-16). In fact, I am an agnostic, with no interest in theology except for its method. Further evidence of Vaughn's wildly off-target remarks is his claim of his proposal of a "post-positivist objectivity" (Vaughn 2003, 410). But this is an absolute contradiction in terms!

12. Finkelstein 2007; A. Mazar 2007b; cf. A. Mazar 2008; and also Faust 2007.

wrung out of their texts almost all the *historical* information they may contain. And by our count here, that is not very much — at least not as much as most would have thought.

That is a bold claim, but a statistical analysis of any of the foregoing chapters, comparing Parts I and II, will bear it out. The biblical data contributed so little of *substance* that in most cases most of it can be eliminated as a truly historical source. To be sure, attaching names to our anonymous actors, or a theological "meaning" to certain events, is of some interest. But for the most part that contribution is not essential, or even necessarily helpful.

Objections to this admittedly "minimalist"[13] assessment will likely come from two quarters: (1) some parochial biblical scholars protecting their own turf, and (2) fundamentalists whose position obviously depends upon a literal reading of Scripture to provide all the truth they need. What is at issue here, however, is neither the demands of academic professionalism nor the demands of faith. It is fundamentally an issue of *history:* what it is, what kinds of data it embraces, how it is written and for what purposes.

Elsewhere I have attempted to distinguish several kinds of history. They would include the following:[14]

1. Natural history: the environment (Pliny's *Naturalis historia*)
2. Technological history: the history of things
3. Political history: the history of public institutions
4. Military history: the art of warfare
5. Cultural history
6. Socioeconomic history
7. Intellectual history: the history of ideas
8. Religious history
9. Narrative history (sometimes oral history)

13. I have observed elsewhere that in some ways all good archaeologists and historians are "minimalists," that is, saying modestly all that our evidence allows us to say. This follows the famous principle of Occam's razor, that the most parsimonious explanation that accounts for the evidence is the best; see Tarnas 1991, 2010-18. On objections to the "minimalist/maximalist" terminology, see Kofoed 2005, 43-48, 109-11; Barstad 2007, 43; Grabbe 2007. Whitelam denies that a "minimalist" school exists; Whitelam 2002. Davies thinks the differences minimal; Davies 2005.

14. See Dever 1997a.

Conclusion

Archaeology is admittedly not well suited for writing the kinds of history that characterize numbers 3, 7-9, where ideas are paramount. Such histories require texts (including the biblical texts that would be relevant here). Archaeology can and will in the future write histories such as those of numbers 1, 2, 4-6 — "histories of things" — where artifacts often speak for themselves.

Here it is relevant that most of the "histories of Israel" written to date, upon examination, turn out to have been *political* (and theological) histories, with a narrow focus on the "great men and public deeds" of the narratives of the Hebrew Bible. Some may think there is still a need for such histories. But the approach is outdated, and it will satisfy few in today's secular, increasingly global environment. If the Hebrew Bible is to continue to have any relevance in the modern world, we must stop trying to make it what it is not — a factual history of ancient Israel and thus supposedly the "ground of faith" (below). There is no word for "history" in the Hebrew Bible, nor is there any evidence that the authors and editors conceived of history writing in the modern sense. They are telling *stories,* as all ancient historians did. And the point of these stories is not what is supposed to have happened, but what the events mean in *larger* perspective. And that perspective is always religious. The Hebrew Bible is "theocratic history," didactic in nature.[15]

My own revered mentor, G. Ernest Wright, claimed in the 1950s, in defense of the then-stylish biblical theology, that "in biblical faith everything depends upon whether the central events actually happened."[16] By "central events" he clearly meant those events developed in the great themes of the Hebrew Bible: the promise to the patriarchs; the exodus and conquest; the Sinai covenant with Moses; Temple and monotheistic cult. Yet today archaeology, far from confirming the historical basis for these themes, has undermined nearly all the events, at least where the biblical texts are to be read literally.[17]

This may sound radical, but it is mainstream scholarship today. Furthermore, the results of the surprising "archaeological revolution" may

15. See above and n. 5.
16. G. E. Wright 1952, 126; cf. my critique in Dever 1981. A useful summary of the discussion (although from an evangelical perspective) will be found in Millard, Hoffmeier, and Baker 1994, 313-40.
17. On the scant historicity of "patriarchal" and "exodus-conquest" tradition, see Dever 2003b, 2003c, and full references there. The views expressed there, once controversial, are now mainstream scholarship.

turn out to be beneficial in the long run. That is because the Hebrew Bible would finally be allowed to be what it actually is: not history, but a testament to faith (above). The result would be, of course, that theology would be liberated from history to be what *it* is: a testament to faith.

The separation of faith from history advocated here will be particularly unsettling to Protestants, even those of liberal persuasion, for whom the motto has been *sola scriptura*. But Judaism, in its Reform manifestation at least, has long since made its peace with such an accommodation. And other non-Christian religions were never so dependent on forced, particularistic historical readings in the first place. Genuine religion should be more about ortho-practice, moral earnestness, than orthodoxy. And if it survives, it will have to be.

I contend here that faith is not rational but is rather suprarational, and therefore it does not depend upon attempts at rational explanations, nor is it enhanced by them. If proof were required, faith would not be faith. Religion is all about magic, but the will to believe is *not* magic. It is a matter of individual temperament and training. Some have it, and some do not. But writing, or rewriting, history, or explaining history — producing yet more "facts" — will make little difference. That is why archaeological proofs that "the Bible is true" are irrelevant (below).

But "What Really Happened?"

The noted Harvard New Testament scholar Krister Stendahl, in his classic dictionary article "Biblical Theology," observed that in biblical studies there are two questions. One is, What *did* the text mean? — the task of exegesis, or scholarly interpretation of the text itself.[18] The other question is, What *does* the text mean? — the task of theology and the church and synagogue.

I would add another question, that of the historian: What really happened? And however we propose to relate faith and history (below), that remains a legitimate question in itself. But can we answer it persuasively? As Lester Grabbe, whose work we noted above, puts it: What do we know about ancient Israel, and how do we know it?

As an archaeologist, I would argue that we now know a great deal, and we know it because the archaeological data, now our primary source for history writing (as Grabbe agrees), have been so productive. Unlike the

18. Stendahl 1962.

static biblical data, with the attendant problems of endlessly reworked and tendentious interpretations, the archaeological data are dynamic — exponentially expanding, much more tangible and less subjective in their interpretation, and truly revelatory. And archaeology possesses an added advantage in that, unlike the elitist perspective of the biblical texts, it allows us to focus as we have done here on ordinary folk and their lives. We are writing history not from the top down but from the bottom up. If numbers mean anything, that matters.

As for "what really happened," the archaeological *realia* that I have presented here stand on their own. Even allowing for inevitable and legitimate differences in interpretation, these data provide the basic information upon which any future reconstructions of life in ancient Israel must depend. Mine is simply one step in that direction.

Faith and History

At this point I must finally address the thorny question of "faith and history," which for some is *the* question. If faith, or religious belief, depends on the biblical accounts being true, what happens if archaeology demonstrates that the events in question did not happen? Is the Bible then not true? That depends on what we mean by "true," as we shall see.

As an example of our dilemma, let us look at the biblical account of the conquest of Canaan and ask what is the truth. In the events according to Joshua, the whole land was seized in a short-lived military conquest. The biblical interpretation is that this was miraculous, a fulfillment of Yahweh's promise to the ancestors of Israel. Here both the event and the meaning assigned to it are straightforwardly presented as truth. On the other hand, the archaeological evidence has demonstrated overwhelmingly that no such conquest ever took place. And thus there can be no event-based meaning since there is no event. The Bible might still be true but only metaphorically (below).

There will be objections to this concept of the Bible and religion. One is that unless it is grounded in historical reality (i.e., in the veracity of the biblical writers' reports, and the authority that derives from the original meaning attributed to these events), religion will degenerate into relativism, mere theosophy. That may happen, indeed perhaps inevitably. But it is not only archaeology that fails at this point, but also critical exegesis of the biblical texts. The kind of certitude that Orthodox Judaism or Christianity requires, and until recently mainstream biblical studies seemed to supply, is simply not obtainable in the modern world (postmodern or not), if it ever was. Faith is faith, not knowledge; it requires no validation except in practice. As the liberal biblical theologian Will Herberg declared, "Biblical faith is faith enacted in history, or it is nothing at all."[19] And as far as I can see, that is true for all religions.

For those who still want to see theology as dependent upon the validation of the Bible as history, there would seem to be only a few options (excluding fundamentalism, which is oblivious to any critical thinking). (1) Stay committed to faith *and* critical methods and accept the newer archaeological reassessment in general. But rationalize the conflict in some cases so as to have it both ways. This appeals to many evangelicals. But what it boils down to is that the Bible is "true" because it satisfies *my need* for certainty in life. (2) A second way of thinking depends partly on the classic work of Hans Frei, *The Eclipse of Biblical Narrative: A Study in Eighteenth and Nineteenth Century Hermeneutics* (1974). The biblical texts are "history-like," or *metaphorically* true. Thus the Bible need not be historically true at all in order to be relevant still for questions of morality and ethics. Here theists and secularists may agree.

(3) The third option is to jettison the Bible and the biblical tradition altogether, as part and parcel of the obsolete Western cultural tradition, with postmodernists (and some revisionists).

What Is Left of the Bible?

The kind of history I have presented here may be seen by many as minimalist. Not only does the emphasis on archaeology question some biblical stories, it eliminates many of them as primary sources for history writing. If the Hebrew Bible is not decisive for faith (above), and now not decisive for history either, of what value is it?

It is ironical that today many biblical scholars would say that the Hebrew Bible is worth studying only as literature. It consists of stories that at best are "history-like." Archaeologists, especially in Israel, tend to reject

19. Quoted in Millard, Hoffmeier, and Baker 1994, 330. Cf. the statement of an evangelical scholar, in this work: "In the end I accept the biblical story not because of historical reasoning, but rather on account of an inner quality of the Gospel, namely its truthfulness" (334 n. 88). That would seem, however, to be a circular argument.

that approach. Nevertheless, their actual use of the Hebrew Bible as history does not retain much of it as truly historical.[20] And since nearly all of them are secularists, they do not read the Hebrew Bible for its religious content either. Without realizing fully the implications of their approach, these archaeologists, too, are writing the history of ancient Israel in essence without the Bible, as I am doing here.

The difference, however, is that they do not address the issues specifically as historians, concerned rather with what is called "culture history." Rarely do they ask the question: What was it really like in ancient Israel? And they seem to be oblivious to the question of faith in history. Their focus is more on pots than peoples. This is where the present work is different, even if it is controversial.

I believe that the controversy will resolve itself in the near future, because most biblical scholars and archaeologists are already tending toward a kind of minimalism, whether they admit it or not. Yet the Hebrew Bible still retains value as a fundamental source for the Western cultural tradition, the ground for the moral and ethical values that distinguish many of us. Its history is our history. And by stripping away extraneous elements to isolate a "core history" in the Hebrew Bible, we enhance its real value.

It is that core history that I defend against the biblical revisionists, who seem intent upon writing Israel out of history. I want to write it back in, but into a *believable* account of ancient Israel that will be true to all that we now know from archaeology.

Setting the Hebrew Bible into a real-life context, illustrating its stories through the archaeological remains now brought to light, does not detract from it. To the contrary, this kind of history of ordinary folk can make the Bible *more* credible, more believable, because it is a story about people like its readers. In my reconstruction here, I can only hope that I have given a voice to those countless anonymous people of ancient Israel, to all "those who sleep in the dust of the earth" (Dan. 12:2).

20. Cf. references in n. 12 above.

Bibliography

Ackerman, Susan

1989   "'And the Women Knead Dough': The Worship of the Queen of Heaven in Sixth-Century Judah." In *Gender and Difference in Ancient Israel*, edited by Peggy L. Day. Minneapolis: Fortress, 109-24.

1992   *Under Every Green Tree: Popular Religion in Sixth-Century Judah*. Harvard Semitic Monographs 46. Atlanta: Scholars Press.

2003a   "At Home with the Goddess." In *Symbiosis, Symbolism, and the Power of the Past: Canaan, Ancient Israel, and Their Neighbors from the Late Bronze Age through Roman Palaestina*, edited by William G. Dever and Seymour Gitin. Winona Lake, IN: Eisenbrauns, 455-68.

2003b   "Digging Up Deborah: Recent Hebrew Bible Scholarship on Gender and the Contribution of Archaeology." *Near Eastern Archaeology* 66/4:172-84.

2008   "Asherah, the West Semitic Goddess of Spinning and Weaving." *Journal of Near Eastern Studies* 67/1:1-29.

Adams, Russell B., ed.

2008   *Jordan: An Archaeological Reader*. London: Equinox.

Aharoni, Yohanan

1967   *The Land of the Bible: A Geography*. Translated by Anson F. Rainey. London: Burns and Oates.

1973   *Beer-Sheba I: Excavations of Tell Beer-Sheba 1969-1971 Seasons*. Publications of Institute of Archaeology 2. Tel Aviv: Tel Aviv University.

1979   *The Land of the Bible: A Geography*. Enlarged edition. Translated by Anson F. Rainey. London: Burns and Oates.

1981   *The Arad Inscriptions*. Jerusalem: Bialik.

Bibliography

Aharoni, Yohanan, and Ruth Amiran

1958   "A New Scheme for the Discussion of the Iron Age." *Israel Exploration Journal:* 171-84.

Aḥituv, Shmuel

2006   *Echoes from the Past: Hebrew and Cognate Inscriptions from the Biblical Period.* Jerusalem: Carta.

Ahlström, Gösta W.

1993   *The History of Ancient Palestine from the Paleolithic Period to Alexander's Conquest.* Journal for the Study of the Old Testament: Supplement Series 146. Sheffield: Sheffield Academic Press.

Akkermans, P. M. M. G., and G. M. Schwartz

2003   *The Archaeology of Syria: From Complex Hunter-Gatherers to Early Urban Societies (ca. 16,000-300 BC).* Cambridge: Cambridge University Press.

Albertz, Rainer

2007   "Social History of Ancient Israel." In *Understanding the History of Ancient Israel,* edited by Hugh G. M. Williamson. Proceedings of the British Academy 143. Oxford: Oxford University Press.

Amiran, Ruth

1958   "The Tumuli West of Jerusalem." *Israel Exploration Journal* 8:205-70.

1967   *Ancient Pottery of the Holy Land.* Jerusalem: Massada Press.

Amit, Yairah

2006   "Looking at History through Literary Glasses Too." In *Essays on Ancient Israel in Its Near Eastern Context: A Tribute to Nadav Na'aman.* Winona Lake, IN: Eisenbrauns, 1-15.

Amit, Yairah, et al., eds.

2006   *Essays on Ancient Israel in Its Near Eastern Context: A Tribute to Nadav Na'aman.* Winona Lake, IN: Eisenbrauns.

Arav, Rami

2000   "Bethsaida Rediscovered." *Biblical Archaeology Review* 26/1:48-49.

Aubet, M. E.

1976   *Bullae and Seals from a Post-Exilic Judean Archive.* Qedem 4. Jerusalem: Institute of Archaeology, Hebrew University of Jerusalem.

1986   *Hebrew Bullae from the Time of Jeremiah: Remnants of a Burnt Archive.* Jerusalem: Israel Exploration Society.

1993   *The Phoenicians in the West: Politics, Colonies, and Trade.* Cambridge: Cambridge University Press.

Avigad, Nahman

1953   "The Epitaph of a Royal Steward from Silwan Village." *Israel Exploration Journal* 3:137-52.

1986   *Hebrew Bullae from the Time of Jeremiah: Remnants of a Burnt Archive.* Jerusalem: Israel Exploration Society.

1987   "The Contribution of Hebrew Seals to an Understanding of Israelite Religion and Society." In *Ancient Israelite Religion: Essays in Honor of Frank M. Cross,* edited by Patrick D. Miller, Paul D. Hanson, and S. Dean McBride. Philadelphia: Fortress, 195-208.

1990   "The Inscribed Pomegranate from the 'House of the Lord.'" *Biblical Archaeologist* 53/3:157-66.

Avigad, Nahman, Michael Heltzer, and André Lemaire

2000   *West Semitic Seals: Eighth–Sixth Centuries* B.C.E. Haifa: University of Haifa.

Avigad, Nahman, and Benjamin Sass

1997   *Corpus of West Semitic Stamp Seals.* Jerusalem: Israel Exploration Society.

Baadsgaard, Audrey

2008   "A Taste of Women's Sociality: Cooking as Cooperative Labor in Iron Age Syro-Palestine." In *The World of Women in the Ancient and Classical Near East,* edited by Beth Alpert Nakhai. Newcastle upon Tyne: Cambridge Scholars Publishing, 13-44.

Baker, David W., and Bill T. Arnold, eds.

1999   *The Face of Old Testament Studies: A Survey of Contemporary Approaches.* Grand Rapids: Baker.

Banks, Diane

2006   *Writing the History of Israel.* London: T. & T. Clark.

Bar-Adon, Pesach

1975   "An Early Hebrew Graffito in a Judean Desert Cave." *Israel Exploration Journal* 25:226-32.

Barkay, Gabriel

1986   *Ketef Hinnom: A Treasure Facing Jerusalem's Walls.* Jerusalem: Israel Museum.

1992   "The Iron Age II." In *The Archaeology of Ancient Israel,* edited by Amnon Ben-Tor. New Haven: Yale University Press, 302-73.

1996   "A Balance Beam from Tel Lachish." *Tel Aviv* 23:75-82.

Barkay, Gabriel, et al.

2004   "The Amulets from Ketef Hinnom: A New Edition and Evaluation." *Bulletin of the American Schools of Oriental Research* 334:41-71.

Barnett, Richard D.

1982   *Ancient Ivories in the Middle East.* Qedem 14. Jerusalem: Institute of Archaeology, Hebrew University of Jerusalem.

Barr, James

2000   *History and Ideology in the Old Testament: Biblical Studies at the End of a Millennium.* Oxford: Oxford University Press.

Barstad, Hans

2007   "The History of Ancient Israel: What Directions Should We Take?" In *Understanding the History of Ancient Israel,* edited by Hugh G. M. Williamson. Proceedings of the British Academy 143. Oxford: Oxford University Press, 25-48.

Bartlett, John R.

1989   *Edom and the Edomites.* Sheffield: Sheffield Academic Press.

1992   "Edom in History." In *Anchor Bible Dictionary,* edited by D. N. Freedman. New York: Doubleday, 2:287-95.

Barton, John

1996   *Reading the Old Testament: Method in Biblical Study.* 2nd ed. London: Darton, Longman and Todd.

Beck, Pirhiya

1982   "The Drawings from Horvat Teiman (Kuntillet ʿAjrud)." *Tel Aviv* 9:3-80.

Becking, Bob, et al., eds.

2001   *Only One God? Monotheism in Ancient Israel and the Generation of the Goddess Asherah.* Biblical Seminar. Sheffield: Sheffield Academic Press.

Beit-Arieh, Itzhak, ed.

1995   *Horrat Qitmit: An Edomite Shrine in the Biblical Negev.* Tel Aviv: Tel Aviv University.

1999   *Tel ʿIra, a Stronghold in the Biblical Negev.* Tel Aviv: Tel Aviv University.

Ben-Tor, Amnon, and Yuval Portugali

1987   *Tell Qiri.* Qedem 24. Jerusalem: Institute of Archaeology, Hebrew University of Jerusalem.

Ben Zvi, Ehud, and M. H. Floyd, eds.

2000   *Writings and Speech in Israelite and Ancient Near Eastern Prophecy.* Atlanta: Society of Biblical Literature.

Bienkowski, Piotr, ed.

1992   *Early Edom and Moab: The Beginning of the Iron Age in Southern Transjordan.* Sheffield Archaeological Monographs 7. Sheffield: Collins.

Bintliff, John, ed.

1991   *The Annales School of Archaeology.* Leicester: University of Leicester.

Biran, Avraham

1994   *Biblical Dan.* Jerusalem: Israel Exploration Society.

1999   "Two Bronze Daggers and the Ḥuṣṣot of Dan." *Israel Exploration Journal* 49:43-54.

Biran, Avraham, and Joseph Naveh

1993   "An Aramaic Stele Fragment from Tel Dan." *Israel Exploration Journal* 43:81-98.

1995   "The Tel Dan Inscription: A New Fragment." *Israel Exploration Journal* 45:1-18.

Blakely, Jeffrey A., and James W. Hardin

2002   "Southwestern Judah in the Late Eighth Century B.C.E." *Bulletin of the American Schools of Oriental Research* 326:111-64.

Bloch-Smith, Elizabeth

1992   *Judahite Burial Practices and Beliefs about the Dead.* Sheffield: Sheffield Academic Press.

2002a   "Life in Judah from the Perspective of the Dead." *Near Eastern Archaeology* 65/2:120-30.

2002b   "Solomon's Temple: The Politics of Ritual Space." In *Sacred Time, Sacred Place: Archaeology and the Religion of Israel,* edited by Barry M. Gittlen. Winona Lake, IN: Eisenbrauns, 83-94.

2004   "Maṣṣēbôt in the Israelite Cult: An Argument for Rendering Cultic Criteria Explicit." In *Temple and Worship in Biblical Israel,* edited by John Day. London: T. & T. Clark, 28-39.

Bloom, Allan

1987   *The Closing of the American Mind: How Higher Education Has Failed Democracy and Impoverished the Souls of Today's Students.* New York: Simon and Schuster.

Borowski, Oded

1998   *Every Living Thing: Daily Use of Animals in Ancient Israel.* Walnut Creek, CA: Alta Mira Press.

2002   *Agriculture in Iron Age Israel.* Boston: American Schools of Oriental Research.

2003   *Daily Life in Biblical Times.* Atlanta: Society of Biblical Literature.

Braun, Joachim

2002   *Music in Ancient Israel/Palestine: Archaeological, Written, and Comparative Sources.* Grand Rapids: Eerdmans.

Bibliography

Brettler, Marc Zvi

1995   *The Creation of History in Ancient Israel.* London: Routledge.

2003   "The Copenhagen School: The Historiographical Issues." *American Jewish Studies Review* 27/1:1-22.

Broshi, Magen, and Israel Finkelstein

1992   "The Population of Palestine in Iron Age II." *Bulletin of the American Schools of Oriental Research* 287:147-60.

Bunimovitz, Shlomo, and Avraham Faust

2002   "Ideology in Stone: Understanding the Four-Room House." *Biblical Archaeology Review* 28/4:32-41, 59-60.

2003a   "Building an Identity: The Four Room House and the Israelite Mind." In *Symbiosis, Symbolism, and the Power of the Past: Canaan, Ancient Israel, and Their Neighbors from the Late Bronze Age through Roman Palaestina,* edited by William G. Dever and Seymour Gitin. Winona Lake, IN: Eisenbrauns, 411-23.

2003b   "The Four-Room House: Embodying Iron Age Israelite Society." *Near Eastern Archaeology* 66:22-31.

Bunimovitz, Shlomo, and Zvi Lederman

2009   "The Archaeology of Border Communities: Renewed Excavations at Tel Beth-Shemesh, Part I: The Iron Age." *Near Eastern Archaeology* 72/3:115-42.

Burgh, Theodore

2006   *Listening to the Artifacts: Music Culture in Ancient Palestine.* New York: T. & T. Clark.

Burke, Aaron

2009   *"Walled Up to Heaven": The Evolution of Middle Bronze Age Fortification Strategies in the Levant.* Studies in the Archaeology and History of the Levant 4. Winona Lake, IN: Eisenbrauns.

Cahill, Jane

2003   "Jerusalem at the Time of the United Monarchy: The Archaeological Evidence." In *Jerusalem in Bible and Archaeology,* edited by Andrew Vaughn and Ann Killebrew. Atlanta: Scholars Press, 13-80.

Campbell, Edward F.

1998   "A Land Divided: Judah and Israel from the Death of Solomon to the Fall of Samaria." In *The Oxford History of the Biblical World,* edited by Michael D. Coogan. New York: Oxford University Press, 206-41.

1994   "Archaeological Reflections on Amos's Targets." In *Scripture and Other Artifacts: Essays on the Bible and Archaeology in Honor of Philip J. King,* edited by Michael D. Corgan, J. Cheryl Exum, and Lawrence E. Stager. Louisville: Westminster John Knox, 32-52.

Canaan, Tewfik

1933   "The Palestinian Arab House: Its Architecture and Folklore." *Journal of the Palestine Oriental Society* 13:1-83.

Carr, David M.

2008   "The Tel Zayit Abecedary in (Social) Context." In *Literate Culture and Tenth-Century Canaan: The Tel Zayit Abecedary in Context*, edited by Ron E. Tappy and P. Kyle McCarter. Winona Lake, IN: Eisenbrauns, 113-29.

Carr, E. H.

1987   *What Is History?* London: Penguin.

Carroll, Robert

1997   "Madonna of Silences: Clio and the Bible." In *Can a "History of Israel" Be Written?* Journal for the Study of the Old Testament: Supplement Series 14. Sheffield: Sheffield Academic Press.

Cassuto, Deborah

2008   "Bringing the Artifacts Home: A Social Interpretation of Loom Weights in Context." In *The World of Women in the Ancient and Classical Near East*, edited by Beth Alpert Nakhai. Newcastle upon Tyne: Cambridge Scholars Publishing, 63-77.

Chambon, Alain

1984   *Tell el-Fârʿâh I: L'âge du Fer.* Paris: Éditions Recherche sur les Civilisations.

Chapman, Rupert

1997   "Weapons and Warfare." In *Oxford Encyclopedia of the Archaeology of the Near East*, edited by J. Sasson. New York and Oxford: Oxford University Press, 5:334-39.

Clark, Douglas R.

2003   "Bricks, Sweat and Tears: The Human Investment in Constructing a 'Four-Room' House." *Near Eastern Archaeologist* 66:1-2.

Clark, Douglas R., and Larry G. Herr

2009   "From the Stone Age to the Middle Ages in Jordan: Digging Up Tall al-ʿUmayri." *Near Eastern Archaeology* 72/2:68-97.

Cogan, Mordechai

1998   "Into Exile: From the Assyrian Conquest to the Fall of Babylon." In *The*

Oxford History of the Hebrew Bible, edited by Michael D. Coogan. New York: Oxford University Press, 242-73.

Cohen, Rudolf, and Y. Yisrael

1995   "The Iron Age Fortress at ʿEn-Ḥaseva." *Biblical Archaeologist* 58:223-25.

1996   "Smashing the Idols: Piecing Together an Edomite Shrine in Judah." *Biblical Archaeologist* 22/4:40-51.

Collins, John J.

2005   *The Bible after Babel: Historical Criticism in a Postmodern Age.* Grand Rapids: Eerdmans.

Connelley, Joan B.

1989   "Standing Before One's God: Votive Sculpture and the Cypriote Religions." *Biblical Archaeologist* 52/4:210-18.

Cornelius, Izthak

2004   *The Many Faces of the Goddess: The Iconography of the Syro-Palestinian Goddesses Anat, Astarte, Qedeshet, and Asherah, 1500-1000 BCE.* Fribourg: Academic Press.

Crowfoot, John W., and Grace M. Crowfoot

1938   *Early Ivories from Samaria.* London: Palestine Exploration Fund.

Crowfoot, John W., Grace M. Crawfoot, and Kathleen M. Kenyon

1957   *Samaria-Sebaste III: The Objects from Samaria.* London: Palestine Exploration Fund.

Dalman, Gustav

1935   *Arbeite und Sitte in Palästina.* Vols. 2-4. Gütersloh: Bertelsmann.

1942   *Arbeite und Sitte in Palästina.* Vol. 7. Gütersloh: Bertelsmann.

Dar, Shimon

1986   *Landscape and Pattern: An Archaeological Survey of Western Samaria, 800 BCE–636 CE.* BAR International Series 308. Oxford: British Archaeological Reports.

Daviau, P. M. Michèle, John W. Wevers, and M. Weigl, eds.

2001   *The World of the Aramaeans II: Studies in History and Archaeology in Honour of Paul-Eugene Dion.* Sheffield: Sheffield Academic Press.

Davies, Philip R.

1992   *In Search of "Ancient Israel."* Journal for the Study of the Old Testament: Supplement Series 148. Sheffield: Sheffield Academic Press.

1997   "Whose History? Whose Israel? Whose Bible? Biblical Histories, Ancient and Modern." In *Can a "History of Israel" Be Written?* edited by Lester L.

Grabbe. Journal for the Study of the Old Testament: Supplement Series 245. Sheffield: Sheffield Academic Press, 104-22.

2000   "The Search for History in the Bible — What Separates a Minimalist from a Maximalist? Not Much." *Biblical Archaeology Review* 26/2:24-27, 72-73.

2005   "Crypto-Minimalism." *Journal of Semitic Studies* 50:117-36.

2007   "Biblical Israel in the Ninth Century." In *Understanding the History of Ancient Israel,* edited by Hugh G. M. Williamson. Proceedings of the British Academy 143. Oxford: Oxford University Press, 49-56.

Davis, Miriam C.

2008   *Dame Kathleen Kenyon: Digging Up the Holy Land.* Walnut Creek, CA: Left Coast Press.

Davis, Thomas W.

2004   *Shifting Sands: The Rise and Fall of Biblical Archaeology.* Oxford: Oxford University Press.

Day, John

2000   *Yahweh and the Gods and Goddesses of Canaan.* Sheffield: Sheffield Academic Press.

Day, John, ed.

2004   *In Search of Pre-Exilic Israel.* Journal for the Study of the Old Testament: Supplement Series 406. London: T. & T. Clark.

Dayagi-Mendels, M., and M. Weigl

1999   *Drink and Be Merry: Wine and Beer in Ancient Times.* Jerusalem: Israel Museum.

Dearman, Andrew, ed.

1989   *Studies in the Mesha Inscription and Moab.* Atlanta: Scholars Press.

de Geus, Cornelius H. J.

2003   *Towns in Ancient Israel and in the Southern Levant.* Leuven: Peeters.

Deist, Ferdinand E.

2000   *The Material Culture of the Bible.* Sheffield: Sheffield Academic Press.

Demsky, Aaron, and Moshe Kochavi

1978   "An Alphabet from the Days of the Judges." *Biblical Archaeology Review* 4/3:23-30.

Dever, William G.

1981   "Biblical Theology and Biblical Archaeology: An Appreciation of G. Ernest Wright." *Harvard Theological Review* 73:1-15.

1984   "Asherah, Consort of Yahweh? New Evidence from Kuntillet 'Ajrûd." *Bulletin of the American Schools of Oriental Research* 255:29-37.

1985   "Syro-Palestinian and Biblical Archaeology." In *The Hebrew Bible and Its Modern Interpreters*, edited by Douglas A. Knight and Gene M. Tucker. Philadelphia: Fortress, 31-74.

1986   "Late Bronze Age and Solomonic Defences at Gezer: New Evidence." *Bulletin of the American Schools of Oriental Research* 262:9-34.

1988   "Impact of the New Archaeology." In *Benchmarks in Time and Culture: Introduction to Palestinian Archaeology*, edited by Joel F. Drinkard Jr., Gerald L. Mattingly, and J. Maxwell Miller. Atlanta: Scholars Press, 337-52.

1991   "Archaeology, Material Culture and the Early Monarchical Period." In *The Fabric of History: Text, Artifact, and Israel's Past*, edited by Diana V. Edelman. Journal for the Study of the Old Testament: Supplement Series 127. Sheffield: JSOT Press, 103-15.

1992   "Archaeology, Syro-Palestinian and Biblical." In *Anchor Bible Dictionary*, edited by David Noel Freedman. New York: Doubleday, 1:354-67.

1993   "Further Evidence on the Date of the Outer Wall at Gezer." *Bulletin of the American Schools of Oriental Research* 289:33-54.

1994   "The Silence of the Text: An Archaeological Commentary on 2 Kings 23." In *Scripture and Other Artifacts: Essays on the Bible and Archaeology in Honor of Philip J. King*, edited by M. D. Coogan, J. C. Exum, and L. E. Stager. Louisville: Westminster John Knox.

1995   "Social Structure in Palestine in the Iron II Period on the Eve of Destruction." In *The Archaeology of Society in the Holy Land*, edited by Thomas E. Levy. London: Leicester University Press, 416-31.

1997a   "Philology, Theology, and Archaeology: What Kind of History Do We Want, and What Is Possible?" In *The Archaeology of Israel: Constructing the Past, Interpreting the Present*, edited by Neil A. Silberman and David Small. Sheffield: Sheffield Academic Press, 290-310.

1997b   "On Listening to the Texts and the Artifacts." In *The Echoes of Many Texts: Essays in Honor of Lou H. Silberman*, edited by William G. Dever and J. Edward Wright. Atlanta: Scholars Press, 1-23.

1998   "Archaeology, Ideology, and the Search for an 'Ancient' or 'Biblical' Israel." *Near Eastern Archaeology* 61/1:39-52.

1999a   "Histories and Non-Histories of Ancient Israel." *Bulletin of the American Schools of Oriental Research* 316:89-105.

1999b   "Archaeology and the Israelite Cult: How the Kh. el-Qôm and Kuntillet 'Ajrûd 'Asherah' Texts Have Changed the Picture." *Eretz-Israel* 26:8*-15*.

2000   "Biblical and Syro-Palestinian Archaeology: A State-of-the-Art Assessment at the Turn of the Millennium." *Currents in Research: Biblical Research* 8:91-116.

2001a   *What Did the Biblical Writers Know and When Did They Know It? What Archaeology Can Tell Us about the Reality of Ancient Israel.* Grand Rapids: Eerdmans.

2001b   "Iron Age Kernoi and the Israelite Cult." In *Studies in the Archaeology of Israel and Neighboring Lands in Honor of James A. Sauer,* edited by Samuel Wolff. Studies in Ancient Oriental Civilization 59. Chicago: Oriental Institute, 119-33.

2001c   Review of *The Bible Unearthed: Archaeology's New Vision of Ancient Israel and the Origin of Its Sacred Texts,* by I. Finkelstein and Neil A. Silberman. *Bulletin of the American Schools of Oriental Research* 322:66-77.

2003a   "Syro-Palestinian and Biblical Archaeology: Into the Next Millennium." In *Symbosis, Symbolism, and the Power of the Past: Canaan, Ancient Israel, and Their Neighbors from the Late Bronze Age through Roman Palaestina,* edited by William G. Dever and Seymour Gitin. Winona Lake, IN: Eisenbrauns, 513-27.

2003b   *Who Were the Early Israelites and Where Did They Come From?* Grand Rapids: Eerdmans.

2003c   "The Patriarchs and Matriarchs of Ancient Israel: Myth or History?" In *One Hundred Years of American Archaeology in the Middle East: Proceedings of the American Schools of Oriental Research Centennial Celebration, Washington, DC, April 2000,* edited by Douglas R. Clark and Victor H. Matthews. Boston: American Schools of Oriental Research, 39-56.

2003d   "The Rural Landscape of Palestine in the Early Bronze IV Period." In *The Rural Landscape of Ancient Israel,* edited by Aren M. Maeir, Shimon Dar, and Z. Safrai. Oxford: Archaeopress, 43-59.

2004   "Histories and Non-Histories of Ancient Israel: Theology, Archaeology, and Ideology." In *In Search of Pre-Exilic Israel,* edited by John Day. Cambridge: Cambridge University Press, 65-94.

2005a   *Did God Have a Wife? Archaeology and Folk Religion in Ancient Israel.* Grand Rapids: Eerdmans.

2005b   "Histories and Non-Histories of Ancient Israel: What Archaeology Can Contribute." In *Recenti tendenze nella ricos tiuzioni della storia antica Israel,* edited by Mario Liverani. Rome: Academia Lincei, 29-50.

2005c   "Social Structure in Palestine in the Iron II on the Eve of Destruction." In *The Archaeology of Science,* edited by Thomas E. Levy. Leicester: Leicester University Press, 416-30.

2007   "Archaeology and the Fall of the Northern Kingdom: What Really Happened?" In *"Up to the Gates of Ekron": Essays on the Archaeology and History of the Eastern Mediterranean in Honor of Seymour Gitin,* edited by Sidnie W. Crawford et al. Jerusalem: Israel Exploration Society, 78-92.

2008   "A Temple Built for Two: Did Yahweh Share a Throne with His Consort Asherah?" *Biblical Archaeology Review* 34/2:4, 54-62.

2010   Review of *Ancient Israel: What Do We Know and How Do We Know It?* by Lester L. Grabbe. *Bulletin of the American Schools of Oriental Research* 357:77-83.

Forthcoming   "The Judean 'Pillar-Base Figurines': Mother and Mother Goddesses?" In *The Rainer Albertz Festschrift*. Münster.

Dever, William G., H. Darrell Lance, and G. Ernest Wright
1970   *Gezer I: Preliminary Report of the 1964-65 Seasons.* Jerusalem: Hebrew
        Union College.

Dever, William G., et al.
1986   *Gezer IV: The 1968-81 Seasons in Field IV, the "Acropolis."* Annual of the
        NGSBAJ. Jerusalem: Hebrew Union College.

Dever, William, and Seymour Gitin, eds.
2003   *Symbiosis, Symbolism, and the Power of the Past: Canaan, Ancient Israel,
        and Their Neighbors from the Late Bronze Age through Roman Palaestina.*
        Winona Lake, IN: Eisenbrauns.

Dijkstra, Meindert
2001   "I Have Blessed You by YHWH of Samaria and His Asherah: Texts with
        Religious Elements from the Soil Archive of Ancient Israel." In *Only One
        God? Monotheism in Ancient Israel and the Veneration of the Goddess
        Asherah,* edited by Bob Becking et al. Biblical Seminar 77. Sheffield: Shef-
        field Academic Press, 17-44.

Dolansky, Shawna
2008   *Now You See It, Now You Don't: Biblical Perspectives on the Relationship be-
        tween Magic and Religion.* Winona Lake, IN: Eisenbrauns.

Dornemann, Rudolph H.
1983   *The Archaeology of the Transjordan in the Bronze and Iron Ages.* Milwau-
        kee: Milwaukee Public Museum.

Dothan, Moshe
1971   *Ashdod II-III: The Second and Third Seasons of Excavations 1963, 1965;
        'Atiqot IX-X.* Jerusalem: Institute of Archaeology, Hebrew University of
        Jerusalem.

Dothan, Moshe, and Trude Dothan
1992   *People of the Sea: The Search for the Philistines.* New York: Macmillan.

Dothan, Trude
1992   "Philistines, History." In *Anchor Bible Dictionary,* edited by D. N. Freed-
        man. New York: Doubleday, 5:326-28.

Eagleton, Terrence
1996   *The Illusions of Postmodernism.* Oxford: Blackwell.

Ebeling, Jennie R.

2010   *Women's Lives in Biblical Times.* London: T. & T. Clark.

Ebeling, Jennie R., and Michael M. Homan

2008   "Baking and Brewing Beer in the Israelite Household: A Study of Women's Cooking Technology." In *The World of Women in the Ancient and Classical Near East,* edited by Beth Albert Nakhai. Newcastle upon Tyne: Cambridge Scholars Publishing, 45-62.

Ebeling, Jennie R., and York Rowan

2008   *New Approaches to Old Stones: Recent Studies of Ground Stone Artifacts.* London: Equinox.

Edelman, Diana V., ed.

1991   *The Fabric of History: Text, Artifact, and Israel's Past.* Journal for the Study of the Old Testament: Supplement Series 127. Sheffield: JSOT Press.

1995   *You Shall Not Abhor an Edomite for He Is Your Brother: Edom and Seir in History and Tradition.* Atlanta: Scholars Press.

Eitam, David

2007   "The Stone Tools from Khirbet ʿAuja el-Foqa." In *"Up to the Gates of Ekron": Essays on the Archaeology and History of the Eastern Mediterranean in Honor of Seymour Gitin,* edited by Sidnie W. Crawford et al. Jerusalem: Israel Exploration Society, 93-106.

Ellis, J. M.

1989   *Against Deconstruction.* Princeton: Princeton University Press.

Eshel, Itzhak, and Kay Prag

1995   *Excavations by K. M. Kenyon in Jerusalem, 1961-67.* Vol. IV, *The Iron Age Cave Deposits on the South-Eastern Hill and Isolated Burials and Cemeteries.* Oxford: Oxford University Press.

Evans, Carl D., William W. Hallo, and John B. White, eds.

1986   *Scripture in Context: Essays on the Comparative Approach.* Pittsburgh: Pickwick.

Falconer, Steven E., and Stephen H. Savage

1995   "Heartlands and Hinterlands: Alternative Trajectories of Early Urbanization in Mesopotamia and the Southern Levant." *American Antiquity* 60:38-44.

Faust, Avraham

2000   "The Rural Community in Ancient Israel during the Iron Age II." *Bulletin of the American Schools of Oriental Research* 317:17-39.

2002   "Accessibility, Defence and Town Planning in Iron Age Israel." *Tel Aviv* 29/2:297-317.

2003a   "The Farmstead in the Highland of Iron Age II Israel." In *The Rural Landscape of Ancient Israel*, edited by Aren M. Maeir, Shimon Dar, and Z. Safrai. BAR International Series 1121. Oxford: British Archaeological Reports, 91-104.

2003b   "Residential Patterns in the Ancient Israelite City." *Levant* 35:123-38.

2005a   "The Settlement of Jerusalem's Western Hill and the City's Status in Iron Age II Revisited." *Zeitschrift des Deutschen Palästina-Vereins* 121:97-118.

2005b   "The Israelite Village: Cultural Conservatism and Technological Innovation." *Tel Aviv* 32:204-19.

2006a   *Israel's Ethnogenesis: Settlement, Interaction, Expansion, and Resistance.* London: Equinox.

2006b   "Farmsteads in Western Samaria's Foothills: A. Reexamination." In *"I Will Speak the Riddles of Ancient Times": Archaeological and Historical Studies in Honor of Amihai Mazar on the Occasion of His Sixtieth Birthday*, edited by Aren M. Maeir and Pierre deMiroschedji. Winona Lake, IN: Eisenbrauns, 477-504.

2006c   "The Negev Fortresses in Context: Reexamining the Phenomenon in Light of General Settlement Processes of the Eleventh-Tenth Centuries B.C.E." *Journal of the American Oriental Society* 26/2:135-60.

2007   "Rural Settlements, State Formation, and 'Bible Archaeology.'" *Near Eastern Archaeology* 70/1:4-9.

2008a   "Settlement and Demography in Seventh-Century Judah and the Extent and Intensity of Sennacherib's Campaign." *Palestine Exploration Quarterly* 140/3:168-94.

2008b   "The Judahite Rock-Cut Tomb: Family Response at a Time of Change." *Israel Exploration Journal* 58:150-70.

2011   *The Archaeology of Israelite Society in Iron Age II.* Winona Lake, IN: Eisenbrauns.

Faust, Avraham, and Shlomo Bunimovitz

2003   "The Four Room House: Embodying Iron Age Israelite Society." *Near Eastern Archaeology* 66/1-2:22-31.

Finkelstein, Israel

1995   "The Archaeology of the United Monarchy: An Alternative View." *Levant* 28:177-87.

1998   "Bible Archaeology or the Archaeology of Palestine in the Iron Age? A Rejoinder." *Levant* 30:167-74.

2001   "The Rise of Jerusalem and Judah: The Missing Link." *Levant* 33:105-15.

2003   "The Rise of Judah and Jerusalem: The Missing Link." In *Jerusalem in Bi-*

ble and Archaeology: The First Temple Period, edited by A. G. Vaughan and Ann E. Killebrew. Atlanta: Society of Biblical Literature, 81-101.

2007   "The Two Kingdoms: Israel and Judah." In *The Quest for the Historical Israel: Debating Archaeology and the History of Early Israel,* edited by Brian B. Schmidt. Atlanta: Society of Biblical Literature, 147-57.

Finkelstein, Israel, Zvi Lederman, and Shlomo Bunimovitz

1997   *Highland of Many Cultures: The Southern Samaria Survey.* Tel Aviv: Institute of Archaeology, Tel Aviv University.

Finkelstein, Israel, and Eli Piasetzkey

2003   "Recent Radiocarbon Results and Biblical History." *Antiquity* 77:876-84.

Finkelstein, Israel, and Neil Asher Silberman

2001   *The Bible Unearthed: Archaeology's New Vision of Ancient Israel and the Origin of Its Sacred Texts.* New York: Free Press.

Finkelstein, Israel, David Ussishkin, and Baruch Halpern, eds.

2000   *Megiddo III/1 & 2: The 1992-1996 Seasons.* Tel Aviv Monograph Series 18. Tel Aviv: Institute of Archaeology, Tel Aviv University.

2006   *Megiddo IV/1 & 2: The 1998-2002 Seasons.* Tel Aviv Monograph Series 24. Tel Aviv: Institute of Archaeology, Tel Aviv University.

Frankel, R., S. Avitsur, and E. Ayalon

1994   *History and Technology of Olive Oil in the Holy Land.* Translated by J. C. Johnson. Tel Aviv: Eretz Israel Museum.

Frei, Hans

1974   *The Eclipse of the Biblical Narrative: A Study in Eighteenth and Nineteenth Century Hermeneutics.* New Haven: Yale University Press.

Fritz, Volkmar

1990   *Kinneret.* Wiesbaden: Otto Harrassowitz.

1995   *The City in Ancient Israel.* Sheffield: Sheffield Academic Press.

2007   "On the Reconstruction of the Four-Room House." In *"Up to the Gates of Ekron": Essays on the Archaeology and History of the Eastern Mediterranean in Honor of Seymour Gitin,* edited by Sidnie White Crawford et al. Jerusalem: Israel Exploration Society, 114-18.

Fritz, Volkmar, and Philip R. Davies, eds.

1996   *The Origins of the Ancient Israelite State.* Sheffield: Sheffield Academic Press.

Galil, Gershon

1996   *The Chronology of the Kings of Israel and Judah.* Leiden: Brill.

Garbini, Giovanni

1998   *History and Ideology in Ancient Israel.* New York: Crossroad.

Garfinkel, Yosef

2007   "The Dynamic Settlement History of Philistine Ekron: A Case Study of Central Place Theory." In *"Up to the Gates of Ekron": Essays on the Archaeology and History of the Eastern Mediterranean in Honor of Seymour Gitin,* edited by Sidnie W. Crawford et al. Jerusalem: Israel Exploration Society, 17-24.

Garfinkel, Yosef, and Vaar Ganor

2009   *Khirbet Qeiyafa Vol. 1: Excavation Report, 2007-2008.* Jerusalem: Institute of Archaeology, Hebrew University of Jerusalem.

Geva, Hillel

2003   "Western Jerusalem at the End of the First Temple Period in Light of the Excavations in the Jewish Quarter." In *Jerusalem in Bible and Archaeology: The First Temple Period,* edited by Andrew G. Vaughn and Ann E. Killebrew. Atlanta: Society of Biblical Literature, 183-208.

Geva, Shulamith

1989   *Hazor, Israel: An Urban Community of the 8th Century BCE.* BAR International Series 543. Oxford: Oxford University Press.

Gilboa, Ayelet

2009   "Notes on Iron IIA ^{14}C Dates from Tell el-Qudeirat (Kadesh Barnea)." *Tel Aviv* 36/1:82-94.

Gitin, Seymour

1990   *Gezer III: A Ceramic Typology of the Late Iron II, Persian and Hellenistic Periods at Tel Gezer.* Annual of NGSBAJ, vol. 3. Jerusalem: Hebrew Union College.

1993   "Scoops: Corpus, Function, and Typology." In *Studies in the Archaeology and History of Ancient Israel: In Honor of Moshe Dothan,* edited by M. Heltzer, A. Segal, and D. Kaufman. Haifa: Haifa University Press, 99-126.

1997   "The Neo-Assyrian and Its Western Periphery: The Levant, with a Focus on Philistine Ekron." In *Proceedings of the 10th Anniversary Symposium of the Neo-Assyrian Text Corpus Project, Helsinki, September, 1995,* edited by Simo Parpola and R. M. Whiting. Helsinki: University of Helsinki, 77-103.

1998   "Philistia in Transition: The Tenth Century BCE and Beyond." In *Mediterranean Peoples in Transition: Thirteenth to Early Tenth Centuries BCE,* edited by Seymour Gitin, Amihai Mazar, and Ephraim Stern. Jerusalem: Israel Exploration Society, 162-83.

2002   "The Four-Horned Altar and Sacred Space." In *Sacred Time, Sacred Place:*

Archaeology and the Religion of Israel, edited by Barry M. Gittlen. Winona Lake, IN: Eisenbrauns, 95-123.

2004a "The Philistines: Neighbors of the Canaanites, Phoenicians, and Israelites." In *One Hundred Years of American Archeology in the Levant: Proceedings of the American Schools of Oriental Research Centennial Celebration, Washington, D.C., April, 2000,* edited by Douglas Clark and Victor Matthews. Atlanta: American Schools of Oriental Research, 55-83.

2004b "A Silver-Based Monetary Economy in the 7th Century BCE: A Response to Raz Kletter." *Levant* 36:203-5.

2006 "The lmlk Jar-Form Redefined: A New Class of Iron Age II Oval-Shaped Storage Jars." In *"I Will Speak the Riddles of Ancient Times": Archaeological and Historical Studies in Honor of Amihai Mazar on the Occasion of His Sixtieth Birthday,* edited by Aren M. Maeir and Pierre de Miroschedji. Winona Lake, IN: Eisenbrauns, 505-24.

Gitin, Seymour, and A. Golani

2001 "The Tel Miqneh Silver Hoards: The Assyrian and Phoenician Connections." In *Hacksilber to Coinage: New Insights into the Monetary History of the Near East and Greece,* edited by Miriam Balmuth. New York: American Numismatic Society, 25-45.

Gitin, Seymour, J. Edward Wright, and J. P. Dessel, eds.

2006 *Confronting the Past: Essays in Honor of William G. Dever.* Winona Lake, IN: Eisenbrauns.

Grabbe, Lester L.

2000 "Hat die Bibel doch Recht? A Review of T. L. Thompson's *The Bible in History." Journal for the Society of the Old Testament* 13:117-39.

2007 *Ancient Israel: What Do We Know and How Do We Know It?* London: T. & T. Clark.

2008 *Israel in Transition. From Late Bronze II to Iron IIA (c. 1250-850 B.C.E.).* Vol. 1, *The Archaeology.* London: T. & T. Clark.

Grabbe, Lester L., ed.

1997 *Can a "History of Israel" Be Written?* Journal for the Study of the Old Testament: Supplement Series 245. Sheffield: Sheffield Academic Press.

Greenberg, Raphael

1987 "New Light on the Early Iron Age at Tell Beit Mirsim." *Bulletin of the American Schools of Oriental Research* 265:55-80.

Gress, David

1998 *From Plato to NATO: The Idea of the West and Its Opponents.* New York: Free Press.

Guy, P. L. O., and Robert M. Engberg
1938   *Megiddo Tombs.* Chicago: University of Chicago Press.

Hadley, Judith M.
2000   *The Cult of Asherah in Ancient Israel and Judah: Evidence for a Hebrew Goddess.* Cambridge: Cambridge University Press.

Hagelia, Hallvard
2004   "The First Dissertation on the Tel Dan Inscription." *Scandinavian Journal of the Old Testament* 18/1:135-45.

Hallo, William W.
1990   "The Limits of Skepticism." *Journal of the American Oriental Society* 110/2 (April-June).

Hallo, William W., James C. Moyers, and Leo G. Perdue, eds.
1983   *Scripture in Context II: More Essays on the Comparative Method.* Winona Lake, IN: Eisenbrauns.

Halpern, Baruch
1985   *The First Historians: The Hebrew Bible and History.* San Francisco: Harper and Row.
1995   "Erasing History: The Minimalist Assault on Ancient Israel." *Bible Review* 11/6:26-35, 47.
1997   "Text and Artifact: Two Monologues?" In *Constructing the Past, Interpreting the Present,* edited by Neil A. Silberman and David Small. Journal for the Study of the Old Testament: Supplement Series 237. Sheffield: Sheffield Academic Press, 311-41.

Hardin, James W.
2010   *Lahav II: Households and the Use of Domestic Space at Iron II Tell Halif; An Archaeology of Destruction.* Winona Lake, IN: Eisenbrauns.

Harris, William V.
1989   *Ancient Literacy.* Cambridge: Harvard University Press.

Harrison, Timothy P.
2004   *Megiddo 3: Final Report on the Stratum VI Excavations.* Oriental Institute Publication 127. Chicago: University of Chicago Press.

Havelock, E. A.
1982   *The Literate Revolution in Greece and Its Cultural Consequences.* Princeton: Princeton University Press.

Heaton, E. W.
1994   *The School Tradition of the Old Testament: The Bampton Lectures for 1994.* Oxford: Clarendon.

Hendel, Ronald S.

1999   Review of *The Israelites in History and Tradition,* by Niels Peter Lemche. *Biblical Archaeology Review* 25/6:59-60.

Herr, Larry G.

1988   "Tripartite Pillared Buildings and the Market Place in Iron Age Palestine." *Bulletin of the American Schools of Oriental Research* 271:47-67.

Herzog, Ze'ev

1984   *Beersheba II: The Early Iron Age Settlement.* Tel Aviv: Institute of Archaeology, Tel Aviv University.

1992   "Settlement and Fortification Planning in the Iron Age." In *The Architecture of Ancient Israel,* edited by Aaron Kempinski et al. Jerusalem: Israel Exploration Society, 231-74.

1997   *Archaeology of the City: Urban Planning in Ancient Israel and Its Social Implications.* Tel Aviv: Institute of Archaeology, Tel Aviv University.

2001   "The Date of the Temple at Arad: Reassessment of the Stratigraphy and the Implications for the History of Judah." In *Studies in the Archaeology of the Iron Age in Israel and Jordan,* edited by A. Mazar. Journal for the Study of the Old Testament: Supplement Series 331. Sheffield: Sheffield Academic Press, 156-78.

Herzog, Ze'ev, Yohanan Aharoni, and Anson F. Rainey

1987   "Arad: An Ancient Israelite Fortress with a Temple to YHWH." *Biblical Archaeology Review* 13/2:16-35.

Herzog, Ze'ev, Anson Rainey, and Shmuel Muskovitz

1977   "The Stratigraphy of Beer-Sheba and the Location of the Sanctuary." *Bulletin of the American Schools of Oriental Research* 225:49-58.

Herzog, Ze'ev, et al.

1984   "The Israelite Fortress at Arad." *Bulletin of the American Schools of Oriental Research* 254:1-34.

Hess, Richard S.

2007   *Israelite Religions: An Archaeological and Biblical Survey.* Grand Rapids: Baker Academic.

Hestrin, Ruth, and M. Dayagi-Mendels

1979   *Inscribed Seals: First Temple Period; Hebrew, Ammonite, Moabite, Phoenician, and Aramaic.* Jerusalem: Israel Museum.

Hodder, Ian

1986   *Reading the Past: Current Approaches to Interpretation in Archaeology.* Cambridge: Cambridge University Press.

Bibliography

Hodder, Ian, and Scott Hutson

2003   *Reading the Past: Current Approaches to Interpretation in Archaeology.* 3rd ed. Cambridge: Cambridge University Press.

Hodder, Ian, and Clive Orton

1976   *Spatial Analysis in Archaeology.* Cambridge: Cambridge University Press.

Hoffmeier, James K., and Alan Millard, eds.

2004   *The Future of Biblical Archaeology: Reassessing Methodologies and Assumptions.* Grand Rapids: Eerdmans.

Holladay, John S.

1986   "The Stables of Ancient Israel: Functional Determinants of Stable Construction; Interpretation of Pillared Building Remains of the Palestinian Iron Age." In *The Archaeology of Jordan and Other Studies Presented to Siefried H. Horn,* edited by T. Geraty and G. Herr. Berrien Springs, MI: Andrews University Press, 65-103.

1987   "Religions in Israel and Judah under the Monarchy." In *Ancient Israelite Religion: Essays in Honor of Frank Moore Cross,* edited by Paul D. Hanson and S. Dean McBride. Philadelphia: Fortress, 249-99.

1992   "House, Israelite." In *Anchor Bible Dictionary,* edited by D. N. Freedman. New York: Doubleday, 3:308-18.

1995   "The Kingdoms of Israel and Judah: Political and Economic Centralization in the Iron Age II A-B (*ca.* 1000-750 B.C.E.)." In *The Archaeology of Society,* edited by Thomas E. Levy. London: Leicester University Press, 368-98.

Holland, Thomas

1977   "A Study of Palestinian Iron Age Baked Clay Figurines with Special Reference to Jerusalem Cave I." *Levant* 9:121-55.

Homan, Michael M.

2010   "Did the Ancient Israelites Drink Beer?" *Biblical Archaeology Review* 36/5:48-56, 78.

Hopkins, David C.

1985   *The Highlands of Canaan: Agricultural Life in the Early Iron Age Israel.* Social World of Biblical Antiquity 3. Sheffield: Almond Press.

Hurvitz, Avi

1997   "The Historical Quest for an 'Ancient Israel' and the Linguistic Evidence of the Hebrew Bible: Some Methodological Observations." *Vetus Testamentum* 47:301-15.

1999   "The Relevance of Biblical Hebrew Linguistics for the Historical Study of

Ancient Israel." In *Proceedings of the Twelfth World Congress of Jewish Studies*. Jerusalem: World Congress of Jewish Studies, 21-33.

James, Francis W.

1966   *The Iron Age at Beth Shan*. Philadelphia: University Museum.

Jamieson-Drake, David W.

1991   *Scribes and Schools in Monarchic Judah: A Socio-Archaeological Approach*. Journal for the Study of the Old Testament: Supplement Series 109. Sheffield: Sheffield Academic Press.

Japhet, Sara

1998   "In Search of Ancient Israel: Revisionism at All Costs." In *The Jewish Past Revisited: Reflections on Modern Jewish Historians*, edited by David D. Meyers and David S. Ruderman. New Haven: Yale University Press.

Jeffers, Ann

1986   *Magic and Divination in Ancient Palestine and Syria*. Leiden: Brill.

Kaiser, Walter C.

1998   *A History of Israel*. Nashville: Broadman and Holman.

Katzenstein, H. J.

1992   "Philistines, History." In *Anchor Bible Dictionary*, edited by D. N. Freedman. New York: Doubleday, 5:326-28.

Kaufmann, Ivan

1982   "The Samaria Ostraca: An Early Witness to Hebrew Writing." *Biblical Archaeologist* 45:229-39.

Keel, Othmar

1997   *The Symbolism of the Biblical World: Ancient Near Eastern Iconography and the Book of Psalms*. Winona Lake, IN: Eisenbrauns.

Keel, Othmar, and Christoph Uehlinger

1998   *Gods, Goddesses, and Images of God in Ancient Israel*. Minneapolis: Fortress.

Kempinski, Aharon, and Ronny Reich, eds.

1992   *The Architecture of Ancient Israel from the Prehistoric to the Persian Period*. Jerusalem: Israel Exploration Society.

Kenyon, Kathleen M.

1974   *Digging Up Jerusalem*. London: Benn.

Killebrew Ann E.

2008   *Biblical Peoples and Ethnicity: An Archaeological Study of Egyptians,*

Canaanites, Philistines, and Early Israel, 1300-1100 B.C.E. Atlanta: Scholars Press.

King, Phillip J., and Lawrence E. Stager

2001   *Life in Biblical Israel.* Louisville: Westminster John Knox.

Kitchen, Kenneth A.

2003   *On the Reliability of the Old Testament.* Grand Rapids: Eerdmans.

Kletter, Raz

1991   "The Inscribed Weights of the Kingdom of Judah." *Tel Aviv* 18/1:121-63.

1996   *The Judean Pillar-Figurines and the Archaeology of Asherah.* BAR International Series 636. Oxford: Temvs Reparatum.

1999   "Pots and Polities: Material Remains of Late Iron Judah in Relation to Its Political Borders." *Bulletin of the American Schools of Oriental Research* 314:19-54.

2001   "Between Archaeology and Theology: The Pillar Figurines from Judah and the Asherah." In *Studies in the Archaeology of the Iron Age in Israel and Judah*, edited by A. Mazar. Journal for the Study of the Old Testament: Supplement Series 331. Sheffield: Sheffield Academic Press, 179-216.

Knauf, Ernst Axel

1991   "From History to Interpretation." In *The Fabric of History: Text, Artifact, and Israel's Past*, edited by D. V. Edelman. Journal for the Study of the Old Testament: Supplement Series 127. Sheffield: Sheffield Academic Press, 26-64.

2008   "From Archaeology to History, Bronze and Iron Ages, with Special Regard to the Year 1200 B.C.E., and the Tenth Century." In *Israel in Transition: From Late Bronze II to Iron IIa (c. 1250-850 B.C.E.)*, vol. 1, *The Archaeology*, edited by L. L. Grabbe. London: T. & T. Clark, 72-85.

Knoppers, Gary N.

1993/94 *Two Nations under God: The Deuternomistic History and the Dual Monarchies.* 2 vols. Harvard Semitic Museum Series. Atlanta: Scholars Press.

1997   "The Vanishing Solomon: The Disappearance of the United Monarchy from Recent Histories of Ancient Israel." *Journal of Biblical Literature* 116:19-44.

Knoppers, Gary N., and J. Gordon McConville, eds.

2000   *Reconsidering Israel and Judah: The Deuteronomistic History in Recent Thought.* Winona Lake, IN: Eisenbrauns.

Kofoed, Jens B.

2005   *Text and History: Historiography and the Study of the Biblical Text.* Winona Lake, IN: Eisenbrauns.

Kramer, Carol, ed.

1979   *Ethnoarchaeology: Implications of Ethnography for Archaeology.* New York: Columbia University Press.

LaBianca, Øystein, and Randall W. Younker

1995   "The Kingdoms of Ammon, Moab and Edom: The Archaeology of Society in Late Bronze/Iron Age Transjordan (*ca.* 1400-500 BCE)." In *The Archaeology of Society,* edited by T. E. Levy. Leicester: Leicester University, 399-415.

Lamon, Robert, and Geoffrey M. Shipton

1939   *Megiddo I.* Chicago: University of Chicago Press.

Lance, H. Darrell

1967   "Gezer in the Land and in History." *Biblical Archaeologist* 30:34-47.

1971   "The Royal Stamps and the Kingdom of Josiah." *Harvard Theological Review* 64:315-32.

Lapp, Paul W.

1964   "Taʿanach by the Waters of Megiddo." *Biblical Archaeologist* 30:2-27.

1969   "The 1968 Excavations at Tell Taʿanach: The New Cultic Stand." *Bulletin of the American Schools of Oriental Research* 195:42-44.

LaRocca-Pitts, Elizabeth C.

2001   *"Of Wood and Stone": The Significance of Israelite Cultic Terms in the Bible and Its Early Interpreters.* Harvard Semitic Monographs 61. Winona Lake, IN: Eisenbrauns.

Lehmann, Gunnar

2001   "Phoenicians in Western Galilee: First Results of an Archaeological Survey in the Hinterland of Akko." In *Studies in the Archaeology of Israel and Jordan,* edited by Amihai Mazar. Sheffield: Sheffield Academic Press.

2003   "The United Monarchy in the Countryside: Jerusalem, Judah, and the Shephelah during the Tenth Century B.C.E." In *Jerusalem in Bible and Archaeology: The First Temple Period,* edited by A. G. Vaughn and A. E. Killebrew. Atlanta: Society of Biblical Literature, 117-62.

Lemaire, Andre

1998   "The Tel Dan Stele as a Piece of Royal Historiograph." *Journal for the Study of the Old Testament* 81:3-14.

2006   "Khirbet el-Qôm and Hebrew and Aramaic Epigraphy." In *Confronting the Past: Archaeological and Historical Essays on Ancient Israel in Honor of William G. Dever,* edited by S. Gitin, J. Edward Wright, and J. P. Dessel. Winona Lake, IN: Eisenbrauns, 231-38.

Lemche, Niels Peter

1993   "The Old Testament — a Hellenistic Book?" *Scandinavian Journal of the Old Testament* 7:163-93.

1996   "Clio Is Also among the Muses: Keith W. Whitelam and the History of Palestine; A Review and a Commentary." *Scandinavian Journal of the Old Testament* 10:88-119.

1998a   *The Israelites in History and Tradition.* Louisville: Westminster John Knox.

1998b   "The Origin of the Israelite State: A Copenhagen Perspective on the Emergence of Critical Historical Studies of Ancient Israel in Recent Times." *Scandinavian Journal of the Old Testament* 12/1:44-63.

2000   "On the Problem at Reconstructing Pre-Hellenistic Israelite (Palestinian) History." *Journal of Historical Study* 3:1-14.

Lemche, Niels Peter, and Thomas L. Thompson

1994   "Did Biran Kill David? The Bible in the Light of Archaeology." *Journal for the Study of the Old Testament* 64:3-22.

Lemert, Charles

1997   *Postmodernism Is Not What You Think.* Oxford: Blackwell.

Levine, Baruch A., and Avraham Malamat

1996   Review of *The Invention of Ancient Israel: The Silencing of Palestinian History,* by Keith W. Whitelam. *Israel Exploration Journal* 46:284-88.

Levy, Thomas E., ed.

1995   *The Archaeology of Society.* Leicester: Leicester University Press.

Levy, Thomas E., and Thomas Higham, eds.

2005   *The Bible and Radiocarbon Dating: Archaeology, Text, and Science.* London: Equinox.

Levy, Thomas E., et al., eds.

2007   *Crossing the Jordan: American Contributions to the Archaeology of Jordan.* London: Equinox.

Lewis, Theodore J.

1989   *Cults of the Dead in Ancient Israel and Ugarit.* Harvard Semitic Monographs 39. Atlanta: Scholars Press.

Lipinski, Edouard, ed.

1991   *Phoenicia and the Bible.* Leuven: Peeters.

Liverani, Mario

2007   *Israel's History and the History of Israel.* London: Equinox.

London, Gloria

2008   "Fe(male) Potters as the Personification of Individuals, Places, and

Things as Known from Ethnoarchaeological Studies." In *The World of Women in the Ancient and Classical Near East*, edited by B. A. Nakhai. Newcastle upon Tyne: Cambridge Scholars Press, 155-80.

Long, V. Philips

1994   *The Art of Biblical History*. Grand Rapids: Zondervan.

Long, V. Philips, ed.

1999   *Israel's Past in Present Research: Essays on Ancient Israelite Historiography*. Winona Lake, IN: Eisenbrauns.

Long, V. Philips, David W. Baker, and Gordon J. Wenham, eds.

2002   *Windows into Old Testament History: Evidence, Argument, and the Crisis of "Biblical Israel."* Grand Rapids: Eerdmans.

Lutifiyya, A. M.

1966   *Baytin, a Jordanian Village: A Study of Social Institutions and Social Change in a Folk Community*. The Hague: Mouton.

Macalister, Robert A. S.

1912   *The Excavations at Gezer*. Vol 1. London: Palestine Exploration Society.

MacDonald, Burton

1992   "Archaeology of Edom." In *Anchor Bible Dictionary*, edited by D. N. Freedman. New York: Doubleday, 2:295-301.

2000   *East of the Jordan: Territories and Sites of the Hebrew Scriptures*. Boston: American Schools of Oriental Research.

MacDonald, Burton, and Randall W. Younker, eds.

1999   *Ancient Ammon*. Studies in the History and Culture of the Ancient Near East 17. Leiden: Brill.

MacDonald, Nathan

2008   *What Did the Ancient Israelites Eat? Diet in Biblical Times*. Grand Rapids: Eerdmans.

Malul, Meir

1990   *The Comparative Method in Ancient and Near Eastern and Biblical Legal Studies*. Neukirchen-Vluyn: Neukirchener Verlag.

Marcus, G. E., and M. M. J. Fischer

1986   *Anthropology as Cultural Critique: An Experimental Moment in the Human Sciences*. Chicago: University of Chicago Press.

Martens, Elmer A.

1994   "The Oscillating Fortunes of 'History' within Old Testament Theology."

In *Faith, Tradition, and History,* edited by A. R. Millard, J. K. Hoffmeier, and D. W. Baker. Winona Lake, IN: Eisenbrauns, 313-40.

Master, Daniel M.

2001 "State Formation Theory and the Kingdom of Ancient Israel." *Journal of Near Eastern Studies* 60:117-31.

May, Herbert G., and Robert M. Engberg

1935 *Material Remains of the Megiddo Cult.* Oriental Institute Publication 26. Chicago: University of Chicago Press.

Mazar, Amihai

1982 "Three Israelite Sites in the Hills of Judah and Ephraim." *Biblical Archaeologist* 45:167-78.

1990 *Archaeology of the Land of the Bible: 10,000-586 B.C.E.* New York: Doubleday.

1997 "Iron Age Chronology: A Reply to I. Finkelstein." *Levant* 27:157-67.

2001 "Beth Shean during Iron Age II: Stratigraphy, Chronology and Iron Age Ostraca." In *Studies in the Archaeology of the Iron Age in Israel and Jordan,* edited by Amihai Mazar. Sheffield: Sheffield Academic Press, 289-309.

2006 *Excavations of Tel Beth-Shean, 1989-1990.* Vol. I, *From the Late Bronze Age to the Medieval Period.* Jerusalem: Institute of Archaeology, Hebrew University of Jerusalem.

2007a "The Spade and the Text: The Interaction between Archaeology and Israelite History Relating to the Tenth–Ninth Centuries B.C.E." In *Understanding the History of Ancient Israel,* edited by H. G. M. Williamson. Oxford: Oxford University Press.

2007b "The Divided Monarchy: Comments on Some Archaeological Issues." In *The Quest for the Historical Israel: Debating Archaeology and the History of Early Israel,* edited by B. B. Schmidt. Atlanta: Society of Biblical Literature, 159-70.

2008 "From 1200 to 850 B.C.E.: Remarks on Some Selected Archaeological Issues." In *Israel in Transition: From Late Bronze IIa (c. 1250-850 B.C.E.),* vol. 1, *The Archaeology,* edited by L. L. Grabbe. London: T. & T. Clark, 86-120.

Mazar, Benjamin, and Eilat Mazar

1989 *Excavations in the South of the Temple Mount, the Ophel of Biblical Jerusalem.* Qedem 29. Jerusalem: Hebrew University of Jerusalem.

Mazar, Eilat

1987 "Excavate King David's Palace!" *Biblical Archaeology Review* 23/1:50-57, 74.

2002 *The Complete Guide to the Temple Mount Excavations.* Jerusalem: Shoham.

2006a "The Solomonic Wall in Jerusalem." In *"I Will Speak the Riddles of Ancient*

Times": Archaeological and Historical Studies in Honor of Amihai Mazar on the Occasion of His Sixtieth Birthday, edited by A. M. Maeir and P. de Miroschedji. Winona Lake: Eisenbrauns, 775-86.

2006b "Did I Find King David's Palace?" *Biblical Archaeology Review* 32/1:16-27, 70.

2007 *Preliminary Report on the City of David Excavations 2005 at the Visitor Center Area.* Jerusalem: Shoham.

McCarter, P. Kyle

1996 *Ancient Inscriptions: Voices from the Biblical World.* Washington, D.C.: Biblical Archaeology Society.

McClellan, Thomas L.

1984 "Town Planning at Tell en-Naṣbeh." *Zeitschrift des Deutschen Palästina-Vereins* 100:53-69.

McCown, Chester C.

1947 *Tell en-Nasbeh I. Archaeological and Historical Results.* New Haven: American Schools of Oriental Research.

McGovern, Patrick E.

2003 *Ancient Wine: The Search for the Origins of Viniculture.* Princeton: Princeton University Press.

McKenzie, Steven L.

1991 *The Trouble with Kings: The Composition of the Book of Kings in the Deuteronomistic History.* Supplements to Vetus Testamentum 42. Leiden: Brill.

McNutt, Paula M.

1999 *Reconstructing the Society of Ancient Israel.* Louisville: Westminster John Knox.

Meshel, Zeev

1978 *Kuntillet 'Ajrûd: A Religious Center from the Time of the Judaean Monarchy on the Border of Sinai.* Israel Museum Catalogue 175. Jerusalem: Israel Museum.

Meyers, Carol L.

1991 "'To Her Mother's House': Considering a Counterpart of the Israelite Bêt 'āb." In *The Bible and the Polities of Exegesis: Essays in Honor of Norman K. Gottwald on His Sixty-fifth Birthday,* edited by D. Jobling, P. L. Day, and G. T. Sheppard. New York: Pilgrim Press, 39-51.

1999 "'Guilds and Gatherings': Women's Groups in Ancient Israel." In *Realia Dei: Essays in Archaeology and Biblical Interpretation in Honor of Ed-*

ward F. Campbell, Jr., edited by P. M. Williams Jr. and T. T. Hiebert. Atlanta: Scholars Press, 154-84.

2002   "Having Their Space and Eating There Too: Bread Production and Female Power in Ancient Israel." *Nahshim: A Journal of Jewish Studies and Gender Issues* 5:14-44.

2003a   "Material Remains and Social Relations: Women's Culture in Agrarian Households of the Iron Age." In *Symbiosis, Symbolism, and the Power of the Past: Canaan, Ancient Israel, and Their Neighbors from the Late Bronze Age through Roman Palaestina*, edited by W. G. Dever and S. Gitin. Winona Lake, IN: Eisenbrauns, 425-44.

2003b   "Engendering Syro-Palestinian Archaeology: Reasons and Resources." *Near Eastern Archaeology* 66/4:185-97.

2007   "Terra Cottas without Texts: Judean Pillar Figurines in Anthropological Context." In *To Break Every Yoke: Essays in Honor of Marvin L. Chaney*, edited by R. B. Coote and N. K. Gottwald. Sheffield: Sheffield Academic Press, 115-30.

2009   "From Field Crops to Food: Attributing Gender and Meaning to Bread Production in Iron Age Israel." In *The Archaeology of Difference: Gender, Ethnicity, Class, and the "Other" in Antiquity; Essays in Honor of Eric M. Meyers*, edited by D. R. Edwards and C. T. McCollough. Boston: American Schools of Oriental Research, 67-83.

Millard, Alan R.

1992   "Arameans." In *Anchor Bible Dictionary*, edited by D. N. Freedman. New York: Doubleday, 1:345-50.

Millard, Alan R., James K. Hoffmeier, and David W. Baker

1994   *Faith, Tradition, and History: Old Testament Historiography in Its Near Eastern Context.* Winona Lake, IN: Eisenbrauns.

1997   "Story, History, and Theology." In *Faith, Tradition, and History: Old Testament Historiography in Its Near Eastern Context*, edited by Alan R. Millard, James K. Hoffmeier, and David W. Baker. Winona Lake, IN: Eisenbrauns.

Miller, J. Maxwell

1992   "Moab." In *Anchor Bible Dictionary*, edited by D. N. Freedman. New York: Doubleday, 4:882-93.

1997   "Separating the Solomon of History from the Solomon of Legend." In *The Age of Solomon: Scholarship of the Turn of the Millennium*, edited by L. K. Handy. Leiden: Brill.

Miller, J. Maxwell, and John H. Hayes

1991   *A History of Ancient Israel and Judah.* 2nd ed. Philadelphia: Westminister.

Moberly, R. W. L.

1999   "Theology of the Old Testament." In *The Face of Old Testament Studies: A Contemporary Approach,* edited by D. W. Baker and B. T. Arnold. Grand Rapids: Baker, 452-78.

Monson, John

2000   "The New ʿAin Dara Temple: Closest Solomonic Parallel." *Biblical Archaeology Review* 26/3:20-35, 67.

Moorey, P. Roger S.

2003   *Idols of the People: Miniature Images of Clay in the Ancient Near East.* Oxford: Oxford University Press.

Naʾaman, Nadav

1979   "Sennacherib's Campaign to Judah and the Date of the *lmlk* Stamps." *Vetus Testamentum* 29:61-86.

2000   "Three Notes on the Aramaic Inscriptions from Tel Dan." *Israel Exploration Journal* 50:92-104.

2006   *Ancient Israel's History and Historiography: The First Temple Period.* Winona Lake, IN: Eisenbrauns.

Nakhai, Beth Alpert

2008   *The World of Women in the Ancient and Classical Near East.* Cambridge: Cambridge Scholars Publishing.

Naroll, R.

1962   "Floor Area and Settlement Population." *American Antiquity* 27:587-89.

Naveh, Joseph

1963   "Old Hebrew Inscriptions in a Burial Cave." *Israel Exploration Journal* 13:74-92.

1982   *Early History of the Alphabet.* Jerusalem: Magnes Press.

Netzer, Ehud

1992   "Domestic Architecture in the Iron Age." In *The Architecture of Ancient Israel: From the Prehistoric to the Persian Period,* edited by A. Kempinski and R. Reich. Jerusalem: Israel Exploration Society, 93-202.

Neufeld, E.

1971   "Hygiene Conditions in Ancient Israel (Iron Age)." *Biblical Archaeologist* 34/2:41-66.

Noll, K. N.

2001   *Canaan and Israel in Antiquity: An Introduction.* Biblical Seminar 83. Sheffield: Sheffield Academic Press.

Ofer, Avi

2001   "The Monarchic Period in the Judean Highland: A Spatial Overview." In *Studies in the Archaeology of the Iron Age,* edited by A. Mazar. Journal for the Study of the Old Testament: Supplement Series 331. Sheffield: Sheffield Academic Press, 14-37.

Olyan, Saul M.

1998   *Asherah and the Cult of Asherah in Israel.* Atlanta: Scholars Press.

Oren, Eliezer D.

2000   *The Sea Peoples and Their World: A Reassessment.* Philadelphia: University Museum.

Ornan, Tally

2001   "Ištar as Depicted on Finds from Israel." In *Studies in the Archaeology of the Iron Age in Israel and Jordan,* edited by A. Mazar. Journal for the Study of the Old Testament: Supplement Series 831. Sheffield: Sheffield Academic Press 235-56.

Ortiz, Steven M.

2004   "Deconstructing and Reconstructing the United Monarchy: House of David or Tent of David (Current Trends in Iron Age Chronology)." In *The Future of Biblical Archaeology: Reassessing Methodologies and Assumptions,* edited by J. K. Hoffmeier and A. Millard. Grand Rapids: Eerdmans, 121-48.

Pasto, J.

1998   "When the End Is the Beginning? Or When the Biblical Past Is the Political Present: Some Thoughts on Ancient Israel, 'Post-Exilic Judaism,' and the Politics of Biblical Scholarship." *Scandinavian Journal of the Old Testament* 12:157-202.

Paz, Sarit

2007   *Drums, Women, and Goddesses: Drumming and Gender in Iron Age II Israel.* Fribourg: Academic Press.

Peckham, B.

1992   "Phoenicians, History of." In *Anchor Bible Dictionary,* edited by David Noel Freedman. New York: Doubleday, 5:349-57.

Perdue, Leo G., Joseph Blenkinsopp, and John J. Collins, eds.

1997   *Families in Ancient Israel.* Louisville: Westminster John Knox.

Pippin, Tina

1986   "Ideology, Ideological Criticism, and the Bible." *Currents in Research: Biblical Studies* 4:51-78.

Pitard, Wayne T.

1987   *Ancient Damascus: A Historical Study of the Syrian City-State from Earliest Times until Its Fall to the Assyrians in 732 B.C.E.* Winona Lake, IN: Eisenbrauns.

Provan, Ian W.

1995   "Ideologies, Literary and Critical: Reflections on Recent Writing on the History of Israel." *Journal of Biblical Literature* 114:585-606.

Rainey, Anson F.

1994   "The 'House of David' and the House of the Deconstructionists." *Biblical Archaeology Review* 20/6:47.

1995   Review of *Early History of the Israelite People from the Written and Archaeological Sources,* by Thomas L. Thompson. *American Jewish Studies* 20:156-60.

Rainey, Anson F., and R. Steven Notley

2006   *The Sacred Bridge: Carta's Atlas of the Biblical World.* Jerusalem: Carta. Cited as Rainey 2006 in notes.

Rast, Walter E.

1978   *Ta'anach 1: Studies in the Iron Age Pottery.* Cambridge, MA: American Schools of Oriental Research.

Reich, R.

1992   "Palaces and Residencies in the Iron Age." In *The Architecture of Ancient Israel from the Prehistoric to the Persian Periods,* edited by Aharon Kempinski and Ronny Reich. Jerusalem: Israel Exploration Society, 202-22.

Reich, Ronny, and Baruch Brandl

1985   "Gezer under Assyrian Rule." *Palestine Exploration Quarterly* 117:41-54.

Reich, Ronny, and Eli Shukron

2000   "The System of Rock-Cut Tunnels near Gihon in Jerusalem Reconsidered." *Revue Biblique* 107:5-17.

2006   "On the Original Length of Hezekiah's Tunnel: Some Critical Notes on David Ussishkin's Suggestions." In *"I Will Speak the Riddles of Ancient Times": Archaeological and Historical Studies in Honor of Amihai Mazar on the Occasion of His Sixtieth Birthday,* edited by A. Maeir and P. de Miroschedji. Winona Lake, IN: Eisenbrauns, 795-800.

Reich, Ronny, Eli Shukron, and Omri Lernau

2008   "The Iron Age II Finds from the Rock-Cut 'Pool' near the Spring in Jerusalem: A Preliminary Report." In *Israel in Transition: From Late Bronze II to Iron IIa (c. 1250-850 B.C.E.)*, vol. 1, *The Archaeology*, edited by L. L. Grabbe. London: T. & T. Clark, 138-43.

Reisner, George A., Clarence S. Fisher, and David G. Lyon
1924 *Harvard Excavations at Samaria (1908-1910)*. Vols. 1, 2. Cambridge: Harvard University Press.

Renfrew, Colin, and Paul Bahn
1991 *Archaeology: Theories, Methods, and Practice*. London: Thames and Hudson.

Rollston, Christopher A.
2008 "The Phoenician Script of the Tel Zayit Abecedary and Putative Evidence for Israelite Literacy." In *Literate Culture and Tenth-Century Canaan: The Tel Zayit Abecedary in Context*, edited by R. E. Tappy and P. K. McCarter. Winona Lake, IN: Eisenbrauns, 61-96.

Rosovsky, M., ed.
1996 *Illness and Healing in Ancient Times*. Haifa: Hecht Museum.

Routledge, Bruce
1995 "Pillared Buildings in Iron Age Moab." *Biblical Archaeologist* 58/4:236.
2004 *Moab in the Iron Age: Hegemony, Polity, Archaeology*. Philadelphia: University of Pennsylvania Press.

Sader, Helene
1992 "The 12th Century B.C. in Syria: The Problem of the Rise of the Arameans." In *The Crisis Years: The 12th Century B.C.; From Beyond the Danube to the Tigris*, edited by W. A. Ward and M. S. Joukowsky. Dubuque: Kendall/Hunt Publishing Co., 1509-63.

Sahlins, Marshall D.
1972 *Stone Age Economics*. Chicago: University of Chicago Press.

Sanders, Seth H.
2008 "Writing and Early Iron Age Israel: Before National Scripts, beyond Nations and States." In *Literate Culture and Tenth-Century Canaan: The Tel Zayit Abecedary in Context*, edited by R. E. Tappy and P. K. McCarter. Winona Lake, IN: Eisenbrauns.

Sass, Benjamin, and Christopher Uehlinger, eds.
1993 *Studies in the Iconography of North Semitic Inscribed Seals*. Orbis biblicus et orientalis 125. Freibourg: University Press.

Sawyer, John F. A., and David J. A. Clines, eds.
1993 *Midian, Moab, and Edom: The History and Archaeology of Late Bronze and*

Iron Age Jordan and North-West Arabia. Journal for the Study of the Old Testament: Supplement Series 24. Sheffield: JSOT Press.

Schmidt, Brian B.
1996   *Israel's Beneficent Dead: Ancestor Cult and Necromancy in Ancient Israelite Religion and Tradition.* Winona Lake, IN: Eisenbrauns.

Schmidt, Brian B., ed.
2007   *The Quest for the Historical Israel: Debating Archaeology and the History of Early Israel.* SBL Archaeology and Biblical Studies 17. Atlanta: Scholars Press.

Schniedewind, William M.
1996a   "The Problem with Kings: Recent Study of the Deuteronomistic History." *Religious Studies Review* 22:22-87.
1996b   "The Tel Dan Stele: New Light on Aramaic and Jehu's Revolt." *Bulletin of the American Schools of Oriental Research* 302:75-90.
2000   "Orality and Literacy in Ancient Israel." *Religious Studies Review* 26/4:327-32.

Seger, Karen, ed.
1981   *Portrait of a Palestinian Village: The Photographs of Hilma Granqvist.* London: Third World Centre for Research and Publishing.

Sered, Susan S.
1992   *Women as Ritual Experts: The Religious Lives of Elderly Jewish Women in Jerusalem.* New York: Oxford University Press.

Shamir, Orit
2007   "Loomweights and Textile Production at Tel Miqne-Ekron." In *"Up to the Gates of Ekron": Essays on the Archaeology and History of the Eastern Mediterranean in Honor of Seymour Gitin,* edited by S. W. Crawford et al. Jerusalem: Israel Exploration Society, 43-49.

Shanks, Hershel
1997   "Face to Face: Biblical Minimalists Meet Their Challengers." *Biblical Archaeology Review* 23/4:26-42, 46.
2008   "Sound Proof: How Hezekiah's Tunnelers Met." *Biblical Archaeology Review* 34/5:51-57, 78.

Sharon, Ilana, and Annabel Zarzecki-Peleg
2006   "Podium Structures with Lateral Access: Authority Ploys in Royal Architecture in the Iron Age Levant." In *Confronting the Past: Archaeological and Historical Essays on Ancient Israel in Honor of William G. Dever,* edited by Seymour Gitin, J. Edward Wright, and J. P. Dessel. Winona Lake, IN: Eisenbrauns, 145-67.

Sharon, I., et al.

2007   "The Early Iron Age Dating Project: Introduction, Methodology, Progress Report and an Update on the Tel Dot Radiometric Dates." In *The Bible and Radiocarbon Dating*, edited by Thomas Levy and Thomas Higham. London: Equinox, 43-54.

Sheffer, A., and A. Tidhar

1991   "Textiles and Basketry at Kuntillet 'Ajrud." *'Atiqot* 20:1-26.

Shiloh, Yigal

1970   "The Four-Room House, Its Situation and Function in the Israelite City." *Israel Exploration Journal* 20:180-90.

1978   "Elements in the Development of Town Planning in the Israelite City." *Israel Exploration Journal* 28:36-51.

1979   *The Proto-Aeolic Capital and Israelite Ashlar Masonry.* Qedem 11. Jerusalem: Institute of Archaeology, Hebrew University of Jerusalem.

1980   "The Population of Iron Age Palestine in the Light of a Sample of Urban Plans, Areas and Population Density." *Bulletin of the American Schools of Oriental Research* 239:25-35.

1987   "The Material Culture of Judah and Jerusalem in the Eighth–Sixth Centuries BCE." In *Recent Excavations in Israel: Studies in Iron Age Archaeology*, edited by S. Gitin and W. G. Dever. Annual of the American Schools of Oriental Research 249. Winona Lake, IN: Eisenbrauns, 113-96.

Shukon, Eli, and Ronny Reich

2000   "The Rock-Cut Tunnels near Gihon Reconsidered." *Revue Biblique* 107:5-17.

Singer-Avitz, Lily

2002   "Arad: The Iron Age Pottery Assemblages." *Tel Aviv* 29:110-214.

Smith, Mark S.

2001   *The Origins of Biblical Monotheism: Israel's Polytheistic Background and the Ugaritic Texts.* New York: Oxford University Press.

2002   *The Early History of God: Yahweh and the Other Deities of Ancient Israel.* Grand Rapids: Eerdmans.

Sneh, Amihai, Ram Weinberer, and Eyal Shalev

2010   "The Why, How, and When of the Siloam Tunnel Reevaluated." *Bulletin of the American Schools of Oriental Research* 359:67-76.

Soggin, J. Alberto

1999   *An Introduction to the History of Israel and Judah.* London: SCM.

2001   *Israel in the Biblical Period: Institutions, Festivals, Ceremonies, Rituals.* London: T. & T. Clark.

Sommers, Benjamin D.

1998   Review of *The Invention of Ancient Israel: The Silencing of Palestinian History*, by Keith W. Whitelam. *Middle East Quarterly*: 85-86.

Stager, Lawrence E.

1985   "The Archaeology of the Family in Ancient Israel." *Bulletin of the American Schools of Oriental Research* 260:1-35.

1995   "The Impact of the Sea Peoples in Canaan." In *The Archaeology of Society*, edited by Thomas E. Levy. Leicester: Leicester University Press, 332-48.

Stager, Lawrence E., and Samuel R. Wolff

1981   "Production and Commerce in Temple Courtyards: An Olive Press in the Sacred Precinct at Tel Dan." *Bulletin of the American Schools of Oriental Research* 243:95, 101.

Stendahl, Krister

1962   "Biblical Theology, Contemporary." In *Interpreter's Dictionary of the Bible*, edited by G. A. Buttrick. Nashville: Abingdon, 1:418-32.

Stern, Ephraim

2001   *The Assyrian, Babylonian, and Persian Periods, 732-332 BCE*. New York: Doubleday.

Stern, Ephraim, ed.

1993   *New Encyclopedia of Archaeological Excavations in the Holy Land*. Vols. 1-4. Jerusalem: Israel Exploration Society.

2008   *New Encyclopedia of Archaeological Excavations in the Holy Land*. Vol. 5. Jerusalem: Israel Exploration Society.

Tappy, Ron E.

2001   *The Archaeology of Israelite Samaria: The Eighth Century BCE*. Winona Lake, IN: Eisenbrauns.

2006   "The Provenance of the Unpublished Ivories from Samaria." In *"I Will Speak the Riddles of Ancient Times": Archaeological and Historical Studies in Honor of Amihai Mazar on the Occasion of His Sixtieth Birthday*, edited by A. M. Maeir and P. de Miroschedji. Winona Lake, IN: Eisenbrauns, 637-56.

Tappy, R. E., and P. K. McCarter, eds.

2008   *Literate Culture and Tenth-Century Canaan: The Tel Zayit Abecedary in Context*. Winona Lake, IN: Eisenbrauns.

Tarnas, Richard

1991   *The Passion of the Western Mind: Understanding the Ideas That Have Shaped Our World View*. New York: Ballantine Books.

Taylor, J. Glen

1993   *Yahweh and the Sun: Biblical and Archaeological Evidence for Sun Worship in Ancient Israel.* Journal for the Study of the Old Testament: Supplement Series 111. Sheffield: Sheffield Academic Press.

Thompson, Thomas L.

1987   *The Origin Tradition of Ancient Israel: The Literary Formation of Genesis and Exodus 1–23.* Journal for the Study of the Old Testament: Supplement Series 55. Sheffield: JSOT Press.

1992   *Early History of the Israelite People from the Written and Archaeological Sources.* Studies in the History of the Ancient Near East. Leiden: Brill.

1995   "A Neo-Albrightian School in History and Biblical Scholarship." *Journal of Biblical Literature* 114:983-98.

1997   "Defining History and Ethnicity in the Southern Levant." In *Can a "History of Israel" Be Written?* edited by L. L. Grabbe. Journal for the Study of the Old Testament: Supplement Series 245. Sheffield: Sheffield Academic Press, 166-87.

1999   *The Mythic Past: Biblical Archaeology and the Myth of Israel.* New York: Basic Books.

2001   "A View from Copenhagen: Israel and the History of Palestine." Online at http//www.bibleinterp.com.

2003   *Jerusalem in Ancient History and Tradition.* Journal for the Study of the Old Testament: Supplement Series 381. London: T. & T. Clark.

Tigay, J. H.

1986   *You Shall Have No Other Gods: Israelite Religion in the Light of Hebrew Inscriptions.* Atlanta: Scholars Press.

Toombs, Lawrence E.

1992   "Shechem (Place)." In *The Anchor Bible Dictionary,* edited by David Noel Freedman. New York: Doubleday, 5:1174-86.

Toorn, Karel van der

2002   "Israelite Figurines: A View from the Texts." In *Sacred Time and Space: Archaeology and the Religion of Israel,* edited by B. M. Gittlen. Winona Lake, IN: Eisenbrauns, 45-62.

2003   "Nine Months among the Peasants in the Palestinian Highlands: An Anthropological Perspective on Local Religion in the Early Iron Age." In *Symbiosis, Symbolism, and the Power of the Past: Canaan, Ancient Israel, and Their Neighbors from the Late Bronze Age through Roman Palaestina,* edited by W. G. Dever and S. Gitin. Winona Lake IN: Eisenbrauns, 393-410.

2007   *Scribal Culture and the Making of the Hebrew Bible.* Cambridge: Harvard University Press.

Tufnell, Olga

1953   *Lachish III: The Iron Age.* London: Oxford University Press.

Ussishkin, David

1977   "The Destruction of Lachish by Sennacherib and the Dating of the Royal Judean Storage Jars." *Tel Aviv* 4:28-60.

1982   *The Conquest of Lachish by Sennacherib.* Tel Aviv: Institute of Archaeology, Tel Aviv University.

1983   "The Conquest of Lachish by Sennacherib." *Tel Aviv* 10:97-105.

Ussishkin, David, et al., eds.

2004   *The Renewed Archaeological Excavation at Lachish (1973-1994).* Institute of Archaeology Monograph Series 22. Tel Aviv: Institute of Archaeology, Tel Aviv University.

Van Seters, John

1983   *In Search of History: Historiography in the Ancient World and the Origins of Biblical History.* New Haven: Yale University Press.

Vaughn, Andrew G.

1999   "Can We Write a History of Israel Today?" In *The Future of Biblical Archaeology: Methodologies and Assumptions,* edited by J. K. Hoffmeier and A. Millard. Grand Rapids: Eerdmans, 368-85.

2003   "Is Biblical Archaeology Theologically Useful Today? Yes, a Programmatic Proposal." In *Jerusalem in Bible and Archaeology: The First Temple Period,* edited by Andrew G. Vaughn and Ann E. Killebrew. Atlanta: Society of Biblical Literature, 407-30.

Vaughn, Andrew G., and Ann E. Killebrew, eds.

2003   *Jerusalem in Bible and Archaeology.* Atlanta: Society of Biblical Literature.

Vaughn, Andrew G., and Carolyn P. Dobler

2006   "A Provenience Study of Hebrew Seals and Seal Impressions." In *"I Will Speak the Riddles of Ancient Times": Archaeological and Historical Studies in Honor of Amihai Mazar on the Occasion of His Sixtieth Birthday,* edited by A. Maeir and P. de Miroschedji. Winona Lake, IN: Eisenbrauns, 757-71.

Vriezen, Karel J. H.

2001   "Archaeological Traces of Cult in Ancient Israel." In *Only One God? Monotheism in Ancient Israel and the Veneration of the Goddess Asherah,* edited by B. Becking, M. Dijkstra, and K. J. H. Vriezen. Biblical Seminar 77. Sheffield: Sheffield Academic Press, 45-80.

Walsh, C.

2000   *The Fruit of the Vine: Viticulture in Ancient Israel.* Harvard Semitic Monographs 60. Winona Lake, IN: Eisenbrauns.

Watson, Patty Jo
1979   *Archaeological Ethnography in Western Iran.* Tucson: University of Arizona.

Whitelam, Keith W.
1996   *The Invention of Ancient Israel: The Silencing of Palestinian History.* London: Routledge.
2002   "Representing Minimalism: The Rhetoric and Reality of Revisionism." In *Sense and Sensibility: Essays on Reading the Bible in Memory of Robert Carroll,* edited by A. G. Hunter and P. R. Davies. Journal for the Study of the Old Testament: Supplement Series 348. Sheffield: Sheffield Academic Press, 194-223.

Whitley, D. S.
1998   *Reader in Archaeological Theory: Post-Processual and Cognitive Approaches.* London: Routledge.

Wiggins, Steve A.
2001   *A Reassessment of "Asherah": A Study according to the Textual Sources of the First Two Millennia* BCE. Neukirchen-Vluyn: Neukirchener.

Willett, Ann R.
2008   "Infant Mortality and Women's Religion in the Biblical Periods." In *The World of Women in the Ancient and Classic Near East,* edited by Beth Alpert Nakhai. Newcastle upon Tyne: Cambridge Scholars Press, 79-98.

Williamson, Hugh G. M., ed.
2007   *Understanding the History of Ancient Israel.* Proceedings of the British Academy 143. Oxford: Oxford University Press.

Windschuttle, K.
1996   *The Killing of History: How Literary Critics and Social Theorists Are Murdering Our Past.* New York: Free Press.

Winter, Irene J.
1976   "Phoenician and North Syrian Ivory Carving in Historical Context: Questions of Style and Distribution." *Iraq* 38:1-22.
1981   "Is There a South Syrian Style of Ivory Carving in the Early First Millennium B.C.?" *Iraq* 43:101-30.

Wolff, Samuel
2007   "Stone Pedestaled Bowls from the Late Bronze Age Iron Ages in the Levant." In *"Up to the Gates of Ekron": Essays on the Archaeology and History of the Eastern Mediterranean in Honor of Seymour Gitin,* edited by S. W. Crawford et al. Jerusalem: Israel Exploration Society, 305-12.

Wright, George Ernest

1952   *God Who Acts: Biblical Theology as Recital.* London: SCM.

1965   *Shechem: The Biography of a Biblical City.* New York: McGraw-Hill.

Wright, G. R. H.

1985   *Ancient Building in South Syria and Palestine.* Vols. I-II. Leiden: Brill.

Yadin, Y.

1959   "Receipts of Owners, a Note on the Samaria Ostraca." *Israel Exploration Society* 19:184-87.

1975   *Hazor: The Rediscovery of a Great Citadel of the Bible.* New York: Random House.

Yadin, Yigael, et al.

1958   *Hazor I.* Jerusalem: Magnes Press.

1960   *Hazor II.* Jerusalem: Magnes Press.

1989   *Hazor III.* Jerusalem: Magnes Press.

Yadin, Yigael, and Amnon Ben-Tor, eds.

1989   *Hazor III-IV, Text.* Jerusalem: Israel Exploration Society.

1993   *The Art of Warfare in Biblical Lands in the Light of Archaeological Study.* 2 vols. New York: McGraw-Hill.

Yeivin, A.

1987   "The Mysterious Silver Hoard from Eshtemoa." *Biblical Archaeology Review* 13/6:38-44.

Yezerski, Irit

1999   "Burial-Cave Distribution and the Borders of the Kingdom of Judah toward the End of the Iron Age." *Tel Aviv* 26:253-70.

2004   "An Iron Age Burial Cave at Rās āl-Tawil." In *Burial Caves and Sites in Judea and Samaria,* edited by H. Hizmi and A. De Groot. Jerusalem: Israel Antiquities Authority, 209-30.

Zertal, Adam

2001   "The Heart of the Monarchy: Pattern of Settlement and Historical Considerations of the Israelite Kingdom of Samaria." In *Studies in the Archaeology of the Iron Age in Israel and Jordan,* edited by A. Mazar. Journal for the Study of the Old Testament: Supplement Series 331. Sheffield: Sheffield Academic Press, 38-64.

Zevit, Ziony

1999   Review of *In Search of "Ancient Israel,"* by Philip R. Davies. *American Jewish Studies Review* 20:153-56.

2001   *The Religions of Ancient Israel: A Synthesis of Parallactic Approaches.* London: Continuum.

2002   "Three Debates about Bible and Archaeology." *Biblica* 83/1:1-27.

Zirmhoni, Ora

2004   "The Pottery of Levels III and II." In *The Renewed Archaeological Excavations at Lachish (1973-1994)*. Institute of Archaeology Monograph Series 22. Tel Aviv: Institute of Archaeology, Tel Aviv University, 178-89.

Zorn, Jeffrey R.

1994   "Estimating the Population Size of Ancient Settlements: Methods, Problems, Solutions, and a Case Study." *Bulletin of the American Schools of Oriental Research* 295:31-48.

1997   "An Inner and Outer Gate Complex at Tell en-Naṣbeh." *Bulletin of the American Schools of Oriental Research* 307:36-53.

Name Index

Page numbers in **boldface** indicate figure credits.

Subject Index

Theory, viii, ix, 17

Threshing, 172-75. *See also* Grain; Harvest; Seasons

Tiglath-pileser III, 330-32, 335, 339, 343

Timnah, 362

Tombs, 215, 216, 283-87

Tools, 173, 178-80. *See also* Metal implements; Stone implements

Towns, 48, 82, 83

Trade, 237-43. *See also* Economics

Travel, 204

Trees, 265

Tribes, 344

'Umayri, Tell al-, 129

Urbanism, 106-28; biblical view of, 133-35, 140, 141

Utensils, domestic, 165-69, 178-85

Villages, 49, 84-88, 101, 142-46

Vocations, 233-35, 248

Votive offerings, 264, 276, 280

Vows, 283

Walls, city, 59, 112-15, 136-38

Warfare, 320-67

Water systems, 57, 125-28, 139, 140, 231, 232, 349-51, 365, 366

Weaving, 160, 165, 179, 180, 189

Weights, 239-41, 354. *See also* Economics; Shequels

Wells, 164. *See also* Cisterns

Western cultural tradition, 25, 26, 34. *See also* Postmodernism; Revisionism

Wine, 170, 178, 194, 238, 239

Women's roles, tasks, 153, 159-69, 187-89, 189, 205, 270, 271, 293. *See also* Baking; Bread; Cooking; Dowry; Grain; Marriage

Writing, 180, 183, 184. *See also* Inscriptions; Literacy

Yahweh, deity, 264, 265, 285, 287

Yanoah, 337

Yoqneam (Jokneam), 340

Zoomorphic vessel, 277, 278

Scripture Index

16:18-20	192	19:35-38	44	12:30-31	289
17:5	137	20:8	312	14:23	290
18:33ff.	192	21:12	134	15:13	289
19:14	192	21:38	312	17:7	46
22:11	178	24:26-27	290	19:6	188
24:6	188, 190			20:30	310, 361
24:10-11	190	**Judges**		20:34	247, 306
24:12-13	190	1:18	301	21:8	246
24:17	190	1:27	44, 134	22	312
24:19	192	6:1-3	44		
25:4	192	16:3	137	**2 Kings**	
25:13-14	192	16:13	188	3:2	290
25:13-16	245	16:13-14	189	3:4	44
25:24	192	21:13-24	196	7:18	244
26:1-4	192	21:25	203	8:28–9:10	312
26:2-14	192			12:7	363, 364
26:17-19	192	**Ruth**		12:17	299
27:17	192	4:1	137	12:17-18	310
28:3-6	193	4:1-12	137	13–21	316
28:12	46			13–20	363
33:26-27	281	**1 Samuel**		13:1ff.	363
		5:10	296	13:1-6	310
Joshua		7:14	296	13:14-17	310
3:16	44	8:10-18	141	13:17	363, 364
7	187	9:8	244	13:22	363
7:21	244	13:21	244, 245	13:22-25	310
9:1	44	17:5	244	13:24	363, 364
10:16	44	17:7	188	14–21	103
10:17	44	20:25	137	14–20	99
11:2	44			14:7	311, 317
11:16	44	**2 Samuel**		14:25-28	363
11:21	44	1:20	301	15:20	244
12:7	44	2:13	139	15:29	99, 100, 333, 335,
12:8-24	44	11:21	188		343, 365
13–19	100	14:26	244	16:5-7	318
13:2-3	296	21:16	244	17	365
13:27	44	24:24	244	17:6	365
15–19	100			17:7	365
15	100, 134	**1 Kings**		17:9	134
15:21-63	100	4:13	44	17:41	365
15:33-42	44	4:17-19	100	18	349
15:45-47	296	5–9	257	18:4	289, 290
17:16	44	9:26	318	18:8	134
19:27	306	10:27	44	18:13	349